MODERN

AMERICAN S [illegible] LISM,

OR [illegible]

BY

EMMA HARDINGE.

Richardson N.Y.

Engraved by John Sartain Phil^a

Emma Hardinge

MODERN

AMERICAN SPIRITUALISM:

A TWENTY YEARS' RECORD

OF THE

COMMUNION BETWEEN EARTH AND THE WORLD OF SPIRITS.

BY EMMA HARDINGE.

VOLUME 1

SNU PUBLICATIONS

First published by the author in 1870

This edition in two volumes
published in 1999 by
SNU Publications
Redwoods
Stansted Hall
Stansted Mountfitchet
Essex CM24 8UD

E-mail: pubs@snu.org.uk
Web-site: www.snu.org.uk

ISBN 0 902036 21 1

Reprinted in England by Booksprint

DEDICATION.

To the Wise and Mighty Beings through whose Instrumentality the Spiritual Telegraph of the Nineteenth Century has been Constructed;

To the Benificent and Powerful Spirits through whose Sublime Labors the Immortal World can Commune with the Mortal Dwellers of Earth;

This Brief, Fragmentary, and most Imperfect Record of their Divine Ministration, undertaken at their Command, and Executed under their Supervision, is Reverently and Gratefully Inscribed by their Faithful and Devoted Medium,

EMMA HARDINGE.

New York City,
229 East 60th Street,
December 15th, 1869.

ILLUSTRATIONS.

TABLE OF CONTENTS.

VOLUME 1

VOLUME 2

PREFACE.

As these pages seem to imply by their title certain specialties both in regard to time and place, whilst the subject of "Spiritualism," or the record of man's spiritual experiences is one which must be commensurate with the physical history of humanity upon this globe, they require a few words of explanation touching the aim and scope of the subject which the author designs to embrace in this work.

The entire history of the race, when recorded in accurate detail and fidelity to fact, ever has, and ever will be found, marked with the shadowy outline of a second world of existence, supersensuous to that of mortality. On the walls of our earthly dwelling-places ever will be seen a writing inscribed by "a part of a man's hand," the form whereof is dimly visible, the full proportions of which no human eye may scan. And these mystic writings are discovered everywhere; they are traced in our holy places, and meet us on the thresholds of our habitations. They are seen in our very city streets, and the stones prate of their whereabouts.

Sometimes we label them "religion," at others denounce them by the weird name of "magic," "witchcraft," or "sorcery;" in a word, we variously denominate them, as time, prejudice, or custom suggests, under all the different titles which are included in the generic synonym of "supernaturalism;" but deem of them as we will, they include a set of experiences, occult and incomprehensible though they be, as irresistible and inevitable in time and space as the more material array of facts which we assume makes up the sum of human history. In truth, this same "supernaturalism" is the woof spun by the hands of a powerful though invisible existence, which incloses all human life and shapes all human destiny. Hitherto, we have either determined to resolve the whole realm of power which makes up man's spiritual existence into the universal solvent of all mysteries, "*God*," *and* "*His Will;*" or else, with still more unphilosophic ignorance, we have striven to stifle the records of its being beneath the pall of unreasoning and senseless materialism. Neither will longer serve our turn. All mental progress tends to the discovery that "God's will" is only manifest in *law.* Religion, ethics, miracle, and supersensuous life, like tides, and times, and seasons, all resolve themselves at last into stern and immutable procedures of a set of mental laws as stringent as any of those that bind our physical existence. The whole realm of visionary supernaturalism melts away, then, before the morning sun of that glorious light that science brings, leaving no refuge for our world of occult facts but to range them within the domain of unexplained but inevitable law, or else, like rude materialism, to deny them altogether, and write upon half mankind's experience the gratuitous charge of "falsehood." Between the horns of this dilemma, and in the age when bold assertions or denial can no longer serve the cause of true philosophy, much less religion, comes the dawning of a day of spiritual science, in the vast and overwhelming tides of occult power that for twenty years have swept the continent of North America. And when we cite this mighty witness to our bar of spiritual inquisition, *we stand alone.* Acknowledging that every fact we have to record, or every case to cite, bears a strict analogy in point of representation to other facts and cases witnessed in every land and age, we still claim that the American phenomena—based, as their authors insist they are, upon the foundations of natural law, and produced only in accordance with the conditions that law affords—form such an array of testimony concerning their origin as renders the modern movement in America a distinct and concrete one in the world's history. Several points of specialty cluster around it, as: first, the astonishing fecundity of its manifestations, crowding up tens of thousands of facts into a period of time that baffles the skill of any earthly recorder to keep track of; next, the marvellous coincidence and similarity of the manifestations, extending over immense surfaces of country—including three millions of square miles of thickly-populated States—within a period of time that renders the possibility of propagandism or the theory of collusion impossible; and next, the deduction arising from this last-named fact, namely, that the same occult and invisible operators that originated the phenomena in one instance, must have been instrumental in producing them in all. It is contrary to the peculiar method of the writer of these pages to attempt the fortification of any position that may be advanced by *human authority*, however high or valuable; hence no such course will be pursued, and few, if any, authoritative quotations, outside of the American history itself, will find a record here. Were it, however, admissible, hosts of opinions world-wide in renown and acceptance could be cited to prove the worth of such wonderfully coincident testimony as the above. The exercise of simple reason, however, should suffice to prove that a unique, well-organized, and highly practical concert of action alone could account for the manifestation of a coincident set of phenomena, spread over the immense geographical area we have indicated, dividing itself throughout the districts of thirty-six separate States, affecting all ranks of persons and classes of mind at once, occupying in this gigantic system of propagandism less than twenty years, and exhibiting on its simply human side scarcely a single evidence of any of the accepted modes of disseminating strange tidings at present in use, much less of promoting physical changes and developments of the most unprecedented nature in thousands of individuals themselves. Still another point of isolated interest presents itself in the modern American movement, and this is in its religious or doctrinal character. Spiritualism, with a large majority of its American adherents, *is a religion*, separate in all respects from any existing sect, because it bases its affirmations purely upon the demonstrations of fact, science, and natural law, and admits of no creed or denominational boundary. With such a foundation, its philosophy must necessarily ramify through immeasurable realms of natural and unceasing revelation; whilst destitute of the hedge of sectarian limitation, its aims must encompass the whole human race in membership. If the American spiritual movement, therefore, did not stand wholly unrivalled in point of unity of design, wonderful, though invisible concert of action, manifest purpose, and overwhelming numerical strength, the doctrinal isolation of its majorities from all other existing sects would distinguish it from the Spiritualism of all other countries, where the generality of believers appear to accept the phenomena as a means of deepening their convictions in credal faiths, rather than as originating such views of the hereafter as destroy reliance upon ceremonial forms or sectarian beliefs. This religious phase of the American movement has ultimated in gathering together in Pentecostal meetings multitudes of persons for Sabbath-day worship, when, chiefly through the lips of entranced or inspired speakers, descriptions of the spheres and conditions of spirit life have been portrayed with such glowing eloquence, and under such an evident afflatus of supernal power, that these utterances have been by millions accepted as truths, received as genuine representations of immortal life, and hence superseded in the minds of the listeners the mere theories of *mortals* concerning the conditions of *immortal* existence. In connection with such teachings, keenly analytical discourses have been given—under circumstances that rendered their production from the normal condition of the speaker impossible—on the various natural sciences, illustrative of the all-wise and beneficent character of the Deity, the guardianship of his ministering spirits, and the propelling causes of such human actions as tend to elevate or deform the spirit. In this category all the various reforms of the day have been discussed with a profound logic and searching acumen that would tax the far-reaching powers of the most highly cultivated intellects. Combined with such subjects as these, popular opinions [both in matters of religion and politics] have been analyzed; and seeing that the discovery and application of *truth* has been the sole object claimed by the intelligences that influence these utterances, and that truth has always been defined as "*that which is*," it may well be supposed that mere fanciful theories or unsound opinions, asseverated upon human authority only, have not been treated with politic leniency or excused by the sophistries of custom and prejudice. And hence it is that American Spiritualism, *as a religion*, based upon facts, proved by science, and defended with an irresistible tide of burning oratory amply demonstrative of a supra-mundane source, has not only taken captive the minds of the masses, but has also appealed, and that most successfully, to the deep thinkers of the land, to whom "religion must be a science" and "science a religion," or one or the other must be false and worthless. As we are not aware of any other country than America, where a popular religion thus appeals to the reason and requires its votaries to do their own thinking, or of any other denomination than "American Spiritualists" who base their belief on scientific facts, proven by living witnesses, so we deem our claim, on these grounds alone, would be justified in describing American Spiritualism as an unique, concrete, and at present isolated movement, demanding from historic justice a record as full, complete, and independent, as itself. Two other considerations induce the author to attempt this record, however unworthy it may seem of the stupendous subject. The first of these is the somewhat remarkable indifference with which modern American Spiritualism has been treated by European writers on kindred topics. From whatever cause the overwhelming importance of the American movement may have been deemed sufficiently disposed of in occasional paragraphs or at most a few chapters of meagre detail, it matters not now to inquire; suffice it to say that Asiatic, African, European, and even *American Indian* Spiritualism has been fully and ably represented in most of the languages spoken by civilized man, and has engaged the attention of the highest talent of every age and country, admirable compendiums of which may be perused by the student of our own time from the ever-fertile pens of a Howitt, Enemoser, Kerner, DeMorgan, Scott, Brevior, Ashburner, Reichenbach, Kardec, Browning, Bushnell, Crowe, and others, whose honored names command the world's attention and respect for the subjects they treat of. William Howitt alone has exhausted the subject, and as far as a world-wide history can be transcribed and bound up in limited space, that noble champion of divine truth has ransacked the ages to bear witness on the side of God, immortality, and religion. Robert Dale Owen, too, with all the acumen of his keenly-analytical mind and the charming style peculiar to his highly-cultivated intellect, has added many a laurel wreath to the triumphs of spiritual versus material philosophy; whilst the venerable and learned Dr. Ashburner has penetrated as far into the adytum of that temple of occult force which enshrines the mystic cord that unites spirit and matter as the investigations of the present time can carry man; and yet the stupendous realities of what the great good God and the spirits have done for man in America, during the last eventful twenty years, remain almost a sealed book, or one which, if opened to the world, no authoritative finger has pointed out to the heedless crowds who think through the leading minds of the day. And who is it, may well be questioned, that dares to raise such an index finger where minds accustomed to grasp the reins which guide the car of popular opinion have deemed the task beyond or beneath their notice? No matter who or what; enough if the task be done, or at least the attempt be made; enough if one grateful hand, that the loving clasp of spirits have guided through life's stormiest paths, now wields the encyclopedist's pen, to record their doings, or as much of them as that feeble pen can note or the narrow page preserve. And how small a portion of that mighty sum can here find place, none better knows on earth than the mind that is now bent with reverend purpose to gather up the fragments of those small loaves and fishes that have yet, in the Providence of God, sufficed to break the bread of spiritual life to America's thronging millions. But a score of years ago the name of "Spiritualist" was unknown on the American continent, whilst all the sum of Spiritualism was contained in the persons of three young girls, ignominously designated the "Rochester knockers." According to the last statistical accounts of this movement, furnished by its opponents in 1867, Spiritualism now numbers eleven millions of persons on the American continent! And it is to trace some of the most prominent footprints made by the invisible hosts who have wrought this stupendous change; to point to the beneficent effects on some individuals, the marvels enacted in the persons of others; preserve the memory of well-timed though evanescent specimens of spiritual literature, bread of the hour, but long since incorporated in the body of the movement and lost almost to recollection, and gather together the scattered blossoms of that garden of spiritual beauty that angel hands have planted, into one immortal wreath, that this record is attempted. Geographically considered, the harvest ground of this great American movement has been spread over a surface of country extending from Maine to California; and not the pathless wastes of two vast oceans have sufficed to cut off or break the telegraphic wires which have conducted the sound of the low tap, tap, of "the Rochester knockers" over three millions of square miles. Modern Spiritualism is rife along the length of the far Pacific shores, and skirts the Atlantic seaboard. It is in the cabin of the miner, in the heart of the Rocky Mountains, on the peaks of the White Sierras, and consoles the toiling emigrant in his nightly camp on the desert waste or the wild prairie. It has breathed its first lessons of freedom and refinement to the Carolina slave, and humbled the pride of the Louisiana planter. It has cheered the hours of toil in Massachusetts factories, and stimulated the energies of Minnesota pioneers. East, West, North, and South, its viewless lines have run; whilst mental science, burning oratory, triumph over pain and death, trust in God and hope for man have followed in its march. To count up its triumphs, number its achievements, do faintest justice to its treasures of hope, consolation, moral improvement, or spiritual elevation, would be as impossible as it has proved for the puny arm of man to stay its progress; but to redeem from cold forgetfulness or ungrateful obloquy the memory of some acts, words, works, and writings, that else might be lost in the whelming floods of chance, change and time—this can be done at least, and to the work, the author's highest and most faithful aims are dedicated.

One pledge more is offered: though in some special cases, names and dates cannot be fully stated, all incidents related are vouched for on the author's keenest sense of honor. The case of each not personally known or verified by individual testimony, has been searched out and scrutinized with the strictest care. Authoritarian names, having no intrinsic value with "the spirits," possess none with their scribe. But little of philosophy is offered, and few deductions or theoretical opinions will be given on what is here presented.

Faithfully to render such well-attested proofs of spiritual intercourse as the multitude of riches with which the author's stores are overloaded can permit her to select from, is all her hope or aim, and yet the half can never be related, and much that is left unsaid may be, and is, of far more worth, perhaps, than what is here preserved.

'Tis said, "the vibration of one single note of music will linger on in motion through the corridors of all eternity." Nothing, then, is ever really lost, and whether written or unwritten on the page of mortal sense, all that has been done is done forever. Farewell, then, regrets for half-attempts or ill-executed purposes. In the eternal printing houses of creation, the types of all that is are found. Accept or reject these pages, then, world, as you may! They and their author's aims and purposes, and all that may be said, or left undone, will meet and greet her on that distant shore where angel reapers gather in God's harvest treasures—"over there!"

INTRODUCTION.

"THE TRUTH AGAINST THE WORLD."

BEFORE entering upon the main object of this work, the author deems that a few remarks are necessary to elucidate the special aim and scope of her undertaking. A feverish appetite for novelty appears to be as much a specialty with the modern American as with the ancient Athenian. Perhaps this is a providential inspiration, which operates in the minds of every pioneer race as a goad to the action required to subjugate a new country. On the other hand, it may be deemed a psychological attribute peculiar to the American character, or a tendency which has been quickened into abnormal activity by the vast and marvellous outpouring of Spiritualism over the land. From whatever cause it may arise, certain it is that the cry of "Tell us something new" seems to be a demand far more urgent amongst a great majority of the American Spiritualists than a requisition for the true, the good, or the beautiful; and because we anticipate this questionable standard of novelty will be very generally applied to measure the value of these pages, we desire on their threshold to declare that they make no provision for the demand of "something new." In the first place, this work has been undertaken chiefly in response to the wish of Spirit Friends, who have urgently pressed upon the author the necessity of gathering up the scattered fragments of spiritual literature that has passed out of circulation, and conserving in concrete form the shreds and patches of broken records, which must else be swept away into the shadowy realms of tradition. When it is remembered that no systematic effort has yet been made to unite the multitudinous lines of interest that Spiritualism has woven into one connected chain of history; that the numbers of the actors who have figured in its wonderful drama must be counted by the millions (scarcely more than one per-cent. of whose experiences have ever been given to the world), full justice may be rendered to our plea that the very best and utmost we can attempt is the work of an encyclopedeist, who labels and catalogues the variety of phenomena and the names of the personages connected with the wonderful movement, and strings together on the thread of history such pearls of truth as the relentless forces of the destroyer Time have left ungathered on the line of his march.

In connection with the groupings of various phenomenal facts, we shall endeavour to present the leading ideas which have grown out of the intercourse between "the two worlds," cite the revelations of spirits concerning the conditions of the after-life and the philosophy of the communion, and quote the utterances of those public teachers who claim to have been spiritually inspired. We shall point to the idiosyncracies of those who have become prominent in the movement, especially the media for the communications from the spirit-world, and when practicable, give such portions of their biographies as may enable us to solve the problem of their seemingly exceptional gifts. It will be necessary for the elucidation of our subject, and in verification of what may be deemed rash statements, that we make frequent quotations from the press notices of the day, and present *verbatim* extracts from the spiritual journals, where facts are to be found recorded with a minutiæ of detail which cannot fail to be valuable to posterity, however tedious such familiar narratives may be to those who are still realizing similar experiences.

The earnest American Spiritualist is one who combines all the restless and inquisitive tendencies of his country with the strong additional propelling power to locomotion which a search after the marvellous supplies; consequently he not only undertakes frequent pilgrimages for the purposes of investigation, but visits distant places and persons on spiritualistic "missions." He reads all the journals of the time and place where he tarries; he visits all the media and joins all the circles held there, whether in garrets, cellars, saloons, halls, steamboats, mines, woods, valleys, Indian wigwams, or amongst the ruins of the "lost races." Either in his own person, or that of some member of his family or acquaintance, he is sure to have available medium power at his command, consequently he has his own store of phenomenal history to add to the general sum.

He is a constant attendant on all the Sabbath spiritual services held now commonly in every town and hamlet he may chance to visit, and there he never fails to gather around him a considerable number of the magnates of the meeting, some member of whom becomes his hospitable entertainer for the day, when the joint experiences of the host and his guest are interchanged and fully canvassed between the morning and evening meetings.

Some portion of each Sabbath is devoted in spiritualistic associations to the public conference, when our sojourner gives his views with that peculiar facility and occasional touch of eloquence which is an almost national characteristic in America. Most commonly the close of the evening service is followed by several invitations from the ranks of the hospitable brethren to join circles, at one of which the welcome guest is greeted by mortals and their celestial visitors with all that cordiality and fraternal feeling which is one of the happy and distinguishing marks of American Spiritualism. And it is as much due to these locomotive and hospitable features in the movement that the phenomena has become so widely diffused, and carefully studied as to any national claim which the American can set up for a peculiarly spiritual nature. From such itinerant experiences, however valuable and often wonderful they may have been, the author freely confesses she has not felt herself at liberty to make many records. Compelled to withdraw within the stern pale of well-proved and thoroughly attested facts, the floating currents of mere hearsay have necessarily been unwrought mines of wealth. Hence, for every fact recorded there will no doubt be found thousands ready to declare they could have furnished testimony of a far more wonderful character. To such we can only say, we write for that posterity to whom our facts of *veritable history* will be of incalculable value, though to us, the living actors therein, they may be of little or no importance. Besides, the memory of these marvels rapidly passes away from us, and their effect upon our minds becomes lessened with the flight of time. Many there are that require a constant succession of phenomena to renew their faith; and few amongst the best-informed Spiritualists have been at the trouble of carefully recording the facts they have witnessed. Spiritual journals, too, though numerous, and often conducted with remarkable abliity, have all—with the exception of the

Spiritual Telegraph and *Banner of Light*—been too short-lived to become points of reference to posterity, and most of the other literature of the movement, though often marked with rare excellence, yet from being issued whilst its events were in *transitu*, are too premature in time and incomplete in detail for historical uses.

Obviously, then, a duty rests on some one to collect the best and most reliable evidence that the circumstances of the case will afford, so as to conserve in a compendious form the records of either the commencement of a new era or an episode in human history as unparalleled in its preternatural marvels as it is rife with instruction, abundant in religious, social, and political influence, and prophetic of a mighty and momentous future for mental and spiritual science. Thus, then, it will be seen that it is not in the interest of the present so much as for future generations that we write; not in the hope of putting forth a volume the tone of which will command, from popular interest, a remunerative sale, but in deep and reverential conviction of a duty performed toward the mighty and beneficent power which has inaugurated this movement, and a grateful desire to share with others the priceless blessings of spiritual revelation which have been so abundantly poured out upon the actors in this marvellous drama.

The whole history of the "Rochester knockings," the disturbances in Dr. Phelps's house at Stratford, the phenomenal life of the "Poughkeepsie Seer," accounts of the Spear, Harris, Spencer, and other fanatical movements, together with a vast array of incidents of a less striking character, are all familiar as household words in the experience of every nineteenth century Spiritualist. But scattered as their records are in solitary volumes, or diffused through a mass of literature which has cost the author years to collect and collate from, they obviously require systematic effort to arrange; and familiar as they may be to the present generation, they demand, in justice to posterity, an orderly place in a compendious history of the whole movement.

Besides this candid statement of what the spiritualistic reader may or may not expect to find in these pages, a few words must necessarily be addressed to the critics, by whom, as is the custom, this work is to be heralded forth to that portion of the world who are in the habit of permitting the said critics to do their literary thinking for them. Although we scorn the petty subterfuge of affecting to disregard the world's opinion at the very time when we are publishing a book for the avowed purpose of appealing to it, yet long experience of the course pursued by a majority of the press in reference to unpopular subjects generally, and Spiritualism especially, has taught the author to expect no better treatment for her work than has been experienced by those whose honorable names should have commanded respect for any subject they wrote of. Where the honest truths detailed by an Ashburner or a Howitt have been received by bold denial or insolent ribaldry, and that by self-styled critics who were utterly ignorant of the subjects they reviled, how can an author without their claims to public respect and "decent observance" hope to escape? Whilst candidly yielding, therefore, to that portion of public opinion which is represented in press criticism all the influence and weight it deserves, the author begs respectfully to state that she has heard the epithets of "trash," "falsehood," "imposture," "impiety," a rehash of old ghost-stories and exploded theories," etc. applied to stubborn facts and unpopular truths before, and is prepared to hear them again. Happy in the belief that the assertions of falsehood do not affect the realities of truth, nor the opinions of bigotry and superstition long retard religious progress or hinder the growth of spiritual freedom, the author, in company with a mighty "cloud of witnesses," is contented to cast her great truths upon the waters of time, and let them sink or swim, as their own inherent vitality shall determine. Well satisfied by the experience of all mankind that truth and logic will survive the shafts which abuse and ridicule aim against them, she commits her record to time and the inevitable justice which this mighty touchstone has ever rendered to the cause of truth. Starting on our undertaking, first, with an overwhelming sense of its magnitude and many difficulties; and next, with but very qualified expectations of a satisfactory recognition from either Spiritualists or outsiders, it may be significantly asked, for whom do we write at all, and on what possible basis do we rest any expectation of public acceptance or sympathy in our work? We answer: "We write for the sake of the spirits, the truth, and humanity," and from each and all we expect to gather such reward as we may merit.

On behalf of the spirits we believe that we write of beneficent beings, of whose very existence, much less of their tender efforts to bless and benefit the world, a large portion of it is profoundly ignorant. If they, from their exalted spheres of blessedness, can be content to labor for a dark and ignorant generation, cannot we, in our human insignificance, emulate their disinterestedness? And again, can none of us afford to labor for love of the good and true, without a certain assurance of temporal reward and human appreciation? It were a libel on the race to deem otherwise. Ninty-nine per cent. of the world's brightest immortals have lived, labored, and died, for the sake of the true, the good, and the beautiful, with no other reward than the tardy and remorseful appreciation of posterity. If there be any amongst us who dare to emulate their martyr-like devotion, and humbly seek to walk in the track of their shining though tear-stained foot-prints, why question or sneer at the choice? It is enough that the subject is more than worthy of all the care, labor, and disinterested effort that the many or the few can bring to bear upon it. Through the beneficent action of the mighty though invisible hosts who constitute the legions of the modern spiritual army, thousands of darkened minds have been snatched from hopeless belief in the horrible doctrine of annihilation. The crippled limbs have been made straight, the blinded eyes opened, the dull ears unstopped, the ebbing life called back to gladden the pathway of rejoicing friends; the homes bereaved of frail mortality have been filled with the glorious presence of arisen angels; the sinner has been startled from the paths of crime, and the fainting strengthened in the thorny road of virtue, by the direct and visible guidance and warning of precious spirit friends. A flood of light has been poured on the long-veiled and awful mysteries of the grave, revealing the solemn and stupendous *realities* of the inevitable hereafter, and a mass of wonderful revelation has illuminated the cherished mysticisms of superstition and sectarianism, breaking the fetters of darkness that have so long hung around the neck of humanity. "Babylon has fallen"—"Mystery, the mother of abominations," is slain, and the angel of truth and judgment has sounded the trumpet of victory in the great outpouring of modern Spiritualism. When we remember that all these results are but a tithe of the blessings which the Spiritualist recognizes as flowing from the dispensation wherewith he has been visited, can it be a matter of astonishment that we deem it the highest of life's privileges to be permitted to write for spirits, and bear witness of their wonderful works throughout the land? To qualify the author for this office, she has borne her part in every phase of the spiritual dispensation. From earliest childhood up to the present time she has seen and conversed with spiritual beings like familiar friends; passed through many of the phases of modern mediumship, and witnessed or taken part in most of the scenes described in these pages. For the performance of professional duties connected with the cause of Spiritualism, she has travelled and lectured through thirty-two of the United States, and gathered her records chiefly from personal observation and the witness of living millions who are still on earth to bear testimony to the truth of her statements. Thus, the facts herein recorded are open to the strictest scrutiny; they are, indeed, still transpiring, and occur constantly in the experience of *eleven millions* of persons in America, whose numbers include authors, editors, doctors, lawyers, clergymen, professors of colleges, magistrates on the bench, statesmen, traders, operatives, and mechanics—in a word, all gradations of rank and all classes of thought. As keen research and sceptical scrutiny has for the most part characterized the progressive belief of American Spiritualism, these vast masses testify of that *which they know and have proved.* On the contrary, it will be found that the loudest and most rancorous opposers of this belief are persons who have either never investigated the subject at all, or so slightly as to be in no position to judge of its subtle and far-reaching realities. Let the world determine between these two classes. Both, no doubt, will be represented amongst the readers and critics of these pages, and to both we close our introductory remarks by affirming that we have lived, written, and purpose to abide by, in time present and to come, and under all circumstances, this axiom of invincible strength and never-failing triumph: "The truth against the world."

MODERN AMERICAN SPIRITUALISM;

OR,

A TWENTY YEARS' RECORD OF THE COMMUNION BETWEEN EARTH AND THE WORLD OF SPIRITS,

FROM 1848 TO 1868.

CHAPTER I.

"VOICES CRYING IN THE WILDERNESS."

"In deep trance-slumbers, when the world, asleep,
Lay in the arms of night and wept or smiled,
His liberated soul raised from its dust.
We led him far beyond the veils, and floods,
And labyrinths of sleep; the clouds of death
And all the shadowed dwellers in the world
Were far beneath him. Through his consciousness
Streamed the celestial sunrise.
Cities and temples of celestial space
Were mirrored in his mind."

T. L. Harris.

The Mesmerizers — Electro-biologists — Adventists of Spiritualism — The Poughkeepsie Seer and his Revelations.

If it be true that the history of humanity moves forward in epochs, then it is certain that the leading characteristics of one era result from the specialties of the age which preceded it, whilst we in turn plant the seed whose fruitage will be gathered by the hands of our posterity.

He who searches for the origin of some great discovery, or the sources from which spring stupendous changes, may invariably trace the germ-thought through a continued series of experimental antecedents.

Sometimes the causative idea is sown in many minds, and springs up in many places at once, but it may always be traced in rudimental stages of growth e'er it is exhibited in the maturity of a fully-perfected work.

What we call "Modern American Spiritualism" forms no exception to this univerasal method of progressive unfoldment.

Startling and unprecedented in many respects as appears to be the achievement of a telegraphic communion between the visible and invisible worlds, the open ear of intelligence will have no difficulty in recognizing the voice of many a John the Baptist who has proclaimed the coming of the New Spiritual Messiah.

Amongst these none has rung out with a more clearly-marked tone than "Mesmerism," with its kindred phenomena of "Electro-biology" and "Clairvoyance." Chemistry, Physiology, Phrenology, Magnetism, and Clairvoyance have all been steps leading up through the once-forbidden mysteries of nature into the realm of imponderable forces, bearing the student onward to the very gates of the temple of mind, within which are now heard the low, telegraphic knocks of the spirit, inviting the earnest inquirers to enter, and prophesying the great day of revelation, when man may ascend, as on a Jacob's ladder, that mighty column where Physics is the base, Science the shaft, Metaphysics the superstructure, and Spiritualism the coronal glory of the capital, whose starry crown pierces the overarching firmament of Heaven.

Mesmerism, with its wonderful results in somnambulism and clairvoyance, has often been assumed by the superficial observer to offer a complete solution of the mysteries of Spiritualism. Without attempting at present to show how totally inadequate is this explanation to meet the case in point, we are prepared to admit that mesmerism has performed an important part in ushering in the more comprehensive movement of Spiritualism. For several years antecedent to the advent of the latter, mesmerism, or "animal magnetism," was largely practiced over every part of America. In nearly every city, town, or hamlet, the itinerant mesmerizer made his rounds, operating upon chance subjects as opportunity offered, and alternately exciting superstitious terror or wrathful antagonism by the exercise of his seemingly magical powers.

Many professional operators were no doubt skilful, and with a higher realization of the valuable gift with which they were endowed, might have become successful healers of the sick. As it was, and despite the fact that the exercise of their art was frequently interrupted by the insensate fury of ignorant mobs, they often succeeded in effecting what were deemed "miraculous" cures, at which they themselves were not less astonished than their subjects.

In view of the superstitious bigotry and *scientific ignorance* which prevailed on this subject when animal magnetism was first practiced in America, continuous experiment and deliberate investigation was impossible. Nevertheless, the exhibitions of itinerant magnetizers, undignified and occasionally riotous as they were, became suggestive to thoughtful observers, and ultimately produced a wide-spread interest on the subject. Intelligent witnesses, assembled by chance in a village school-house or country barn, set themselves to work to discover the source of the marvels they beheld. Magnetic experiments were practiced in the home circle; more favorable conditions were followed by more remarkable results; the inquiry deepened into profound interest, and the phenomena of animal magnetism became familiarly known to the most progressive classes of the community. Ignored by those scientists who were too proud to investigate anything they did not originally discover, and anathematized by a superstitious and creed-bound priesthood, animal magnetism was openly denounced as "the latest invention of the enemy of mankind," or, "a profound humbug" whilst the luckless itinerant exhibitor was often cited before some grave magistrate, who, in the seclusion of his own home, was a more interested investigator and a better operator than the criminal he was called upon to punish. In a word, magnetism became a fashion, and its legitimate claim to be considered as a science was at length fully established. The result of this movement upon Spiritualism has now become obvious.

Thousands of persons who are warm advocates of the spiritual phliosophy acknowledge that their attention was first attracted to the subject by their interest in magnetism. In all the principal cities of the Union, gentlemen distinguished for their literary abilities, progressive opinions, or prominence in public affairs, have graduated from the study of magnetism and clairvoyanee to become adherents to the cause of Spiritualism, whilst many of the best mediums—especially the trance speakers and magnetic operators—have taken their first degree in Spiritualism, as experimentalists in the phenomena of mesmerism.

All popular movements in America are spread over such immense surfaces of country that nothing less than a question of national interest can form a focalizing point for popular opinion, or its representation in foreign countries; hence, whilst magnetism, electro-biology, and clairvoyance have swept over the land in vast tides of influence, they have acquired more notoriety in a few solitary instances in France and Germany, than in all their magnitude in the United States.

Admitting that the modern spiritual manifestations in America first began to assume the form of a concrete movement at Rochester in 1848, it would still be impossible to separate the influence which the prevalence of the magnetic idea exercised upon minds prepared to receive Spiritualism and organisms already imbued with the necessary force to develop mediumship.

Between the epochs in which these two great movements have dominated, is an interregnum, rife with the advent of a human phenomenon, connecting both, belonging to both, yet standing alone, and unrivalled in the marvellous character of his occult endowments, and the irresistible nature of the influence he has exercised upon humanity. This personage is Andrew Jackson Davis, more commonly called "the Poughkeepsie Seer." At about the age of fifteen, young Davis first became remarkable in New York and Connecticut for his skill in diagnosing and prescribing for disease through his wonderful clairvoyant faculty. Of a slight and delicate temperament, the young physician possessed a degree of intuitive refinement which in some sense compensated for his total deficiency of educational culture, and an artificial grace which could not be expected from his exceedingly humble origin, which was that of the son and apprentice of a poor country shoemaker.

About the age of fourteen he was casually magnetized by a Mr. Livingston, of Poughkeepsie, who, discovering that the shoemaker's boy possessed wonderful clairvoyant powers, and an unusually successful gift of prescribing for the sick, gradually drew him from his trade into association with himself until at length they travelled and practiced together as operator and subject, with unbounded success and benefit to the world.

From the period when Mr. Livingston accidentally discovered young Davis's wonderful endowments, his whole time was so disposed of that neither then nor at any subsequent period of his career could he have found leisure, even if he had the capacity, to add one iota of literary information to his slender stock of village scholasticism. The exceedingly humble rank and limited means of his parents deprived young Davis of all chances of culture, save five months at a rustic school and the association of the rude boors of wild country districts. The extraordinary celebrity to which he has now attained has rendered even the minutest details of his early childhood public property; hence it is well known that his highest accomplishment, at the time of what may be called his spiritual illumination, was limited to the capacity to read, write, and cipher very indifferently, whilst his whole stock of remembered literature was a tale called "the Three Spaniards."

Mr. Davis was about eighteen years of age when he announced to the circle of admirers who had become interested in his wonderful lucidity as a clairvoyant, that a new and astounding phase of spiritual power was about to be revealed through his instrumentality, commencing with the delivery of a course of lectures which were destined ultimately to revolutionize the scientific world and produce a striking effect upon the religious opinions of mankind.

In fulfilment of this prophecy Mr. Davis proceeded to give the promised course of lectures, for the production of which he selected Dr. Lyon, of Bridgeport, as his magnetizer, the Rev. William Fishbough as his scribe, the Rev. Y. N. Parker, R. Lapham, Esq., and Dr. L. Smith, of New York, as his special witnesses, whilst several other gentlemen, high in place or distinguished for literary and scientific attainments, were from time to time invited in, or permitted to be present at the delivery of the lectures; and thus was produced the vast compendium of literary, scientific, philosophic, and historic knowledge, entitled "Nature's Divine Revelations." Of the work itself, together with a more detailed account of its author and his subsequent career, we shall speak more fully in our biographical sketches; suffice it to say that the marvellously abnormal character of the book, emanating as it did from a person so utterly incapable of its production under ordinary circumstances, excited the most profound astonishment in all ranks and classes. "The Revelations" were quickly followed by "The Great Harmonia," "Penetralia," "Present Age and Inner Life," and other voluminous productions, the sum of which, combined with Mr. Davis's lectures, editorial labors, associative movements, and wide-spread personal influence, have effected a complete revolution in the minds of a large and distinguished class of thinkers in the United States, who are known as the advocates of the "Harmonial Philosophy," a belief which emphatically owes its origin to *the poor shoemaker's boy*, A. J. Davis. Even at the early age of eighteen (the period when the first of the "Revelations" were given) the remarkable attainments of Mr. Davis as a medical clairvoyant, together with the exceeding purity of his life and the modesty of his manners, had drawn around him a circle of distinguished persons who became his warmly-attached friends. Mr. James Victor Wilson, a gentleman of New Orleans, renowned for his literary talents and the author of an excellent treatise on magnetism, writes of him thus, during the delivery of his first lectures:

> "The world will shortly be apprised of a triumph in clairvoyance through the celebrated Mr. Davis, which it will be totally unprepared for. During the past year this uneducated, unsophisticated, and amiable young man has been delivering verbally, day by day, a comprehensive, well-planned, and extraordinary book, relating to all the vast questions of the age; to the physical sciences; to nature in all her infinite ramifications; to man in his innumerable modes of existence; to God in the unfathomable abysses of his love, wisdom, and power. . . . . . .
>
> "Thousands of persons who have witnessed him in his medical examinations or scientific disclosures, live to testify to the astounding exaltation of mind possessed by Mr. Davis in his abnormal state.
>
> "The two new planets of our system, conjectured recently, were described in Davis's manuscripts fourteen months ago, namely, March 15 and 16, 1846."

Shortly after the lectures commenced, Mr. Davis's rooms in New York City were thrown open to the public for medical examinations, on which occasions his manuscripts were often submitted to the highest intellects of the country for investigation, and his whole career — especially the impossibility of his having acquired the knowledge he exhibited in his clairvoyant state

Andrew Jackson Davis

by any ordinary means—was made the subject of searching and rigid scrutiny. One of the most marked results established by the life of this phenomenal personage was the actuality of clairvoyance and the triumphant revelation that the soul of man could commune spiritually with supra-mundane as well as mundane minds, and aspire far beyond this terrestrial sphere in its acquisition of knowledge. The latter, indeed, was still a mooted point, and a vast amount of logic was expended on young Davis's case in the attempt to prove that all the "revelations" poured through his lips were only the reflex of minds still upon earth, or stereotyped in books, and that the seer's gift was simply clairvoyant perception of mundane existences. It was doubtless very gratifying to the egotism of certain individuals to believe that the clairvoyant had found the source of his remarkable and varied revelations in their own highly-illuminated minds, and they professed themselves willing to become the subjects of this original system of mental piracy for the sake of appropriating the merit of his comprehensive philosophy and disposing of the awkward problem of supra-mundane interference; but whilst many of Mr. Davis's writings give obvious evidence of human clairvoyance, there is still a large amount of original matter which can only be accounted for by admitting the hypothesis of spiritual perception in realms of super-sensuous existence and inspiration from a world of supra-mundane knowledge. Besides this, there are points of coincidence in the testimony of other illuminated persons which must not be lost sight of. Whilst it must be admitted that Mr. Davis's lucidity and breadth of mental power was unparalleled in the records of history, the gift of clairvoyant sight was by no means limited by his experience, even in his own time. The various magnetic subjects who abounded at the period we write of, not only gave evidences of a highly exalted condition and remarkable interior perception, but frequently perplexed their operators by speaking of *spirits*, declaring they could converse with "dead people," perceive them in life, enter their habitations, and describe the homes or "spheres in which they dwelt." All this was contrary to the experience of the magnetizers, hence declared by them to be no reflex of their minds or opinions; and as these unaccountable vagaries of entrancement seemed to be on the increase, considerate and candid inquirers began to connect them with the wonderful mental flights achieved by young Davis, and conjecture that the freed spirit in its "sleep waking" condition, might pass into realms of being, super-sensuous in their nature, and supra-mundane in their population.

Meantime, as the transcendent powers of Mr. Davis seemed to concentrate into one focal point all the lesser lights of magnetic marvel, so the whole ranks of materialistic antagonism rushed pell-mell upon him, as the head and front of all spiritualistic offending. Nero-like, the anti-spiritual world seemed, to think that in striking at him they could sweep out of being all the obnoxious, occult people and forces that outraged their materialism or bigotry; hence the "Poughkeepsie Seer" earned his newly-acquired fame at the price of becoming a target for the shafts of every form of abuse, ridicule, and slander that ignorance and prejudice could heap upon him.

About the early part of December, 1847, the general understanding of spiritual philosophy received a valuable impetus from the publication of an excellent weekly journal entitled *The Univercœlum, or Spiritual Philosopher*. This paper was started at the instance of a few gentlemen whose friendship for and high appreciation of Mr. Davis induced them to make this attempt to popularize his opinions, and call around them a circle of such wise and progressive minds as would sympathize with their views. The projectors and chief contributors to the undertaking were Mr. Davis, then just twenty-one years of age; Rev. William Fishbough, Rev. Thomas L. Harris, the inspired author of the "Epic of the Starry Heavens," and other equally renowned poems; and the Rev. S. B. Britain, to whose scholarly charge and highly-polished intellect the editorial department was wisely intrusted.

Besides this accomplished editorial staff, contributors of the highest talent filled the columns of the *Univercœlum.* Amongst these were the Rev. W. M. Fernald, J. K. Redfield, Mr. F. M Baker, J. V. Ingalls, Charles Worth, and D. T. H. Chivers. So brilliant an array of writers procured for the *Univercœlum* a high reputation, and besides being the first spiritual periodical of modern date in America, it became a compendium of the best thoughts and purest philosophy of the age. In addition to its own intrinsic merits, this journal was favored with the usual amount of advertising, which resulted from the bitter antagonism provoked by the spiritualistic reputation of its authors and editors.

Unfortunately the latter gentlemen were richer in mental than material endowments; hence they had to struggle with the usual amount of financial disability, that seems to be the fate of genius; and hence, too, in all probability, they were as much indebted to the publicity afforded to their paper by the rancor of their opponents as to their own merits; the combination of the two causes, however, enabled them to fill a hiatus in the literature of the time for above two years, during which their paper, sustained by the most indomitable perseverance and bitter self-sacrifice, laid the foundation of a noble and genuine tone of thought, the fruits of which will be felt in all ages where true spiritual life and philosophy can be appreciated.

Besides their untiring efforts in connection with the paper, its noble staff of editors endeavored to distribute the bread of life with which they felt they had been so richly blessed, in lectures given at home and abroad, to which they added public discussions, newspaper and magazine controversies; in a word, they threw their hearts and talents into the work, and formed a nucleus from which the irradiations of spiritual thought and influence flowed out in abundant and startling force. It is simple justice to affirm that "Nature's Divine Revelations," the *Univercœlum*, and the personal influence and diffusive labor of their talented authors, inaugurated a new era in the world of thought, and opened up a new channel of inspiration, whose source, like that of the mighty Nile, may long remain a hidden mystery, but when explored by the enterprise of future ages, will date back to a human Nyanza in the person of the "Poughkeepsie Seer," upheld by the strong hands and sunlit minds of the noble gentlemen who rallied around him.

"Honor to whom honor is due." The despised itinerant lecturers on magnetism, the still more contemned experimenters in electro-biology, even the unsophisticated children and rustics who were their subjects, these, as forerunners of the culminating marvel of modern ages—A. J. Davis—were amongst the first to hear the divine command to "prepare the way of the Lord," and re-echo the solemn charge in the wildernesses of materialism.

The obscurity of the personages, and the humility of their pretensions, may throw over the origin of the movement the veil of unkind forgetfulness, or ungrateful repudiation, yet the vital fires of magnetism and the subtle forces of psychology will yet be found to underlie the whole science of life and mind, whether incarnate in mortal clay or enfranchised in the free spiritual existence in life beyond the tomb. The waters of Oblivion, muddied by the thick night of human ignorance and human ingratitude, may engulph in dim forgetfulness the name of the author of "Nature's Divine

Revelations," but his phenomenal life-work and teachings have already formed a glittering star which is set in the firmament of eternity, surrounded by the constellation of unworn minds whom he focalized about him, and through whom the spiritual yearnings of the nineteenth century first found expression, in the shape of a true and harmonious philosophy.

A. J. Davis and his friends, ridiculed, despised, contemned and slandered as they were, on the one hand startled the age from the worship of atoms, in which material science pretended to discover the sources of mind; and on the other, embodied the vague transcendentalisms of credal faiths in the distinct and tangible form of an electric, living, silver cord, uniting the shadowy phantasmagoria of matter with the deathless and changeless principle of spirit.

Though not the origin of or immediately connected with the phenomenal movement called Modern Spiritualism, though indeed, up to this date, *The Harmonial Philosophy* of A. J. Davis, and the doctrines of Spiritualism, may maintain lines of separative demarcation between them, the great spiritual unfolding revealed in Mr. Davis's person, and the irresistible influence which he has exercised upon the opinions of the age, unquestionably formed the John Baptist which inaugurated that sunlit day when faith became knowledge, hope of immortality a glorious realization, and the dark, spectral shadow of death became transfigured into the radiant form of a ministering spirit, in the bright illuminating beams of modern Spiritualism.

CHAPTER II.

"AND THERE SHALL BE NO MORE DEATH."

THE SHAKERS AS "JOHN THE BAPTISTS" OF SPIRITUALISM — HYDESVILLE — THE FIRST RAPPINGS — THE FIRST SPIRITUAL TELEGRAPH.

A FEW years ago, the author, being on a lecturing tour in the vicinity of a large village of the community known as "Shakers," was waited on by some of their members for the purpose of communicating certain facts which they seemed to think it was essential to the cause of truth should be laid before her. One of the party, a man distinguished for his literary talents and the integrity of his character, read a document which purported to be an account of a special visitation of the "guardian spirits" who openly communed with the members of that society. It seemed that manifestations of spiritual presence, through rappings, movings of furniture, visions, trance, clairaudience, and clairvoyance, had been common amongst the Shakers since the time of their foundation, some seventy years ago; but the particular visitation to which the visitors desired to call attention, took place about 1830, when a multitude of spiritual beings, with the most solemn and forcible tokens of their presence, in a variety of phenomenal ways indicated the approach of a great spiritual crisis, in which they designed for a season to withdraw the special gifts enjoyed by the Shakers, and pour them out in mighty floods upon the "world's people," who, for the realization of certain divine purposes, faintly shadowed forth, were to be visited by unlooked-for and stupendous tokens of spiritual presence.

The commencement of the promised new era was to be inaugurated by an extraordinary discovery of material as well as spiritual wealth. *Mines of treasure* were to be discovered in the earth, and floods of spiritual light were to descend from the heavens, and both these vast outpourings were, it was predicted, to occur in the year 1848, and to continue until about 1870, when fresh sensuous and super-sensuous demonstrations were to proclaim the inauguration of another era. The record of this spiritual visitation, together with the details of the communication, was shown to the author, duly attested by numerous witnesses, and bearing date about 1829 or '30. The document stated further, that the Shakers, fearing lest their beloved "guardian angels" purposed to withdraw from them altogether, wept in such abundance that their tears fell on the ground like rain, and bedewed the sacred floor on which the angelic presence shone. The authenticity, together with the date of this prophecy, has been confirmed by numerous communications from other Shaker communities; and in further corroboration of its truth, we call attention to the fact that the discovery of gold in California and the breaking out of Spiritualism through the "Rochester knockings" both occurred in 1847–8.

In a most excellent work, published as early in the progress of modern American Spiritualism as 1855, giving a detailed account of its facts and fanaticisms up to that period, Mr. E. W. Capron, its author, relates, chiefly upon his own authority as an eye-witness, a full and interesting account of that initiatory phase of the manifestations known as the "Rochester knockings." Dr. Hare, Judge Edmonds, Hon. R. D. Owen, and other American writers of celebrity have repeated in substance Mr. Capron's narrative, while several journals and a great many ephemeral pamphlets, now out of print, have given the sum of the history with more or less fidelity, so that a repetition of this oft-told tale in these pages might appear supererogatory and almost impertinent, were its insertion not in strict accordance with the principal aim of a work which promises rather a compendious *resumé* of the facts already patent to the public mind than any originality of detail or novel revelation in connection with it. Even the privilege enjoyed by the author of an intimate acquaintance with the famed "Poughkeepsie Seer," the "Rochester mediums," and Dr. Phelps, of Stratford, affords no new sources of information in addition to the facts already detailed in former publications; but as these facts form the opening wedges that rent asunder the rock of ancient supernaturalism, converting it into the light of modern Spiritualism, so the omission of these details from our history would shear effects from their legitimate causes, and display the blossom and fruitage of a great movement severed from the root which gave it birth. The astonishing power of the human mind revealed through the magnetic sleep were not phenomena peculiar to Mr. A. J. Davis alone, nor unfamiliar to the investigators of occult science; nevertheless, it was in his person that they assumed such magnitude and orderly development as to crystalize in one example the experience of preceding ages, and represent magnetism and clairvoyance as facts which admit of no dispute. Strange sounds and apparitions of the so-called *dead* were not peculiar to the house at Hydesville, inhabited by the Foxes, neither was the aura through which spirits could manifest their presence an attribute special to this family alone. Besides the spiritual manifestations of other times and countries, rappings, movements of ponderable bodies, and all the variety of unaccountable phenomena witnessed at Hydesville, had often startled the inhabitants of other districts before; and although the weird manifestations at Dr. Phelps's house at Stratford, exceeded in power and persistency any equally well attested facts of modern Spiritualism, their nature was not unfamiliar to those who had ever examined the subject of haunted houses or the doings of the German "Poltergheist." Still the concrete and scientific characteristics of the spiritual movement in America take their origin in the first attempt at telegraphy, commenced at Hydesville and followed out in Rochester, and hence we cannot do justice to the subject without a careful review of this portion of it. From the first working of the spiritual telegraph by which invisible beings were enabled to spell out consecutive messages, they ["the spirits"] claimed that this method of communion was organized by scientific minds in the spirit spheres; that it depended mainly upon the conditions of human and atmospheric magnetisms, and pointed to the ultimation of a science whereby spirits, operating upon and through matter, could connect in the most intimate relations the worlds of material and spiritual existence.

They referred to the house at Hydesville as one peculiarly suited to their purpose from the fact of its being *charged with the aura requisite to make it a battery for the working of the telegraph;* also to the Fox family as being similarly endowed.

They called this aura the "life principle," represented it as a force which constituted the person or place in which it existed in abundance a medium, or channel through which spirits could communicate. These glimmerings of philosophy form the first stepping-stones to a spiritual science; hence it is to the inauguration of a communion based upon these principles that we trace the commencement of the present era, and we should deem our history incomplete unless it started from that point.

In pursuance of this object, we shall now invite the attention of the reader to a few extracts from certain pamphlets, written by E. E. Lewis, Esq., of Canandaigua, New York; D. M. Dewey, of Rochester, published in 1850; J. B. Campbell, M.D., of Alleghany, published in 1851; E. W. Capron, of Auburn; and the testimony of various members of the Fox family, rendered in familiar conversations with the author. It should be stated that the scene of the following manifestions was a small wooden house in the little village of Hydesville, Wayne County, New York. The place, not being directly accessible from a railroad, was lonely, and unmarked by those tokens of progress that the locomotive generally leaves in its track, hence it was the last spot where a scene of fraud and deception could find motive for or possibility of a successful execution. The family so prominently identified with the phenomena were persons of worth and integrity. Their little dwelling, though so small and simply furnished as to leave no shadow of opportunity for concealment or trick, was the residence of honest piety and rural simplicity. All who have ever known them will bear witness to the unimpeachable character of the good mother, now happily removed from the scene of her overwhelming earthly trials, while the integrity of the simple-minded farmers who were father and brother to the ladies who have since become so celebrated as "the Rochester knockers," stands proved beyond all question. At the time of the manifestations, the house was tenanted by Mr. and Mrs. Fox and their two youngest children, Margaret and Catharine, the respective ages of whom Mrs. Fox's published statement represents as twelve and fifteen years.

These details, insignificant as they may now appear, are due alike in justice to the family and posterity. When the future of this wonderful movement shall have become matter of history, and antiquity, if not reverence for spiritual truth, shall induce mankind to follow the example of their ancestors and label the records "sacred," the names now sunk in obscurity and masked by slander may perchance be engraved in monuments of bronze and marble, and the incidents deemed too slight for notice may be reverenced as "*Holy Writ.*" These changes of chance and time have happened before. If history repeats herself they will occur again.

From a published statement of the early investigations connected with this house, entitled "Report of the Mysterious Noises, etc.," we learn that some disturbances had affected the inhabitants before Mr. Fox and his family came to reside there. Nothing of the kind was noticed, however, until the tenancy of a Mr. and Mrs. ——, who, according to the statement of Lucretia P. [a girl who occasionally resided with them], occupied that house for a short time during the winter of 1843–4. Miss P., in the deposition called forth by subsequent investigations, states that one afternoon a pedler, apparently about thirty years of age, dressed in a black frock coat, light pantaloons and cap, and carrying with him a pack of goods, called on Mrs. ——, who seemed to recognize him as an acquaintance. Shortly after his arrival, Mrs. —— called her, and told her, very much to her surprise, that she thought she could not afford to keep her any longer, and, as she was going to Lock Berlin that afternoon, she wished Lucretia to leave the house with her. This the latter agreed to do, but before going she looked at a piece of dress delaine in the pedler's pack, and requested him to call with it at her father's house the next day. The man promised to do so, but she never saw him more. Mrs. —— and Lucretia then left the house, the pedler and Mr. —— remaining behind, the former being apparently likely to remain there for the day.

After the lapse of three days, Mrs. —— sent for Lucretia P. from her home and requested her to return to her again. From this time Lucretia P. began to hear knockings in the bedroom, and on one occasion, when her employers had gone to Lock Berlin, she sent for her little brother and a companion named Aurelia to pass the night with her. All the young people that night distinctly heard noises which, as they declared, sounded like the footsteps of a man passing from the bedroom into the buttery, then down the cellar stairs, traversing the cellar for a short distance, and then suddenly stopping.

They were very much frightened, and scarcely slept the remainder of the night. In the "Report of Mysterious Noises," Mrs. P., the mother of Lucretia, who resided near, deposed that, having called on Mrs. —— one day, after the foregoing circumstances, she found her quite ill from want of rest on the previous night. On inquiring the cause, Mrs. —— declared that she was sick of her life, and that she heard the footsteps of a man traversing the house all night; a statement which she often subsequently repeated. About a week after the visit of the pedler to the house, Lucretia, having occasion to go down into the cellar, stumbled and fell into some soft soil. Aware that this was unusual, she screamed for assistance, and when Mrs. —— came to her, she asked "whatever had Mr. —— been doing in the cellar?" Mrs. —— replied that it was only *rat-holes;* and a few nights afterwards, the witness related that Mr. —— was busy for a long time in the cellar filling up "the rat-holes" with earth which he carried there himself. The house, as has been stated, was an humble frame dwelling, consisting of two fair-sized parlors opening into each other, a bed-room, and buttery or pantry, opening into one of the rooms; and a stairway between the buttery and bedroom, leading down to the cellar and up to the half-story above. It seems that those who had inhabited this house previously had never noticed any unusual sounds or disturbances in it. A few months from the occurrences above detailed it was occupied by a Mr. Michael Weekman, whose testimony we extract from Dr. Campbell's published account of the spirit rappings at Hydesville, which states that—

"The first well-authenticated history that we have of the sounds so unaccountable to those who have heard them was in a house occupied by Mr. Michael Weekman, in a little village known by the name of Hydesville, in the township of Arcadia, Wayne County. He resided in the house for about eighteen months, and left some time in the year 1847. Mr. Weekman makes the statement in substance as follows: That one evening, about the time of retiring, he heard a rapping on the outside door, and, what was rather unusual for him, instead of familiarly bidding them 'come in,' stepped to the door and opened it. He had no doubt of finding some one who wished to come in, but, to his surprise, found no one there. He went back and proceeded to undress, when, just before getting into bed, he heard another rap at the door, loud and distinct. He stepped to the door quickly and opened it, but, as before, found no one there. He stepped out and looked around, supposing that some one was imposing on him. He could discover no one, and went back into the house. After a short time he heard the rapping again, and stepped up [it being often repeated] and held on to the latch, so that he might ascertain if any one had taken that means to annoy him. The rapping was repeated; the door opened instantly, but no one was to be seen! He states that he could feel the jar of the door very plainly when the rapping was heard. As he opened the door, he sprung out and went around the house, but no one was in sight. His family were fearful to have him go out lest some one intended to harm him. It always remained a mystery to him, and finally, as the rapping did not continue at that time, passed from his mind, except when something of the same nature occurred to revive it.

"They were at one time disturbed by a manifestation of a different nature, which might be thought more incredible than the former, had not facts proved that such occurrences were common in the families where the early manifestations were heard. One night their little girl, then about eight years of age, was heard to scream from fright, so that the family were alarmed by her cries and went to her assistance. This was about midnight. She told them that something like a hand had passed over her face and head; that she felt it on the bed and all over her, but did not become so much alarmed until it touched her face. It seemed cold, and so badly had she been frightened that it was a long time before she could tell the cause of her alarm. It was several days before she could be induced to go into the same room to sleep.

"All this *might* have occurred, and been only 'the idle fabric of a dream;' and we should be inclined to the belief that such was the case had we not had the most conclusive evidence that such manifestations were quite common, not only in that house, but in various others where any of these strange occurrences have happened.

"We hear nothing more of Mr. Weekman being disturbed by the rappings or other manifestations, or there being anything of the kind with that exception, until after the house was occupied by the family of Mr. John D. Fox. It was reserved to that family to be the instruments of communicating to the world, or to this part of it, this most singular affair. They were the ones who first, as if by accident, found out that there was an intelligence manifested even in this rapping, which at first appeared nothing more than an annoying and unaccountable noise.

"The family of Mr. Fox were well known in the neighborhood where they resided. Mr. and Mrs. Fox were connected with the Methodist Episcopal Church, of which they had for many years been exemplary members, and had sustained a character unimpeachable for truth and veracity. No one who knew them had the least suspicion of their honesty or truthfulness. At the time these occurrences first took place in the family, there were living with the parents three daughters, the youngest about twelve years of age.

"There are probably few families in which such an occurrence could have taken place where it would have created a greater degree of surprise and fear than in this one. They were entirely unacquainted with the history of any similar occurrence in the world, and brought up in the common routine of religious belief they were, as in fact all the world really was and still is, entirely unprepared for such a development of the power of spirits to make themselves known to us by sounds or other ways."

From the family themselves the author learns that they heard knocking very frequently before the period when they first called in the neighbors, and that they generally seemed to proceed from the bedroom or the cellar beneath. Mrs. Fox was at first disposed to attribute these sounds to a neighboring shoemaker, but the cause soon began to be plainly located in the house itself, and not only seemed to jar the furniture, but even to occasion a slightly oscillating movement of the bed in which the children slept. Sometimes the sounds resembled footsteps, and occasionally the children complained of being touched by something invisible, which at one time seemed like a cold hand, and again a large dog. The family had moved into the house in December, 1847, and in the February of the following year the noises had become so distinct and continuous that their rest was broken night after night, and they were worn out by their efforts to discover the cause. Up to the March of 1848 these disturbances, harassing and even serious as they were, affecting their rest and tranquility of a night, had never been heard during the day.

At length, however, they became so incessant and distressing that Mrs. Fox communicated the matter to her son David, a farmer, who resided about three miles distant from the troubled house. Her story, however, was listened to with incredulity, and regarded simply as the work of imagination "or something of the simplest kind in the world." On Friday evening, March 31st, the family had retired to bed earlier than usual, being completely worn out with the restlessness induced by former disturbances. The mother had strictly charged the children "to lie still" and take no notice whatever of the sounds; but, as if in rebuke of her determined insensibility, they were on this occasion louder and more pertinacious than ever. Rest or silence was impossible; the parents had not yet retired, but were about to do so. The children kept exclaiming, and sitting up in bed to listen to the sounds. Mr. and Mrs. Fox tried the windows and doors, but all in vain; the raps were evidently answering the noise occasioned by the father's shaking the window-shashes, as if in mockery. At length the youngest child, Kate—who, in her guileless innocence, had become familiar with the invisible knocker, until she was more amused than alarmed at its presence—merrily snapped her fingers and called out, "Here, Mr. Split-foot, do as I do!" The effect was instantaneous; the invisible rapper responded by imitating the number of her movements. She then made a given number of motions with her finger and thumb in the air, *but without noise*, and her astonishment and childish delight was redoubled to find that it *could see as well as hear*, for a corresponding number of knocks were immediately given to her noiseless motions. "Only look, mother!" she cried; "look, it can see as well as hear!" What an announcement were these few simple words! *It can see as well as hear* should have been a text which all the doctors, professors, sceptics, and scoffers who have subsequently tried to crush out the sublime truth of spiritual intercourse with earth should have studied and learned by heart ere they entered on their rash and irreverend crusade. Happily for the momentous work which the spiritual telegraphers had undertaken to initiate in this humble dwelling, the first manifestations did not appeal to the high and learned of the earth, but to the plain common-sense of an honest farmer's wife, and suggested that whatever could see, hear, and intelligently respond to intelligent queries, must have in it something in common with humanity; and thus prompted she continued her investigations, an act doubtless far beneath the dignity of mighty professors and learned savans, who can work out problems in Euclid, but scorn to descend to the simple task of putting two and two together to make four.

Addressing the viewless rapper, Mrs. Fox then said, "Count ten." The raps obeyed. "How old is my daughter Margaret?" then "Kate." Both questions were distinctly and correctly rapped out. The next response was wrong, however. Querying, "How many children have I?" the raps answered "seven." Mrs. Fox only had six living, but having become surprised and interested enough to wish that the invisible rapper should be correct, she repeated her question, and was again answered by seven knocks. Suddenly she cried, "How many have I *living?*" six raps responded; "How many dead?" a single knock; and both these answers proved correct. To the next question, "Are you a man that knocks?" there was no response; but "*Are you a spirit?*" elicited firm and distinct responsive knocks. To the question whether "it would knock" if she called in her neighbors, an answer was given, whereupon she sent her husband for a Mrs. Redfield, who, after questioning the knocker in the same manner and receiving numerous and always correct responses, in great agitation proceeded to summon others, by whom similar investigations were conducted, with equal success, far into the night.

The reader must endeavor to picture to himself the scene which followed the introduction of the neighbors to this weird and most novel court of inquiry.

Imagine the place to be an humble cottage bedroom in a remote and obscure hamlet; the judge and jurors, simple, unsophisticated rustics; and the witness an invisible, unknown being, a denizen of a world of whose very existence mankind has been ignorant; acting by laws mysterious and inconceivable, in modes utterly beyond all human control or comprehension, and breaking through what has been deemed the dark and eternal seal of death, to reveal the long hidden mysteries of the grave and drag to the light secrets which not even the fabled silence of the tomb could longer hide away. Those who have been accustomed to dream of death as *the end* of all whom its shadowy portals inclose, alone are prepared to appreciate the awful and startling reality of this strange scene, breaking apart, as it did, like a rope of sand, all the preconceived opinions of countless ages on the existence and destiny of the *living* dead.

Those who have become familiar with the revealments of the spirit circle will only smile at the consternation evoked in this rustic party by the now-familiar presence and manifestations of "the spirits;" but to those who still stand in the night of superstition, deeming of all earth's countless millions as dead! dead! lost! gone! no one knows whither; never to return; to give no sign, no echo, no dim vibration from that vast gulf profound of unfathomed mystery—what a picture is that which suddenly brings them in an instant face to face with the mighty hosts of vanished dead, all clothed in life, and girded round with panoply of power, and light, and strength; with vivid memory of the secret wrongs deemed buried in their graves! The wrong doer and his victims face to face; earth's murdered ones in life again; her loved ones, supposed to be crumbling into dust, in busy, active life, fanning our cheeks with threads of golden hair! Why, sirs, the very air is full of them! Our city streets are thronged with an unseen people who flit about us, jostling us in thick crowds, and in our silent chambers, our secret closets, and our busiest haunts; their piercing eyes, invisible to us, are scanning all our ways. The universe is teeming with them; "THERE ARE NO DEAD." Those who went out from the humble chamber on that night of mingled fear and awe beheld the world they lived in with changed eyes. Every familiar thing to them seemed to wear a different aspect. Something was altered; some mighty, nameless change had fallen on all around them, and though they knew not how to phrase their thoughts in speech, they all and each felt that they were another man or woman, whilst the air, the earth, the dust beneath them, and the sky above, were filled with a viewless host of spirit-witnesses; and that for all they had loved and lost, as for themselves, "*there is no death.*"

Returning from this digression to the house at Hydesville on the memorable night of March 31st, 1848, we again invite the reader to the perusal of the statements collected by Dr. Campbell. After reiterating the questions already quoted, the pamphlet continues the narrative thus:

"Mrs Fox then inquired in the same way—*i. e.* by the raps— if it was an injured spirit, and to request an answer in the same way, and the rapping was repeated. In this way it answered her until she ascertained that it purported to be the spirit of a man, and that he was murdered for his money. To the question of how old he was, there were *thirty-one* distinct raps. She also ascertained by the same means that he was a married man, and had left a wife and five children; that his wife was dead, and had been dead two years. After ascertaining so much, she asked the question, 'Will the noise continue if I call in the neighbors?' The answer was, by rapping, in the affirmative. They then for the first time began to call in their neighbors, to help, if possible, to solve this great mystery.

"At first they called in their nearest neighbors, who came thinking they would have a hearty laugh at the family for being frightened; but when the first lady that came in found that the noise, whatever it might be, could tell the age of herself as well as others and give correct answers to questions on matters of which the family of Mr. Fox was entirely ignorant, she concluded that there was something beside a subject of ridicule and laughter in these unseen but audible communications. These neighbors insisted on calling in others, who came, and after investigation were as much confounded as at first.

"The family, being somewhat alarmed and much fatigued, left the house for the night. The next day the excitement began to spread, and the house was filled with anxious seekers for the unknown and invisible visitor. Through that day and up to that time there were no sounds heard in the daytime.

"On Sunday morning, April 2d, the noise commenced in the daytime, and was heard all that day by all who could get into the house, as the crowd which came from all quarters was much greater than the house would hold. We have heard it estimated that at one time there were as many as five hundred people who had gathered to hear the sounds, so great was the excitement at the commencement of these strange occurrences. On Saturday evening, there was a committee appointed to ask questions and report what the result was, but it was nothing of any importance differing from what is here related."

As a confirmation of what we have above stated, we give the following extracts from the testimony of William Deusler, of Arcadia, an immediate neighbor of Mr. Fox at the time of the transaction. This statement was published in a pamphlet by E. E. Lewis, Esq., of Canandaigua, New York, which contains the testimony of many persons in the neighborhood. Mr. Deusler says:

"I live in this place. I moved from Cayuga County here last October. I live within a few rods of the house in which these noises have been heard. The first I heard anything about them was one week ago last Friday evening [31st day of March]. Mrs. Redfield came over to my house to get my wife to go over to Mr. Fox's. Mrs. Redfield appeared to be very much agitated. My wife wanted I should go with them, and I accordingly went. When she told us what she wanted us to go for I laughed at her, and ridiculed the idea that there was anything mysterious in it. I told her it was all nonsense, and that it could easily be accounted for. This was about nine o'clock in the evening. There were some twelve or fourteen persons there when I got into the room. I went into the room and sat down on the bed. Mr. Fox asked questions, and I heard the rapping which they had spoken of, distinctly. I felt the bedstead jar when the sound was produced.

"Mrs. Fox then asked if it would answer my questions, if I asked any, and if so, rap. It then rapped three times. I then asked if it was an injured spirit, and it rapped; I asked if it had come to hurt any one who was present, and it did not rap. I then reversed this question, and it rapped. I asked if I or my father had injured it [as we had formerly lived in the house]; there was no noise. Upon asking the negative of these questions, the rapping was heard. I then asked if Mr. —— [naming a person who had formerly lived in the house] had injured it, and if so, to manifest it by rapping, and it made three knocks louder than common, and at the same time the bedstead jarred more than it had done before. I then inquired if it was murdered for money, and the knocking was heard. I then requested it to rap when I mentioned the sum of money for which it was murdered. I then asked if it was one hundred, two, three or four, and when I came to five hundred the rapping was heard. All in the room said they heard it distinctly. I then asked the question if it was five hundred dollars, and the rapping was heard.

"After this, I sent over and got Artemus W. Hyde to come over.* He came over. I then asked over nearly the same questions as before, and got the same answers. Mr. Redfield sent after David Jewel and wife, and Mrs. Hyde also came. After they came in I asked the same questions over and got the same answers. . . . . . . I then asked it to rap my age—the number of years of my age. It rapped thirty times. This is my age, and I do not think any one about here knew my age, except myself and family. I then told it to rap my wife's age, and it rapped thirty times, which is her exact age; several of us counted it at the same time. I then asked it to rap A. W. Hyde's age; then Mrs. A. W. Hyde's age. I then continued to ask it to rap the ages of different persons—naming them—in the room, and it did so correctly, as they all said. I then asked the number of children in the different families in the neighborhood, and it told them correctly in the usual way, by rapping; also the number of deaths that had taken place in the different families, and it told correctly. . . . . . .

"I then asked in regard to the time it was murdered, and in the usual way, by asking the different days of the week and the different hours of the day, learned that it was murdered on Tuesday night, about twelve o'clock. The rapping was heard only when this particular time was mentioned. When it was asked if it was murdered on a Wednesday, or Thursday, or Friday night, etc., there was no rapping. I then asked if it carried any trunk, and it rapped that it did. Then how many, and it rapped once. In the same way we ascertained that it had goods in the trunk, and that —— took them when he murdered him; and that he had a pack of goods besides. I asked if its wife was living, and it did not rap. If she was dead, and it rapped. . . . . . . This was tried over several times and the result was always the same.

"I then tried to ascertain the first letters of its name by calling over the different letters of the alphabet. I commenced with A, and asked if it was the initial of its name; and when I asked if it was B the rapping commenced. We then tried all the other letters, but could get no answer by the usual rapping. I then asked if we could find out the whole name by reading over all the letters of the alphabet, and there was no rapping. I then reversed the question, and the rapping was heard. . . . . . . There were a good many more questions asked on that night by myself and others, which I do not now remember. They were all readily answered in the same way. I staid in the house until about twelve o'clock and then came home. Mr. Redfield and Mr. Fox staid in the house that night.

"Saturday night I went over again about seven o'clock. The house was full of people when I got there. They said it had been rapping some time. I went into the room. It was rapping in answer to questions when I went in. . . . . . .

"There were as many as three hundred people in and around the house at this time, I should think. Hiram Soverhill, Esq., and Volney Brown asked it questions while I was there, and it rapped in answer to them.

"I went over again on Sunday between one and two o'clock P. M. I went into the cellar with several others, and had them all leave the house over our heads; and then I asked, if there had been a man buried in the cellar, to manifest it by rapping or any other noise or sign. The moment I asked the question there was a sound like the falling of a stick about a foot long and half an inch through, on the floor in the bedroom over our heads. It did not seem to rebound at all; there was but one sound. I then asked Stephen Smith to go right up and examine the room, and see if he could discover the cause of the noise. He came back and said he could discover nothing; that there was no one in the room, or in that part of the house. I then asked two more questions, and it rapped in the usual way. We all went up-stairs and made a thorough search, but could find nothing.

"I then got a knife and fork, and tried to see if I could make the same noise by dropping them, but I could not. This was all I heard on Sunday. There is only one floor, or partition, or thickness between the bedroom and the cellar; no place where anything could be secreted to make the noise. When this noise was heard in the bedroom I could feel a slight, tremulous motion or jar. . . . . . .

"On Monday night I heard this noise again, and asked the same questions I did before and got the same answers. This is the last time I have heard any rapping. I can in no way account for this singular noise which I and others have heard. It is a mystery to me which I am unable to solve. . . . . . .

"I lived in the same house about seven years ago, and at that time never heard any

* The son of the proprietor of the house at Hydesville.

noises of the kind in and about the premises. I have understood from Johnston and others who have lived there before —— moved there, that there were no such sounds heard there while they occupied the house. I never believed in haunted houses, or heard or saw anything but what I could account for before.

(Signed)

"*April* 12, 1848. WILLIAM DEUSLER."

To the same effect is the testimony of the following persons, whose certificates are published in the work alluded to, namely: John D. Fox, Walter Scotten, Elizabeth Jewel, Lorren Tenney, James Bridger, Chauncey P. Losey, Benjamin F. Clark, Elizabeth Fox, Vernelia Culver, William D. Storer, Marvin P. Losey, David S. Fox, and Mary Redfield.

CHAPTER III.

THE FIRST SPIRITUAL TELEGRAPH ON EARTH.

"We are the first that ever burst
Into that silent sea."

ANCIENT MARINER.

So blind, so ignorant is man,
That did not God withhold in mercy what we ask
We would be ruined at our own request."

HANNAH MORE.

THE FIRST SPIRIT CIRCLE—THE REMOVAL TO ROCHESTER—PERSECUTION—THE BEGINNING OF SORROWS—THE SPIRITS REJECTED—THEIR RETURN AND GREAT JOY OF THE MEDIUMS—PRELIMINARY ARRANGEMENTS FOR PUBLIC INVESTIGATIONS.

As it was deemed best for Mrs. Fox and her children to seek the shelter of a neighbor's house on the night of March 31st, when they had departed, Mr. Fox and his neighbors, to the number of seventy or eighty persons, remained to question as best they could their mysterious visitor by the knocks. Through these, obtaining affirmative answers or silence to their suggestions, they learned that the rapper purported to be the spirit of a pedler, who had been, as it was stated in the preceding chapter, murdered in that house between four and five years ago. On naming over the various inhabitants of the house who might have destroyed him, the knocks emphatically and repeatedly pointed to one who had lived there at the time indicated by the spirit. It was in this way ascertained [as far, at least, as answers to leading questions could be held as testimony], that the pedler was murdered on the Tuesday night that Lucretia P., the hired girl, was sent away; that —— was alone in the house, and that "the body was dragged through the parlor, into the buttery, and thence down the cellar stairs, and buried ten feet deep in the cellar." When the party adjourned to the cellar, the knocks accompanied them, and repeatedly confirmed the above story in every particular; these sounds also indicated the place where the body was buried, and the rappings were given on the spot above the place pointed out in the cellar. An attempt was made to receive communications through raps, by calling the letters of the alphabet; the sounds responded to C and B, but it was not until a later period that Mr. David Fox succeeded in obtaining the full name of Charles B. Rosna. To the practiced investigator in

Eng'd by A. H. Ritchie

Kate Fox

spiritual phenomena, it will be readily understood that the confused magnetic spheres of the highly-excited crowd assembled in the cellar at Hydesville on the night of the 31st of March, prevented the success of the first attempt of spirits to communicate through raps by the alphabet; and the same considerations show why Mr. Fox, in a calm and prayerful spirit, did succeed on a later occasion. The only marvel is that this attempt was not again resorted to until four months afterwards, when Isaac Post, a member of the Society of Friends and an acquaintance of the Fox family, weary of the unsatisfactory method of prompting questions and only obtaining negative or affirmative replies, suggested the same method of communication as that used by David Fox in the cellar. The result of this experiment has been, as all investigators know, eminently successful, where the conditions have not been broken by over-anxiety, fear, antagonism, or any strong emotion on the part of those present; conditions which, by causing disturbance in the delicate, imponderable aura that surrounds the circle, as conclusively break the affinities through which the manifestations are made as unscientific arrangements will destroy the effect of a voltaic pile or galvanic battery. Notwithstanding the crude methods in which the first investigators at Hydesville endeavored to communicate with their invisible respondent, their report, and the astounding implication of murder involved in it, drew all the inhabitants from far and near to the house. Up to seven o'clock on the evening of April 1st, however, no noises were heard, after which they re-commenced, and answered the questions as before, when amongst the hundreds there assembled, it was asserted that not a single incorrect response was given. On the Monday following Mr. David Fox and others commenced digging in the cellar, but as the house was built on low ground, and in the vicinity of a stream then much swollen by rains, it was not surprising that they were baffled by the influx of water at the distance of three feet down. In the summer of 1848, when the ground was dry and the water lowered, "the diggings" again commenced, when they found a plank, a vacant place or hole, some bits of crockery, which seemed to have been part of a wash-bowl, charcoal, quicklime, some human hair, bones [declared on examination by a surgeon to be human], and a portion of a human skull.

Such were the results of the examination of the cellar; such the only corroborative evidences obtained of the truth of the spirit's tale of untimely death; and hence it may be proper to add that Mr. ——, the party to whom the spirit emphatically pointed as his murderer, came forward from the town of Lyon, N. Y., to which he had removed in 1846, and produced a certificate of good character, signed by forty-four persons, to the effect that they had "never known anything against him," and "*believed* him to be a man of upright and honest life, and incapable of committing the crime of which he was suspected." By way of throwing discredit on the tale rapped out by the spirits, several other missing persons were *said* to have been murdered, and after various parties had been accused falsely "by the spirits," reappeared again. Most of these stories proved "bogus," and none of them bear the least relation to the unsought and unexpected spontaniety of the revelations at Hydesville. No further investigations, however, have been deemed necessary into this affair.

The presence of human remains in the cellar proves that *some one* was buried there, and the accompanying quicklime and charcoal testify to the fact that all traces of that mysterious inhumation were *purposely destroyed.*

The Fox family did not immediately quit the scene of this mysterious haunting, but remained to witness still more astonishing phenomena. The furniture was frequently moved about; the girls were often clasped by hard, cold hands; doors were opened and shut with much violence, their beds were so shaken that they were compelled to "camp out," as they termed it, on the ground; their bed-clothes were dragged from off them, and the very floor and house made to rock as in an earthquake. Night after night they would be appalled by hearing a sound like a death struggle, the gurgling of the throat, a sudden rush as of falling blood, the dragging as if of a help less body across the room and down the cellar stairs; the digging of a grave, nailing of boards, and the filling up as of a new-made grave. These sounds have been subsequently produced by request, and spontaneously also, in the presence of many persons assembled in circles at Rochester; but occurring as they did in that "lonely dreadful house," in the stillness of the dim evening, or dark night, and startling them, when not thinking of the subject, with all the ghastly sounds of a murder then enacting in tragic reality close to them, produced upon them the most painful and distressing feelings, aggravated, too, by other circumstances of annoyance that now began to thicken around them.

It was perceived that "the spirits" seemed to select or require the presence of the two younger girls of the family for the production of the sounds, and though these *had been made without them*, especially on the night of the 31st of March, when all the family save Mr. Fox were absent from the house, still, as curiosity prompted them to close observation of, and conversation with the invisible power, it was clear that the manifestations became more powerful in the presence of Kate, the youngest sister, than with any one else.

As the house was continually thronged with curious inquirers, and the time, comfort, and peace of the family were consumed in these harassing disturbances, besides the most absurd though injurious suspicions being cast upon them, they endeavored to baffle the haunters by sending Kate to reside with her eldest sister, Mrs. Fish, at Rochester; but no sooner was she gone than the manifestations re-commenced, with more force than ever, in the presence of Margaretta, the second sister. In course of time, Mrs. Fox, with both her daughters, took up their residence in Rochester; but neither change of place nor house, nor yet the separation of the family, afforded them any relief from the disturbances that now evidently attached themselves to persons rather than to places, as formerly. Although the Fox family had for months sedulously striven to banish the power that tormented them, praying with all the fervor of true Methodism to be released from it, and enduring fear, loss, and anxiety in its continuance, the report of its persistent manifestation began to spread abroad, causing a rain of persecution to fall upon them from all quarters.

The respectable parents were so severely censured and so impertinently lectured by their minister—who should have been the foremost to sustain them in their heavy visitations—that they were obliged to sever their long-cherished and hitherto unblemished relations with their church. Old friends looked coldly on them, and strangers circulated the most atrocious slanders at their expense.

Mrs. Fish, the eldest sister, who was a teacher of music in Rochester, began to lose her professional connections; and whilst the sudden blanching of the poor mother's hair *in a single week* bore testimony to the mental tortures which supra-mundane terrors and mundane cruelties had heaped upon them, the world was taunting them with originating, in wilful imposture, the very manifestations which were destroying their health, peace of mind, good name, and fortunes. Notwithstanding their dislike of the notoriety that these manifestations brought upon them, however, it was impossible to avoid it.

They had solicited the advice of their much-respected friend, Isaac Post, a highly esteemed Quaker citizen of Rochester, and, at his suggestion, succeeded in communicating by raps with the invisible power, through the alphabet. Thus telegraphic numbers were given to signify "yes," "no," "doubtful," etc., and sentences were spelled out, by which were learned the astounding facts that not only "Charles Rosna," the supposed murdered pedler, but hosts of spirits, good and bad, high and low, could, under certain conditions not understood, and impossible for mortals yet to comprehend, communicate with earth; that such communication was produced through the forces of spiritual and human magnetism, in chemical affinity; that the varieties of magnetism in different individuals afforded "medium power" to some, and denied it to others; that the magnetic relations necessary to produce phenomena were very subtle, liable to disturbance, and singularly susceptible to the influence of mental emotions; that the spirits chiefly concerned in the inauguration of this telegraphy were philosophic and scientific minds, many of whom had made the study of electricity and other imponderables a specialty in the earth-life, and prominent among them the name of Dr. Benjamin Franklin was frequently given. In addition to communications purporting thus to explain the object and something of the *modus operandi* of the communion, numerous spirit friends of the family, and those who joined in their investigations, gladdened the hearts of their astonished relatives by direct and unlooked-for tests of their presence. They came spelling out their names, ages, and various tokens of identity correctly, and proclaiming the joyful tidings that they all "still lived," "still loved," and with the tenderness of human affection, and the wisdom of a higher sphere of existence, watched over and guided the beloved ones who had mourned them as dead, with all the gracious ministry of guardian angels.

The spirits recommended the assembling of the friends of the family together in harmonious meetings, which have since obtained the name of "spirit circles," and at these, the practice of animal magnetism to some of the parties present was suggested, as a means of evoking the phenomena of clairvoyance.

But redolent of joy and consolation as is the intercourse with beloved spirit friends at this time when orderly communion has succeeded to doubtful experiment, it must not be supposed that any such harmonious results characterized the initiatory proceedings of the spiritual movement in Rochester. Within and without the dwellings of the mediums, all was fear, consternation, doubt, and anxiety.

Several persons possessed of clairvoyant and clairaudient powers had been developed as mediums by magnetism. But in the meantime fanatical religionists of different sects had forced themselves into the family gatherings, and the wildest scenes of rant, cant, and absurdity often ensued. Opinions of the most astounding nature were hazarded concerning the object of this movement; some determining that it was a "millenium," and looking for the speedy reign of a personal Messiah and the equally speedy destruction of the wicked. Boisterous sounds accompanied the fervent prayers of the ranters, and wild confusion, in which invisible actors played their weird part, added to the distraction of the already tortured mediums.

A Mr. Calvin Brown, who resided in the house of Mrs. Fish, and afterwards became her husband, being particularly opposed to the manifestations, seemed to be selected by the spirits as a marked butt for their Puck-like pranks. They threw books, pamphlets, and other small articles about his person, and though—one occasion alone excepted—they never struck him with sufficient force to cause him the least injury, they persecuted him by intelligent signs and movements of so violent, erratic, and even spiteful a character, as to compel him at last to own and respect their power. They often threw about the house blocks of wood with sentences written on them for the encouragement and instruction of the family, who uniformly conducted themselves gently, piously, and in fact admirably, in the midst of the trying scenes they were passing through.

It must not be supposed that the clergy were idle spectators of the tumultuous wave that was sweeping over the city. On the contrary, several of them called on Mrs. Fox with offers to "exorcise the spirits;" and when they found their attempts were futile, and that though the spirits would rap in chorus to the "amens" with which they concluded their incantations, they were otherwise unmoved by these reverend performances, they generally ended by proclaiming abroad that the family were "in league with the evil one" or the authors of a "vile imposture." Honorable exceptions, however, were found to this cowardly and unchristian course, and amongst these was the Rev. A. H. Jervis, a Methodist minister, of Rochester, in whose family remarkable manifestations occurred of the same character as in that of the Foxes, and whose appreciation of the beauty and worth of the communications he received several of his published letters bear witness of. Mr. Lyman Granger, Rev. Charles Hammond, Deacon Hale, and several other families of wealth and influence, both in Rochester and the surrounding towns, also began to experience similar phenomena in their own households, while the news came from all quarters, extending as far as Cincinnati and St. Louis, West, and Maine, Massachusetts, Pennsylvania, and New York, East, that the mysterious rappings and other phases of what is now called "medium power" were rapidly spreading from town to town and State to State, in fulfilment of an assurance made in the very first of the communion to the Misses Fox, namely, "that these manifestations were not to be confined to them, but would go all over the world." Notwithstanding the fact that many persons besides the Fox family became distinguished as mediums for the sounds, movements of furniture, and other manifestations of supramundane intelligence, and that every day saw some new development of "the power" in families whose wealth and position placed them beyond the reach of suspicion or the possibility of collusion, so startling and unparalleled had been the first appearance of the phenomena that it seemed impossible for the public mind to dissever their origin and continued practice from the Fox family.

They were still called the "Rochester knockers," the "Fox girls," the "rappers," and other epithets, equally foolish and cruelly obnoxious to their interests and feelings. Catharine Fox, the youngest girl, had been removed to the house of Mr. E. W. Capron, of Auburn. Mrs. Fish, though generally present when phenomena were transpiring, was not in its earliest phases conscious of being a medium. Margaretta, the second sister, was then in reality the only one through whom the manifestations appeared to proceed, when in November, 1848, the spirits, who had long been urging them to permit public investigations to be made through her mediumship, informed them by raps that "they could not always strive with them," and since they were constantly disobedient to the spirits' requests, and obviously opposed to their presence, they should leave them, and in all probability withdraw for another generation, or seek through other sources for the fulfilment of the high and holy purposes with which this spiritual outpouring had been designed.

To these appeals the family were inflexible. They constantly prayed that the cup of this great bitterness "might pass from them." They "did not wish to be mediums," and abhorred the notoriety, scandal, and persecution which their fatal gift had brought upon them, and when warned that the spirits would leave them they protested their delight at the announcement, and expressed their earnest desire that it might be fulfilled. There were present at a circle, when communications of this character were made, several influential persons of the city, who had become greatly interested in the manifestations and were warm friends of the family. They could not, however, realize that the threat here implied would actually be fulfilled until the spirits, by rappings, spelled out several messages of a particularly affectionate and valedictory character. The scene became, says an eye-witness, solemn and impressive. The spirits announced that in twenty minutes they would depart, and exactly as that time expired, they spelled out, "We will now bid you all farewell;" when the raps entirely ceased. The family expressed themselves "glad to be rid of them;" the friends present vainly tried to obtain, by solicitations, made, as it would seem, to empty air, some demonstration that this beneficent and wonderful visitation had not indeed wholly ceased. All was useless. A mournful silence filled the apartment which had but a few minutes before been tenanted with angels, sounding out their dear messages of undying affection, tender counsel, wise instruction, and prescient warning. The *spirits indeed were gone;* and as one by one the depressed party separated and passed out into the silent moonlit streets of Rochester, all and each of them felt as if some great light had suddenly gone out, and life was changed to them. There was a mighty blank in space, and a shadow everywhere, but spirit light came no more to illuminate the thick darkness.

A fortnight passed away, during which the former investigators called constantly on the Fox family to inquire if their spirit friends had returned. For the first few days a stoical negative was their only reply; after this, they began more and more fully to recognize the loss they had sustained. The wise counsellors were gone; the sources of strange strength and superhuman consolation were cut off. The tender, loving, wonderful presence, no more flitted around their steps, cheered their meals, encouraged them in their human weakness, or guided them in their blindness. And these most wonderful and providential beings their own waywardness had driven from them. At last, then, they met their inquiring friends with showers of tears, choking sobs, and expressions of the bitterest self-reproach and regret. On the twelfth day of this great heart-dearth Mr. E. W. Capron, being in Rochester on business, called at the house of Mrs. Fish, with George Willetts, a member of the Society of Friends, and one of their earliest spiritual investigators. On receiving the usual sorrowful reply "that the spirits had left them," Mr. Capron said, "Perhaps they will rap for us if not for you." They then entered the hall, and put the usual question if the spirits would rap for them, in answer to which, and to the unspeakable joy and delight of all present, they were greeted with a perfect shower of the much-lamented sounds. Mrs. Fish, now Mrs. Underhill, often declares to this day that if suddenly, fortune, friends, and all they had ever loved had been snatched from them, and as suddenly returned in an hour of despair and agony, their emotions could have scarcely equalled the ecstacy with which they once more greeted those precious returning proofs that their spirit friends had not deserted them. In fact, in the enthusiasm of that returning morning of long-quenched spiritual light, they knelt down and kissed the ground made sacred by the electric tones of the heavenly telegraph. And now once more the spirits urged them to make the manifestations public.

Again they reiterated the charge with solemn earnestness, and despite of the mediums' continued aversion to the task imposed upon them, the fear of a fresh and final bereavement of the inestimable boon of spirit communion prevented their continued resistance to the course proposed. When the persons who were called upon to aid the mediums and take somewhat prominent parts in the work urged the awkwardness of the positions assigned them, the spirits only replied, "Your triumph will be so much the greater." There is no doubt that the severe warning they had just received, and the fear of its repetition, acted upon the whole party with more force than any argument that could have been used to induce their submission. Certain it is that they at length consented, one and all, to do the bidding of the spirits; but as their first public demonstration of the modern spiritual movement requires more accuracy of detail than history has yet assigned to it, we shall reserve its description for another chapter.

CHAPTER IV.

CORINTHIAN HALL, OR THE FIRST PUBLIC INVESTIGATION OF SPIRITUALISM.

"'Tis bitter to endure the wrong
  Which evil hands and tongues commit;
The bold encroachments of the strong,
  The shafts of calumny and wit;
The scornful bearing of the proud,
The sneers and laughter of the crowd.
  Conscious of purity and worth,
We may with calm assurance wait
  The tardy recompense of earth:
And e'en though justice come too late
  To soothe the spirit's homeward flight,
  Still heaven at last the wrong shall right."

PSALMS OF LIFE.

ROCHESTER SCIENCE AND PIETY IN 1849 — LAW AND DIVINITY TRYING THE SPIRITS — THE BRAVE FOLLOWERS OF GEORGE FOX — TESTIMONY OF GEORGE WILLETTS, REV. C. HAMMOND, AND A. H. JERVIS — DR. BENJAMIN FRANKLIN AS A SPIRIT AND SPIRITUAL ELECTRICITY.

THE first public investigation into the possibility of communion between the world of spirits and the earth they once inhabited — between bereaved mourners and the mysterious dwellers of an unknown land, claiming identity with the beloved ones thus mourned — should, as it would seem, have inspired the whole community with feelings of the most profound interest and solemn reverence. The scene of inquiry should have been a place dedicated to the sacred offices of religion, and the inquisitors the men who, above all others, profess to teach the doctrine of the soul's immortality.

Far otherwise, however, did the ignorance and bigotry of the times decree that the investigation should be conducted. The spirits, through the rappings, both in the presence of Margaretta Fox in Rochester, and Catharine in Auburn, simultaneoulsy spelled out the same urgent requests that the family would challenge public scrutiny and scientific investigation. The compliance which they finally yielded was not only made on the grounds mentioned in the last chapter, but also on the promise of the spirits that they would take part in a public inquiry by rapping loud enough to be heard by an assembled audience. After several trials in private houses, it was conceded that the raps were loud enough to sound distinctly in a large hall, before a crowded auditory.

The order of proceedings indicated by the spirits arranged that "Corinthian Hall," the largest public place of meeting in Rochester, should be hired, and a lecture given, narrating in plain and terse language the origin and progress of the manifestations from their commencement to their present date. Afterwards it was directed that a committee should be chosen from the most respectable of the audience present, who should have charge on the following day to investigate the subject in private, and report to an audience each evening on three successive occasions. It was promised that the sounds should be made during the progress of the proceedings with sufficient force to be heard throughout the hall; a promise that was amply redeemed by the spirits in clear and distinct rappings. Mr. E. W. Capron, of Auburn, was selected to deliver the address; Mr. George Willetts and Mr. Isaac Post to attend to the business arrangements; Mrs. Amy Post, a few other ladies, and the Rev. A. H. Jervis, N. Draper, Lyman Granger, and other well-known citizens, to accompany the mediums on to the platform.

Many of the parties thus honored by the selection of the spirits were exceedingly unwilling to accept the equivocal and embarrassing positions assigned to them; better feelings and the urgency of the communications at length prevailed, however, and the first meeting in the exact order prescribed by the spirits took place on the evening of November 14th, 1849. The address was given by Mr. Capron in a manner at once so truthful and interesting that it commanded the respectful attention of a numerous audience. The silence was only broken by the clear tones of the speaker, and the distinctly audible, though muffled sounds of the raps, which constantly emphasized the striking passages of the address. At its close, a committee to investigate the subject and report on the next evening was chosen by the audience, consisting of the following persons, all highly respectable and responsible citizens of Rochester: Messrs A. J. Combs, Daniel Marsh, Nathaniel Clark, A. Judson, and Edwin Jones. From unquestionable authority we learn that in the office of the *Rochester Democrat*, an elaborate article was prepared, announcing "the entire explosion of the rapping humbug;" but though the article in question, to save time, was actually set up in type, yet the editors, to save credit, *deferred* its publication *after* the report of the committee was publicly rendered in the following terms:

"That without the knowledge of the persons in whose presence the manifestations are made, the committee selected the hall of the Sons of Temperance for investigation; that the sounds on the floor near where the two ladies stood were heard as distinctly as at other places, and that part of the committee heard the rapping on the wall behind them; that a number of questions were asked, which were answered not altogether right nor altogether wrong; that in the afternoon they went to the house of a private citizen, and while there the sounds were heard on the outside of the front door, after they had entered, and on the door of a closet. By placing the hand upon the door, there was a sensible jar felt when the rapping was heard. One of the committee placed one of his hands upon the feet of the ladies and the other on the floor, and though the feet were not moved there was a distinct jar on the floor. On the *pavement* and on the *ground* the same sounds were heard. When the ladies were separated at a distance no sound was heard, but when a third person was interposed between them the sounds were heard. The ladies seemed to give every opportunity to the committee to investigate the cause fully, and would submit to a thorough investigation by a committee of ladies, if desired. They all agreed that the sounds were heard, *but they entirely failed to discover any means by which it could be done.*"

This report was delivered to an eager and excited audience on the second public night, and seemed to fall like a thunder-bolt on many of those assembled, who had obviously come in the expectation of receiving one of a very different and far less favorable character.

After some discussion, which already pointed to a disapproval of the report, and a wish to find the mediums guilty of imposture, another committee was appointed by the audience, such persons being named as were least likely to be favorable to the spiritual hypothesis of the sounds.

The gentlemen thus selected were Dr. H. H. Langworthy, Hon. Frederick [Counsellor] Whittlesey, D. C. McCallum, William Fisher, and Hon. A. P. Hascall, of LeRoy.

The ladies had been subject to examinations by the former committee, the rigidity of which was not one of the statements brought before the public. Their feelings were often outraged, their statements doubted, and their peculiarly sensitive natures wounded to agony by the cold, severe, and often sneering scrutiny to which they were subjected. Happily for them the spirit friends behind the scenes encouraged and cheered them, often warning them of the disagreeable nature of what they would have to encounter, of the "hard and angular characters" of some of their judges, and the amenable and spiritual natures of others.

The little great men whose verdict was to render forever to mankind the truth or falsehood of man's relations with ministering spirits, had no idea what a shrewd and analytical spirit painting of themselves had already unmasked them to those they pretended to judge, ere they themselves entered on the farce of trying the spirits.

Still these two committees were so far honest in their search, and candid enough in their report, as greatly to incense the audiences which each night assembled, not to hear the truth, but rather in expectation of a report which should proclaim the Fox family impostors.

The second investigation was conducted, to avoid all possibility of deception, at the office of Counsellor Whittlesey. The ladies were placed in various positions, together and separate, but though the only avowed medium was Margaret, Mr. Fish not deeming she had the "power," and Catharine being absent at Auburn, the sounds were heard on the floor, chairs, table, walls, door, and, in fact, everywhere. Dr. Langworthy tested the possibility of their being ventriloquism by the use of the stethescope, and the joint report of the committee was that "the sounds were heard, and their thorough investigation had conclusively shown them to be produced neither by machinery nor ventriloquism, though what the agent was, they were unable to determine."

It would be impossible to describe the indignation that was manifested at this second failure, and a third committee was immediately chosen, whose sneers and scoffing remarks seemed their chief recommendation to the office. As a specimen of the animus of these investigations, it may be mentioned that one of them — Mr. Lewis Burtis — declared, "the girls wouldn't have him on the committee for a hundred dollars." Another — Mr. L. Kenyon — "that if he could not find out the trick he would throw himself over Genessee Falls." In addition to these persons were Drs. Langworthy and Gates, and William Fitzhugh. To the honor of this committee be it said, that despite the most severe and inquisitorial treatment, conducted with circumstances of severity that are quite as well omitted from the record, they reported entirely in the ladies' favor, although Mr. Burtis frankly owned himself beaten, and Mr. Kenyon did not either throw himself over the Falls or pretend that he could "find out the trick." In addition to this final examination under public auspices, the committee appointed another to assist them in their investigation, composed of ladies, by whom the clothing of the mediums was thoroughly searched, and even their shoes, stockings, and under-garments minutely examined. The poor girls wept bitterly during this ordeal; still they submitted to it, though shame and indignation wrought up their feelings to so severe a pitch that their sobs and lamentations were heard by some of their friends who had been purposely excluded from the room. One of these, a sweet Quaker lady — Mrs. Amy Post — who throughout the whole of their bitter trials had lent them the aid of her gentle counsel and the strength of her irreproachable name, at last insisted upon forcing her way into the chamber where the poor girls were disrobed and undergoing examination. No sooner did the sight of her friendly face greet them than they threw themselves into her arms, and the favorable revulsion of feeling occasioned by her presence had the effect of producing what the severe scrutiny of antagonism had neutralized, namely, a perfect shower of raps, from which point the sounds were loud and frequent, responding to questions, and rapping whilst they stood with bare feet on pillows, glass, and other substances [*supposed to be non-conductors of electricity*], or with their dresses tightly tied to their ankles. In all these positions the raps were distinctly heard on the floor and walls, in proof of which we extract the following passage from the certificate of the Ladies Committee:

> "When they were standing on pillows, with a handkerchief tied around the bottom of their dresses, tight to the ankles, we all heard the rapping on the wall and floor distinctly.
>
> [Signed] "MRS. STONE,
> MRS. J. GATES,
> MRS. M. P. LAWRENCE."

Notwithstanding the confidence which the poor family had in their own integrity and the strength and fidelity of the spirits, the power of public opinion was so strong against them, and the reports from without were of so alarming a character, that they almost shrank from the final trial that was demanded of them, namely, to present themselves for the fourth time on the platform, during the presentation of the last report.

The two first committees had frankly declared to Miss Fox their opinions of her perfect honesty; but it was evident they disliked the task of presenting themselves before the excited crowds that had threatened to assemble at Corinthian Hall that night, and "lynch the rappers and their advocates too," provided the report of the third committee should be in their favor. Although the feeling of those who had come prepared for mischief was unmistakable, the committee, opposed as they had been to the mediums the night before, were honest in their statements. "They had heard the sounds," they said, "and *failed utterly to discover their origin.* They had proved that neither machinery nor imposture had been used, and their questions, many of them being mental, were answered correctly." . . . .

Each member of the committee reported separately, and fully corroborated the others; and then it was that a scene of confusion ensued, equally impossible to describe and discreditable to record.

Mrs. Fish and Amy Post, though, to use their own words, they were "no mediums," had accompanied the pale and shrinking Margaretta on the platform, ready to defend or share her danger.

But the poor ladies were not alone; Isaac Post, the Rev. A. H. Jervis, and a few other true men, and therefore gentlemen, were on guard, determined to protect, or if need be "perish with the martyrs to this unpopular but unquestionable truth," whilst George Willetts, whose peaceful religion as a Quaker lent peculiar emphasis to his words, declared "that the mob of ruffians who designed to lynch 'the girls,' should do so—if they attempted it—over his dead body."

Sustained by this faithful little band, Margaretta Fox and her friends presented themselves on the platform; but immediately following the reports of the different members of the committee, Josiah Bissell, writing himself "Esq." and "gentleman," proceeded to distribute torpedoes amongst "the boys," and on every side the explosion of these noisy tormentors distracted the ears and stimulated the ribald jokes of the mob against the "rappers." A "gentleman," who had recently filled the post of alderman, led another gang of disturbers; whilst two more prominent citizens, by the name of Jerome, *gentlemen*, who, as attached to a *daily American paper*, were supposed to be leaders of public opinion, together with a certain Major Packard, undertook to state that the sounds were made by leaden balls fastened to the "females'" dresses. They then mounted the platform and invited up the "rowdies" for "investigation," until the police, perceiving the disgraceful turn the proceedings were taking, urged the ladies and their friends to retire, and after carefully guarding them home, were compelled to disperse the meeting by threatening the principal gentlemen present to arrest them as authors and instigators of the disturbance.

And thus ended an investigation into the sublime and occult mysteries of the communion between the natural and spiritual worlds, in which gentlemen, magistrates, editors, and professional men were the judges, and enlightened American citizens the jury; and thus too ended the experiment of entrusting any truth that has not yet been endorsed with the label of popularity, to the censorship of the men who assume to be leaders of public opinion. Spiritual agencies were wiser in days of yore, and entrusted the promulgation of divine truth to fishermen and Galileans rather than to Scribes and Pharisees; nevertheless, though the *élite* of Rochester citizenship was "called but not chosen," the cause they attempted to disgrace rose triumphantly out of the ruins they strove to create. The aim of wide-spread publicity was attained. The very bitterness of the opposition provoked disscussion, and thousands heard of, wondered at, investigated, and finally believed in, spiritual communion who would never have dreamed of the subject but for the persecution and slander that was publicly directed against the "Rochester knockings." But the spirit of persecution did not cease at Corinthian Hall. A feeling of determined and relentless antagonism was excited against the subject by the very impossibility of finding it out or crushing it down. Believers began to multiply; mediums sprang up in families whose wealth and position removed them from the least suspicion of imposture; and since it was impossible to reach these, or strike the hydra-headed monster in its now hourly-increasing magnitude, the only resort of the unreasoning spirit of persecution, which seems to be an unaccountable element developed by the advent of all new movements, was to strike at the humble and obnoxious Fox family.

Notwithstanding the fact that up to the date of the first manifestations they had lived in the enjoyment of respect and an unblemished name from all who knew them, from this time forth the malignant blows that were aimed against the cause of Spiritualism were first levelled at them, and even now, their fair fame is blurred in the city of Rochester by meaningless slanders that once launched upon the relentless billows of time drift on forever, and though they may ultimately be swept away by the tides of oblivion, yet never return upon their track to render justice at the point from whence they started.

Before taking leave of the fortunes of this remarkable family, it will be necessary to the clear understanding of the influence for good which Spiritualism from the first assumed towards mankind, that we should present some of the views of the earliest investigators into this subject, in the form of certain letters which they themselves wrote in private correspondence, but which the irresistible logic of events has converted into testimony, rendered invaluable from its unpremeditated character and the obvious disinterestedness of its authors.

The first letter which we shall present is from the pen of Mr. George Willetts, who was known to all his acquaintances as a man of the most unimpeachable integrity and truthfulness. Mr. Willetts's conviction of the spiritual origin of the rappings became strong enough to induce him to take the noble and prominent part in the Corinthian Hall inquisition above noticed. His letter is addressed to Mr. E. W. Capron, of Auburn, who publishes it in his work on "The Facts and Fanaticisms of Modern Spiritualism." Our extract is taken from Dr. Campbell's pamphlet on the Rochester knockings:

"DEAR FRIEND, E. W. CAPRON:—It is with some reluctance that I furnish you with the following statement; not that I am afraid to tell you the truth, but that the world, as I conceive, is not ready to receive such truths yet. Ridicule, probably, will be heaped upon me; but when I consider that it is the ignorant only who use that weapon, perhaps I can afford to stand up and say, 'let the storm come.' All who know me can say whether I have been truthful from my youth up, yea or nay; and the strongest language that I can use is to say that the following statement is *strictly and entirely true:*

"'In the summer of 1848, I had concluded, from the best judgment that I could bring to my aid, that it was right for my family to remove somewhere amongst the wilds of the West. Accordingly I took a tour of observation, and finding some land in Michigan that suited me better than any other, belonging to a gentleman living in Rochester, I stopped there on my return, in order, if possible, to negotiate for it. I staid with my friend and relative, Isaac Post, and while there he told me of certain sounds being heard in the city, and that they displayed intelligence and purported to be made by spirits, or persons invisible to us. I was really sceptical about any such things, but at his solicitation went to examine it. The person with whom these sounds seemed to be I had never seen or heard of before, and my friend was careful not to tell them who I was or where I had been. It seems that the question was asked whether there was any communication for me, and the direction from the sounds was that three persons be magnetized; two of them were present, and one was sent for from a neighboring family. I did not know the name of any person present; and I was also certain that no one knew me. After the three persons were put in the 'clairvoyant state,' one of them said, 'We have to go to Michigan.' They all agreed that they had to go there, and began to describe places and things which I had seen, and at length came to a piece of land which they said was the place they came to look at. They then described the land so accurately which I had stopped in Rochester to buy that I began to wonder 'who had told them.' They all with one accord then said, 'But he must not go there. His father says he had better not go.' As they said this, there came a loud sound close by my chair, and *I sat some distance from any other person.* They spoke much of my father, and what his mind was, and at each time that same sound was heard and the jar distinctly felt close by myself. They then said, 'His *mother* thinks it is not best.' As they spoke this a different sound, not quite so loud, was heard, still close by me. Then, 'that my *sister* said it was not best.' Another and different sound still was heard. Up to this time I had not spoken a word, but found the big drops of perspiration starting from my face. I gathered courage and thought I would dispel that illusion directly; I said, 'As you assume to know my father and what his mind is concerning me, *perhaps* you can tell his name.' They all seemed to look steadily for some time, then commenced and spoke slowly and deliberately these letters: William Willetts. At each letter the loud sound that I first heard was again heard and felt immediately under my feet. I never was so astonished in my life, and involuntarily said, 'What does all this mean?' The sounds then said, by the alphabet being called over, 'that they had better be awakened;' and the first loud sound said, 'I will talk with George and tell him all about it.' The direction was for Mr. Post, myself, and a little girl [Catharine Fox] thirteen years old, to go by ourselves. And here I wish it distinctly understood that all which I shall relate as obtained from these sounds was in the presence only of my friends Mr. and Mrs. Post, myself, and the little girl spoken of. As what follows all purported to be from my father, I will say that his name was William Willetts, a member of the Society of Friends, widely known at Westbury, Long Island, where he lived until nearly sixty years of age, and subsequently at Skaneateles, Onandagua County, where he died in 1841. The communication by sounds then went on to say that it was my father that was present and talking with me, and three hours were consumed at the first interview. In saying to me what his counsel was it always assumed to counsel and advise, but never to dictate. He said that it was not best for us to go to Michigan, and gave various reasons, among which were that we should not enjoy ourselves in a new country, and that my health would not be competent for the task of clearing up new land, and he foresaw, if we did go, we should come back again and would be less in number than when we went. I then asked what was best to do. The answer was, 'Come to Rochester.' I replied that I knew of no business that I could do in Rochester. The sounds said, 'I will tell thee when thee comes.' I asked if I might know now. The answer was, 'No, I did not need any business until I came, and then he would tell me.' The sounds then said that after a time it would be best for me to buy some land. I asked where. The sounds then spelled out the name of a man whom no one present knew, and said that he owned fifty acres of land on such a street adjoining the city, and such a distance from the centre of the city; that he would sell any part. I asked the price that would be asked. The sounds were heard and counted by three of us—one hundred and fifty times in succession—to tell us the number of dollars per acre that would be asked. The sounds said that we had better go the next day and see if this was so, and said that we should not see the man until ten o'clock, although we might look for him as early as we pleased. In the morning I looked in the Directory and there found the name spelled out to us, and went to his residence at seven o'clock, and was informed that he was gone to a distant part of the city, and would not be home until twelve o'clock. We then went to find him, and had some difficulty to do so, but after talking with him five or six minutes looked at the time and it *was seven minutes past ten!* This person said that he owned fifty acres on the street told us by the sounds, and said that he would sell any part. When I asked him the price he showed me a map with the price of each lot marked, and taking the number of acres said by the sounds to be best to buy, and averaging the price, it was just upon one hundred and fifty dollars per acre. I then went home to my family and pondered over these strange things. Many were the conflicts in my own mind, and I heard the cry from all quarters, 'humbug,' 'deception,' 'fraud,' but I could not believe that I wanted to deceive myself. Three months I thought of these things deeply, and *I could not go* to Michigan. I concluded if it was deception it would do the world some good to find it out. The first of December, 1848, I moved from Waterloo to Rochester. A few days after getting here, the little girl spoken of came round to our house and said that the 'spirit' had directed her to come, for what purpose she did not know. We inquired what it was, and this was the communication: 'I told thee if thee would come to Rochester I would tell thee where thee could find employment; in four days from this I will tell thee. In the meantime the anti-slavery folks are going to hold their Fair; would it not be well for thee to help them?' No one was present at this time except my wife, the little girl, and myself. The four days went by, and again, without solicitation and without thinking the time was up, the little girl came again. The communication was, 'Apply to William Wiley, Superintendent of the Auburn and Rochester Railroad, to-morrow at two o'olock, at his office, for a situation, and thee will have one before this week is out.' This was Thursday. I was a stranger to Mr. Wiley, and I called on Mr. Post and told him the direction, and asked him if the next day he would go with me. That evening he, happening to be at the depot, inquired if Mr. Wiley was at home, and was told that he was in Boston, and by a letter just received would not be at home till Friday night. I was told by the sounds on Wednesday to apply on Thursday at two o'clock. Thursday at half-past one, instead of going to the railroad office, I went round to where these sounds were heard, and said, 'How is this? I am told to apply to William Wiley, and he is in Boston.' The sounds said, '*Go to his office now; he is there.*' I called for Mr. Post and walked immediately there, and *found Mr. Wiley in his office.* He said that he had returned sooner than he expected to when he wrote the letter. Mr. Post said that I was a relative of his and wished employment, and Mr. Wiley replied that they were all full, with abundant applications, and he could give no encouragement whatever. We walked back, thinking deeply, and I went where the sounds were heard again. I inquired, 'How is this? Mr. Wiley has no place for me.' The answer was, '*Thee will have a place on the cars, and will know it before the week is out.*'"

"On Saturday night, at dark, I met Mr. Post, and he asked if I had heard anything from Mr. Wiley, I replied, 'Not a word.' At eight o'clock on that same evening, Mr. Post called at my house, and said that Mr. Wiley had just been at his store and said that he had a place for me, and wished me to call at his office on Monday morning. As Mr. Wiley did not tell what place I was to fill, I again asked the sounds what it was; and they said 'that it was to go as baggage-master between this place and Auburn.' On Sunday morning I wrote to my friend James Trueman, of Waterloo, stating that I should pass through that place on Monday following—in the capacity above stated—before I knew from Mr. Wiley what place he wanted me to fill, and he can testify to that fact. One month after I had been running on the cars, I learned that the person whose place I took had done things worthy of a dismissal previous to my being directed to make application, and which did not come to Mr. Wiley's notice till the day on which I received the appointment. These things have only been known to a few friends; you and the world now have them. I have many communications, penned down at the time they were received, purporting to be from my father, all of the most elevating character, inciting me to goodness, purity, and honesty of heart, and ever pointing to the endless progression of man. In conclusion, I may say that I have examined the matter attentively for one year and a half, and have had abundant opportunity to do so, and am prepared to say, although the sounds may cease to-day and never be heard again, they have displayed a remarkable degree of intelligence, and were not made by any person visible to us.

"George Willetts."

The next letter we shall quote is from the Rev. C. Hammond, and though it contains no proofs of spirit identity of a very striking character, it is inserted in reference to the singular worth of the writer and the weight which is due to his respected testimony. Mr. Hammond, subsequent to the dictation of this letter, became an excellent writing medium himself, and the publisher of a voluminous collection of "communications from the spirit-world," written through his mediumship.

Considering that Mr. Hammond was content to sacrifice good name, fame, and livelihood in his defence of the unpopular cause he espoused, credence should be assigned to him for his sincerity, if denied on behalf of his moral worth.

LETTER FROM THE REV. C. HAMMOND.

"Mr. D. M. Dewey: *Dear Sir*,—In compliance with your solicitation, I will proceed to lay before you a brief statement of what has fallen under my observation, in regard to the 'mysterious sounds' and 'demonstrations,' purporting to be made by intelligent spirits, who once inhabited an earthly tabernacle. It is quite probable that many others may have had more convincing and satisfactory evidences of the real presence of their departed, or, as I should say, deceased friends, than myself; yet I am free to acknowledge my inability to account for these marvellous manifestations by any law recognized in science or philosophy; nor am I aware of having an organization so extra-credulous as to admit theoretical propositions, without facts to sustain them. If, therefore, imposition and deception have 'humbugged' me into a conviction that the 'sounds' and 'demonstrations' which I have witnessed originate in any cause other than those assigned in this narrative, the person who shall disclose the mystery and detect the fraud will receive my grateful acknowledgments.

"In the early part of January last, in company with other persons, I gained an introduction to the family in this city in whose residence these sounds had been heard. They received us politely, and seemed rather more cheerful than what I had supposed would be natural for those who were hourly exchanging communications with the spirits of the dead. A company of twenty or more persons had assembled; the 'three sisters' came into the room; the sounds were heard, and through the medium of the alphabet, they, and about half the company, were directed to retire to another apartment. Our company in the absence of the 'three sisters,' whose presence is generally deemed essential to these spiritual communications, were all seated closely around an ordinary dining table, when one of the ladies, bowing her head, inquired in rather a solemn tone, 'Will the spirit answer questions now?' No response being made, I felt the disappointment of the lady, and was half inclined to smile at the ludicrous scene, when the searching glance of her suspicious eye, falling upon me, bade me maintain my usual gravity and respect toward the company and the occasion which had called us there. After several ineffectual attempts to get responses, the sounds were heard, and the company generally were privileged with answers to their respective interrogatories. I availed myself of the opportunity, but gained no other satisfaction than a prompt assurance that all my 'test questions' should be answered when I should come there again. I went away sceptical, though unable to account for the 'sounds' which caused the floor occasionally to vibrate under my feet.

"On my next visit I was much more successful. During the interval, I had prepared my mind with certain questions touching events unknown to the family, and of a remote date. The sounds told me my age precisely, though my appearance is such as to indicate a difference of eight or ten years. The names of six of my nearest deceased relatives were given me. I then inquired, 'Will the spirit who now makes these sounds give me its name?' Five sounds directed me to the alphabet, which I repeated until the name of 'Charles' appeared, which answered to an infant child whom we consigned to the grave in March, 1843. To my inquiries, it gave me a true answer in regard to the time it had been in the spirit land, and also the period since my eldest sister's death, which was nearly eighteen years; the latter fact not being recollected then, I found true by dates on my return home. Many other test questions were correctly answered; and yet, notwithstanding the origin of these sounds seemed inexplicable, I was inclined to impute them to mesmerism or clairvoyance. However, as the spirit promised to satisfy me by other demonstrations when I came again, I patiently awaited the opportunity.

"On the third visit I was selected from half a dozen gentlemen, and directed by these sounds to retire to another apartment, in company with the 'three sisters' and their aged mother. It was about eight o'clock in the evening. A lighted candle was placed on a large table, and we seated ourselves around it. I occupied one side of the table, the mother and youngest daughter the right, and two of the sisters the left, leaving the opposite side of the table vacant. On taking our positions the sounds were heard, and continued to multiply and become more violent until every part of the room trembled with their demonstrations. They were unlike any I had heard before. Suddenly, as we were all resting on the table, I felt the side next to me to move upward. I pressed upon it heavily, but soon it passed out of the reach of us all—full six feet from me, and at least four from the nearest person to it. I saw distinctly its position—not a thread could have connected it with any of the company without my notice, for I had come to detect imposition, if it could be found. In this position we were situated when the question was asked, 'Will the spirit move the table back where it was before?' And back it came, as though it were carried on the head of some one who had not suited his position to a perfect equipoise, the balance being sometimes in favor of one side, and then the other. But it regained its first position. In the meantime the 'demonstrations' grew louder and louder. The family commenced, and sung the 'spirit's' song,* and several other pieces of sacred music, during which accurate time was marked on the table, causing it to vibrate. A transparent hand, resembling a shadow, presented itself before my face. I felt fingers taking hold of a lock of hair on the left side of my head, causing an inclination of several inches; then a cold hand was drawn over my face; three gentle raps on my left knee; my right limb forcibly pulled, against strong resistance, under the table; a violent shaking, as though two hands were applied to my shoulders; myself and chair uplifted and moved back a few inches, and several slaps, as with a hand, on the side of my head, which were repeated on each one of the company, more rapidly than I could count. During these manifestations, a piece of pasteboard, nearly a foot square, was swung with such velocity before us as to throw a strong current of air in our faces; a paper curtain attached to one of the windows was rolled up and unrolled twice; a lounge immediately behind me was shaken violently; two small drawers in a bureau played back and forth with inconceivable rapidity; a sound resembling a man sawing boards, and planing them, was heard under the table; a common spinning-wheel seemed to be in motion, making a very natural buzz of the spindle; a reel articulated each knot wound upon it, while the sound of a rocking cradle indicated maternal care for the infant's slumbers. These were among many other demonstrations which I witnessed that evening, amid which I felt a perfect self-possession, and in no instance the slightest embarrassment, except a momentary chill when the cold hand was applied to my face, similar to a sensation I have realized when touching a dead body. That any of the company could have performed these things, under the circumstances in which we were situated, would require a greater stretch of credulity on my part than it would to believe it was the work of spirits. It could not,

* "The Spirit's Song." At one of these circles the spirits rapped out by the alphabet a simple melody, which being given by letters to Mrs. Fish with instructions how to divide it into bars and rhythm, that lady being a musician, readily arranged the given letters into the air. The spirits then requested the circle to sing to those notes the words of Mrs. Heman's charming poem, "The Haunted Spring;" requiring the singers, however, to substitute the word *sacred* for *haunted*.

by any possibility, have been done by them, nor even attempted, without detection. And I may add, that near the close of the demonstrations at this visit, there was a vibration of the floor, as though several tons in weight had been uplifted and suddenly fallen again upon it This caused everything in the room to shake most violently for several minutes, when the force was withdrawn.

"I have also tested the intelligence of these spirits in every way my ingenuity could invent. On one occasion, I wrote a word on a slip of paper privately, placed it in my wallet, went there—and the sounds, through the alphabet, spelled that word correctly as I had written it. That word was 'Sibyl.'

"On the 20th of February, the two youngest sisters made my family a visit. Here the sounds were heard; questions involving subjects wholly unknown to them, were answered; a large, heavy dining-table was moved several times; and on expressing thanks at the table to the Giver of all Good, some six or eight sounds responded to every sentence I uttered, by making loud and distinct sounds in various parts of the room.

"Yours, truly,

"C. HAMMOND.

"ROCHESTER, *February* 22, 1850."

A great variety of other manifestations began to appear in families residing in and about Rochester, besides the rappings. Volumes might be written on the extraordinary intelligence manifested by spirits in various ways, especially through clairvoyance, premonition, and mental telegraphy. A short but rather striking instance of the latter kind is inserted here, occurring in the family of the Rev. A. H. Jervis, a Methodist minister of Rochester, who was warmly interested in the Fox family, and who had the advantage of the same kind of medium power as theirs, produced in members of his own household. It will suffice to illustrate multitudes of similar cases that were now transpiring hourly. Writing to E. W. Capron, Mr. Jervis says:

"There are many facts that have come under my observation equally convincing of the intelligence and utility of the communications from these unseen agents, who I believe are now continually about us, and more perfectly acquainted with all our ways and even our thoughts than we are with each other. But the fact in reference to our friend Pickard is what you require. He was at my house on Friday, April 6, 1849. None of the Fox family were present. While at the tea-table we had free communication on different subjects. Mr. Pickard was requested to ask questions. He desired to know who it was that would communicate, and was answered, 'I am your mother, Mary Pickard.' Her name, or the fact of her death, was not known to any of us. The next Monday evening Mr. Pickard was at Mr. G—'s, and tarried there over night. He then received a communication purporting to be from his mother, saying, 'Your child is dead.' He came immediately to my place, and said he should take the stage for home [Lockport, sixty miles distant]; accordingly [and wholly on the faith of the spirit's communication, remember], he left in the stage at eight A. M. At twelve that same day I returned to my home, my wife meeting me with a telegraph envelope, which I first read mentally, and then breaking the seal, read out as follows:

"'ROCHESTER, *April* 10, 1849.

"'*By Telegraph from Lockport, to Rev. A. H. Jervis, No.* 4 *West Street:*

"'Tell Mr. Pickard, if you can find him, his child died this morning. Answer.

R. MALLORY.'

• • "I then added to my wife, 'God's telegraph has outdone Morse's altogether.'

"Yours, truly,

"To E. W. CAPRON, *Auburn.* A. H. JERVIS."

Several attempts were made by the spirits to reduce the communications to something like an orderly system of spiritual telegraphy. One of the most frequent names spelled out in the Rochester manifestations was that of "Benjamin Franklin," who claimed to be actively interested in promoting them; a claim not at all at variance with the pursuits of this renowned philosopher whilst an inhabitant of earth. Had the instructions of this wise and beneficent spirit been strictly followed out, there might possibly have long since resulted that order which was sadly lacking in the chaos of the earlier manifestations; but in the meetings which now began to take place in hundreds of families, the ignorance and superstition which had formerly prevailed on all subjects connected with the life beyond the grave, either continued to characterize the communications or became apparent in an excess of fanatical credulity.

The *séances* of the Misses Fox were constantly broken up by inharmony, rudeness, and determined opposition, on the part of some of the visitors. The company were driven from room to room by incessant intrusions; and the nervously excited state of the poor mediums' minds, together with their entire ignorance of the necessary conditions for scientific communion, rendered orderly experiments almost impossible. In some of the circles where entranced clairvoyant or impressional media presided, the wildest scenes of confusion would often prevail. Two or three of "the prophets" would be jabbering in unknown tongues at once, whilst others would be shouting the war-whoop of the red Indian. "Apostolic" letters, in miserable grammar and worse spelling, were palmed off as genuine productions from the seventh sphere; and all the crudities of impressible minds, stimulated half to frenzy by the contagious excitement of the times, were set down as direct communications from exalted ancients whose authoritative teachings no doubt emanated from the fantastic imaginings of self-psychologized persons. It would indeed have required a more re-creative power than any that Divine wisdom has yet intrusted to spirits or mortals to fashion these elements into order, or to bring forth the wise dicta of science from such disturbed magnetic conditions. A few phenomenal evidences were from time to time developed out of the chaos, proving the power possessed by spirits to achieve marvellous results in mental science, could favorable conditions be afforded. One of these experiments has been so amply recorded by Mr. N. Draper, of Rochester, a very worthy gentleman and the husband of a most excellent magnetic clairvoyant, that we subjoin his statement in full:

"*To Messrs. Jervis, Willetts, Jones, and others:*

"GENTLEMEN,—As we are required by authority, that we think we have no right to disregard, to make public the extraordinary communications witnessed at my dwelling, it becomes necessary to give you, and through you the public, the facts which gave rise to the first interview, on Friday, the 16th inst. The novelty of the subject and the state of the public mind are such that I feel prompted to do this, not only correctly but as minutely as possible. Circumstances had placed me in a way to witness those remarkable communications called the 'mysterious rappings,' from the time of their origin in this city in the summer of 1848. After the severest tests, under a variety of circumstances and at various places, for about one year, incontestible evidence addressed to my senses baffled my scepticism, and fully convinced me that they were the production of no human agencies. And as they profess to emanate from invisible intelligences, called spirits, I had not allowed myself the liberty to attribute them to any other source, at least until some other origin could be detected. In hope of eliciting some further light on the mysterious subject, I proposed to a member of my family, who is susceptible to magnetic influence, to be put into a clairvoyant state, and see what might be presented in relation to it. She complied, and for this purpose was magnetized on the evening of the 12th inst.

"The questions and answers were as follows:

"*Q.* Do you see anything? *A.* I see a stranger who I never before saw. He is not prepossessing in appearance, but is very elevated in his position, and is busily employed. *Q.* What is he doing? *A.* He is preparing work for you. *Q.* What is the nature of the work? *A.* He is establishing a line of communication. *Q.* Ask him 'Is it practicable to the communications between two distant points by means of these rappings?' *A.* 'To be sure,' he says. *Q.* Can you ascertain who this stranger is? *A. Benjamin* [and after a pause] *Franklin. Q.* Will you ask him to give you some signal by which we may know it is really Benjamin Franklin? After a silence of one or two minutes, a violent shock of her person induced me hastily to say, 'What is the matter; are you waking up? *A.* No; you wanted a signal and I told him if it was Dr. Franklin he might electrize me, and he did it. *Q.* Has it injured you? *A.* No; I feel better; my head is clearer; I can see plainer. *Q.* Will you ask him where communications between distant points at the same time can be tested. *A.* He says at your own house. *Q.* Is there anything required of us in the matter? *A.* He says, get two of these young ladies about whom there is so much excitement in your city, place them in extreme parts of two rooms, and you [meaning herself] be put in the same state in which you now are, and I will communicate with you. *Q.* Who else may be in attendance? *A.* Mr. Jervis and a few others who have been acquainted with the subject. *Q.* Will he direct as to time? *A.* He says consult the convenience of those concerned, and I shall be advised of it. *Q.* Are there any further directions to be given at this time? *A.* That is the end of the chapter.

"In compliance with the above, the interview on Friday, the 16th, was called, you and others notified, and the attendance of the two young ladies, Margaretta and Catharine Fox, secured; from whom, for prudential reasons, the above facts and preliminaries were withheld.

"Respectfully yours, N. DRAPER."

"*To the Editor of the Daily Magnet:*—

"Pursuant to the notice as above stated, we, the undersigned, met at the house of Mr. Draper on Friday, the 15th inst., about four o'clock P. M. We inquired for directions, and were answered by alphabet, 'Let Mrs. Draper be magnetized.' Through her the two young ladies were directed to retire to another room. The directions then were for Mr. Jervis, Mrs. Fox, and Catharine Fox, to be placed in a room at the opposite end of the house, and for Mr. Jervis to take notes. Margaretta Fox should be with the company in the parlor, and Mr. Draper take notes. This was done. The sounds were then heard in both rooms by either company, exactly similar to the sound heard in the telegraph office.

"*Question to the Clairoyant*—What does that rapping mean, unlike any other sounds before heard by rapping? *Answer*—He is trying the batteries." The signal for the alphabet was heard, and on calling the letters it was spelled, 'She must be waked in ten minutes.' A watch was placed on the table, after noting the time, and covered up, and the question asked, if we could have a signal by sounds at the exact time, and was answered affirmatively. At the *precise* time the signal was heard. The question was then asked, 'Who shall wake her?' and she was instantly awakened with an apparent electric shock.

"At this point there was much interruption, by persons coming into both rooms. The question was asked for further directions, and the answer was by alphabet, 'Things are not as I directed; therefore, you cannot proceed at this time. There should be but four in each room.' Mr. Jervis and company came into the parlor, and his notes read as follows: 'Things are not as I directed them; therefore, you cannot proceed at this time.' *Q.* Can we have another opportunity? *A.* If I set the time and name the company there shall be no fail. *Q.* Shall the appointment be now made? Answered affirmatively. The following persons were then named by the alphabet: Mr. Jervis, Mr. Jones, Mr. Draper, Mr. Willetts, Mrs. Jervis, Mrs. Draper, Mrs. Brown, Mrs. Fox, Margaretta Fox, and Catharine Fox. *Q.* May we know the time? *A.* Wednesday next, at four o'clock P. M. *Q.* The place? *A.* Here. On the day appointed, February 20th, the above-named persons convened; some of the company were late, and as soon as order was observed, the question was asked 'What are the directions of Benjamin Franklin? *A.* Hurry, first magnetize Mrs. Draper.' This was done, she immediately saying: 'He says we are behind the time, but he will forgive us this time; we must do better in future.' The company was divided as follows: Mr. Jervis, Mr. Jones, Mrs. Fox, Mrs. Brown, Catharine Fox, in a retired room, with two doors closed between them. Mrs. Draper, Mrs. Jervis, Mr. Draper, Mr. Willetts, and Margaretta Fox remained in the parlor. Sounds unusually loud were heard in each room by either company, as before, resembling the telegraphic sounds. They were so unusual that Miss Fox became alarmed and said, 'What does all this mean?' Mrs. Draper, while her countenance was irradiated with animation, replied, 'He is trying the batteries.' Soon there was the signal for the alphabet, and the following communication was spelled to the company in the parlor: 'Now I am ready, my friends. There will be great changes in the nineteenth century. Things that now look dark and mysterious to you will be laid plain before your sight. Mysteries are going to be revealed. The world will be enlightened. I sign my name, Benjamin Franklin. Do not go into the other room.'

"After waiting a few minutes, Mr. Jervis came into the parlor, saying that he was directed by the sounds to come and compare notes. They read as follows: *Q.* Are we all right? Answered affirmatively; signal for alphabet, and the following was spelled: 'There will be great changes in the nineteenth century. Things that now look dark and mysterious to you will be laid plain before your sight. Mysteries are going to be revealed. The world will be enlightened. I sign my name, Benjamin Franklin. Go in the parlor and compare notes.' Mr. Jervis returned to his company, and by alphabet was spelled: 'Now all go into the parlor.' The notes were then compared in presence of the whole company. *Q.* Is there anything more from Dr. Franklin? *A.* I think I have given tests enough for this day. *Q.* Will it not be better to keep this matter private? *A.* No; it should be published. *Q.* In what paper? *A.* In *Democrat* or *Magnet*. *Q.* Who shall prepare it for publication? *A.* George Willetts.' Time and place were then designated for the same company to meet again, with two other persons added to the number.

"We sign our names as no parties, but as witnesses. If our testimony is incredible, impeach and reject it; if admissible, hand it over to the judge and jurors—the public—and charge them that we claim no interest aside from their own in their verdict.

"Rev. A. H. Jervis,
Edward Jones,
Rachael Draper,
Mary Brown,
Nathaniel Draper,
George Willetts,
Mary Jervis,
Margaret Fox.

"Rochester, *February* 23, 1850."

And here for the present we must close our account of doings of the spirits in Rochester, and that rather from the pressure of other subjects than the lack of material, as the records of that city alone would amply suffice to fill up many volumes in connection with the early history of Spiritualism in America.

Many highly interesting narratives are necessarily omitted, and above two hundred letters, printed and in MSS., in the author's possession, containing graphic accounts of first interviews with the spirits and subsequent conviction of their truth, are withheld for want of space.

Many gentlemen connected with the press of different cities joined in the Rochester investigations, and many reported in favor of the honesty and truth of the mediums.

Frequent acknowledgments were made that the phenomena exhibited were marvellous, the intelligence unquestionable, generally correct, and out of the sphere of the mediums' knowledge, but admissions made thus far generally concluded by declaring that, while acquitting the media of any concocted plan in the production of said phenomena, "they were not prepared; or could not, would not, *must not believe*, etc., that it was the work of spirits." There were many others connected with the press, especially the *religious* papers, who first refused scornfully to investigate "the thing," and after pluming themselves on their virtuous ignorance, proceeded in unmeasured terms to revile it, heap scandal and denunciation on the heads of all connected with it, and fill their columns with unreasoning abuse of that which they "knew nothing at all about."

Whole columns of the daily journals were filled with trash of this character, which though temporarily injurious to the feelings of those concerned, served the purpose of giving the manifestations precisely that publicity which the spirits demanded, and for which, as it would seem, a great majority of the press actually became "mediums." And thus the fiery cross, carried by the hands of unseen messengers, sped from point to point; the beacon fires lighted by invisible hands gleamed on every mountain-top, and the low muffled sound of the spirit-raps that first broke the slumbers of the peaceful inhabitants of the humble tenement at Hydesville, became the clarion peal that sounded out to the millions of the western hemisphere, the anthem of the soul's immortality, chorused by hosts of God's bright ministering angels.

CHAPTER V.

SPIRITUALISM IN AUBURN, NEW YORK.

"The argument that nothing ever came
From spirits or the spiritual world
Is very ancient. The philosopher
Said to the seer, 'All that you see I know.'
The seer in his deep wisdom made reply,
'All that you know I see.'"

T. L. HARRIS.

PROGRESS OF SPIRITUALISM FROM 1849 TO 1855 — CATHARINE FOX AT AUBURN — MRS. TAMLIN AND MRS. BENEDICT — SPIRIT MUSIC — THE OPPOSITION — TROUBLES WITHIN THE CAMP — THE APOSTOLIC CIRCLE.

IT was in November, 1849, that the scenes were enacted in Corinthian Hall, Rochester, described in the last chapter.

The immense geographical areas embraced in the thirty-six States of the Union, and the fact that no regular system of human propagandism issuing from a central source and ramifying through the country, or, indeed, anything analagous to such a procedure, has ever been attempted, to account for the spread of Spiritualism, embarrasses the historian in describing its progress. "Progress," in fact, it can scarcely be called; for, if modern Spiritualism had been promulgated as well as inaugurated by the Rochester mediums, its course might have been traced in their footprints; but whilst we are considering the effects upon some town or State which the visits of the Misses Fox produced, behold we find a great spiritual outpouring in sections of country where the echoes of the Rochester vibrations could never even have reached.

Spiritualism did not radiate from a definite centre, but sprang with a spontaneous and irresistible life of its own, independent of human propagandism, the contagious force of public sentiment, or the psychological effect of common report. If the ends of the countless threads that with sudden and magical rapidity appeared to be inclosing the whole continent of America in one vast woof of spirit-power, were not spun, held, and intelligently directed by the unseen people of the spirit country, then all theories of causation must fail, and the marvellous growth and blossoming of Spiritualism, the germs of which no visible hands had planted, will forever remain one of the unfinished problems of the universe. Apart from the obviously supramundane character of its production in various sections of country at once, it is not difficult to trace the secondary causes of its rapid growth in the all-absorbing nature of its revealments and the passionate emotions of love and hatred which it excited in its friends and foes. In fact it would be difficult to determine which was the most effective form of propaganda for the spread of the belief, namely, the zealous enthusiasm of its admirers or the bitter persecution of its antagonists.

To do justice to the uprising of this mighty power, we must consider its manifestations in different States about the same period of time. The first point which we shall notice is the State of New York, in which the communion between mortals and spirits first took the form of a scientific telegraphy.

In the city of Auburn, New York State, resided Mr. E. W. Capron, to whom allusion has already been made in connection with the earliest manifestations and the Corinthian Hall investigation. To strengthen the convictions of a spiritual source for the phenomena, an opinion which had irresistibly forced itself upon his reason, Mr. Capron induced Mrs. Fox to permit her youngest daughter, Catharine, to spend some time in his family. During the *séances* conducted through the mediumship of this young lady, many of the principal inhabitants of Auburn had the opportunity of witnessing the most astounding phenomena under circumstances which precluded even the suspicion of deception. Spirit music was produced; hands were seen, felt, and even examined, forming and melting apparently in the clasp that held them; messages of affection, timely warning, and prescient intelligence were constantly spelled out through the raps; the furniture moved in supra-mundane feats of power, and almost every conceivable phase of intelligent spiritual phenomena was exhibited to all who chose to come and witness it. Two remarkable results followed the first introduction of "the power" into Auburn. The first was the fact that though the press were permitted free access to the circles, and the most abundant opportunity for investigation, yet the strength of the occult force, whose evidences they beheld, only seemed to arouse in the most of their number a vindictive and unreasoning spirit of antagonism, which broke forth in unqualified and often senseless slander.

For example: The *Auburn Daily Advertiser* coolly stated that old Mr. Fox [a quiet, inoffensive farmer, chiefly remarkable for simple-minded devotion to the Wesleyan Church and his retired, peaceful habits] had by a cunning contrivance of springs and wires managed to produce all the marvels witnessed at Hydesville! The fact that every plank, board, and brick, or inch of matter connected with the possessed house had been ransacked in vain by hundreds of persons in the attempt to detect any trickery, all went for nothing with this shrewd editor. The still more awkward fact that the phenomena had continued to increase in strength and variety for upwards of a twelvemonth, moving about from place to place, house to house, person to person, involving the action of above a hundred different mediums; and that the poor old gentleman accused of its production had never, except in the first two or three months of the Hydesville excitement, been in the spirit circles or in any way connected with the movement—all this was with equal *sense* and *candor* utterly disregarded, and good Mr. Fox's "springs and wires," invisibly fixed into *nothing*, still continued to stretch from the cottage at Hydesville and to rap over hundreds of miles, sounding down to the valley of the Mississippi, along the vast seaboard of the New England States, and up to the northern regions of Lake Superior! Wonderful invention of a quiet little New York farmer! and marvellous springs and wires, the intelligent action of which could reveal past, present, and future with an accuracy that would have put to shame Egyptian magic or Chaldean astrology! We must here remark that if from time to time we insert the puerilities and baseless slanders which have been levelled against "the cause" and its adherents, it is not for their worth or efficacy, but rather to show the utter futility and even desperation of that opposition which has been forced to create such childish fictions in order to discredit the spiritual hypothesis.

The second result of Miss Kate Fox's visit to Auburn seemed to be the unfoldment of medium powers not less remarkable than her own in many persons who attended her *séances*. The most prominent cases of this kind occurred in the persons of Mrs. Tamlin and Mrs. Benedict, mediums whose names have since become an integral part of the great American spiritual record. Several other ladies were also developed in the Auburn circles as mediums and clairvoyants. A great variety of gifts in the direction of physical, writing, healing, seeing, and trance mediumship also became rapidly manifest in various families of the highest respectability, and the great majority of these developments took place irrespective of Miss Fox's presence, although her visit first called the attention of the community to the subject, and induced the formation of the circles in which these powers in the various media became externalized. In Mr. Capron's work on the early Spiritualism of America are recorded some very interesting accounts of the manifestations at Auburn; amongst others, the following incidents, which were also verified to the author by Mr. Henry C. Wright, an eye-witness of the scenes. Mr. Capron writes:

"Mrs. Tamlin was, so far as I have been able to learn, the first medium through whom the guitar or other musical instruments were played, without visible contact, so as to recognize tunes. In her presence it was played with all the exactness of an experienced musician, although she is not acquainted with music, or herself able to play on any instrument. The tones varied from loud and vigorous to the most refined touches of the strings that could be imagined."

At a circle held at Mrs. Tamlin's, when about seven or eight persons were present, whose testimony was afterwards publicly tendered for the truth of what follows, Mr. Capron goes on to say:

"I had magnetized the medium, and, after various manifestations of the spirits, she said that they were about to do something new which she could not understand. After sitting a few minutes, we heard a low sound like a distant locomotive whistle. Soon, however, the sound grew louder, and softened into the most exquisite music. One of the company was requested to sing and she did so; the most beautiful music accompanied. It was like the notes of an exquisite Æolian harp, but any attempt to describe its beauty would fail. . . . . . . We frequently had the same kind of music in the presence of Mrs. Tamlin. . . . . . At times it would resemble the finest conceivable tones of the human voice, and almost seem to be dissolved into words.

"Another phase of this musical manifestation was the imitation of 'Fabyan's' horn. This was first produced when Henry C. Wright was present. He called for the spirit of N. P. Rogers and asked him to sound the horn, when immediately a sound came like the sounding of a horn and its reverberation among distant hills, echoing and re-echoing for a long time. Mr. Wright had visited the White Mountains in company with N. P. Rogers some years before, and there had heard Fabyan, the hotel-keeper, wind his horn among the hills, and it was this sound that was so exactly imitated. Mr. Wright afterwards published a description of this scene in a pamphlet."

So long as the manifestations continued to be of the character above narrated, their appearance in Auburn was hailed with delight by bereaved mourners, to whom conclusive evidences of the presence and watchful guardianship of beloved spirit friends was clearly proven.

It excited the interest of the scientific from the fact that wonderful phenomena of a novel and interesting character were produced. It startled the learned by the exhibition of ignorant adults and uninstructed children speaking in foreign languages, and often with marvellous eloquence. Clairvoyance, psychometry, and healing by the laying on of hands or spiritual prescriptions, testified to the beneficent character of the intelligence and the vast range of uses which it included.

But the profound ignorance of all psychological phenomena in which this material age has been steeped, soon operated to mar and deform the infant movement.

The world had to learn that the spirit country is peopled from earth, and that spirit-life commences from the point where mortal existence ends. Unconscious of this solemn truth, the early communicants with the unseen world were unprepared for the visitation of the *dark spirits* whom the sad experiences of earth had manufactured into criminals. Unaware that life, whether here or hereafter, is *progress*, not violent and unnatural change, investigators were appalled at the representations, produced through media, of the same vicious tendencies in spirits which they had beheld with indifference from the same spirits whilst inhabitants of earth; in a word, they did not realize the fact that spirits were still human, and that the soul in many respects remained unchanged by the mere act of physical dissolution. In this state of perplexity and ignorance the return of earth's criminals was generally met, either by the superstitious and unavailing exercises of old Catholic rites, or submitted to blindly in the idea that all spirits must necessarily be authoritative, until the unwary medium became the subject of the distressing condition now known as "obsession." Still, though the first circles were conducted in a condition of mental blindness scandalous to the religious teachers who should long since have instructed mankind concerning "spiritual gifts" and spiritual existences, in course of time the investigators learned *experimentally* to realize the true character of the spirit-world, and that more conclusively by their failures than they could have done by contemplating the sunlit side of the picture only. But whilst the philosophical Spiritualist began to realize the true conditions of immortality from communion with the beings who were living in its experience, the egotist and fanatic appropriated as their share of the great spiritual outpouring, precisely those elements which were best calculated to stimulate their vanity and pander to their superstitious imaginings. Amongst the Auburn Spiritualists were to be found several extremely ignorant but strongly bigoted persons of the Second Advent persuasion. The phenomena of modern Spiritualism, interpreted through their own narrow credal views, appeared to them to be the actual inauguration of the long-promised "millennium," whilst they—the "true believers"— must of course be the chosen ones through whom the millennial dynasty was to be established on earth.

Quite early in the movement a circle had been formed, which at first had received the modest title of "The Auburn Circle;" but no sooner did the "chosen few" of the millennial belief gain a foothold in this happy gathering than they bent themselves to the work of converting it to their own purposes and using the manifestations as an endorsement of their peculiar opinions; in fact, as an eye-witness of the scenes here enacted described to the author, "in return for their conversion to Spiritualism they strove to convert the spirits to Second Adventism."

In pursuance of this notable idea they secured the services of Mrs. Benedict, an impressible rapping medium, through whom the influences mortal and immortal that operated in this circle, dictated plans of action designed to make "the universe rock," and that portion of it which they modestly called *this little planet*, a convert to their faith and a subject to the spiritual authority of *John the Divine*, *Daniel the Prophet*, *Paul the Apostle*, and other Biblical worthies whom they assumed to have become temporarily reincarnated in their mediumship. The title of the circle was changed from the "Auburn" to the "Apostolic Circle;" Mrs. Benedict, the medium, was dispatched to New York, where, under *spirit direction*, she summoned a certain Baptist preacher, named James D. Scott, to come to Auburn to minister in the work. A series of papers were published purporting to emanate from various distinguished personages of Jewish origin and of the Apostolic age. Some of these publications were well calculated to produce the results which their authors predicted for them, namely, a revolution, though not exactly in the universe, or even in the "little planet" earth, but simply in the fortunes of the luckless publishers, who found the issue of the said pamphlets exciting a very revolutionary effect upon their worldly prosperity. To the disbelievers in the Divine origin of these papers they certainly created no little feeling of indignation at the audacity which could append the names of prophets and apostles to their absurd puerilities, whilst even the most credulous of the well-educated Spiritualists had cause to mourn over the deterioration in grammar and orthography which befalls the exalted dead by a long residence in the spirit-world.

About the commencement of the year 1850 the "Apostolic Brotherhood" assumed a more respectable literary shape under the authority of the Rev. James Scott, and actually rose into eminence by the accession to their ranks of the renowned poet, preacher, and medium, the Rev. Thomas L. Harris, who was also spiritually called to "the work." With the leadership of these accomplished gentlemen,—who claimed to act under the highest spiritual guidance,—the movement gained in numbers and in importance until it seemed to absorb and control nearly all the Spiritualism in Auburn, reflect itself through the chief of the communications, crystallize into a numerously attended religious meeting, and finally to culminate in the famous "Mountain Cove movement," of which a detailed description will be given in a later chapter. And here it may be asked whether these shadows, cast by human pride, presumption, and fanaticism, did not irrevocably quench the dawning light of the still embryotic spiritual movement? We answer, most unquestionably not; although many were the confident predictions of such a result; indeed certain journalistic magnates who had hitherto been indefatigable in castigating the cause through their columns, now abandoned their efforts with the complaisant remark that "the Spiritualists themslves were performing the work of self-destruction, and it was only necessary to give them rope enough and they would inevitably hang themselves." In view of what has been already narrated, there is no doubt but that this enlightened policy would have had the desired effect had it so happened that *all* the Spiritualists of Auburn were included by the followers of *Pope Harris* and *Cardinal Scott;* but besides a very considerable number outside of their ranks, even some of those who had been subject to their authority gained by their experience some very wise and useful lessons, and not a few of these deluded ones, instead of rushing to the destruction so liberally predicated for them, exchanged their leadership for *Pope Judgment* and *Cardinal Reason,* dignitaries who were henceforth enshrined in plenary authority over the spiritualistic circles at Auburn. Amongst the lessons that these rulers taught was the very important one that no spirit, mortal or immortal, should stand between the creature and the Creator; that it was necessary to try the spirits *out of the form* by precisely the same rules of good and use as those which applied to spirits *in the form*, and finally that the spirit-world was of no more authority as spirits unbodied than the earth-world as spirits still embodied. These lessons the recipients deemed cheaply learned, even though the price paid for them was the ridicule of a community profoundly ignorant of the subject they ridiculed.

As to the "faithful" amongst the "Apostolic Brotherhood," they soon disposed of the question, as far as the people of Auburn were concerned, by quitting that "reprobate community" for the holy retreat of "Mountain Cove" under the leadership of their inspired shepherds. After this instructive episode Spiritualism in Auburn rose, Phœnix-like, resurrected from the ashes of fanaticism into purified life, strength, and increasing numbers. Mediums began to multiply, the gifts of the spirit became constantly more abundant, and the ranks of Spiritualism were swelled with daily added converts.

Sunday meetings were in due time established, and a well written weekly paper entitled *The Spiritual Clarion*, together with an annual statistical register, was issued from the office of the Rev. Uriah Clark, an ex-Universalist minister, who established the above-named periodicals in Auburn, from whence they long continued to go forth as welcome evangels of the spiritual Gospel to the world. The city now numbers thousands of Spiritualists; nor, with all the "rope" that Christian ministers and learned editors so generously allowed them, have they yet "hanged themselves," or permanently hindered the progress of their glorious cause.

CHAPTER VI.

SPIRITUALISM IN NEW YORK FROM 1849 TO 1855.

"They wrought with sad sincerity;
Themselves from God they could not free;
They builded wiser than they knew
The conscious stone to beauty grew."

SPIRITUAL SPRING-TIME IN NEW YORK — REV. S. B. BRITAIN, HIS SPIRITUAL BIRTH — THE "UNIVERCŒLUM" — DR. HALLOCK AND THE PROPHETIC CLAIRVOYANT — A LITERARY CIRCLE — JAMES FENIMORE COOPER, GEORGE BANCROFT, N. P. WILLIS, WILLIAM CULLEN BRYANT, AND OTHER INVESTIGATORS — THE PRESS EXPLAINING, IGNORING, ABUSING, DECRYING, DEFYING, AND MYSTIFYING THE MYSTERY — THOSE ROCHESTER KNOCKINGS AGAIN — GRIMES, CHAUNCY, BURR, AND MRS. CULVER.

No year in the first epoch of modern Spiritualism has been more fruitful with events of interest than 1850. It was in that year that manifestations of the most violent and astounding character appeared in the family of Dr. Eliakim Phelps, D.D., of Stratford, Connecticut. It was then also that rappings, automatic writing, and other intelligent modes of communing with spirits became familiar in Boston through the mediumship of Mrs. Margaret Cooper, daughter of the eminent lecturer and writer, LeRoy Sunderland.

On February 1, 1850, a party of ladies and gentlemen, in Philadelphia, Penn., formed themselves into an experimental circle, and after a very few sittings succeeded in obtaining, through raps, clairvoyance, and other methods, satisfactory communion with the spirit-world. Circles were inaugurated in the same year in Providence, Rhode Island; Binghamton, Westfield, Albany, Troy, Waterford, and numerous other places in New York State; in Cincinnati, where the test rappings were remarkably powerful and intelligent; in Memphis, Tennessee; St. Louis, Missouri; California, Oregon, Texas, South America, Maine, Vermont, and New Hampshire, similar manifestations appeared, and all before the personal influence of the "original Rochester

Eng'd by A. H. Ritchie

mediums" could give the least color to the supposition, put forth in many instances by the press, that these persons were the authors or "teachers" of the "awful delusion" that had seized on the dwellers of these wide-spread districts of America.

In New York State it cannot be questioned that the rumor of the Rochester investigations, the visits of the mediums to its different towns, combined with the powerful effect which the phenomenal career of A. J. Davis produced, contributed to fill up the overflowing measure of spiritual life which has specially distinguished this State.

In the cities of Troy and Albany, with the neighboring villages of Waterford and Lansingburgh, most excellent mediums were developed, at a very early period of the movement, for various phases of "the power." The visits of the Misses Fox and the reports from Rochester first called attention to the subject, but communion with the spirit-world by no means depended on these agencies. For example: In the family of Mr. Anson Attwood, of Troy, a gentleman of prominent position and high character, one of his little daughters, a child of about ten years of age, became suddenly developed for marvellous phases of the strongest physical character, besides rapping, writing, and clairvoyance; and similar manifestations continued to spring up like grass beneath the feet in every place and with every variety of development.

For the present, however, we shall limit our observations to the progress of Spiritualism in New York City.

One of the main features of interest in tracing a movement for which a supra-mundane origin is affirmed, must necessarily be derived from the proofs that can be offered in verification of that claim. The history of the rise and progress of Spiritualism in New York City forms as valuable an item in this class of testimony as can well be selected, for we see the principal actors in the great drama being prepared in methods peculiar to themselves long before they were called upon to take part in the *séances* by which they have since become publicly identified with Spiritualism. A striking illustration of this occurs in the person of the Rev. S. B. Britain, a gentleman widely known as an author of eminent literary and scientific attainments, but more especially distinguished as one who has filled the various positions of editor, lecturer, essayist, magnetizer, psychologist, and magnetic physician in the spiritual ranks. By his eloquent advocacy, public discussions, and editorial labors, Mr. Britain has rendered services to the cause of Spiritualism which can never be over-estimated; yet his adherence was not secured through phenomenal evidence or any of the ordinary channels of human propagandism. Whilst officiating as pastor to the First Univeralist Church in Albany, New York, and during the progress of a severe fit of sickness, Mr. Britain was thrown into a state of profound trance, which for a period of twelve days held his consciousness in abeyance, neither did he receive the least nourishment for twenty-one days. From this condition, hovering between sleep and death, Mr. Britain returned to life, awakening from the trance as mysteriously as he had sunk into it. With the restoration of health and consciousness, however, his feelings experienced a complete revulsion, which marked him for a changed man. Either a fresh train of thought was infused into his mind by the still, small voice whose utterances can never be interpreted into human speech, or the presence of a *strange spiritual visitor* [whom he described as of majesic aspect and benevolent bearing, often standing near him during the period of his trance] engraved on his mind a set of impressions wholly distinct and at variance from those which his former life's images had left. Certain it is that he arose from his couch of suffering like a soul resurrected from the ashes of a buried past. For a brief period only, he resumed his ministerial duties; and though earnestly entreated by his congregation to remain with them and distribute the living bread of which it was evident that he had partaken, he felt a strong mental pressure compelling him to sever his connection with any credal organization where he might be fettered in the free range and expression of the newly-born thoughts that were animating him. It has already been noticed that the appearance of Mr. A. J. Davis's extraordinary work, "Nature's Divine Revelations," was followed by the publication of the *Univercœlum* of which the Rev. S. B. Britain was the editor. Mr. Britain had taken a warm interest in the young "Poughkeepsie Seer's" supra-mundane development; and having himself become an earnest investigator into magnetism, clairvoyance, and those occult mysteries of which he reasonably judged his own case was an evidence, he naturally gravitated to the ranks of the philosophic Spiritualists, amongst whom his literary attainments and highly-cultured intellect procured him a distinguished place.

Thus it was that he became, by universal consent of his new associates, the editor of a paper which was designed to embody the most spiritually illuminated thoughts of the age. But Mr. Britain's phenomenal preparation for entering the ranks of Spiritualism was by no means an isolated evidence of spirit agency. Nearly all the persons connected directy or indirectly with Spiritualism have some remarkable experiences to relate—some evidence to give that they were each being prepared in their place to become one of the highly-wrought and polished stones in the great temple of the "New Jerusalem"—so that when at last they came together as if by the force of mutual and inevitable attraction, they found that they had but been instruments in the hands of the supreme power, who was fashioning each, through their separate experiences, to the work of Divine ministration.

At the New York Conference, established in 1851, for the discussion of psychological subjects, Dr. Hallock, one of the most able and prominent advocates of the truth of Spiritualism, related several experiences he had enjoyed with magnetic subjects about the time of the advent of the Rochester knockings; amongst these is a case strikingly illustrative of hundreds of others that were occurring in various parts of the country. Dr. Hallock, being a skilful operator, was asked by a clairvoyant to magnetize her for the purpose of examining an article which had just appeared in the New York *Tribune* of December, 1848, on the subject of the "rappings" at Hydesville.

"The clairvoyant passed," says the doctor, "into a kind of religious ecstacy, and in a solemn but happy frame of mind, evinced by a great change in her manner and appearance, went on to say that the newspaper statement of the Rochester phenomena was true. That it would not end there, but would be repeated in various places in America, Europe, and Asia. That its object was to convince the world of the realities of spiritual life and communion, and that these manifestations would not cease until the end was accomplished. She said it appeared to her as if a man by the name of Swedenborg had a great deal to do with it. That the rapping seemed to be made by the strong will of a man trying to impress himself on others. She described the appearance of Swedenborg while on earth, related anecdotes of his life, and added, "Why, he was like me; that is, he could be in one place, and tell what was going on in another." All her statements with regard to Swedenborg were verified by history, and those concerning the Rochester mediums, besides other collateral circumstances, were found upon inquiry to be strictly true; yet this person was very illiterate, and could have had no instruction upon the historical and scientific points she discoursed of. When questioned in her normal state if she had ever heard of Swedenborg, she replied, with unmistakable sincerity, "No; does he live in New York?" and thus the effects which magnetism and clairvoyance exerted in preparing the public mind and mediumistic organizations for the reception of Spiritualism was strikingly illustrated, and the advent of the Rochester knockings in New York found the ground ploughed, harrowed, and seed-bearing, long before the first visit of the Misses Fox to the city.

Notices of "the mysterious rappings in Hydesville" had already been widely circulated in the papers. Startling accounts of similar manifestations had reached the citizens from their friends in different parts of the States. "Rappings," it was said, had "broken out" in several towns in the immediate vicinity of Rochester, but above all, public attention was painfully excited by the report of the manifestations occurring at the house of the Rev. Dr. Phelps, of Stratford. The unquestionable veracity and high ecclesiastical position of Dr. Phelps, and the frightfully preternatural character of the events transpiring in his family, had excited a feeling of curiosity mingled with terror which was heightened by the accounts of marvels transpiring in other places with which the public were made familiar through the press, especially the New-York *Tribune*, the columns of which, through the influence of its progressive editors, were open to a free representation of the subject from all quarters, and on both sides of the question. It is from a file of this paper for the year 1850 that the author is enabled to present an account of a circle which was held through the mediumship of the Fox family soon after their first professional visit to New York City in the spring of 1850. The reader will perceive that the whole recital points to the mere infancy of the movement, and does not offer a view of any phenomena even commonly interesting or startling; but as presenting a fair specimen of the cautious tone of newspaper narratives of that period—however favorable the writer's opinions might be on the subject—but still more in view of the interest with which we must associate investigations, connected with names so distinguished in literature as those which figure in this circle, we deem the *verbatim* report of the *Tribune* may prove an acceptable record. The paper from which we extract this report being torn and the date defective, we are only enabled to indicate the time as being about the spring of 1850. The report was drawn up by one of the editors, a man of great learning and intelligence, Mr. Ripley.

"AN EVENING WITH THE 'SPIRITS'—NEW YORK, 1850.

"We were present on Thursday evening at a party of gentlemen who had been invited to the chambers of the Rev. Dr. Griswold, in Broadway, to meet the Rochester ladies, whose connection with the mysterious knockings has called forth such general curiosity. The party had been arranged by Dr. Griswold, who has been incredulous from the first with regard to any preternatural character in the manifestations. . . . . . .

"It consisted of persons whose general character for intelligence and probity was a guarantee against their being deluded by hasty impressions, and who probably without exception had no prepossession in favor of the principal actors in the movement. . . . .

"Among the guests of Dr. Griswold we may without impropriety mention the names of Mr. J. Fenimore Cooper, Mr. George Bancroft, Rev. Dr. Hawks, Dr. J. W. Francis, Dr. Marcy, Mr. N. P. Willis, William Cullen Bryant, Mr. Bigelow of the *Evening Post*, Mr. Richard B. Kimball, Mr. H. T. Tuckerman, and General Lyman. . . . . . .

"The ladies had been previously consulted, and after ascertaining that manifestations would take place, consented to meet the party. In order to prevent any suspicion as to the arrangement of the room, furniture, closets, etc., the *reunione* was appointed at the house of Dr. Griswold, which neither of the ladies had ever entered before the party was assembled. A little past eight o'clock they made their appearance—Mrs. Fox, an elderly lady, the mother of the 'ghost-seers' [which word we use for want of a better], Mrs. Fish, a married daughter, and her two younger sisters. . . . . . .

"For some time, perhaps a little over half an hour, after the arrival of the ladies no sounds were heard, and the company gave obvious symptoms of impatience. They were then requested to draw nearer the table, which was in front of the ladies, and form themselves into a compact circle. Soon after faint sounds began to be heard from under the floor, around the table, and in different parts of the room.

"They increased in loudness and frequency, becoming so clear and distinct that no one could deny their presence nor trace them to any visible cause. The question was now asked by the 'ghost-seers,' 'Will the spirits converse with any one present?' . . . . . .

"After a good deal of coquetting it was said that replies would be given to any questions proposed by Dr. Marcy. He inquired whether the spirit which he wished to converse with was a relation, was a child, and what was its age at the time of its death, etc. We understood Dr. Marcy to say that the answers were correct. . . . . . .

"Mr. Henry T. Tuckerman was the next to propound inquiries which, contrary to the usual custom, he expressed audibly, so as to be heard by the ladies and the whole company. Having fixed in his mind the name of an individual he asked, 'Did he live in New York?' No answer. 'In Baltimore? In Cambridge? In Boston?' Three distinct raps, which is the sign of an affirmative answer. A negative reply is indicated by silence. Mr. T. continued, 'Was he a lawyer? A merchant? A physician? A clergyman?' Knocks. 'Was he an Episcopalian? A Presbyterian? A Unitarian?' going over the names of the principal sects. No answer. At the suggestion of a gentleman, Mr. T. asked, 'Was he a Christian?' Knocks. Mr. T. then asked the age of the person in a series of tens. 'Was he twenty years old at the time of his death? Was he thirty? Fifty? Sixty?' Knocks. 'Has he left a family?' Knocks. 'Children?' Knocks. 'Five? Three? Two?' Knocks. 'Did he die in Boston? In Philadelphia? In Albany? In Northampton? In Bennington?' Knocks. 'Did he die of consumption? Of fever? Of cholera? Of old age?' Knocks.

"The person in Mr. Tuckerman's mind was the late Rev. Dr. Channing, of Boston, who died in Bennington, Vermont, while on a journey. The degree of correctness in the answers may be judged by the reader. It may be stated, however, that for the last few years of his life Dr. C. disclaimed the use of all sectarian names, preferring to be called only *Christian*, and that, though under seventy, his physical powers had long suffered from premature exhaustion. . . . . . .

"Rev. Dr. Hawks was then urgently requested by several of the party to propose inquiries, to which, after some hesitation, he reluctantly consented. He did not meet with any great success. The sounds uttered were faint. . . . . . .

"After several more ineffectual attempts he resigned the floor to Dr. Francis, who was welcomed with a general roll of knockings from the mysterious agents, seeming to claim the privilege of old and intimate acquaintance. With his proverbial urbanity, seating himself as if at the bedside of a patient, Dr. F. asked in terms of the most insinuating blandness whether the spirits present would converse with any member of the company. Would they vouchsafe to speak to his illustrious friend, the world-renowned author, Mr. Cooper? Would they converse with the great American poet, Mr. Bryant? To these flattering invitations no reply was given. Would they speak to so humble an individual as himself? *Loud knocks.* Dr. F. then asked, fixing on a person, 'Was he an American? Was he an Englishman? Was he a Scotchman?' The knocks were loud and unanimous. 'Was he a merchant? Was he a lawyer? Was he an author?' *Loud knocks.* 'Was he a poet?' *'Yes,' in distinct knocks.* 'Will you tell his name?' Here the spirits called for the alphabet, by sounds intelligible to the 'ghost-seers.' The answers by this method are given in knocks at the letter desired, when the alphabet is repeated by one of the ladies. It then spelled out B-u-r-, when the company indiscreetly, but spontaneously, interrupted, by crying out, 'Robert Burns.' This was the true answer, and after the interview with the favorite Scotch poet Dr. F. declined any further communication.

"Mr. J. Fenimore Cooper was then requested to enter into the supra-mundane sphere, and proceeded to interrogate the spirits with the most imperturbable self-possession and deliberation. After several desultory questions from which no satisfactory answers were obtained, Mr. C. commenced a new series of inquiries. 'Is the person I inquire about a relative?' 'Yes,' was at once indicated by the knocks. 'A near relative?' 'Yes.' 'A man?' No answer. 'A woman?' 'Yes.' 'A daughter? A mother? A wife?' No answer. 'A sister?' 'Yes.' Mr. C. then asked the number of years since her death.

To this the answer was given in rapid and distinct raps, some counting forty-five, others forty-nine, fifty-four, etc. After considerable parleying as to the manner in which the question should be answered, the consent of the invisible interlocutor was given to knock the years so slowly that they might be distinctly counted. This was done. Knock, knock, knock, for over a minute, till the number amounted to fifty, and was unanimously announced by the company. Mr. C. now asked, 'Did she die of consumption?' naming several diseases to which no answer was given. 'Did she die by accident?' 'Yes.' 'Was she killed by lightning? Was she shot? Was she lost at sea? Did she fall from a carriage? Was she thrown from a horse?' 'Yes.' Mr. Cooper did not pursue his inquiries any further, and stated to the company that the answers were correct, the person alluded to by him being a sister who, just fifty years ago the present month, was killed by being thrown from a horse.

"The evening was now far advanced, and it was not thought desirable to continue the colloquies any further. At the suggestion of several gentlemen, the ladies removed from the sofa, where they had sat during the evening, and remained standing in another part of the room, producing a vibration on the pannels which was felt by every one who touched them. Different gentlemen stood on the outside and the inside of the door at the same time, when loud knockings were heard on the side opposite to that where they stood. The ladies were at such a distance from the door in both cases as to lend no countenance to the idea that the sounds were produced by any direct communication with them. They now went into a parlor, under the room in which the party was held, accompanied by several gentlemen, and the sounds were then produced with great distinctness, causing sensible vibrations in the sofa, and apparently coming from a thick hearth-rug before the fire-place, as well as from other quarters of the room. Such are the most important facts which we can recall of the manifestations of the evening. We believe we have stated them without any coloring whatever, as they appeared to every one present; but with regard to their origin or their nature, we are as much in the dark as any of our readers. The manners and bearing of the ladies are such as to create a prepossession in their favor. They have no theories to offer in explanation of the acts of their mysterious attendants, and apparently have no control of their incomings or outgoings."

Many of the persons then present for the first time at a spiritual *seance* have since become firm believers in the truth of the communion between the natural and spiritual worlds, while some have themselves entered into the sphere of those sublime verities which they then began to investigate as a matter of simple curiosity or pastime.

Amongst these, it is gratifying to know that the distinguished author and poet Fenimore Cooper and N. P. Willis partook of the illuminating influence of the bright homes to which they were so soon after summoned, as premonitory whispers which cheered their earthly way and prepared their pilgrim feet for the brighter path they are now treading. In how many thousands of ears have these same low telegraphic raps sounded the triumphant words, "O death, where is thy sting? O grave, where is thy victory?" on the eve of the very hour when some earthly pilgrim was about to take his "leap in the dark?" How many a footprint to the tomb has been illumined into the highway of eternity by the spirit lights which flashed before the eyes of mortals at these same "evenings with the spirits."

Precisely the same results which followed the introduction of Spiritualism in Auburn, grew out of the Misses Fox's visit to New York, namely, the unmitigated bitterness with which the press and pulpit commenced to assail the cause, and the unmistakable progress which it seemed to make under the stimulus of their fierce denunciations. In fact, the opposition became so violent and unreasonable that it provoked investigation, were it only to inquire into the calumnies that were launched against the mediums and their friends, and the absurdly fallacious theories that were set up to account for the phenomena. The result of this feverish excitement was the formation of circles in every other house in town, and the rapid development of media in every other family.

We have before stated that a psychological society of which A. J. Davis's revelations formed the concretive power, was in existence at the time of the Hydesville disturbances, whilst the issue of the *Univercœlum* preceded that event for more than a year. The visit of the Misses Fox in 1850 was most opportune, however.

That which had hitherto been regarded as the *mysterious power of clairvoyance and the revelations of the magnetic sleep*, now assumed a normal place as part of the direct communication which had ever subsisted between "the two worlds," and all the preternatural spontaniety of the magnetic movement was justly regarded as the inspiration of wise spirits; a belief that was perpetually being strengthened by a variety of fresh phases of mediumship, all rife with intelligent proofs of the agency of individuals who had long been deemed lost to earth and its interests in the dim mystery of the grave.

To arrive at any just conception of the excitement to which the public mind was stimulated by the development of open spiritual communion with the so-called "dead," and to appreciate the motives which compelled the wise and candid to enter upon the field of investigation with the generous purpose of protesting against the calumnies and one-sided action of the press towards Spiritualism, it will be necessary to quote some of the journalistic slanders that were thus put forth, and in so doing we shall make a few extracts from a small pamphlet on the early facts of Spiritualism by Messrs. Capron and Barron, in which the authors, amongst other matters of interest, give a statement of the New York *Express* to which we especially desire to call attention.

It would seem that some time antecedent to the Rochester knockings, a certain Professor Loomis had set forth a theory in the *Scientific American*, concerning the vibratory effects of mill-dams, and this the sapient editor of the *Express* tortured into a full explanation of all the mysteries of modern Spiritualism, no doubt thinking that if he could destroy the spiritualistic basis of the rappings, the entire hydra-headed monster, whose existence he innocently attributed to the Fox family, would be destroyed at one fell swoop. His *explanation* reads thus:

> "THE ROCHESTER SPIRITS.—We have referred in our literary notices to various noises heard at Rochester, New York, and attributed to supernatural causes.
>
> "In the New York *Scientific American* we find the following very plausible and very simple explanation:
>
> "'SUPERNATURAL KNOCKINGS.—A 'knocking at the door at nights,' which has alarmed the good people of Rochester who attributed it to spiritual agency, is explained in the *American Journal of Science*, by Prof. Loomis, as the effect of the vibration of a dam over which the water falls. Prof. Loomis describes this vibration as producing sounds like a loud knocking on the doors and walls of buildings, and gives a particular account of the phenomena as observed at the dams of Cayuga Falls, Ohio; East Windsor, Conn.; Springfield and Northampton, Mass., etc. He attributes the vibrations to the friction of the water falling over the dam, and shows how these sounds are transmitted to a distance by the earth and produce that sudden and alarming knocking sound in dwellings. Prof. Loomis has pointed to a very simple and easy method of checking this vibratory action of the dam, and the people of Rochester, who have been troubled by an invisible spirit, will find it easily exercised by mechanical means.'
>
> "'O philosophy and common sense, ye play the devil with theories!' said one of the snarlers in the days of the Encyclopedists."

It will be seen that the New York *Express* makes no allowance for the locomotive character of these sounds, nor provides for their exorcism in its own city, nor in any other place except those afflicted by vibratory noises from the neighborhoood of waterfalls, whilst the agency by which these noises could communicate intelligence is disdainfully untouched altogether.

On the other hand, one Professor Dewey, of Rochester, challenged the "respectable papers in New York, Boston, etc," to discredit the vibratory theory because it was [as he justly declared] inapplicable to the facts of the case; but in its place he substituted the bold and wholly unsustained assertion that the Rochester manifestations were the simple production of fraud, on the part of the Foxes, a statement which if true in their case, never touched similar manifestations which were now beginning to thicken in every part of the country; nevertheless, the New York papers, unable to furnish weapons of their own wherewith to annihilate Spiritualism, eagerly repeated Prof. Dewey's assertions as facts, instead of perceiving that they were simply the ghosts of dead arguments, and as such could never enter into successful warfare with living spirits.

One of the committee who had been appointed to examine the mediums at Rochester, and had actually signed a report in their favor which was read at Corinthian Hall, without any further investigation or assignable reason, save the desire to swim with the tide of popular opinion, coolly published in several papers an uncalled-for denunciation of the Rochester mediums, on the ground of fraud, a charge which his own former report had utterly repudiated.

A number of base and groundless falsehoods were published also by one John W. Hurn, of Rochester, and though they were noted, answered, and triumphantly refuted one by one in the spiritual literature of the day, the papers that circulated the scandal almost invariably refused to give place to the refutation.

A man calling himself Reverend (?) and a Doctor of Divinity, stood on the platform in Corinthian Hall, Rochester, and before a literary association whom he was called upon to instruct, and with less skill than would have been exhibited by an itinerant conjurer at a country fair, cracked his boots to the delight of his literary auditory, and declared *that* to be the explanation of all the disturbances at Hydesville. The learned and Christian gentleman's "complete explanation" was another item which found a wide and ready circulation in the leading journals of the day.

Several other theories of equal value and pertinence were afforded extensive publicity through the same sources. Amongst these, "ankle joints," "toe joints," and "finger snapping;" "machinery," and every description of imposture generally, largely figured; the characters of nearly every person connected with the movement, were recklessly assailed, and scarcely a single opportunity of redress was afforded to the victims of these falsehoods by the press through their columns. One or two more specimens of the blindness which partisan feeling imposed upon the antagonists of this movement are selected from hundreds of similar lucubrations, not for their worth, but rather to show the exhaustive and illogical positions the opposition were compelled to assume.

The New York *Commercial Advertiser* writes:

"THOSE ROCHESTER KNOCKINGS.—We perceive that a gentleman in town* is lecturing on divers matters of inscrutable physiology, and endeavoring to establish some connection between them and the rappings of the *pretended spirits at Rochester*. We are satisfied, so far as the rappings are concerned, the gentleman may spare himself the trouble of discoursing on the subject.

* (Rev. S. B. Brittain.)

"We have had a long and instructive conversation with a gentleman of intelligence from the vicinity of Rochester, and his account makes it clear to our minds that the mystery is not only an imposture, but a very clumsy one; indebted for its success entirely to the credulity of the auditors and spectators who are impressed by it. We say entirely to the credulity, for the clumsiness of the imposture is so great, there is so little art in the means adopted to avert detection, that people have literally to shut their eyes to avoid seeing. The only point upon which there is any successful trick is the manner in which the rapping is effected. It is easy enough to see, if people will not shut their eyes *wilfully*, that the girls effect the rapping *somehow*. For instance, if they are prevented from placing themselves in close proximity to a door, a table, a piano, or some object to rap on, the rapping soon ceases. . . . As for the moving of the table, *anybody can see how that is done.* A slight impulse with the foot gives a movement to a table which runs very readily on rollers, and as the spectators are required to gather close round the table when it is to be moved, nothing can be easier than to give it a start, or an imperceptible push merely with the toe of a boot." etc.

Other statements of a personal character were made in relation to the friends and associates of the mediums in this article, so grossly false that Mr. E. W. Capron wrote to demand, in simple justice, a contradiction of the *misstatements*, in reference to himself at least. This was refused, and the editor who claimed to represent the piety as well as the commercial interests of New York, wilfully committed himself to the circulation of known and proven falsehoods.

Since the day when the New York *Commercial Advertiser* warned the world "only just to open its eyes" and they would discover the whole thing, and discover it to be the trick of girls and the impulses of "boot toes," upwards of five thousand portraits of deceased persons have been executed under circumstances that rendered deception or mistake as impossible as to mistake the light of the mid-day sun for the glaring lamps of the city gas; thousands and thousands of heavy, ponderable bodies have floated in space without human contact; spirit-hands have been formed and melted in the grasp of the examinant; pages, even to the amount of volumes, have been written by *spirit hands alone;* millions of forms have been seen, described and recognized as well-remembered friends, through the mediumship of total strangers; hidden things have been dragged to light; secret crimes revealed; thousands of darkened souls have been convinced of their immortal destiny by facts tested through the severest and most exhaustive scrutiny, and the few hundreds of "credulous, gullible" believers, in the genuine character of the manifestations, whom this editorial sage so bitterly satirizes, have swelled to a mighty army of eleven millions of persons!

And who are they whom he declares have only to open their eyes to detect the imposture? Magistrates on the bench; statesmen in the Senate; lawyers, counsellors, judges, professors of learning and divinity, schoolmen and editors, doctors and divines, writers, thinkers, chemists, and men and women of science, learning, intelligence and high repute; plain farmers, shrewd mechanics, common-sense operatives; the wise and the ignorant, the rich and the poor — every class and every grade of mind but those whom bigotry determines to remain blind, prejudice keeps so, lack of opportunity deprives of the knowledge, or those in whom lack of common-sense prevents its appreciation.

The *Northern Christian Advocate*, the organ of the Methodist Episcopal Church, and as such, no doubt, the source from which the members of that respectable body felt authorized to expect *truthful* instruction concerning spiritual subjects, writes thus:

"For the information of several friends at a distance who have written to us to know about the strange noises which are heard in this city we would say, that we know nothing of the matter.

"Not being overstocked with gullibility and having very little taste for the low marvels which furnish entertainment to some people, we have left the thing to take care of itself.

"The class of persons who deal in those mysteries — we mean juggling, sight-seeing, and sceptical — makes all inquiry into the subject disgusting to a firm believer in revelation."

After this cool assurance that the writer "knew nothing at all about the matter," and was deterred from inquiry about "the thing," from the character of the "*class* of persons" that generally took an interest in such subjects, this faithful "watchman on the walls of Zion" proceeds to make deliberate assertions of the fraud, imposture, and impiety of all the actors in the scene, with as much assurance as if he had actually performed his duty by a thorough and searching investigation of "the thing" he denounced.

But still more audacious warriors were provoked to do battle with the spirits than the flock of illogical scribblers whose only arguments were abuse and slander.

Perceiving that the success of Spiritualism was based upon *facts*, against which mere theories were but as swords brandished to the winds, a tribe of heroes arose who concluded that as the strength of Spiritualism lay in its facts, the force of the opposition must be based upon the same ground. Foremost in the van of these attacks appeared Mr. John Stanley Grimes, a professional mesmerist and exhibitor of the art of electro-biology.

Amidst a mass of other daring affirmations published in the *Tribune*, defamatory of the character and pretensions of all spirit mediums, Mr. Grimes goes on to assert that Mrs. Benedict, of Auburn, *confessed to him*, "that the raps heard in her presence were made by a board under the floor, poised like a lever, and so arranged that when she stood near the window she could rap upon a peg which was connected with one end of the lever and cause the other end to rise and knock against the middle of the floor." For the production of all the other marvels occurring in her presence, Mr. Grimes added "she — Mrs. Benedict — charged a young woman living in the next house, and two male cousins as confederates;" and as a climax to this confession, the trickster is made to declare, "that she had become acquainted with the women who practiced the same deception at Rochester, and had learned the art of them."

As a full exposition of the value of this kind of testimony against Spiritualism, let it be remembered that Mrs. Benedict's mediumship was constantly exhibited in other houses besides her own, where pegs, loose boards, and mechanical contrivances were impossible; also in various other towns besides Auburn, where her only *acknowledged confederates* resided; that she appeared and acted as a medium on numerous occasions with the most acute and analytical investigating circles; that her own house, boards, walls, carpets, and flooring had been repeatedly searched by sceptics, and above all, that up to the time of the pretended confession, Mrs. Benedict and the "Rochester women" had never met, and except by report, could have had no knowledge of each other's existence.

Of the same character and value was the pretended *expose* afterwards elicited in 1851 by the bold attempt of the Rev. Chauncy Burr to present as genuine the statement of a woman who from family differences had become an enemy of the Foxes, after having been at one time on intimate terms with them.

This person — a Mrs. Norman Culver — deposed to having been the mother confessor to Catharine Fox, who informed her that the manifestations were the artful concoction of herself, her sister, and cousin; that the sounds were produced by the snapping of their ankle joints, and that when their feet were held by the committees in Rochester, the working of this wonderful piece of human machinery was supplied by a Dutch servant-girl, who rapped with her knuckles on the floor from the cellar below.

Without attempting to controvert a statement so miserably flimsy in all its bearings that it cannot cover a single phase of "the manifestations," had they all been made, as this explanation would require, by raps on the ground and by the feet of the Fox sisters, it is enough to say that on the night when upwards of three hundred people conversed by these same raps with the invisible knocker at Hydesville, not one of the Fox family was in the dwelling; that at the time when the investigating committee at Rochester held the young ladies' feet, they were not in their own house, but in places selected by the committee, and that if they had been at home, they could scarcely have availed themselves of the presence of the Dutch servant-girl, no such appendage ever having formed a part of their household.

And yet there is scarcely a leading journal of the day which did not retail this bold falsehood, and so few were willing to admit the clear, candid, and well-attested refutation of the family and their friends, that to this day the "confession of Mrs. Norman Culver" is quoted as an argument why Spiritualism, slain at the hands of Rev. Chauncey Burr in 1851, cannot be alive this day, although eleven millions of American Spiritualists arise to testify to the fact of its existence.

Truly it may be said that the hand that once ventures to launch a slander on the ocean of public opinion has signed the death-warrant of truth in that direction, and committed an act irrevocable even in his own person. No matter how frail be the craft in which the falsehood is launched it never returns to its source, but drifts on forever!

He who encounters the poison rarely finds the antidote by its side, and so the tides of eternity bear onward forever the condemnatory verdict which brands the slanderer as the murderer of truth and a traitor to the well-being of humanity.

CHAPTER VII.

SPIRITUALISM IN NEW YORK—CONTINUED.

"O pure reformers, not in vain
  Your trust in human kind,
The good which bloodshed could not gain,
  Your peaceful zeal shall find.
The truths ye urge are borne abroad
  By every wind and tide;
The voice of Nature and of God
  'Speaks out upon your side.'"

J. G. WHITTIER.

HON. HORACE GREELEY AND THE FOX FAMILY—THE NEW YORK CIRCLE AND CONFERENCE—THE PRESS—OUR VIEWS OF SPIRITS AND SPIRITUALISM NOW AND THEN.

AMONGST the many instances of ignorance, bigotry, and misrepresentation, which assailed through the press the first attempts of spirits to communicate with mortals, it is gratifying to notice the candid spirit in which the New York *Tribune* opened its columns to evidence on both sides of the question.

About the time when the Misses Fox took up their temporary residence at Barnum's Hotel, in the city, several letters from investigators were published in its columns, detailing their experiences at the various circles they had attended, and even when the writers withheld their own conclusions on the results of the *séances*, their narrations—presenting as they did an array of evidence of a test character—impressed the public mind, and prompted a wide-spread spirit of investigation.

Some of the leading journals became rabid in their denunciations, others considerably modified their tone, but the rappings went on; circles were formed in every direction, and fresh phases of the phenomena perpetually sprung up to meet and overwhelm the vain theories that professed to explain them away. Little children, sensitive women, grave men, and even learned professors found themselves suddenly possessed of the gifts that had been so ridiculed or questioned. The leading minds of the city thronged the hotel of the Rochester mediums, and distinguished visitors from far and near took part in their *séances* with ever-increasing astonishment and interest. Numerous good test-mediums became developed for "the power," and filled the city with available means for general information and research into this new and occult telegraphy with the "beloved ones gone before."

The following letter from the Hon. Horace Greeley, containing a statement of his views respecting the rappings produced through the Fox family, though written with characteristic caution, becomes highly interesting from the fact that, as editor of the *Tribune*, Mr. Greeley's generous and manly treatment of the matter through its columns had already exposed him to the calumnious sneers which were everywhere directed against those who, without avowed partisanship for the subject, ventured even to treat it with candid impartiality:

"Mrs. Fox and her three daughters left our city yesterday, on their return to Rochester, after a stay here of some weeks; during which they have subjected the mysterious influence by which they seem to be accompanied to every reasonable test and to the keen and critical scrutiny of hundreds who have chosen to visit them, or whom they have been invited to visit. The rooms which they occupied at the hotel have been repeatedly searched and scrutinized; they have been taken without an hour's notice into houses they had never before entered; they have been unconsciously placed on a glass surface, concealed under the carpet in order to interrupt electrical vibrations; they have been disrobed by a committee of ladies, appointed without notice, and insisting that neither of them should leave the room until the investigation had been made, etc., etc.; yet we believe no one to this moment pretends that he has detected either of them in producing or causing the 'rappings,' nor do we think any of their contemnors has invented a plausible theory to account for the production of these sounds, nor the singular intelligence which [certainly at times] has seemed to be manifested through them. Some ten or twelve days since they gave up their rooms at the hotel, and devoted the remainder of their sojourn here to visiting several families, to which they had been invited by persons interested in the subject, and subjecting the singular influence to a closer, calmer examination than could be given to it at an hotel, and before casual companies of strangers, drawn together by vague curiosity more than rational interest, or predetermined and invincible hostility. Our own dwelling was among those they thus visited, not only submitting to, but courting the fullest and keenest inquiry with regard to the alleged 'manifestations' from the spirit-world by which they were attended.

"We devoted what time we could spare from our duties, out of three days, to this subject; and it would be the basest cowardice not to say that we are convinced beyond a doubt of their perfect integrity and good faith in the premises.

"Whatever may be the origin or cause of the 'rappings,' the ladies in whose presence they occur do not make them. We tested this thoroughly, and to our entire satisfaction. Their conduct and bearing is as unlike that of deceivers as possible; and we think no one acquainted with them could believe them at all capable of engaging in so daring, impious, and shameful a juggle as this would be if they caused the sounds. And it is not possible that such a juggle should have been so long perpetrated in public.

"A juggler performs one feat quickly, and hurries on to another; he does not devote week after week to the same thing over and over, deliberately, in full view of hundreds who sit beside or confronting him, in broad daylight, not to enjoy, but to detect his trick. A deceiver naturally avoids conversation on the subject of his knavery, but these ladies converse freely and fully with regard to the origin of these 'rappings' in their dwellings, years ago; the various sensations they caused in the neighborhood; the excitement created; the progress of the developments; what they have seen, heard and experienced, from first to last. If all were false, they could not fail to have involved themselves ere this in a labyrinth of blasting contradictions, as each separately gives accounts of the most astounding developments at this or that time. Persons foolish enough so to commit themselves without reserve or caution could not have deferred a thorough self-exposure for a single week.

"Of course a variety of opinions of so strange a matter would naturally be formed by the various persons who have visited them, and we presume that those who have merely run into their room for an hour or so, and listened, among a huddle of strangers, to a medley of questions—not all admitting of very profitable answers—put to certain invisible intelligences, and answered by 'rappings,' or singular noises on the floor, table, etc., as the alphabet was called over, or otherwise, would naturally go away, perhaps puzzled, probably disgusted, rarely convinced.

"It is hardly possible that a matter, ostensibly so grave, could be presented under circumstances less favorable to conviction. But of those who have enjoyed proper opportunities for a full investigation, we believe that fully three-fourths are convinced, as we are, that these singular sounds and seeming manifestations are not produced by Mrs. Fox and her daughters, nor by any human being connected with them. 'How they are caused, and whence they proceed,' are questions which open a much wider field of inquiry, with which way marks we do not profess to be familiar. He must be well acquainted with the arcana of the universe who shall presume dogmatically to decide that these manifestations are natural or supernatural. The ladies say that they are informed that this is but the beginning of a new era, or economy, in which spirits clothed in the flesh are to be more closely and palpably connected with those who have put on immortality; that the manifestations have already appeared in many other families, and are destined to be diffused and rendered clearer, until all who will may communicate freely with their friends who have shuffled off this mortal coil.

"Of all this we know nothing, and shall guess nothing; but if we were simply to print [which we shall not] the questions we asked and the answers we received, during a two hours' uninterrupted conference with the 'rappers,' we should at once be accused of having done so expressly to sustain the theory which regards these manifestations as the utterances of departed spirits. H. G."

The ball once set rolling in New York City, sped on with an impetus which soon transcended the power of the press, pulpit or public to arrest, despite of every force that was brought to bear against it.

In January, 1851, Judge Edmonds, whose potential influence on the progress of Spiritualism is too widely known to need comment here, commenced a series of investigations which even in their earliest stage formed the nucleus of most important developments, extending far beyond the circle of even his wide-spread influence. Many other distinguished persons, strengthened by the example of the learned Judge, devoted themselves to the investigation of the subject with the almost invariable results of conviction that follow.

One of the most important conversions to Spiritualism that marks this period was that of Mr. Charles Partridge, a merchant of New York, whose probity and public spirit had already secured for him the highest consideration of his fellow-citizens. After the return of the Rochester mediums to their home, Mr. Partridge and wife, being on a tour in Western New York, took occasion to visit the Fox family at Rochester, and there pursued their inquiries into Spiritualism with more leisure and deliberation than the crowded *séances* in New York City afforded.

Mr. Partridge was an entire stranger to the mediums, and a man of keen perception, and acute power of observation. These, together with his usual habits of business-like preparation, he brought to bear upon his researches, and so astonishing were their results, both in respect to physical power and mental intelligence, that the whole structure of his preconceived opinions was overthrown, and an array of testimony presented which completely "rolled back the stone from the door of the sepulchre" for him, and disclosed within it the glorified forms of the white-robed angels of eternal life, instead of the corruptible ashes of death's unfathomable mystery.

To afford the most perfect opportunities for deliberate investigation to himself and his circle of friends, Mr. Partridge procured the services of Kate and Margaretta Fox at his residence in New York City, when the most extraordinary and varied forms of intelligent phenomena became so common and abundant that to resist conviction on the part of those who were privileged to attend these circles became impossible.

Although Mr. Partridge's conclusions were only arrived at through slow processes of rigid and exhaustive scrutiny, their results [when once his powerful mind apprehended the fulness of the stupendous truth of spirit communion] were practical and important.

In the summer of 1851 Mr. Partridge became one of a society entitled the "New York Circle." It was the first organic movement that had yet been established in connection with spirit communion.

The principal medium of the circle was Mr. Edward P. Fowler, then a student, but subsequently a distinguished member of the medical profession. Accompanied by many physical signs of a startling character, Mr. Fowler's mediumship was of the most varied and interesting kind.

The spirits wrote manuscripts in different languages and Oriental characters without the aid of human hands, and his communications, spoken or written in the trance condition, were often of the most exalted and scientific nature.

Fortunate in securing from one of their own number the aid of a telegraphic operator whose position removed him beyond the suspicion of interested motives, the "New York Circle" continued for some years to meet together with delight and profit to themselves, and benefit to the world, which was occasionally favored with reports of their wonderful and instructive manifestations.

Amongst the earliest members of this association were Hon. J. W. Edmonds, Dr. J. B. Gray and lady, Charles Partridge and lady, Dr. and Mrs. Warner, Dr. and Mrs. R. T. Hallock, Robert T. Shannon, W. J. Baner, Dr. Hull, Mr. Edward Fowler, Miss Fowler, Professor Bush, Rev. S. B. Britain, Almon Roff, etc.

Besides these, many persons eminent for their talent or of distinguished public position, were from time to time invited to take part in the *séances*, and mediums of remarkable phenomenal gifts were not unfrequently developed under their influence; in fact it has been asserted that all the regular members of this interesting association were baptized with the Pentecostal fire, and became in their own persons mediums for various forms of spirit communion.

It was at one of these sittings that Mr. Henry Gordon, a medium from Springfield, Massachusetts, first exhibited in New York the astonishing feat of floating in the air. After the first manifestation of this kind, the marvel was frequently repeated in the person of this same medium, and his transit through the air for a distance of sixty feet at the residence of Dr. Gray, in

Lafayette place, occurred in the presence of a large number of unimpeachable witnesses, including the venerable master of the house and Mr. Charles Partridge. But these new and grand fields of observation seemed to their deeply-interested participants to be misused when limited within the circle of private families, especially of the distinguished position occupied by most of Dr. Gray's visitors.

It was resolved that a conference should be established where the experiences of all present could be freely exchanged, and to which strangers from a distance could be admitted without the formalities attending more exclusive gatherings.

Mr. Partridge, whose wealth and standing shielded his motives from the least suspicion of interest, but whose genial, large-hearted, reformatory nature was peculiarly attractive to the community, generously tendered a handsome suite of reception rooms in his own house for the accommodation of the proposed conference.

As the initiatory step towards forming a basis for the future guidance of those attending the conference, a circular was issued of which the following is a copy:

"DEAR SIR,—Understanding that you entertain the following views, I cordially invite you to a social meeting of persons of like sentiments to be held at —— on, etc.

"1st. That the Divine Author of the Universe is a conscious Spiritual Being.

"2d. That he has revealed somewhat of the spiritual world in ages long since passed, and especially that the Jewish people were a medium of such revelation.

"3d. That in our own day and through our own American people, manifestations are being made from the spiritual into the natural world, whereby the immortality and unbroken continuity of the personal existence of all men is being daily demonstrated.

"4th. That an honest, frank, and tolerant interchange of views and conclusions will tend to promote a beneficial use and extension of such spiritual manifestations.

"My purpose in inviting this meeting is furthermore, after due consideration, to ascertain whether anything, and what, can be done by associative action in reference to the advancement of harmonious and profitable intercourse with the world of spirits.

"I am, etc., ——."

This unassuming little circular was not issued even under the authority of the gentleman whose house was the place of gathering, so careful were the real leaders of the spiritual movement to avoid any appearance of dictation or assumption of a power which they justly felt was in the hands of higher and wiser beings than themselves.

Astounded with the revealments which had been made to them, convinced, if the communion between this and higher worlds was a truth, it was one of the most solemn and important kind that humanity had ever been blessed with, and predicated future revelations of almost illimitable use and grandeur to mankind, the early pioneers of Spiritualism felt they had been entrusted with the discovery of mines of wealth which it would be sacrilege for them to reserve to themselves, yet blind and helpless as they were in the hands of a world almost unknown to them either in power or purpose, they were unable to acknowledge aught but the agency of intelligent spiritual beings, and the assurance that they were dealing with them, in a wisdom beyond their own, and a control which was as resistless as the breath of life that animated them.

The first meeting of the New York Conference, took place on the 14th of November, 1851, when several persons besides the members of the New York Circle were present.

The views of the assemblage were kindly solicited, and their personal experiences listened to and discussed, and during their deliberations, the frequent movements of the table and the sounds of rappings, etc., testified that the interest of the scene was shared in by a host of invisible witnesses.

From that time the weekly conferences continued without interruption for more than two years in their original form; that is, in the semi-private character of social gatherings. Being obliged to seek another place of meeting in consequence of the repairs going on in Mr. Partridge's house, the conference assumed a more public though somewhat heterogeneous character. In connection with the Sunday meetings of the Spiritualists, or at halls hired for the purpose, they have now continued with but little intermission for some eighteen years.

It is not, however, from a casual visit to the New York Conference under its present aspect that the faintest idea can be gathered of its utility in promoting the dissemination and discussion of spiritual verities. The free and unconservative character of its present platform renders it liable to intrusion from all classes of mind, and all shades of opinion; hence the meetings are now often inharmonious, controversial, and even *anti-spiritual;* but in its earlier sessions, it faithfully fulfilled the original design of its founders, and formed a rallying point for the believers, a source of instruction and information to the auditory, and a fountain of inspiration for those who, assembling together under the stimulus of high and often sublime thoughts, felt "the tongues of fire descending on their heads" in the unity of these accordant gatherings.

Media were often present at these meetings, and either by rappings or trance speaking, afforded the invisible projectors of the mighty spiritual movement an opportunity of representing their views and offering wise counsel on the various plans of action that were suggested for the wider dissemination of spiritual truths.

In the following chapter we shall present a few extracts from the minutes of the first conferences held in New York prior to the publication of the *Spiritual Telegraph.* A faithful record of these interesting meetings was made and preserved by the Secretary, Dr. R. T. Hallock, to whose courtesy we are indebted for the valuable testimony it affords. It may seem a matter of surprise and even of indignation, that the early facts of modern Spiritualism should have found no wide-spread or truthful field of representation until the publication of organs especially devoted to the subject could be accomplished.

It is almost incredible that in America, where the newspaper is the necessity of the people's life, its columns should have left either unrepresented, or worse still, *misrepresented*, a subject of such vast and universal interest and phenomena so wonderful and well attested as Spiritualism abounds with. Yet the marvel of this treatment ceases when we attempt to compare the nature of the movement with our own preconceived opinions concerning the possibilities of spiritual existence. Were not these of the most vague and undefined character? and have not all our views of disembodied spiritual life been full either of the sepulchral awe which threw over it the veil of mysticism and terror, or else we were taught to treat this most sublime and momentous subject with the fool's arguments—ridicule, unreasoning denial, and senseless satire.

The immortal soul of man has either been imprisoned by dreary superstition in the loathsome charnel house, or banished by ignorance to the nursery and ale house. There has been no midway in man's unphilosophical treatment of the great theme; hence when Spiritualism came, with its common-sense realities, scientific methods of communion, and analytical philosophy, its form was so totally at variance with all preconceived notions of what a spirit should do, or how a "ghost" should act, that the human soul was an unrecognized stranger in the land of its birth and the world of its kindred humanity.

To the superstitious, its dignity was shorn of its shroud and the attendant horrors of the grave. To the pious, a spirit was a bodiless idea, a *gnome*, a *sylph*, an *archangel* or *arch fiend;* anything, rather than the ripe fruit of a purified humanity; and nothing, rather than aught that humanity could conceive of. To the bigot, all spiritual existence but that which was manifested in Judea eighteen centuries ago was "satanic" in its origin and "evil" in personality. To the scoffer, the only idea of any existence that could not be pounded in a mortar or manipulated in a chemist's retort was "humbug," imposture, "old woman's fables, or nursery tales," and thus, as there is but a step from the sublime to the ridiculous, the demoniac theory on the one hand, and the illogical breath of ridicule on the other, was all that the world's representatives in press and pulpit could bring to bear on the subject. In fact they only knew enough to condemn the souls of their ancestors to the keeping of the evil one, or drive them back from their work of angelic ministry by the jibes of cold materialism. Whilst our sense of reverence for the exalted themes of immortality and our gratitude to the beloved immortals is shocked and offended by the denunciations of bigotry, and the painfully irrelevant misconceptions of ignorance, let us with modest humility ask ourselves, with such teachings as the world has received on such subjects, what right we have to look for a more general spirit of enlightenment.

The status of human opinion on the sublime questions of immortal life are precisely what priestcraft and indolent superstition have made it. If the spirits had come in accordance with the cherished fables of antiquity, or the shapes which this same superstition had devised for them, they would doubtless have been received with more welcome and credit than in the simplicity of their risen humanity. But whilst the true believers had great cause to be thankful that the scales had fallen from their eyes, who could censure the multitude for "walking in gross darkness" so long as the people and their teachers were "the blind leading the blind?"

CHAPTER VIII.

SPIRITUALISM IN NEW YORK CITY AND STATE.

"The weapons which your hands have found
Are those which heaven hath wrought—
Light, truth, and love; your battle ground,
The free, broad field of thought."

J. G. WHITTIER.

THE CONFERENCE AND ITS INFLUENCE—SPIRITUALISM IN WATERFORD, N. Y.—THE ECCLESIASTICAL COMMISSION AND WHAT CAME OF IT—NARRATIVES GIVEN AT THE CONFERENCE, NEW YORK—MR. HOOPER'S INVOLUNTARY MEDIUMSHIP—EDWARD FOWLER AND WARREN BOYNTON—EXCOMMUNICATION.

As the meetings of the New York Conference became more fully attended by strangers from a distance, the recital of the phenomenal facts transpiring in various sections of the country increased the interest of the gatherings and tended to disclose the universality of the movement.

During the first session of the conference in 1851 Mr. Smith, of Norwich, related many instances of fine test communications received through various media residing in that city, who presented *the then rare faculty* of imitating the writing of deceased persons, and by pantomimic action graphically representing their peculiarities, and identifying their names by symbolical pictures psychologically impressed upon the media.

The Rev. R. P. Ambler, the editor of the *Spiritual Messenger*, already in successful operation in Springfield, Massachusetts, related many extraordinary facts of spiritual phenomena occurring in that city, where the number of mediums, public and private, was believed already to exceed two hundred.

Drs. Brewer and Beebe testified to the extraordinary interest that was manifested in the city of Brooklyn, New York, on the subject of Spiritualism. At circles held in their own families, many media had been rapidly developed, and within the range of their immediate acquaintance above fifty circles had been formed, at which rapping, writing, spirit-lights, movement of heavy bodies, and various other phases of "the power" were abundantly manifest. Rev. William Fishbough related still more striking and numerous proofs of the progress of the cause in Williamsburgh, New York, where he stated that hundreds of circles were being held nightly, and openly-avowed believers were multiplying on every side. Several other gentlemen gave similar reports from other sections of New York State, especially from Troy, Waterford, Utica, Central and Western New York. Although not in connection with the New York Conference, it belongs to our subject and period to relate the origin of Spiritualism in Waterford, a village about four miles from Troy, where the manifestations had already taken strong hold of a large number of the community.

The reports from this city were so startling, and the effect of conviction was becoming so obvious and wide spread, that a reverend gentleman, one of the officiating pastors of the large manufacturing village of Waterford, waited upon General Bullard, a distinguished lawyer of the place, and begged him, in company with four other of the most prominent men of the district, to institute inquiries into the "obnoxious thing," with a view to crushing its infidelic and satanic tendencies.

Without questioning as to how far the reverend gentleman's duty, as a minister to human souls, might have required his *personal* inquisition into the "dangerous delusion," the good-natured friend to whom he delegated the duty promised compliance with his request, and as himself and two others of the investigating party were famed for their legal acumen, and the whole number were selected for the qualities which especially fitted them for the office of spiritual "detectives," it was confidently believed that if Spiritualism had not already been exploded—a consummation which each succeeding day was expected to produce—its annihilation at the hands of the Waterford investigators was so inevitable that their reverend employer already began to busy himself in preparations for celebrating its funeral obsequies in his ensuing Sabbath-day sermon.

Having learned that "spirit rapping" was to be found in its most startling prominence in the person of a little daughter of Mr. Anson Attwood, of Troy, and that the parents of the child had generously opened their house free of charge to investigators, the party, headed by General Bullard, proceeded to fulfil their mission by calling at the house in question.

They were freely admitted by Mrs. Attwood, who, without requesting even the formality of their names, introduced them to her little girl, who at the time was amusing herself with the toys proper to her age.

This total unconcern, together with the childish appearance and occupation of the young priestess, somewhat disconcerted the grave magisterial party who had come prepared to detect well-laid plans of imposture, or confront the impious craft of satanic agency, but "not to play doll games with children, or learn metaphysics from babes and sucklings."

The little medium was "out of sorts," the mother said, and having been tortured into ill temper and impatience by "incessant attendance on circles," she had to be coaxed by a liberal supply of *candy*, under the stimulus of which she consented to "sit for the gentlemen." At this crisis there was not one of the party but would have gladly retreated from a scene where they felt their dignity as "sensible men and magistrates" ridiculously compromised by the initiatory steps of their mission.

They could well understand—and some of them even reverently accord their belief to—the idea that the Supreme Being, the Ruler of the Universe, had delegated to man the right to sell passports to a Roman Catholic heaven at so much a head, put a tariff on the liberty to commit sins at so much apiece, or that a Deity of infinite goodness and wisdom should commission *two she-bears to come out of a wood and tear forty and two little children because they called Elisha the Prophet, bald head.** All this and volumes more of the same nature, "they could believe and still adore;" but the idea of bribing a child with a piece of candy to telegraph a message from a departed spirit! The very bare thought was so full of impiety and absurdity that, but for the lady-like self-possession of Mrs. Attwood, the doughty champions of truth would have run away and hid themselves for sheer shame. A single quarter of an hour's experience of the marvels outwrought through this most undignified means, however, soon changed their views, rivetted their profoundest interest, and made them forget the agency of the unconcerned little one altogether.

Seated on a high chair, with her tiny feet resting on a footboard, the medium all-unconsciously munched away at her sweetmeats whilst the spirits lifted her about and moved her from place to place with the ease of a feather blown by the winds.

Meantime the heavy table around which the party were gathered rocked and rolled like a ship at sea; the chairs of the gentlemen, with their occupants, were moved bodily, whilst loud raps sounding from various parts of the room spelled out names, dates, and messages, identical with numerous deceased friends of the astounded witnesses. The wonderful and occult science hidden in these mysterious forces, and the preternatural mass of intelligence spelled out in choice and characteristeric phrases, soon stamped the dignity of a stupendous revelation from the hitherto mysterious realms of immortality upon this phase of spiritual telegraphy.

The sitters became the deeply-moved recipients of many an affecting token of a love that death cannot change and a mental fire that the grave cannot quench, and thus they soon forgot the youth and insignificance of the little *telegraphic wire* that the spirits were using.

The lonely and bereaved heart of one was cheered by the precious tokens of identity which proved the undying love of a still living friend. Another, who had long groped in the blindness of cold materialism, beheld the glorious sunlight of immortality proved in the continued life of a cherished parent. Others perceived the key which unlocked the dim mysteries of religion and the problem of miracles wrested from the skeleton hand of death and cast

* *Vide* II. Kings, ii. 24.

into the open lap of humanity. All felt that they stood on the threshold of the once-closed temple of immortal mind—that they were in the sublime presence of "the mighty dead," and, putting the shoes of their materiality from off their feet, they felt that they were treading "on holy ground."

This deeply interesting *séance* was prolonged to an unusual length, and just as it was about to terminate a spirit, identifying himself with a deceased brother of General Bullard's, expressed a desire to communicate. Up to this time the "detectives" had wholly forgotten that the purpose of their visit was to *expose* the manifestations and disprove their spiritual origin rather than to yield up their own convictions in the opposite direction. Struck with a sudden sense of his duty towards his reverend friend, and with something of remorseful feeling for his breach of faith in the premises, the General determined to make one final effort to prove the whole thing a delusion.

His reason was strongly in favor of the communicating spirit's identity with that of his brother, but ere he would allow his judgment to pronounce in favor of his reason, he *mentally* framed this sentence:

"If this be indeed the spirit of my brother, let him move that child in her chair towards me."

General Bullard was sitting at the side of the table opposite to the medium, and as it was a very large one there was room between any of the party for the movement of a chair. His wish was that the child's chair should be moved a little towards the end of the table which was nearest to himself, but before he could conclude the sentence in his own mind which he was endeavoring to frame, the child, chair and all, was lifted, carried, or moved, none present could define how, completely round the table and set lightly down by the side of General Bullard. The whole party were so paralyzed by the sudden action, the little girl herself was so unconscious of any force being exerted to cause this change of *locale*, involving the movement of the chair, without the least disturbance of her attitude, for a space of at least ten feet, that no one could utter even an ejaculation, until General Bullard, to whom alone the movement was peculiarly significant, started up with an irresistible impulse, exclaiming, "By Heaven, it is all true!"

When the investigating party at length returned with their very unexpected report, the reverend gentleman in whose behalf they had undertaken it was so struck with consternation at the result that he concluded to continue the inquiry in his own person, and as the spirits had promised mediumistic gifts to some of the party if they would "sit for development," the worthy minister joined them, and actually became a fine writing medium, and ultimately a confirmed believer in the truths of Spiritualism.

Our space does not allow us to follow up the interesting records of circles which grew out of this first introduction of the subject to Waterford.

Many remarkable mediums were developed soon afterwards, amongst whom was Mr. Warren Boynton, a most excellent writing medium; a lady who subsequently became the wife of General Bullard; Mr. John Proper, a celebrated and reliable test medium, and many others of equally remarkable mediumistic gifts. Miss Fanny Davis, a young lady residing at Lansingburg, about two miles from Waterford, also caught the afflatus and at a somewhat later period became the subject of a protracted trance, during which she lay motionless and unconscious for forty-five days.

On awakening from this remarkable condition of *coma*, Miss Davis became a highly-developed trance speaker, in which character her ministrations have instructed and delighted public audiences of many thousands of persons from that period to the present day.

At Ballston Spa, Saratoga, Glenn's Falls, and especially in the capital city of New York — Albany — new and wonderful phases of spirit-power began to arise about this time.

The rumor of the "opening of the gates" reached these places, and induced the members of various families to "sit round the table to see what would come of it."

When the New York Conference were first holding their sessions in 1851, and earnestly discussing the means of extending the knowledge and cultivating the gifts of spiritual communion, thousands of circles were being held in different sections of the State.

Few if any experiments of this kind continued beyond the third sitting without unfolding mediumistic powers in one or more of the parties present, and the reports which were weekly rendered at that conference tended to show that there was at least one public medium for every town, city, and hamlet in the Empire State of America, besides thousands of individuals in families whose names were denied to the public, though their gifts as spirit mediums were the subject of popular comment and notoriety.

At a meeting of the conference early in the year 1852, Dr. Greaves, of Milwaukee, a gentleman eminent for his truthful character and success as a physician, related a new development of "the power," as it occurred under his own observation in the city of Milwaukee, Wisconsin. As a scientific man, ever prosecuting his researches into nature's laws with the humility of a scholar, Dr. Greaves had investigated animal magnetism, and realized with considerable interest its singular results in clairvoyance and the cure of diseases.

In the year 1850, and before he had more than heard a faint rumor of the "Rochester knockings," a clairvoyant of remarkable lucidity informed him in the magnetic sleep that the spiritual manifestations now so rife in the East would appear in that city in a few days, mentioning two individuals [patients of the Doctor's], who would become mediums.

To the mother of one of these young ladies the Doctor soon after communicated the singular prophecy, when the lady expressed herself greatly pleased with the intelligence, as being likely to account for certain strange noises which they had heard for several nights past, and which had caused them equal alarm and annoyance. At that time the family had never even heard of the "Rochester knockings;" but, acting under the advice of their trusted physician, they formed a circle, obtained loud rappings and intelligent responses, and within a few weeks afterwards, the father of the young lady informed Doctor Greaves with great emotion that "they had received, through Mary, communications from all their friends that had died, and that strangers visiting them could obtain equally satisfactory responses."

In this, as in one or two other cases he detailed, Dr. Greaves could trace his own agency, and occasionally the influence of his magnetic operations, in evolving medium power in this city, but he added that it no sooner became known that he was interested in the subject than he was invited to attend circles in every part of Milwaukee, and witness the mediumistic gifts of at least thirty or forty families, who had but just caught the faint echo of the glad tidings of the communion, as it made its way thus far West, inducing them, as in New York, "to sit round the table" for mere curiosity, and arise from it startled by the conviction that the humble domestic board had become the family altar, at which the beloved immortals had been the ministering spirits.

At one house the most astonishing feats of strength were performed through the mediumship of a fragile young girl. A sofa on which four full-grown persons were seated was rocked to and fro as violently as the strength of the sofa would permit. Odic lights of a deep red color floated around a darkened room, forming, melting, and being subjected to the closest scrutiny, affording to the narrator [a scientific chemist] the most conclusive assurance that they were not of mundane origin or composition.

On several occasions a very heavy dining-table was held suspended in the air with several persons seated on it whose feet did not even touch the floor.

Mr. Train, of Kenosha, Wisconsin, detailed at the same conference many equally astonishing evidences of phenomenal Spiritualism, which had arisen in his section of the State. Mr. Train seemed disposed to attribute the origin of the manifestations in part to the influence of magnetism. His own investigations, he stated, had conducted him from the study of Swedenborg to the writings of A. J. Davis, and from thence to the practice of animal magnetism, in the course of which his subjects not only became clairvoyant, but were often attended by loud rappings and strange movements of the furniture. Up to the time when the reports of spirit circles at the East reached them, they attributed these unusual sights and sounds to magnetism, or a peculiar action of electricity evolved by the condition of magnetized subjects. After reading the experiences of others, they resolved to test by alphabetical signs the possibility of communing with spirits through these means; and in their success, numbers were induced to form circles, and thus, he added, during the last year [1851] Spiritualism had extended over the State, and into adjoining sections of country, with inconceivable rapidity and power.

Mr. Nimthorne, of Bridgeport, Connecticut, related instances of the rapid development of medium powers in quite one half of any given number who would consent to sit in circles. He mentioned a striking case of phenomenal power that had been exhibited at a recent circle in Bridgeport, in which a spirit who had died by a railway accident produced the sounds of the whistle and locomotive, and besides imitating the sound of escaping steam, succeeded in imparting to more than a dozen people assembled the sense of strong currents of air rushing through the room.

Early in February, 1852, Mr. Partridge, having returned from a visit to Massachusetts, gave a most encouraging account of the progress of the cause in that State.

About the beginning of the year 1850, a gentleman of Fitchburg, Massachusetts, Mr. Edward Hooper, whilst sitting writing at his desk, found his hand moved by a strange and irresistible influence to inscribe, without any volition of his own, these words on the page—*Your father is dead.* Mr. Hooper's father at that time resided in England, and at the last account received from him was in the enjoyment of perfect health; hence, the writing, strange as it seemed to be, originating from no impression on his mind, caused little anxiety until it was repeated under precisely similar circumstances a few hours later, and was confirmed in five days by the receipt of a letter from England, announcing his father's death.

The singularity of this involuntary and prophetic act of mediumship stimulated Mr. Hooper and several of his friends to hold circles, from which had arisen a great variety of phenomenal facts, strong medium powers, and a remarkable degree of interest in the subject.

Mr. Partridge, at the request of a large body of Spiritualists in Templeton, Massachusetts, gave a lecture on the subject, which was listened to by an immense auditory with the most profound interest.

Many other places in Massachusetts and the rest of the New England States, were represented in the conference to be progressing with astonishing celerity in the knowledge of spiritual communion, and the unfoldment of new and powerful phases of mediumship.

Tidings of this nature, however, were still more remarkable from the West, and even from California and the Pacific Islands. Visitors brought the assurance that circles for spirit communion were being held simultaneously with the meetings that were discussing the best means of reaching them in New York. Besides constituting a focal point, where all the radiating lines of wide-spread interest could converge and be gathered up for future edification, several important modes of action were devised and executed by the good pioneers engaged in these New York Conferences. A circular was issued and sent to various parts of the country, calling for facts and requesting the narration of experiences in different States. The result of this wise measure was the accumulation of a vast amount of information, forming an almost inexhaustible treasury for research in future time.

A committee was drafted also to attend to the formation of circles in various parts of the city, which, being numbered and communicating with the Conference or New York Circle as head centre, for a long time supplied a very satisfactory chain of telegraphic offices, whose records were full of interesting phenomena.

The rapid progress of Spiritualism, and the privacy and reticence which has marked its reception in hundreds of families since the time of which we write, has completely outgrown the fostering care of a parent circle, the influence of which was only temporarily felt in the infancy of the movement.

Another highly important step was taken when the conference came to the conclusion to represent their views in the most public and forcible manner possible through the rostrum.

For this purpose the services of the Rev. S. B. Britain were secured, and a series of addresses commenced, the first of which was given at Hope Chapel, Broadway, on the evening of February 26th, 1852. From this time, with few interruptions, Spiritualism, its claims, facts, theories, and all its general features of interest, have been ably represented on New York platforms on an average once in every week, until regular Sunday services, morning and evening, and an afternoon conference, has placed it prominently before the New York public as a great religious no less than a reformatory and scientific movement. The most momentous result which the deliberations of the conference achieved, however, was the publication of a weekly journal, entitled the *Spiritual Telegraph*, which for a period of several years formed one of the most complete and well-conducted records of the spiritual movement of which its literature can boast.

It was started in the first place by the enterprise of Mr. Charles Partridge and Rev. S. B. Britain, who, with certain financial guarantees from many of the leading Spiritualists of the city, commenced their admirable and valuable serial on May 8th, 1852.

The publication of this paper was an era in the history of New York Spiritualism from whence a stupendous impetus was derived. As its character and influence will be particularized in treating of the literature of Spiritualism, we need enter no further at present into the details of this important undertaking. Several pamphlets of timely use and value in the early stages of the cause were published by aid of liberal subscriptions from the members of the conference. Amongst these was an excellent essay on circles by Mr. Hunt, and some remarkable communications from the spirit-world through the mediumship of Mr. Edward Fowler. Large issues of this pamphlet were made for gratuitous circulation.

The conference also made large contributions towards the publication of many printed communications, which, at that particular stage of knowledge, or rather ignorance, on the subject of spirit-life and communion, became of great importance. Amongst these, we find printed for gratuitous circulation a number of communications purporting to come from spirits whose exalted names on earth were freely used as authority for the instructions conveyed. They were given through the mediumship of Mr. Warren Boynton, of Waterford, New York, of whom Mr. King, a gentleman of good standing from the same place, gives the following sketch:

"He [Mr. Boynton], having sat in circles for spirit influence, found his hand automatically controlled to write whole pages of matter, the sentiment of which was often at total variance with his own opinions on religious subjects. Mr. Boynton was a devoted adherent to the tenets of the Wesleyan Methodists, and yet for many months he found himself impelled, under an influence he could not resist, to write sentiments whose broad liberality he knew to be inimical to the dogmas of his own creed, and, what was to him a still more perplexing act, to sign to many of the heretical papers he so bitterly condemned the honored name of the founder of Methodism, 'John Wesley' himself. Amongst these infidelic protests against his convictions was an essay, [which formed a part of the printed pamphlet above alluded to], commencing thus: 'Salvation is progression. Christ is a principle. Reason is a divine attribute of the soul. Nature is a book unfolding the wisdom and goodness of the Deity,' etc. Before the publication of this pamphlet, however, Mr. Boynton's convictions had become harmonized with those of his spiritual teachers, and to some extent in a feeling of disgust and revulsion produced by the action of his *Christian* instructors, who no sooner heard that he had become 'a spirit medium' than they forthwith excommunicated him from their fellowship."

It is proper here to remark that ecclesiastical thunder of this description was now becoming a very frequent resort for the purpose of quenching the spiritual lightning that preceded it; but, as in the case of Mr. Boynton, it generally had the effect of stimulating the excommunicated to seek consolation in a more *Christ-like*, if not a Christian community, whilst its effect upon the world in general was precisely that which abuse or injustice ever produces on the brave and true—namely, to arouse a spirit of indignant resistance which ended in making a hundred Spiritualists for every excommunicated Christian.

CHAPTER IX.

SPIRITUALISM IN NEW YORK CITY AND STATE—CONTINUED.

"The wind bloweth where it will, and thou hearest its voice, but knowest not whence it cometh or whither it goeth. So is every one that is born of the Spirit."

"Verily, verily, I say unto thee, we speak what we know and testify what we have seen, and ye receive not our testimony."

SPIRIT AUTOGRAPHS—SPIRITUAL LITERATURE—JUDGE EDMONDS—THE EARLY INVESTIGATORS AND THEIR TREATMENT—REACTION—MARGARETTA FOX AND HER ASSAILANTS—GOVERNOR TALLMADGE AND HIS NOBLE TESTIMONY—Y. C. CALHOUN AS A SPIRIT.

AMONGST the most remarkable manifestations which were preserved in the archives of the New York Conference, none are more interesting than those which relate to the mediumship of Mr. Edward Fowler, the medical student to whom allusion has already been made.

Besides the faculty of seeing and conversing intelligently with spirits, Mr. Fowler's mind, being of a scientific cast, was frequently instructed through vivid pictorial imagery or direct communications with the methods adopted by spirits to effect their communion with mortals by means of raps, movements of bodies, entrancement, etc. Languages of the most unfamiliar nature, hyeroglyphical figures, and Oriental writings, were constantly found in his chamber inscribed on scraps of paper, vases, and other objects, under circumstances that rendered the action of human agency impossible.

Many excellent and philosophical descriptions of spirit-life and teaching were written or spoken by him in the trance condition, some of which will be found under the head of "spiritual communications," but the one which excited the most interest at the time was a sentence of which a facsimile and brief account will be found in the subjoined extract from the *Spiritual Telegraph* of 1852.

It is proper to add that a number of the signatures were facsimiles of the hand-writing of *private individuals* of whose existence as spirits or mortals Mr. Fowler could have had no knowledge; also that their relations—some of whom were members of the New York Circle—testified to the correctness of the signatures, and the perfect resemblance which each signature bore to that of the writers whilst on earth.

The "sentiment" contained in the document was often referred to by Spiritualists during the late great American conflict, and its prophetic character as regards the issue of the war must not be overlooked:

SPIRITUAL TELEGRAPH—1852.—NEW YORK.

"AUTOGRAPHS OF THE SPIRITS.—Many of our readers are perhaps aware that among the Spiritual manifestations in this city have been a number of *mystical manuscripts*, mostly in foreign and ancient languages, and other documents to which the names of numerous individuals who have left the earth have been signed.

"These we have had engraved at great expense, and for the satisfaction of our readers we shall publish them in the *Telegraph*. We submit the following brief history of its origin:

"'At a regular meeting of a circle convened for spiritual intercourse at the residence of Charles Partridge, in New York, December 11th, 1851, the subject of Kossuth's mission to this country having been incidentally referred to, the spirits addressed the medium, E. P. Fowler, as follows: 'Edward, put a paper on your table and we will write a sentiment and subscribe our names, then you may all sign it too.'

"'In accordance with the above directions Edward placed a paper on his table in his sleeping-room, which was duly written upon in the course of the night and signed by forty-three spirits. It was subsequently signed by the members of the circle, but owing to the omission of the history and the irregular mode of affixing the signatures of the members, the spirits made the following communication at the succeeding regular meeting: 'Burn that, and we will write upon another.'

"'Accordingly, the first paper was destroyed, and a parchment was procured and placed on Edward's table on his retiring for the night. On the morning of the 23d of December, when the medium arose, he found the sentiment, '*Peace, but not without freedom*,' and the signatures, as here published, inscribed on the parchment.

"'At the meeting of the circle held on the 25th of December Dr. Hull asked the spirits whether each spirit executed his or her own name as they occurred on the parchment, when the spirits answered emphatically, '*Yes!*'

"'We, the undersigned, believing that these are the signatures of the spirits themselves, and fully concurring in the sentiment expressed, hereunto affix our names this 25th day of December, one thousand eight hundred and fifty-one:

"'JOHN GRAY,
JOHN F. GRAY, M.D.,
S. T. FOWLER,
F. F. CAREY,
MRS. CHARLOTTE F. WELLS,
ROBERT T. SHANNON,
DANIEL MINTHORN,
CHARLES PARTRIDGE,
EDWARD P. FOWLER,
WILLIAM J. BANER,
MISS ALMIRA L. FOWLER,
MRS. S. A. PARTRIDGE,
ALMON ROFF,
WARD CHENEY,
DR. R. T. HALLOCK,
MRS. MARTHA H. F. BANER.'"

About the year 1851 New York Spiritualism received a great impulse from the fact that Mrs. Fish, the eldest of the Fox sisters, took up her residence in the city, and opened rooms for public *séances* which were constantly thronged by eager and intelligent investigators. At this time also the *Shekinah*, a fine literary monthly journal, devoted to the interests of Spiritualism, entered upon its second year of successful propagandism.

Its talented editor, S. B. Britain, joined Mr. Charles Partridge in the production of the *Spiritual Telegraph*, the first issue of which appeared in May, 1852. The *Spiritual Messenger*, edited by R. P. Ambler and Apollos Munn, of Springfield, Massachusetts, was already enjoying a wide circulation, and New England Spiritualism was further represented in Boston by the commencement of an excellent paper, conducted by the Rev. S. Crosby Hewitt, called the *New Era*.

Even the far West was represented in this constellated mass of spiritual journalism, as a large and ably-conducted paper was started in St. Louis, Missouri, called *Light from the Spirit World*, which detailed the spread of "the cause" from the banks of the Hudson in the East, to the shores of the Mississippi in the Southwest.

Besides the periodicals already named, there was a great mass of ephemeral literature constantly issuing from the press, containing narratives of new and wonderful phenomena; reports of lectures, circles, discussions, and also of conventions, the first of which, held at Cleveland, Ohio, was speedily followed by others in Boston, Worcester, and other parts of the country.

Amongst the more important publications of this period were the works of A. J. Davis, which, besides "Nature's Divine Revelations" and three volumes of the "Great Harmonia," comprised a considerable number of tracts and widely-circulated pamphlets. A list of the spiritual publications in the *New Era* of November, 1852, announced as of recent date and American authorship, a volume of communications called "Light from the Spirit-World," received through the mediumship of Rev. C. Hammond, of Rochester; "The Spiritual Pilgrimage of Thomas Paine," from the same source; "Elements of Spiritual Philosophy," a finely-written and scholarly production by the Rev. R. P. Ambler, of Springfield, Massachusetts; "Voices from the Spirit-World," by Isaac Post, medium, of Rochester; "The Clairvoyant Family Physician," by Mrs. Tuttle; several pamphlets published at Cincinnati, Rochester, and Auburn, giving a history of the manifestations up to that time; "Modern Miracles," and other works, by S. B. Britain; "The Spiritual Experiences of Mrs. Lorin L. Platt, medium;" "Spirit Manifestations," by the Rev. Adin Ballou; "The Microcosm and Macrocosm of the Universe," by the Rev. William Fishbough; "Messages from the Superior State," by the Rev. John M. Spear; "The Spiritual Teacher," by the Rev. R. P. Ambler; "Supernal Theology," and "The Spiritual Instructor," etc. All these works were produced during the first three years of the modern manifestations; and that the shadowy side of the picture should not be wholly left to the uncandid coloring of the opposition, a publication, was issued, called *The Mountain Cove Journal*, fuller notice of which will be given hereafter; but as a specimen of human audacity, impiety, and egotism, this paper, though professedly indited by orders of "apostolic, angelic, and arch-angelic spirits," was only prevented from destroying Spiritualism by the transient nature of its existence and its very limited circulation.

From the year 1851, spiritual manifestations engaged the attention of Judge Edmonds, one of the ablest and most prominent legal men that has adorned the New York bar since America could boast of an historical record. Miss Laura Edmonds, a daughter of the Judge, also pursued her researches in the same direction, and became developed as an excellent medium for trance speaking, the discerning of spirits, the gift of tongues, including several dead and living languages utterly unknown to herself, the ability to travel clairvoyantly to distant places, and communicate with absent friends by the mental telegraph. All these gifts Miss Edmonds nobly devoted, without money or price, without distinction of rank or fortune, to the service of the world; and as her *séances* were held in her father's private residence, amidst those surroundings of wealth and refinement which rendered the suspicion of complicity or fraud impossible, her influence upon the minds of her vast throng of visitors can never be fully appreciated, until her own transfigured spirit shall stand face to face with the glorious host of enfranchised souls who have wrought out their mission of revelation through the ministrations of this estimable lady.

It cannot be supposed that a man of Judge Edmonds's distinguished position, could be long permitted to throw his powerful advocacy into the scale of an unpopular cause, without becoming a target for all the shafts of ridicule and mendacity which were being levelled against Spiritualism and its friends.

Keenly must those shafts have rankled, aimed as they were at the man whom public opinion had before lauded to the skies, and promoted to the highest places of trust and honor; but though the Judge must have suffered with all the acuteness of those finely-strung sensibilities which are at once the bane and blessing of rare genius, no expression of contempt or anger testified to his disdain of his mean and inconsistent assailants, until some two years of settled conviction had given him that impregnable anchor of truth to lean upon, from which he could afford to bear witness against human injustice and falsehood without fear lest his superstructure of metaphysical philosophy, based upon physical facts, should be injured by the fierce storms of public discussion in which he soon found himself compelled to take an active share.

The legal acumen which had heretofore commanded the highest meed of public admiration, and the same amount of carefully-sifted evidence which he had been wont to gather up in the public service, he now hurled in thunderbolts of proof for the despised truths of Spiritualism.

In company with other gentlemen who became distinguished as advocates of Spiritualism, Judge Edmonds was actually pointed at in the streets "as a crazy Spiritualist." As believers in Spiritualism, himself and various members of the bar and medical profession were treated with contumely, and shouldered out of practice, office, and the good opinion of their fellow-men.

Wealthy merchants like Mr. Charles Partridge were compelled to assert their claims to be considered sane, and maintain their commercial rights, by the most firm and determined action. Professional men and tradesmen were often reduced to the very verge of ruin by the evil reputation that clung around the dreaded name of "Spiritualist," and a relentless persecution, originated by the press, maintained by the pulpit, and stimulated to frenzy by the rank and number of the powerful adherents that began to swell its ranks, directed the full flow of its evil tides against "the cause" and its representatives. Many of the houses where circles were being held were disturbed by crowds, who would gather together after night-fall, and with yells, cries, whistles, and occasionally with the breaking of windows by stones and other missiles, endeavor to molest the quiet investigators in their "*unholy work of waking the dead*," as one of the Brooklyn papers piously denominated the act of seeking for the "Ministry of Angels."

The principal leaders of the movement, no less than the mediums themselves, were seriously obnoxious to this kind of rowdyism.

The mediums, especially the ladies, were turned out of their offices and boarding-houses. Hotel-keepers often declined to receive them, and in the streets they were constantly subject to the most insulting and sometimes even threatening language. Their public meetings were disturbed, the characters of every person connected with the movement indiscriminately assailed; the appearance of a Spiritualist in any public trial was the signal for immediate decision against their side of the question, and their mere opinions in favor of the cause subjected them to inquisitorial persecutions, and the excommunicating ban of the church to which they belonged.

Those who have not endured the ordeal of this strange paroxysm of civilized barbarism could never imagine the pitch of injustice to which it was carried, nor the sufferings of the victims.

It is a remarkable and significant token of "the retributive and compensative power behind the throne," that nearly all who suffered in the first years of spiritual persecution, loss of fortune, practise, custom, or reputation, have experienced a reaction in their favor, which seems to proceed from an involuntary appreciation, on the part of the public, of the superior intelligence which some of the Spiritualists display.

Thus, after Judge Edmonds, General Bullard, and other distinguished legal practitioners had been robbed of the well-earned laurels of an honored career at the bar, because, as Spiritualists, "*they must be insane;*" whilst merchants who had long been esteemed as first on change and in the market were compelled to threaten legal prosecution, in order to obtain the erasure of the word "*Spiritualist,*" *labelled publicly against their names;* after teachers had been ignominiously thrust out of their places, operatives dismissed, and tradesmen almost reduced to ruin, a period of reaction came, when spirtualistic lawyers were found to be "possessed of sources of knowledge" which rendered their services invaluable; the most skilful doctors were found to be "those wonderful magnetic physicians," and the word "Spiritualism" began to be interpreted as a challenge to the world to expect superior excellence in art and science, wisdom in judgment, or success in commerce.

But this happy revulsion of feeling was still but partial, and only became manifest at a late period of the movement.

Its first initiatory steps necessarily demanded and obtained its martyrs, like every other great reform, which has had to march to its success over the conquered legions of ignorance, prejudice, and superstition. Even the sufferings endured by the Rochester mediums were not ended with the public inquisition at Corinthian Hall.

Absurd and far-fetched theories were still put forth by so-called scientific men in their useless attempts to kill the hydra-headed monster through the original promoters of its notoriety, and their failure in so doing seemed to incite the opponents to a bitterness which found vent in forms of persecution not always stopping short of peril to life itself, as will be shown in the following case, one out of many similar annoyances that tracked the footsteps of the unfortunate mediums.

When Miss Margaretta Fox visited the city of Troy, New York, in 1850, an evidently organized attempt was made on her life by a party whose agents consisted chiefly of a set of rough men, said to be Irish Catholics.

After dogging her footsteps, trying under various pretexts to get admission to the house where she was holding circles, and seriously endangering the peace and safety of the family she was visiting by hurling stones and other missiles against the windows, they proceeded to fire several shots at the house, which were no doubt aimed at Miss Fox.

The circumstances of the case are best detailed in a letter written to a friend of the cause by Mr. Bouton, the gentleman at whose house Miss Fox was staying. A portion of that letter we subjoin, as follows:

"WEST TROY, *November* 13, 1850.

. . . . "We are endeavoring to make an arrangement for her [Margaretta] to go to another place. If she has mentioned the name to you, do not mention it to others, as you value her life. A deep plot is laid to destroy her. My house is beset every night by assassins after her, and we guard her every moment.

"We think, if we can place her where we wish to, she will be safe. I shall defend her and her reputation at the risk of my fortune and my life. I will advise you of our progress. Suppress the name of the place if you can. I write with difficulty, not having rested for some nights. Five Irishmen, from some motive, are watching Margaretta. We have seen them all together.

"She has never left my family without being attended, which has given them no opportunity yet.

"In returning from Troy, late the night before last, with my family and Margaretta, in a coach, we came to the river and found no boat. Five Irishmen tried to persuade our driver to go to the long 'Troy bridge,' a glorious place for murder. We did not go, but they followed us home, and, after we had retired, they attempted to break into the room occupied by Margaretta and my sister-in-law.

"They were furious on being foiled, and threw stones against the house. I have prepared means of defence, and cannot sleep much, and my family less. I fear they will return again to-night, but they will meet with a warm reception.

"Last night Mrs. B. and Margaretta went to the door of a shed together, and a stone was thrown at them. One man on the roof made an angry exclamation on finding that the two were together, instead of Margaretta alone. They were large, stout men." . . . . . .

A postscript to this letter, dated the next day, the 14th, says:

"As I feared, the Irishmen did return last night, and threw a stone through the window, and broke into the house; but we were prepared for them, and they did not effect anything. We would like to have you come here immediately, if you can."

The small party of "Irishmen" continued to increase until at last Mr. Bouton's house was surrounded by a mob, and when Mrs. Fish, the elder sister, arrived on an imperative telegraphic summons from Rochester, she had to be escorted to her hotel by a party of brave and well-tried friends, in disguise.

The ladies were finally conducted in safety and secrecy to Albany, where a better and more genial reception awaited them, and then it was found that Catholics and Irish did not make up the bulk of the rude and jibing mobs that surrounded Mr. Bouton's house, fired the shots, and threw stones at the windows, uttering meanwhile threats and imprecations against the "unholy witch woman within."

Yet these very demonstrations it was that ultimately caused a strong and irresistible spirit of investigation in Troy, and ended in confirming the belief in that place to an extent which time and the mutations of public opinion elsewhere have never shaken. Troy, in fact, is now one of the spiritual fortresses of New York State.

Similar results, but of far more striking and important character, grew out of the malevolent attacks that were levelled against Judge Edmonds.

Some of these being circulated in the *National Intelligencer*, of Washington, attracted the attention of the members of the Legislature, many of whom were warm friends and admirers of the Judge, and caused an eager interest in Spiritualism to arise in the very heart and focus of national influence. Many excellent mediums were developed in the progress of the investigations that followed, and the visit of the Fox family completed the triumph of the cause in Washington.

Amongst those who protested most justly and indignantly against the vituperative spirit in which the remarks of the Washington *National Intelligencer* denounced Judge Edmonds and his belief, was the Hon. N. P. Tallmadge, a distinguished Senator, ex-Governor of Wisconsin, and a warm personal friend and colleague of the Judge.

In a letter equally fearless and judicially acute, Governor Tallmadge wrote to the *National Intelligencer*, indignantly repudiating his denunciations of the Spiritualists, of whom he proclaims himself to be one. He adds:

"And, let me assure you, there are throughout this widely-extended country, some of the brightest and most exalted intellects, who have, from a thorough investigation of the matter, come to the same conclusion."

In writing of Judge Edmonds he says:

"I had heard for a long time of the 'Rochester knockings,' but had paid no heed to them; on the contrary, had considered them a delusion which would soon pass away. I continued under these impressions till some time last spring [1852], when my attention was called to a newspaper attack on Judge Edmonds for being a believer in these spiritual manifestations. I had known Judge Edmonds for thirty years, had practiced law in the same courts, had served in the Senate of New York, and been associated with him as a member of the Court for the Correction of Errors, the highest court in the State; had known him since that time as a Justice of the Supreme Court, and more recently as a Judge of the Court of Appeals, where he holds a deservedly high and distinguished rank amongst the able judges of that court, the last resort in the State of New York. I also knew him as a gentleman of finished classical education, and as a lawyer of acute mind and decided talent for investigation; and, above all, I knew him to be a man of unimpeachable integrity. Knowing all these things, I concluded that if he had become a believer in 'spiritual manifestations,' it was at least a subject worthy of investigation."

In connection with this letter Governor Tallmadge published several others, addressed to some of the most distinguished persons in the country, who were numbered amongst his intimate friends. As all of these were replete with incidents of the most astounding character, their perusal excited the utmost interest and astonishment, especially when the unquestionable nature of the authority is considered from whence they emanated. Our space will only allow us to reproduce one or two of these narrations, for which purpose we select, in the first instance, a published letter of Governor Tallmadge's addressed to Mrs. Helen N. Whitman, the celebrated poetess of Rhode Island.

This letter has already been published in substance, but the author prefers to quote from the manuscripts supplied by the honored writer himself, as, though occasionally varying in language, it is possible that the memoranda, made immediately after the manifestations were produced, may contain a truer transcript of the writer's feelings at the time of their reception than the entire letter as it was subsequently prepared for publication.

"BALTIMORE, *April* 12, 1853.

"*Hon. N. P. Tallmadge to Mrs. Helen N. Whitman:*

"DEAR MADAM, — I seize a few moments whilst detained here to give you a more extended account of the physical manifestations alluded to in a former letter.

"In this account I shall confine myself to those which purport to come from the spirit of John C. Calhoun. I have received numerous communications from him from the time of my commencing this investigation. They have been received through rapping, writing, and speaking mediums, and are of the most extraordinary character. . . . . . After the arrival of the Misses Fox in Washington, in February last, I called on them by appointment, and at once received a communication purporting to come from Calhoun. I then propounded mentally the following question:

"'Can you do anything to confirm me in the truth of these revelations, and remove from my mind all shadow of unbelief?'

"To which I received the following answer:

"'I will give you a communication on Monday, at seven and a half o'clock. Do not fail to be here. I will then give you an explanation. JOHN C. CALHOUN.'

"I must here remark that *all* the communications referred to in this letter were made through the alphabet; every letter being rapped out, letter by letter, and taken down by me as received, until they spelled out words and sentences.

"I called on Monday, as appointed, and received the following communication:

"'My friend, the question is often put to you, 'What good can result from these manifestations?' I will answer. 'It is to draw mankind together in harmony, and convince sceptics of the immortality of the soul.'

"I will here interrupt my narrative to remark that when in Bridgeport, in 1850, I received a communication through other mediums from a spirit purporting to be W. E. Channing, which strongly reminds me of the above sentence.

"In answer to the question, 'What do spirits propose to accomplish by these manifestations,' it was spelled out, 'To unite mankind, and convince sceptics of the immortality of the soul.'

"During the above communication, at Washington, the table was moved first one way and then the other, and when we all moved back, so that no one was touching it or within two feet of it, it moved — wholly without contact — some three or four feet, and then returned to its original position. This was repeated on the other side, and then one side of it was raised for a few moments and was again rested on the floor. Desirous to test its weight, it being a heavy dining table capable of seating some dozen persons, I placed my hands under the leaf and endeavored to raise it, but without succeeding in stirring it an inch. I then stood up and exerted all the force I was master of in vain. I requested the three ladies to take hold and try all together to lift it. We lifted upon it until the top began to crack, but without raising it a particle. Perceiving that a spiritual force was being exerted to keep it down, I said: 'Will the spirits permit me to raise the table?'

"I then took hold of it alone and raised it without the least effort. After this the following dialogue ensued:

"*Q.* Can you raise the table entirely from the floor with me on it? *A.* Yes; get me the square table. The square table required was of cherry, with four legs — a large-sized tea-table.

"Being brought out and the leaves raised I took my seat in the centre, the three ladies sitting at the sides with their hands and arms resting on it and thus adding to the two hundred pounds weight already on it. Two legs were first raised from the floor, then the other two to a level with the first, until the whole table was held suspended in the air about six inches from the floor. While thus seated on it, I could feel a gentle vibrating movement as if floating in the air. After being thus suspended for a few moments the table was gently set down again to the floor.

"At a subsequent meeting, the spirit claiming to be my friend Calhoun directed me to bring — for the purpose of exhibiting physical signs of spirit-power — three bells and a guitar. These were accordingly procured, the bells being of different sizes, the largest a dinner-bell. A drawer was to be put under the table upside down, and the bells placed on the drawer.

"The three ladies and myself then took our seats, leaning our hands and arms upon the table. The bells were played upon in a sort of melodious and rhythmical chime, whilst numerous raps were made, as if keeping time to a march. When the raps ceased the bells rang violently for several minutes; they were also pressed on my feet and knocked most vehemently against the under side of the table, raising up the candlesticks by the concussion.

"After the bells had ceased, I distinctly felt a hand grasping my foot, ankle, and knee, several times. I was then directed to place the guitar on the drawer. When all were seated as before, the guitar was at first touched softly and gently, giving forth sweet and delicious sounds like an accompaniment. Presently the tones grew louder and louder, and struck into a bold symphony. Then they diminished, becoming softer, sweeter, and almost dying away, as if at a long distance; then they returned, increased in power, grew louder and nearer, and anon died away again in long, vibrating echoes of the most indescribable beauty and sweetness.

"I have heard the guitar played by the most skilful and scientific hands, but I never could have conceived of that instrument being able to produce sounds of such marvellous and fascinating beauty, power, and even grandeur as this invisible performance that night executed.

"After the music had ceased, it was spelled out by the raps, 'It was my hand that touched you and the guitar. CALHOUN.'

"The following phenomena occurred at my next sitting with the Misses Fox, there being then present General Hamilton, General Waddy Thompson, of South Carolina, and myself. We were directed to place the Bible, closed, on a drawer under the table. It was a small pocket Bible in very fine print.

"For some time numerous raps were heard beating time to a march that had been suggested. These raps died away like receding feet, until the sound entirely ceased, when other loud raps gave the signal for the alphabet, by which was spelled out the single word, 'Look.' I took up the book most carefully, finding it was open, and desirous to preserve the place. It was then spelled out, 'Read'; and the verses of the open chapter which it was desired I should read were also spelled out. During the reading loud and vehement rappings seemed to indorse the sentiments rehearsed with a power that was fearfully startling, as coming from an invisible source.

"The book was open at St. John's Gospel, third chapter, and the verses indicated to be read were the 8, 11, 19, 34, and were as follows:

"'8. The wind bloweth where it will, and thou hearest its voice, but knowest not whence it cometh or whither it goeth; so is every one that is born of the spirit.'

"'11. Verily, verily I say unto thee, we speak what we know and testify what we have seen, and ye receive not our testimony.'

"'19. And this is the condemnation, that light is come into the world, and men love darkness rather than light because their deeds are evil.'

"'34. For he whom God hath sent speaketh the words of God; for God giveth not the spirit by measure.'

"After this I was directed to place several sheets of letter-paper, together with a pencil, on the drawer beneath the table. We soon heard the sound of the pencil on the paper; when it was rapped out, 'Get the pencil and sharpen it.' I looked under the table, but at first could not find the pencil until, on continuing my search, I found it lying three or four feet from the table with the lead broken off within the wood.

"I sharpened it as directed and replaced it again upon the drawer. Again I heard the sound of the pencil, but when directed by the raps to take up the paper, we found it marked on each side, but no intelligible writing could be found. By the raps, however, it was spelled out,—

"'The power is not strong enough to write a sentence, but I wish to convince you I can write. If you meet on Friday exactly at seven, I will try a short sentence.

"'JOHN C. CALHOUN.'

"We met pursuant to appointment, took our seats as usual, all our hands and arms resting on the table. I placed my silver pencil-case on the drawer beneath the table, and being in communication with the spirit of Calhoun through the raps, I said, 'My friend, I wish the sentence to be in your own handwriting, so that your friends will recognize it.' He replied, 'You will know the writing.' We soon heard a rapid movement of the pencil on the paper, the rustling of the latter, and the movement of the drawer. I was then directed to look *under* the drawer. I found my pencil outside the drawer, and all the sheets I had placed on the top now underneath it; they were disarranged, and on the outside sheet was written, 'I'm with you still.'

"I have shown that sentence to General Hamilton, former Governor of South Carolina, General Waddy Thompson, late Mexican Minister; General Robert Campbell, of Havana, together with many other intimate friends of Mr. Calhoun. I also showed it to one of his sons, and he, as well as the rest, pronounced it to be a *perfect facsimile of the handwriting of John C. Calhoun.* General Hamilton and Mrs. General Macomb—both of whom are in possession of many private letters from Calhoun—state as a fact of peculiar significance, that he was constantly in the habit of abbreviating 'I am' into 'I'm,' hence this sentence, short as it is—I'm with you still—is peculiarly characteristic of his expression no less than his singularly terse style.

"Very truly yours,

"N. P. TALLMADGE."

On this, as on other and constantly-recurring occasions, it has been remarked that a communication so brief, pointless, and therefore so inconsistent with the character of a statesman as dignified and eloquent as the late John C. Calhoun, was either at variance with his earthly career or unworthy of his exalted spirit. To such arguments, let us apply the responses so often rendered by spirits on similar occasions. "The power by which spirits can act upon matter at all is limited, ill understood even by themselves, and at present in a merely experimental state of control; hence the quantity and power of the manifestations is determined by conditions too complex and subtle, and as yet too remote from the sphere of material science, for human comprehension. Moreover, every communication, howsoever transmitted through a human organism, partakes so closely of the idiosyncracies of the medium that whilst the idea may originate in the spirit-world, the form of the communication must assume the shape of the medium's mind and the measure of their force. Beyond the occasional introduction of a few words, sentences, or forms of writing and expression, it is almost impossible for the mightiest controlling spirit far to transcend these limits; hence their ideas not only sink to the level of the medium's capacity in transmission, but often become so merged in their magnetism as to lose the stamp of their spiritual origin altogether.

"The communion may grow into more-assured identity, and a better system of telegraphy may supervene when mortals industriously study the *science* of Spiritualism, and reverendly prepare themselves to honor it *as a religion.*"

CHAPTER X.

SPIRITUALISM IN NEW YORK CITY AND STATE—CONTINUED.

"Stand for the right! though falsehood rail
And proud lips coldly sneer,
A poisoned arrow cannot wound
A conscience pure and clear.

"Stand for the right! and with clean hands
Exalt the truth on high,
Thou'lt find warm, sympathizing hearts
Among the passers-by."

PSALMS OF LIFE.

SPIRITUALISM EXPLAINED BY CHAUNCY C. BURR — S. GRIMES — MR. JOEL TIFFANY — LEO MILLER — SAUL AND PAUL — JUDGE EDMONDS'S "APPEAL TO THE PUBLIC"— THE PRESS AND THEIR CHANGE OF TONE — DR. DEXTER —"THE SACRED CIRCLE."

FROM the time when the truth of spirit communion with the earth became a fact so fixed that investigators could venture to call public attention to the subject with the most perfect confidence in the results, an infatuation appeared to have possessed certain individuals with little or no reason for their action, determinately to array themselves for a war of opposition, which they conducted with singular bitterness and indiscriminate rashness.

Thus at Buffalo, New York, three gentlemen, whose position as leaders of science should have deterred them from the committal of their names to a published verdict of which subsequent events should have made them heartily ashamed, gravely rendered their testimony to the effect that the manifestations produced through the Fox sisters were all the result of the snapping of their knee and ankle joints!

The details of the notable theory announced by "the Buffalo doctors," together with all the physiological definitions involved in their astounding discovery, will be found in a subsequent chapter. It is only necessary to state here that like all similar attempts to explain away a substantial truth on visionary grounds, the discussion to which the affair gave rise served as exceedingly valuable propaganda for the cause of Spiritualism.

The resort to deliberate falsehood on the part of the professed mesmerist, Grimes, has already been noticed, and soon after the sage Buffalo doctors had assigned to knee and ankle joints the new function of producing the whole range of varied and intelligent spiritual phenomena, the ex-Rev. [?] C. Chauncy Burr took the field to expose the whole "trick" in several public lectures delivered at Hope Chapel, New York, and other places, in which all the former exploded theories were re-hashed, with the addition of several grave and utterly unfounded falsehoods.

It would scarcely be in keeping with the spirit of serious narrative to recur to these pitiful arts, were it not advisable to note the flimsy and desperate character of the opposition.

After *making a living*, such as it was, for a few weeks out of platform "expositions" of Spiritualism in various places, where himself and his confederates *cracked out by their toe joints*, etc., names and sentences previously agreed upon; after disgusting and disappointing even their best friends by the shallow character of their imposture, and subjecting themselves to far more bitter and contemptuous remarks from the press than had ever been levelled against the cause they sought to defame, Messrs Burr & Co. were finally prosecuted for slander by Mrs. Fish [Leah Fox], and in the encounter with that lady's lawyer — Mr. Joel Tiffany — lost even the rags of public credit, wherewith they had been striving to clothe themselves as antagonists of Spiritualism. It may here be mentioned that Mr. Joel Tiffany became so deeply interested in the manifestations through the Fox family that he not only undertook their defence against the slanders of Burr, but devoted his talents as an orator and writer to the advocacy of the cause. His lectures at the Spiritualists' Sabbath meetings, his pungent replies to the attacks of the clergy and secular press, and his able conduct of one of the most popular periodicals of spiritualistic literature — namely, *Tiffany's Monthly Magazine*" — entitle him to a foremost place amongst the ranks of spiritual celebrities, and challenge our gratitude even to the venomous Chauncy Burr, for first prominently identifying Mr. Tiffany with Spiritualism, in Cleveland, Ohio. Antagonists of a similar character to the above were multiplying on every side, encouraged by the unchristian ardor with which their juggling attempts were received by the clergy, many of the press, and a large proportion of the community.

A young lawyer named Leo Miller, who was studying for the bar and anxious to fit himself for forensic display, determined to exercise his talents in a course of lectures through New York which should enlist public interest in his favor, and for this purpose he found no theme so generally acceptable as the announcement that he would "expose the pretended spiritual manifestations."

For many weeks Mr. Leo Miller ran a most successful career in this direction. His lectures were crowded, his addresses lauded to the skies by the press, while notices of his meetings were read from many of the popular pulpits, and his handbills industriously circulated by the clergy.

As Mr. Miller was an eloquent and attractive speaker, his services in conducting "the attack" in Central New York were gladly accepted in lieu of the broken fragment of the Grimes and Burr forlorn hope. Unfortunately, however, for the peace of mind of his Christian supporters, Mr. Miller suddenly became a "speaking medium." A spiritual trance overshadowed him in one of his most powerful flights of defamatory oratory, and Baalam-like, he who came to curse Israel was compelled with unwilling lips to pronounce a blessing instead, and to pour forth prophetic assurances of the unconquerable triumphs of the power he had hitherto assailed. Returning from his truly improvised lecture scarcely less confounded and dismayed than his audience, he retired to his couch to find himself serenaded by "raps," and assailed by voices of invisible beings who tenderly rebuked his past perversity, assured him of the consoling presence of loved and loving spirit friends, and urged upon him the solemn duty of going forth to atone for the errors he had committed by proclaiming the irresistible truths of Spiritualism to the ends of the earth. In the midst of the perplexity which this overwhelming change occasioned in his mind, he received from a man of whose very name and existence he had had no previous knowledge, an exquisite drawing of a female head, which the stranger informed him had been executed whilst in a trance and blindfolded. He—the artist—declared that he had no knowledge whatever of who the lady was, or why it should be given to Mr. Miller, beyond the request of the spirit, whose portrait it was.

Mr. Miller inquired the name of the artist, and learned that he was a Mr. Rogers, of Columbus, Ohio, a tailor by trade; totally unacquainted with drawing; an involuntary automatic medium for the production of spirit portraits, hundreds of which had been eagerly claimed and recognized as beloved departed ones by their astonished relatives.

In some instances, as in Mr. Miller's case, Mr. Rogers was instructed by the spirits to whom he should send or give the pictures, and it was under a charge of this kind that he had presented to Mr. Miller a drawing which the latter instantly recognized as the most inimitably faithful portrait of a beloved sister of whom there was no other likeness extant. It was impossible to mistake the resemblance; the friends of the young lady, as well as her brother, at once perceived the correctness of the portrait, whilst the most careful inquiry into the circumstances of its production only strengthened the facts as detailed by the artist.

Scores of similar cases, many of them far more marvellous than the above, were brought to Mr. Miller's notice in connection with this same artist, and the result was that Mr. Rogers became celebrated for his success as a delineator of the forms of the beloved inhabitants of the spirit country, and Mr. Leo Miller a renowned and powerful champion of the truths of spiritual existence, and communion with mortals. One of the chief results to Mr. Miller in his capacity as a public speaker was the remarkable fact that within a few weeks from the time of his "change of base," his audience fell off in numbers about the ratio of ninety per cent.; whilst his revenue from this source of course endured a proportionate decrease. All this was more than compensated for, however, by the enthusiasm of the young orator's purpose, the joy of his heart, the peace of his conscience, and the manifest improvement of his style; still, no sooner was it discovered that around his pathway hovered an angel sister, who by her pure and glorified influence made him a better and wiser man, than the pious withdrew their countenance; the press no longer advertised his lectures, or devoted a column's admiring criticism to "his able *exposé* of spirit rapping;" and saddest of all, the clergy either forgot to announce his meetings and distribute his notices, or only remembered him in their sermons to cry "Maranatha," and warn all followers of Christ to shun the daring infidel who presumed to give the signs which their master had promised should follow those who believed in him.

It was in the year 1853 that a course of virulent and scandalous attacks made upon Judge Edmonds through the public press, determined him to resign the high office of Judge, which he had so nobly and honorably filled to the satisfaction of his fellow-citizens and the benefit of the community.

The incitements to this course of action are briefly stated in the simple yet dignified "Appeal to the Public," which the learned gentleman published on the occasion. The mental trials which forced this statement from Judge Edmonds must necessarily have been very severe, but it is impossible that any one can peruse it without coming to the conclusion that "in the sufferings of the just, the world is made wise unto salvation," and that whatever may have been the inducing motive, the cause of justice and truth were greatly benefitted by the publication of so noble and manly a document, and such a clear and succinct account of the aspect and status of Spiritualism at the date of the following "appeal:"

"*To the Public:*

"On my recent return from an excursion into the country, I found that during my absence a decision lately pronounced by me had been seized upon as an occasion for an attack, in several quarters, on my religious belief. I was fully aware that that judgment, running counter as it would to popular sentiment, would subject my action to severe criticism; but I confess, I did not anticipate that thence would flow an assault on my religious opinions. Were I a private citizen, I should content myself with merely claiming the right, which belongs to every one in this country, of entertaining such faith on this—the most important of all topics—as my conscience might dictate. And as it is, I might perhaps rest satisfied with challenging those who assail me, to point out a single article in my creed that aims at aught else than exalted private worth and public virtue. But as the position which I occupy renders the soundness as well as the integrity of my judgment a matter of public interest, I am bound to acknowledge the right of others to question my faith, and my own obligation to defend it.

"I acknowledge a still further obligation. And inasmuch as I accepted my present position under the implied understanding, at least, that I believed in the Christian religion, and would administer our civil law according to the principles of the divine law, as it had been revealed to us, on which all our institutions were based, so I am bound to certify to those who have intrusted me with the divine attribute of administering justice among men, that my reverence for that revelation has not been shaken, nor my obedience to that moral law impaired.

"I have not, however, waited for these assaults, to be impressed with these obligations, but have already so far felt them that I have prepared to publish a volume on the subject, which, but for my other avocations, would ere this have been in the printer's hands. To that I must refer for much in elucidation and proof of my belief, which the limits of this communication will not allow me to dwell upon, and content myself on this occasion with such general statements as may tend to give a correct idea of what it is that I believe or have done. Even this would not have been necessary if those who assail me had but done me the justice themselves to have published anything I have said or written on the subject. But hitherto I have been able to reach the public only through publications of very limited circulation; and the wildest and most erroneous notions have therefore been imbibed as to my belief, and the mischief has been increased by the recklessness with which those erroneous statements have been fabricated by those who could not know them to be true, but who could easily have ascertained them to be false.

"Thus one writer,* with a want of feeling not perhaps surprising, speaks of my 'consulting my dead wife' in making up my decisions. Another says, that it is 'rumored' that I have consulted spirit manifestations in regard to my decisions. Another, that my belief is 'at irreconcilable variance with all divine revelation,' and is 'fit for no other system than devil worship;' and still another, that 'it constitutes an abandonment of all self-control, and a surrender of the supremacy of reason, as informed and enlightened by the senses, to the most nonsensical jugglery.'

"All these statements are as wide as they can be of truth, and I might with some justice complain at being subjected to such grievous imputations, merely because I had made a decision which was unacceptable to a portion of the community.

"But it is not for the purpose of complaining that I sit down to write. I am aware that it is not so much me as it is the faith which I profess, which is the object of attack.

"It is 'the mighty theme, and not the inconsiderable advocate,' which offends. I am also aware why it is that so much error exists in the public mind on that subject; and my whole purpose is, so far as I am concerned, to correct that error; to state truly, as far as I can in

* *Daily Chronicle*, of New London.

this connection, what it is that I do believe, and generally the grounds on which my belief is founded, that all who take interest in the matter to read what I may say, may have the means of judging for themselves as to what I really do believe, rather than what others erroneously impute to me as a belief.

"I am sincerely grateful to my assailants for not imputing to me any unworthy or selfish motives, for conceding that as a private citizen I 'stand exempt from public criticism,' and that I am 'not a fool,' and for confining themselves to the mere imputation that I am laboring under a delusion. It is, therefore, to that point I shall confine myself in what I have now to say.

"It was in January, 1851, that my attention was first called to the subject of 'spiritual intercourse.' I was at the time withdrawn from general society. I was laboring under great depression of spirits. I was occupying all my leisure in reading on the subject of death and man's existence afterwards.

"I had in the course of my life read and heard from the pulpit so many contradictory and conflicting doctrines on the subject, that I hardly knew what to believe. I could not, if I would, believe what I did not understand, and was anxiously seeking to know if after death we should again meet with those whom we had loved here, and under what circumstances.

"I was invited by a friend to witness the 'Rochester knockings.' I complied, chiefly to oblige her and to while away a tedious hour. I thought a good deal on what I witnessed, and I determined to investigate the matter and find out what it was. If it was a deception, or a delusion, I thought that I could detect it. For about four months I devoted at least two evenings in a week, and sometimes more, to witnessing the phenomena in all its phases. I kept careful records of all I witnessed, and from time to time compared them with each other, to detect inconsistencies and contradictions. I read all I could lay my hands on, on the subject, and especially all the professed 'exposures of the humbug.'

"I went from place to place, seeing different mediums, meeting with different parties of persons; often with persons whom I had never seen before, and sometimes where I was myself entirely unknown; sometimes in the dark and sometimes in the light; often with inveterate unbelievers, and more frequently with zealous believers. In fine, I availed myself of every opportunity that was afforded, thoroughly to sift the matter to the bottom. I was all this time an unbeliever, and tried the patience of believers sorely by my scepticism, my captiousness, and my obdurate refusal to yield my belief.

"I saw around me some who yielded a ready faith on one or two sittings only; others again under the same circumstances, avowing a determined unbelief; and some who refused to witness it at all, and yet were confirmed unbelievers. I could not imitate either of these parties, and refused to yield unless upon most irrefragible testimony. At length the evidence came, and in such force that no sane man could withhold his faith.

"Thus far the question I was investigating was, whether what I saw was produced by mere mortal means, or by some invisible, unknown agency; in other words, whether it was a deception, an imposition, or what it professed to be—the product of some unknown, unseen cause. To detail what I witnessed would far exceed the limits of this communication, for my records of it for those four months alone fill at least one hundred and thirty closely written pages. I will, however, mention a few things, which will give a general idea of that which characterized interviews now numbering several hundred. Most of them have occurred in the presence of others besides myself. I have preserved their names in my records, but do not give them to the world, because I do not desire to subject them to the obloquy which seems, most strangely, to be visited upon all who look into the matter with any other feeling than a resolute and obstinate incredulity, whatever the evidence. But these considerations grow out of this fact: first, that I have thus very many witnesses, whom I can invoke to establish the truth of my statements; and second, that if I have been deluded and have not seen and heard what I think I have, my delusion has been shared by many as shrewd, as intelligent, as honest, and as enlightened people, as are to be found anywhere among us.

"My attention was first drawn to the intercourse by the rappings, then the most common, but now the most inconsiderable mode of communing. Of course I was on the look-out for deception, and at first relied upon my senses and the conclusions which my reason might draw from their evidence. But I was at a loss to tell how the mediums could cause what I witnessed under these circumstances: the mediums walking the length of a suite of parlors forty or fifty feet, and the rappings being distinctly heard five or six feet behind them, the whole distance, backward and forward, several times; being heard near the top of a mahogany door, above where the mediums could reach, and as if struck hard with a fist; being heard on the bottom of a car when travelling on a railroad, and on the floor and the table, when seated at lunch, at an eating-house, by the side of the road; being heard at different parts of the room, sometimes several feet distant from the medium and where she could not reach; sometimes on the table and immediately after on the floor, and then at different parts of the table, in rapid succession, enabling us to feel the vibration as well as hear the sounds; sometimes, when the hands and feet of the medium were both firmly and carefully held by some one of the party, and sometimes on a table when no one touched it.

"After depending upon my senses as to these various phases of the phenomena, I invoked the aid of science, and with the assistance of an accomplished electrician and his machinery, and eight or ten intelligent, educated, shrewd persons, examined the matter. We pursued our inquiries many days, and established to our satisfaction two things: first, that the sounds were not produced by the agency of any person present or near us; and, second, that they were not forthcoming at our will and pleasure.

"In the meantime another feature attracted my attention, and that was 'physical manifestations,' as they are termed. Thus, I have known a pine table with four legs lifted bodily up from the floor in the centre of a circle of six or eight persons, turned upside down and laid upon its top at our feet, then lifted up over our heads and put leaning against the back of the sofa on which we sat. I have known that same table to be lifted up on two legs, its top at an angle with the floor of forty-five degrees, when it neither fell over of itself, nor could any person present put it back on its four legs. I have seen a mahogany table, having only a centre leg, and with a lamp burning upon it, lifted from the floor at least a foot, in spite of the efforts of those present, and shaken backward and forward as one would shake a goblet in his hand, and the lamp retain its place though its glass pendants rang again.

"I have seen the table tipped up with the lamp upon it so far that the lamp must have fallen off unless retained there by something else than its own gravity, yet it fell not, moved not. I have known a dinner-bell taken from a high shelf in a closet, rung over the heads of four or five persons in that closet, then rung around the room over the heads of twelve or fifteen persons in the back parlor, and then borne through the folding doors to the further end of the front parlor, and there dropped on the floor. I have frequently known persons pulled about with a force which it was impossible for them to resist, and once, when all my own strength was added in vain to that of the one thus affected. I have known a mahogany chair thrown on its side and moved swiftly back and forth on the floor, no one touching it, through a room where there were at least a dozen people sitting, yet no one was touched, and it was repeatedly stopped within a few inches of me, when it was coming with a violence which, if not arrested, must have broken my legs.

"This is not a tithe—nay, not a hundredth part of what I have witnessed of the same character, but it is enough to show the general nature of what was before me.

"At the same time I have heard from others, whose testimony would be credited in any human transaction, and which I could not permit myself to disregard, accounts of still more extraordinary transactions, for I have been by no means so much favored in this respect as some.

"While these things were going on there appeared in the newspapers various explanations and 'exposures of the humbug,' as they were termed. I read them with care, in the expectation of being assisted in my researches, and I could not but smile at once at the rashness and the futility of the explanations. For instance, while certain learned professors in Buffalo were congratulating themselves on having detected it in the toe and knee-joints, the manifestations in this city changed to ringing a bell placed under the table. They were like the solution lately given by a learned professor in England, who attributes the tipping of tables to a force in the hands which are laid upon it, overlooking the material fact that tables quite as frequently move when there is no hand upon them.

"What I have thus mentioned has happened in the presence of others as well as myself. I have not alluded to any of the things which have occurred to me when I have been alone, for as that would depend upon my testimony only, I have preferred not to subject my veracity to the rash and reckless contradictions of those who venture to denounce as an 'atrocious imposture' that of which they are profoundly ignorant, and which has been examined and is believed in by thousands and tens of thousands of their fellow-citizens, who are, to say the least, every whit as honest and as intelligent as they are; nor am I very anxious to submit my faith to the judgment of those who would have persecuted Galileo nigh unto death for discovering our planetary system, and have united in the cry of 'folly' at Fulton's steamboat, 'humbug' at Morse's telegraph, and 'insanity' at Gray's iron road.

"Having thus by a long series of patient inquiries satisfied myself on this point, my next inquiry was, Whence comes the intelligence there is behind it all? For that intelligence was a remarkable feature of the phenomena.

"Thus I have frequently known mental questions answered—that is, questions merely framed in the mind of the interrogator, and not revealed by him or known to others. Preparatory to meeting a circle I have sat down alone in my room and carefully prepared a series of questions to be propounded, and I have been surprised to find my questions answered, and in the precise order in which I made them, without my even taking my memorandum out of my pocket, and when I knew that not a person present even knew that I had prepared questions, much less what they were. My most secret thoughts, those which I have never uttered to mortal man or woman, have been freely spoken, too, as if I had uttered them. Purposes which I have privily entertained have been publicly revealed; and I have once and again been admonished that my every thought was known to and could be disclosed by the intelligence which was thus manifesting itself.

"I have heard the mediums use Greek, Latin, Spanish, and French words, when I knew they had no knowledge of any language but their own; and it is a fact that can be attested to by many, that often there has been speaking and writing in foreign languages and unknown tongues by those who were unacquainted with either.

"Still the question occurred, May not all this have been, by some mysterious operation, the mere reflex of the mind of some one present? The answer was that facts were communicated which were unknown then, but afterwards found to be true; like this, for instance: when I was absent last winter in Central America my friends in town heard of my whereabouts and of the state of my health seven times; and on my return, by comparing their information with the entries in my journal, it was found to be invariably correct. So in my recent visit to the West, my whereabouts and my condition were told to a medium in this city while I was travelling on the railroad between Cleveland and Toledo. So thoughts have been uttered on subjects not then in my mind, and utterly at variance with my own notions. This has often happened to me and to others so as fully to establish the fact that it was not our minds that gave birth to or effected the communication.

"Kindred to this are two well-authenticated cases of persons who can read the thoughts of others in their minds. One is an artist of this city, of high reputation; and the other the editor of a newspaper in a neighboring city. The latter wrote me that in company with three friends he had tried the experiment, and for over forty successive attempts found he could read the secret thoughts of his companions as soon as they were formed, and without their being uttered. So, too, there is the instance of two persons, one of them also resident in this city, who can give a faithful delineation of the character, and even the prevailing mood of mind of any person, however unknown to them, upon whom they fix their attention.

"These are not apocryphal cases; the parties are at hand, and in our very midst, and any person that pleases may make the investigation, as I have, and satisfy himself.

"But all this, and much, very much more of a cognate nature, went to show me that there was a high order of intelligence involved in this new phenomenon—an intelligence outside of, and beyond, mere mortal agency; for there was no other hypothesis which I could devise or hear of, that could at all explain that, whose reality is established by the testimony of tens of thousands, and can easily be ascertained by any one who will take the trouble to inquire.

"If these two points were established—and there are now in these United States hundreds of thousands of sentient beings who have investigated and believe they are—then came this important question, *cui bono*—to what end is it all? For what purpose? With what object?

"To that inquiry I have directed my earnest attention, devoting to the task, for over two years, all the leisure I could command, and increasing that leisure as far as I could by withdrawing myself from all my former recreations. I have gone from circle to circle, from medium to medium, seeking knowledge on the subject wherever I could obtain it, either from books or from observation, and bringing to bear upon it whatever of intelligence I have been gifted with by nature, sharpened and improved by over thirty years' practice at the bar, in the legislature, and on the bench.

"I found there were very many ways in which this unseen intelligence communed with us, besides the rappings and table tippings, and that through those other modes there came very many communications distinguished for their eloquence, their high order of intellect, and their pure and lofty moral tone. At the same time I discovered many inconsistencies and contradictions that were calculated to mislead; I saw many puerile and some very absurd statements, and many that were admirably calculated to make man better and happier, and I set to work to see if I could not, out of this chaos, gather something that might be valuable.

"I was satisfied that something more was intended than the gratification of an idle curiosity; something more than pandering to a diseased appetite for the marvellous; something more than the promulgation of oracular platitudes; something more than upsetting material objects to the admiration of the wonder-lover; something more than telling the age of the living or the dead, etc.

"For that something I have industriously searched. I thought that was wiser than to condemn without investigation, and denounce without knowledge. What I have discovered in that regard I have intended to give to the world, that all may judge for themselves whether there is anything in it worthy the attention of intelligent beings. It would have been done ere this if my leisure would have allowed me time to prepare my manuscript for the press. Now I expect that my book will be published by the first of September, and to that I refer, as I have already said, for particulars. . . . . . .

"I went into the investigation originally thinking it a deception, and intending to make public my exposure of it. Having, from my researches, come to a different conclusion, I feel that the obligation to make known the result is just as strong. Therefore it is, mainly, that I give the result to the world. I say mainly, because there is another consideration which influences me; and that is the desire to extend to others a knowledge which I am conscious can not but make them happier and better.

"If those who doubt this could but spend a few days with me in my library, and witness the calls I have from strangers from all parts of the country; if they could but look over my portfolio, and read the letters which pour in upon me from all sections, and from persons whom I have never seen, and never may see, they would be able, from the evidence thus furnished of the good that has been done, to form some idea of what may yet be accomplished; and they would not wonder that I find a compensation for the obloquy that is so freely heaped upon me by the ignorant, in the grateful outpourings of hearts which have, by my means, been relieved. One of them says [and it is a fair specimen of the whole] 'you have acted the part of the good Samaritan, and poured oil into the wound of one like to die, and you will have rendered a death-bed, sooner or later, calm and hopeful, which might have been disturbed by doubts.'

"This, then, is the offence for which I am arraigned at the bar of the public with so unsparing a condemnation, declared unworthy of my high office, falsely accused of consulting aught else than the law of the land and my own reason in the judgments which I officially pronounce, and have had invoked against me 'the fires of Smithfield and the hangings of Salem.' From such a condemnation it is that I appeal to the calm, unbiased judgment of my countrymen, with a firm reliance upon its justice.

"J. W. EDMONDS.

"NEW YORK, *August* 1, 1853."

One result of Judge Edmonds's appearance in public as *defendant* against the reckless attacks of his adversaries, was a change of tone in the press, which, though strongly confirmatory of his triumphant position, is nevertheless characteristic of the truth of an old proverb which suggests a close alliance between the *bully* and the *coward*. The following extracts will suffice to justify this insinuation:

From the New York Courier.

"The letter from Judge Edmonds, published by us on Saturday, with regard to the so-called spiritual manifestations, coming as it did from an eminent jurist, a man remarkable for his clear common-sense in the practical affairs of life, and a gentleman of irreproachable character, arrested the attention of the community, and is regarded by many persons as one of the most remarkable documents of the day. Judge Edmonds has at least shown that he does not shrink from a full investigation of his case; and his error is, perhaps, upon the right side, under the circumstances. . . . .

"With regard to the extraordinary phenomena which Judge Edmonds testifies to, as having occurred in his presence, it is worthy of note that others far more incredible are testified to by other persons equally eminent with himself. We have the word of a gentleman of acknowledged high social and professional position, one whose bare word on any other subject we would receive without question, that he saw a man carried through the air for seventy feet at the height of three yards, although no one touched him or brought any mechanical power to bear on him. The story is entitled to exactly the same faith which is due to those of Judge Edmonds; no less, and no more."

The *Evening Mirror* remarks:

"John W. Edmonds, the Chief Justice of the Supreme Court for this District, is an able lawyer, an industrious judge, and a good citizen. For the last eight years, occupying without interruption the hightest judicial stations, whatever may be his faults, no one can justly accuse him of a lack of ability, industry, honesty, or fearlessness. No one can doubt his general saneness, or can believe for a moment that the ordinary operations of his mind are not as rapid, accurate, and reliable as ever. Both by the practitioners and suitors at his bar, he is recognized as the head, in fact and in merit, of the Supreme Court for this District."

After reviewing that portion of the letter in which Judge Edmonds records the experiences which led him to embrace the spiritual faith, the *Mirror* remarks:

"Judge Edmonds, with characteristic energy, has not been silent on the subject of his recently-formed opinions. He has repeatedly published his experiences in some of the periodicals devoted to the new faith, and several of his articles were copied extensively by the daily press. Of course, these have furnished food for those editors who prowl about in search of a paragraph or a satire, and have afforded a target for many blunt but not inocuous arrows."

It may be unjust to hold the individual members of the press responsible for the tone assumed by the majority, but the organization of that mighty body in America no more admits of these nice distinctions than the case of Judge Edmonds, and the circumstances cited above, can be considered apart from the gigantic movement of which this distinguished jurist was but an integral part. Judge Edmonds himself defines the truth of this position when he says, "I am aware that it is not so much me as the faith which I profess, which is the object of attack. It is the mighty theme, and not the inconsiderable advocate, which offends."

It has been the general tone of the press, as a body—not the opinion of its individual members, hundreds of whom are devoted Spiritualists—which makes its insolent, profane, and persistent persecution of Spiritualism a subject of equal surprise and discredit.

In 1852, Judge Edmonds formed the acquaintance of Dr. Dexter, who with his two young daughters of the respective ages of nine and fourteen, had become developed, by sitting in a family circle, as excellent mediums. In company with Dr. and Mrs. Dexter, Mr. Owen G. Warren, the author of "Supernal Theology," and Mr. and Mrs. Sweet, the latter a medium of the highest intellectual nature, Judge Edmonds formed a circle the result of which was a series of communications, chiefly written through the hand of Dr. Dexter, or spoken by Mrs. Sweet and written down by the Judge in short-hand, which he gave to the world in September, 1853, under the title of "Spiritualism, by Judge Edmonds and Dr. Dexter."

A second volume, differing somewhat in character and style from the first, was published by Judge Edmonds and Dr. Dexter in the following year—namely, 1854. The changes manifest in this work are attributed by the Judge, in his preface, to the addition of Miss Laura Edmonds, and Miss Keyes, her cousin, to the circle of mediums, besides aid received from Mrs. A. T. Hall and Mrs. Helen Leeds, mediums of Boston. As these productions have been long and widely circulated amongst the American public, it is needless to make any other comment upon them than to record the profound impressions which their issue from such a distinguished source created, and to add the fact that the press and pulpit found in *garbled extracts* from their pages all the fresh food for ribaldry and insult which the literary and Christian spirit of these two potential leaders of public opinion could demand.

CHAPTER XI.

SPIRITUALISM IN NEW YORK CITY AND STATE—CONTINUED.

"It is a faith sublime and pure,
That ever round our head
Are hovering on noiseless wing
The spirits of the dead.

"It is a beautiful belief,
When ended our career
That it will be our ministry
To watch o'er others here."

J. H. PERKINS.

CHARACTER OF THE PHENOMENA—STATISTICS OF SPIRITUALISM IN 1853-4-5—MEDIUMS IN NEW YORK—SPEAKING WITH NEW TONGUES—SPIRIT PORTRAITS—FLOATING IN THE AIR—MRS. METTLER—CORRESPONDENCE—MRS. WHITMAN AND SENATOR SIMMONS—REV. C. HAMMOND—THE RING EXPERIMENT IN WASHINGTON.

BEFORE proceeding with the historical course of Spiritualism in New York it would be well to review the character of the manifestations which had during five years only, grown out of the first simple raps that awakened the inhabitants of the humble "spirit house" at Hydesville to the conscious presence of disembodied human souls. By a reference to the admirable compendium of Spiritualism in 1853, as detailed by Judge Edmonds in his "appeal," given in the last chapter, the character and standing of the personages interested in the cause may be understood, together with the nature of the phenomena which was most operative at that time. It was roughly estimated by Mr. N. P. Willis, editor of the *Home Journal*—himself an interested investigator—that the number of Spiritualists in New York City could not be less than forty thousand; the magnetic circles held at this time about three hundred; in Brooklyn and Williamsburgh at least twice that number; whilst several thousand mediumistic persons, over twenty public test mediums, and at least a hundred clairvoyant and medical mediums could be found in and about the city through whom strangers could acquaint themselves with the phenomenal facts then transpiring. Besides the ordinary phases of rapping, the movement of conderable bodies, and the production of many varied and wonderful feats of power, spirits afforded the most striking proofs of supra-mundane intelligence.

Hundreds of mediums were astounding the world by speaking fluently in many tongues, of which they had no previous knowledge.

In New York, Miss Laura Edmonds conversed fluently, when under special influences of that kind, in Greek, Latin, Italian, Portuguese, Polish, Hungarian, and several Indian dialects; her only branches of lingual education having been English and French. Miss Jenny Keyes was influenced to sing in Italian and Spanish. Mrs. Shepherd, Mrs. Gilbert Sweet, Miss Inman, Mrs. Tucker, Miss Susan Hoyt, A. D. Ruggles, and several others whose names we are not privileged to give, all residents of New York, spoke frequently, under influence, in Spanish, Danish, Italian, Hebrew, Greek, Malay, Chinese, and Indian.

Of Mr. Edward Fowler's writings in Oriental languages we have already spoken. They were often submitted to eminent scholars, amongst others to the learned Professor Bush, of New York, and pronounced to be pure Hebrew, Greek, Sanscrit, etc.; Mr. Fowler being, according to the testimony of his friends and family, utterly incapable of writing, speaking, or comprehending any of the languages in which these communications were given. On one occasion Professor Bush being present with Mr. Fowler and desirous to test the possibility of communicating in Hebrew through the raps, called the alphabet in that language, and received highly satisfactory answers which he afterwards translated, bearing testimony to the indisputable test character of the communication, and its purity and correctness of orthography. The value of the gift of tongues may be estimated from the recital of an incident that occurred in the experience of the late celebrated agricultural chemist, Professor Mapes, who vouched for the verity of the statement. A medium of great phenomenal powers—whose name we are forbidden to mention—was one day influenced to go into the streets in company with Mr. Henry Vail, a pupil of Professor Mapes, when she was accosted by a miserable-looking woman, who addressed her in a foreign language.

The medium, who was an uneducated person, was immediately controlled to answer the stranger intelligibly, and under an irresistible spirit influence, was led into a low quarter of the town, where she found fourteen Italians crowded together in one room, in a state of deplorable destitution and sickness, but unable, from their ignorance of the English language, to make their necessities known.

The medium conversed with them fluently, administered to their relief, and prescribed clairvoyantly and in their own language for the sick amongst them.

Governor Tallmadge, the Honorable J. M. Giddings, and many prominent New York Spiritualists, have testified to numerous cases of a similar nature, in which the same medium, besides performing wonderful cures through clairvoyant agency, conversed with poor strangers in the streets in various foreign languages, she being, from defective education scarcely mistress of her own.

The above incident will remind many New York Spiritualists of a person who for years was famous amongst them as one of the most remarkable mediums of the age, but whose name—on *her own solemn charge*—will find no record in these pages. We must here add that, actuated by different motives from the party above alluded to, and we regret to say, most commonly from the unworthy one of fear of public, opinion thousands of the most striking proofs of spiritual communion are suppressed, because the parties concerned refuse their names or other tokens of authenticity absolutely indispensable to the plan of this work.

Amongst other varieties of phenomena was the production of magnetized water, by which many sick persons were cured, and the changing of the color of the water whilst enclosed in tightly-corked and sealed bottles. The following extract is a specimen of the latter phenomena:

"MR. S. B. BRITAIN: *Dear Sir*,—The cause of Spiritualism in this vicinity is moving forward, regardless of the opposition which it meets on various hands, though mostly from the Church. We have all kinds of manifestations, such as are common in the East with you; but the newest are *the spirit lights and the coloring of water*. The lights are seen by all present in different parts of the room. But lately the medium was directed to take a bottle and fill it half full of water, and cork the same tightly, when the spirits promised to appear in it. This has been done, and the light appeared so bright that objects in the room could be distinctly seen. The bottle was passed around the circle, and all saw and handled it.

"The water is placed in a bottle and left on a table from five to fifteen minutes, when it is changed to any color desired. These things are being constantly witnessed in this vicinity. I saw them myself last evening in a crowded circle. They can be attested by hundreds. Water was changed to various colors; and when a sceptical lady present requested that it be colored red, it was instantly done, and afterwards, by request, it was turned to a pale yellow. The orthodox folks have called it 'humbug,' 'collusion,' 'magnetism,' and various other things, till they are headed in them all, and now they cry, lastly, that it is 'the *devil.*'

"We have all kinds of media here, but these last manifestations are produced through a gentleman who is quite unlearned. He has submitted to the most rigid examination, and the people are satisfied that he is not in possession of any art by which to produce these things.

"Yours for philosophical truth,

"E. P. WILSON.

"FARMINGTON, Fulton County, Illinois."

About this time the papers began to circulate tidings of the most astounding phenomena occurring in Athens County, Ohio, in the family of Mr. Koons, who had built a "spirit room" in the woods to facilitate the performances of "the invisibles."

Without anticipating details which belong to a separate notice, it may be mentioned that the spirits commenced, through the mediumship of the Koons family, to perform upon many instruments in concert, and through a speaking trumpet actually dictated a small volume of communications, and drew diagrams of the spheres and other remarkable details of the unknown country which they claimed to inhabit.

In Columbus, Ohio, Messrs. George Walocutt and Rogers—the medium who was instrumental in the conversion of Leo Miller—were convincing sceptics by hundreds through their astounding gifts of spirit painting, reproducing faithful portraitures of deceased persons wholly unknown to them, and often sending them to strangers at distant places under spirit direction.

To increase the marvel of these productions, they were mostly drawn either in darkened apartments, or when the mediums were blindfolded and surrounded by crowds of carping sceptics. In Springfield and Boston, Massachusetts, D. D. Home—afterwards renowned for his extraordinary mediumistic gifts throughout the courts of Europe—Henry C. Gordon, George Redman, and Rollin Squire, were all developed for physical manifestations of the most wonderful character.

These young men were frequently lifted up in the air and floated over several feet of ground in the presence of hundreds of witnesses.

Notices of these performances were freely circulated in the secular as well as the spiritual press, and because from such a source the statements are never in danger of erring on the side of credulity, we select the following from the New York *Dispatch:*

"'SUPER-MUNDANE,' WITH A VENGEANCE—'MEDIUM FLOATED IN THE AIR.'

"Mr. Henry Gordon, a well-known medium for spiritual manifestations, being at a circle in this city one evening last week, was repeatedly raised from his seat and carried through the room, without any visible power touching him. The room was partially darkened, and the members of the circle could distinctly see him floating, with his lower extremities some two or three feet from the floor and some fifteen or twenty feet from the nearest person to him. The idea of any mechanical contrivance in this case is out of the question, as the circle was gotten up extemporaneously by persons too intelligent to deceive themselves and too honest to deceive others; and the occurrences took place at a house where Mr. Gordon was an invited guest only for the evening. Full particulars of the affair were related by eye-witnesses, at the spiritual conference in Bond street, on Tuesday evening last. Our friend Dr. Hallock was one of the party who witnessed this phenomenon, and perhaps may be induced to write out a more detailed account of it.

"The same event took place with Mr. Gordon in this city some two years ago, of which an account was published."

In Buffalo, the most intense excitement was prevailing on the subject of the manifestations. Besides a number of mediums for the ordinary phases of spirit telegraphy, Miss Brooks, a young and interesting girl of a highly-respectable family, became developed for the production of spirit music, which was performed in her presence in the most masterly and brilliant manner by an invisible piano-forte player, whose magnificent symphonies were produced when the instrument was turned with the keys to the wall, whilst one hand of the medium rested lightly on the cover and the other was held by a member of the circle.

Hundreds of healing mediums were also exercising their beneficent gifts at this time. Amongst many who have since acquired a wide and deserved renown, none was more instrumental for the working of "miraculous" cures than Mrs. Mettler, of Hartford, Connecticut. The suffering and afflicted crowded her rooms from morning till night, whilst the records of the cures she performed under the avowed influence of spirits would fill a volume. The four daughters of Governor Tallmadge, of Wisconsin, became mediums, and by their influence and the exercise of their admirable gifts of seership, trance, musical improvisation, writing, and tongues, created an immense sensation in the fashionable circles in which they moved.

Reports from the West and California were far more startling and abundant even than those at the East, and no day passed in which the spiritual journals were not filled with narratives of the marvels that were transpiring on every part of the continent.

The following extract, from the "Telegraph Papers" of 1853, is taken from the notes of the distinguished writer and tourist James Sargent, Esq., of Boston:

"Mr. Sargent's route lay principally through tracts of country most remote from the influences of civilization. He was for a portion of the time surrounded almost exclusively by an Indian population in a state but little removed from barbarism. It need hardly be added that no vestige of literature, even to the establishment of a district post for the benefit of travellers, had ever penetrated these wilds. No means for the dissemination of information existed, yet Mr. Sargent found that *the rappings and all the other Spiritual manifestations were of common occurrence.*

"It was not by any means unusual, on entering a log cabin, to find the good, simple people seated round the rude table upon which raps were being made, and replying in the usual mode, to questions put by the auditory. There were to be found, moreover, both writing, talking, and seeing media, and these in considerable numbers.

"The villagers themselves appeared to be in total ignorance of the nature and character of the phenomena; only replying, when questioned, that they 'did not understand it; didn't know but that it might be the devil,' etc.

"These sylvan rappings first occurred, it appears, when a number of people were sitting together in conversation, and created no small consternation.

"Soon tables and chairs were moved, tipped over, and lifted, and many other Puck-like gambols performed. The idea that these wonders originated in some superhuman intelligence, seems to have occurred to these unsophisticated beings *naturally*, and without any kind of prompting or suggestion from persons already acquainted with the demonstrations; and having arrived at this conclusion, and ascertained that the rappings could *reply* to them, they no longer hesitated to enter into conversation with them."

Amongst records of incidental phenomena poured iuto the editorial sanctums of the New York spiritual journalists, the author selects, from over *five thousand* similar paragraphs, a few that have been thoroughly well attested, as specimen signs of the times. The letter from which the following extract is taken was written for the *Spiritual Telegraph* by a thoroughly reliable correspondent.

"Mr. Vinson Stockwell, in Thomson, Geauga County, Ohio, has in his family a little girl about twelve years old, who became first a rapping, then a writing, and lastly a clairvoyant medium.

"She describes the nature of disease, tells the symptoms and feelings of the patient, prescribes for the same, and has performed wonderful cures. One case is as follows: A little girl nine years old had been under the care of four very eminent medical gentlemen nearly two years, and during that time over one hundred pieces of bone had been taken from her limbs. The physicians finally gave her up as incurable, at which time she could only be moved from one bed to another on pillows. She is now entirely cured by a prescription made by spirits through this medium.

"Another was a case of deafness of four years' standing. The patient is a lady, a neighbor of mine, and I knew her to be so deaf that it was with much difficulty that she could be made to understand by loudly speaking in her ear. This case, too, had baffled the skill of several physicians. She was entirely healed by spiritual agency through this medium.

"Another astonishing fact is as follows: Mr. Stockwell, father of the medium, left here for California; afterwards his family had news of him by spiritual agency almost daily, stating his whereabouts, and many little incidents occurring in his journey, which statements were found to correspond exactly with his letters afterward received. But the most astonishing fact of all was, that after being absent about one year, and the family not hearing from him for some time, they sat for spiritual communications, and to their surprise the spirit informed them that Mr· Stockwell was on his way home. This information was quite unlooked for, as Mr. Stockwell was not expected home until the year following. The question was asked, 'Is he on the water?' *Answer*, 'No he is on the Isthmus.' The spirit stated at the same time on what day of the month he would be at home; and, strange as it may appear, he arrived on the very day foretold,and stated that he was on the Isthmus at the time stated in the communication.

The *Hartford Times*, Connecticut, publishes in March, 1853, the account of a *seance* which one of its regular correspondents held with Mr. D. D. Home. After relating at length the extraordinary feats of marvel performed through tables, bell-ringing, playing on various instruments, and moving about of heavy pieces of furniture, etc., the writer goes on to relate an incident of such an interesting character that we quote the description entire, only premising that the editor vouches for the full faith and reliability of his correspondent's statements:

"Later in the evening, when the company were preparing to retire, and after some of the party had gone from the room, the spirits requested us to wait; and those that remained were permitted to see the most remarkable part of that evening's proceedings. The gas-light had been turned down, but sufficient light remained in the room to render ourselves, and most objects, quite visible, and the hands of the party, which rested on the table, could be distinctly seen. The spirits asked:

"'How many hands are there on the table?' There were six of us in the party, and the answer, after counting, was 'twelve.'

"*Reply*—'There are *thirteen*.'

"And there, sure enough, on that side of the table which was vacant, and opposite to the medium, appeared a *thirteenth* hand! It faded as we gazed, but presently up it came again—*a hand and an arm*, gleaming and apparently self-luminous; and it slowly moved onward toward the centre of the table! To make sure that we were not deceived or laboring under a hallucination, we counted our own hands, which were all resting in sight upon the table. There it was, however, an arm and a hand, the arm extending back to the elbow, and there fading into imperceptibility. We all saw it, and all spoke of it, to assure each other of the reality of the thing. It had the color and appearance of *silver*, but with this difference—it seemed to be, to a certain extent, self-luminous; it emitted a faint but perceptible *light*. Presently it vanished, but we were soon permitted to see not only the same thing again, but *the process of its formation*. It began at the *elbow*, and formed rapidly and steadily, until the arm and hand again rested on the table before us. It was so plainly seen that I readily observed it to be a *left* hand. I inquired:

"'Can you *write* with that hand, in plain sight?'

"*Answer* (by raps)—'Perhaps.'

"A sheet of paper and a pencil were placed in the centre of the table, the hand receded meanwhile from view. In a moment it came up again [always appearing from the vacant side of the table] and slowly moved forward to the paper, which it grasped and drew back to the edge, and there shook and rattled it for some moments, but failed to write anything legible. It then disappeared, and the next moment the bell was taken from beneath the table, carried from the circle some six feet toward the centre of the room, and there rung by invisible means, and so distinctly that persons in another room, beyond an intervening wall or passage-way, plainly heard it.

"Presently it was brought back and dropped upon the table—and this while each of us sat quietly, without moving. The hand again appeared, was seen to take the bell from the table and place it in the hands, first of one, and then of another of the party. At length it was placed in mine; but, slipping my hand over the bell, I grasped the hand that held it, desiring some more tangible knowledge of its character than that afforded by sight. It was a real hand—it had knuckles, fingers, and finger-nails; and what was yet more curious [if possible], it was soft and warm, feeling much like the hand of an infant, in every respect but that of size. But the most singular part of this [to me] strange occurrence is yet to be told—the hand melted in my grasp! dissolved, dissipated, became annihilated, so far as the sense of feeling extended. It subsequently reappeared on the table and again vanished, after a statement [by the raps] to the effect that this hand had been produced by a near relative of some of those in the circle, who had been in the interior life a number of years. This question was then spelled out:

"'Would you like to see the hand of a colored person?'

"In a moment more there appeared a rather dull-looking *gray* hand, somewhat shadowy, and not quite so clearly defined as the first, but it was unmistakably there, and its gray hue could be clearly seen.

"But this account grows lengthy, and must close. Occurrences yet more astounding than any here related remain untold. Perhaps in another chapter I may give some of them, and also a glance at one theory concerning the philosophy of the production of these startling realities.

FACT.

"HARTFORD, *March* 18, 1853."

"SPIRITS IN CALIFORNIA—1852.

"Jesse Hutchinson writes from California that the spirit rappings are quite prevalent in the land of gold. There are now said to be some twenty good mediums in San Francisco. They have seized upon the editors and conductors of the public press. The *Herald* is now the only sheet as yet unblest by their presence. One of the editors of the *Alta* has become a medium; also the principal editor of the *Whig*, and one of the editors of the *Placer Times* is an enthusiastic believer and medium." *Spiritual Telegraph.*

In a very interesting article written by Hon. Horace Greeley for *Putnam's Monthly Magazine* the talented author gives several striking narratives of the spiritual experiences of some of his friends, together with his own keenly acute though non-committal comments thereon.

Amongst others, the following recital, though it has frequently been republished, will not be out of place, as illustrative of the character of early phenomenal facts, vouched for on the authority of Mrs. S. Helen Whitman, the celebrated poetess of Rhode Island.

The narrative is given in part of a letter addressed by Mrs. Whitman to Mr. Greeley, who introduces it with strong affirmations of the unimpeachable character of the testimony he cites, also with the following postscript added to his letter in *Putnam's Magazine:*

"P. S.—Since the foregoing was in type, the writer has received the following letter from Mrs. Sarah H. Whitman, of Providence, R. I., in reply to one of inquiry from him as to her own experiences in Spiritualism, and especially with regard to a remarkable experience currently reported as having occurred to Hon. James F. Simmons, late U. S. Senator from Rhode Island, and widely known as one of the keenest and clearest of observers, most unlikely to be the dupe of mystery or the slave of hallucination.'

"The most material portion is as follows:

"'DEAR SIR,—I have had no conversation with Mr. Simmons on the subject of your note until to-day. I took an early opportunity of acquainting him with the contents, and this morning he called on me to say that he was perfectly willing to impart to you the particulars of his experience in relation to the mysterious writing *performed under his very eyes in broad daylight, by an invisible agent.* In the fall of 1850 several messages were telegraphed to Mrs. Simmons through the electric sounds, purporting to come from her step-son, James D. Simmons, who died some weeks before in California.

"'The messages were calculated to stimulate curiosity and lead to an attentive observation of the phenomena. Mrs. S. having heard that messages in the handwriting of deceased persons were sometimes written through the same medium, asked if her son would give her this evidence. She was informed — through the sounds — that the attempt should be made, and was directed to place a slip of paper in a certain drawer at the house of the medium, and to lay beside it her own pencil, which had been given her by the deceased. Weeks passed on, and although frequent inquiries were made, no writing was found on this paper.

"'Mrs. Simmons happening to call at the house one day, accompanied by her husband, made the usual inquiry, and received the usual answer.

"'The drawer had been opened not two hours before, and nothing was seen in it but the pencil lying on the blank paper. At the suggestion of Mrs. S., however, another investigation was made, and on the paper was found a few pencilled lines, resembling the handwriting of the deceased, but not so closely as to satisfy the mother's doubts. Mrs. Simmons handed the paper to her husband. He thought there was a slight resemblance, but should probably not have remarked it had the writing been casually presented to him. Had the signature been given him he should at once have decided on the resemblance. He proposed, if the spirit of his son were indeed present — as alphabetical communications, received through the sounds, affirmed him to be—that he should, then and there, affix his signature to the suspicious document.

"'In order to facilitate the operation, Mr. S. placed the closed points of a pair of scissors in the hands of the medium, and dropped his pencil through one of the rings or bows, the paper being placed beneath. Her hand presently began to tremble, and it was with difficulty she could retain her hold of the scissors. Mr. Simmons then took them into his own hand, and again dropped his pencil through the ring. It could not readily be sustained in this position. After a few moments, however, it stood as if firmly poised and perfectly still. It then began slowly to move. Mr. S. saw traced beneath his eyes the words JAMES D. SIMMONS. The letters were distinctly and deliberately written, and the handwriting was a facsimile of his son's signature. But what Mr. S. regards as the most astonishing part of this seeming miracle is yet to be told.

"'Bending down to scrutinize the writing more closely, he observed, just as the last word was finished, that the top of the pencil leaned to the right; he thought it was about to slip through the ring, but to his infinite astonishment he saw the point slide slowly back along the word Simmon's, till it rested over the letter *i*, where it deliberately imprinted a dot. This was a punctilio utterly unthought of by him; he had not noticed the omission, and was therefore entirely unprepared for the amendment. He suggested the experiment, and hitherto it had kept pace only with his will or desire; but how will those who deny the agency of disembodied spirits in these marvels, ascribing all to the unassisted powers of the human will or to the blind action of electricity—how will they dispose of this last significant and curious fact? The only peculiarity observable in the writing was that the lines seemed sometimes slightly broken, as if the pencil had been lifted and then set down again.

"'Another circumstance I am permitted to relate, which is not readily to be accounted for on any other theory than that of spiritual agency: Mr. S., who had received no particulars of his son's death until several months after his decease, intending to send for his remains, questioned the spirit as to the manner in which the body had been disposed of, and received a very minute and circumstantial account of the means which had been resorted to for its preservation, it being at the time embalmed.

"'Improbable as some of these statements seemed, they were, after an interval of four months, confirmed as literally true by a gentleman, then recently returned from California, who was with young Simmons at the period of his death. Intending soon to return to San Francisco, he called on Mr. Simmons to learn his wishes in relation to the final disposition of his son's remains.

"'I took down the particulars in writing by the permission of Mr. S., during his relation of the facts. I have many other narratives of a like character from persons of intelligence and veracity; but they could add nothing to the weight of that which I have just reported to you.'"

The following "test" of spiritual identity is inserted both on account of the ingenious method of representation employed by the spirits, and for the sake of Mr. Bartlett's valuable and well-accredited testimony.

TELEGRAPH PAPERS.

"Among the numerous investigators of the subject of spiritual philosophy is Mr. Bartlett, the well-known Mexican boundary commissioner. Mr. B. is a man thoroughly versed in science and natural philosophy, and is widely known, either personally or by reputation, throughout a large section of the United States.

"On the occasion of which I speak, Mr. Bartlett had gone, in company with ex-Senator Tallmadge, to the residence of Mrs. C. Laurie, of Washington, for the purpose of witnessing some of the manifestations. Mr. L.'s family are all mediums. Mr. B. was a stranger to the family, and was merely introduced by Governor Tallmadge as Mr. Bartlett, a friend of his. Soon the hand of Mr. L.'s daughter was moved to write the letters 'M. B.'

"No one present recognized the personage whose presence was thus indicated, and it was asked:

"'Were you a relative of this gentleman?' [Mr. Bartlett.]

"'No.'

"The hand of the medium was then made to draw the picture of a covered baggage or camp-wagon, drawn by a team of mules. To these objects were added, at a little distance, a large tree and the prostrate figure of a man, apparently dead, beneath it.

"'This,' said Mr. B., 'looks like a scene in Mexico. The wagon and the mules are just like those we used there. But I do not understand the man lying under the tree.'

"Hereupon Mrs. L., who is a very impressible medium, remarked:

"'I receive the impression that that man died a vioient death; and further, that his Christian name was *Marcus*.'

"Soon after, she added:

"'He lost his life by some means in connection with that tree, and I think his body must be buried beneath it.

"At this jnncture Mr. Bartlett was startled by the thorough recognition of the individual who was thus endeavoring to make himself known. He recollected him at once, as a man who had been attached to the boundary commission and whose name was *Marcus B.* This individual, in company with two others, had acquired a bad name among the members and *attachés* of the commission, and at length the three committed a high and daring crime, for which they were arrested and tried before a jury empanelled by Mr. Bartlett upon the spot, consisting of six Americans and six Mexicans, and the result was a condemnation to be hung upon the nearest tree. This sentence was promptly executed, and the three bodies were buried beneath the tree on which they had been hung!

"The invisible presence showed unmistakable evidence of satisfation at the recognition, and proceeded to say that he had come to ask Mr. B.'s pardon for his wrong deeds, adding that he did not impress Mrs. L. with his whole name, for the reason that he had a brother and a mother living in the State of ——, who did not know of his death or his journey through Mexico, and he did not wish to lacerate their feelings by any announcement which might spread from others.

"Mr. B. subsequently said that this statement was strictly true. He remembered the surname of the man who had thus unexpectedly and strangely come to him, and stated that his family were actually living in the remote State which had been designated by the spirit.

"No member of Mr. Laurie's family had ever heard of 'Marcus B.' or knew aught of his tragic death."

"NEW PHASE OF THE MANIFESTATIONS—SPIRITUAL TELEGRAPH, 1853.

"WAUKEGAN, *June* 7.

"DEAR BRITAIN, — Among numerous and remarkable facts occurring all over the land, furnishing incontestable proof of spiritual communion, the one I am going to relate may not be considered the least curious or interesting.

"A lady medium in this vicinity, Mrs. Seymour, when entranced, is in the habit of writing communications on her arms with the point of her finger — first on the left arm with the index finger of the right hand, and then *vice versa*. The writing is for some minutes illegible, but soon it begins to appear in raised letters that can be both seen and felt distinctly.

Yours truly
C Hammond

"At first these lines have a whitish appearance, but afterwards become a bright red, and can be as plainly seen and deciphered as chalk-marks on a wall. When examined by the sense of feeling, they impart the same unyielding impression to the finger as the ridges inflicted by the stroke of a whip, though the finger, in writing, is passed over the surface very lightly and rapidly. To the eye they look like a burn, or not unlike erysipelas. They remain thus distinct and legible for fifteen or twenty minutes, causing no pain or even unpleasant feeling, and then gradually fade away as they came, leaving the skin natural, smooth, and uncolored.

"The lady is also a speaking medium, and at the close of her address, in this manner, usually gives the name of the spirit who has been speaking, or answers questions by '*yes*' and '*no.*' Sometimes, however, she will write short communications, covering the whole arm from wrist to shoulder, in two or three lines, often commencing on one arm and finishing on the other. It is curious to witness the facility with which the arm is twisted to receive the successive lines. The philosophy and *rationale* of this is as puzzling to the sceptic—and I may say also to the believer—as many other wonders of this wonderful visitation to man.

"How the unseen operators manage to thus use the different portions of the living organism, the finger for a stile, the vital fluid as ink, and the living cuticle as parchment, it remains, perhaps, for Dodds, or the Devil, or some other aspirant for fame to account for, on the score of 'the involuntary powers of the mind,' or some such theory equally satisfactory and assininely luminous. W. B."

Since the publication of the above letter, written by an esteemed and reliable correspondent, many hundreds of persons have seen and borne witness to Mrs. Seymour's remarkable mediumship.

Several other mediums have recently been developed for the same phase of spirit-power, but as the above is the first public notice that appeared of this phenomenon it is deemed worthy of insertion here.

The following is an extract from the "notes of travel," written for the Boston *New Era* by the Rev. Charles Hammond, of Rochester, New York. This gentleman, it may be remembered, was one of the earliest investigators of Spiritualism through the mediumship of the Fox family. At the first few interviews which Mr. Hammond enjoyed with "the spirits" he became powerfully controlled as a personating, speaking, and trance medium. His physical system was violently exercised, and that contrary to his wish, or—in view of his ministerial capacity—to his sense of propriety.

In course of time, however, he became a writing medium and gave several interesting and voluminous works to the world, purporting to be communications dictated by spirits. He subsequently became a popular inspirational speaker, and it was in this mission that the observations were made, a few of which will be found as follows:

"NOTES OF TRAVEL.

"ROCHESTER, *July* 14, 1852.

"FRIEND BRITAIN,—Believing that the readers of the *Telegraph* would be gratified with a brief account of what I witnessed during my six weeks' tour to the West, I am induced to write to you, leaving you to judge and dispose of the matter as you may think proper. . . . . . .

"Along the entire path of my journey I found individuals of the highest respectability anxiously inquiring into the truth, and gladly receiving the light of spiritual communications. I made a short stay in Chautauque, where I found one rapping medium who received such instruction through my hand as resulted in developing her condition so as to become a writing medium. Several other persons were exercised very powerfully, even beyond their power of resistance. One young man took the pen without the least expectation that he could be moved, and in less than five minutes his hand began to shake, and shake more violently, as he offered resistance, then both hands, and afterwards his limbs, so that he could not sit or stand still, but began to dance to the astonishment of himself and friends. This exercise was continued for more than an hour, when he was released. He said it did not tire him in the least. . . . . . .

"From this county, I passed on to Cleveland, where I arrived on Sunday too late for the meeting of the Spiritualists. I, however, found a circle in the evening, far advanced in the philosophy of spiritual intercourse.

"During ten or twelve days, I had the pleasure of attending circles of Spiritualists every evening, beside visiting some forty or fifty families in the daytime. It is nearly impossible to describe the peculiar manifestations which I beheld, or the manner in which persons are exercised by spirits.

"The most remarkable are the speaking, pointing, and dancing mediums. The speaking mediums sometimes act and speak in a dialect wholly unintelligible to me, yet apparently well understood by those who are conversing. The circles being formed, mediums are instantly affected, as it were with a magnetic shock; their eyes become closed, and yet they act and move about the room with as much readiness as though they were conscious of everything about them. When the medium rises, however silent they may be, by a simple motion of the finger another is brought on the feet, and another, and so on, till the required number are unwillingly led into a circle, when the speaking commences, each alternately participating in the subject, under the control of spirits, who act upon the organs in such a manner as to force the utterance of words very readily and correctly. I have in my possession a very interesting dialogue which was repeated at the house of Mr. Kirkpatrick, in Ohio city. This dialogue was uttered in the Indian language, and was not at first understood until a translation was written out by my hand. The manner of its delivery was purely characteristic of the red man, and yet I had no idea of the subject until my hand involuntarily wrote it out. I also heard a French dialogue spoken by the same mediums, not one of whom understood the language. And however incredible it may seem, these mediums do not, as they inform me, become unconscious of the presence of the company, nor have they the power to sit down or do differently than they do. All that is done seems to be wholly mechanical, and the mediums may be regarded as the machinery, acted upon by an invisible power so as to induce manifestations of spirits, who control the voice, words, and gesticulation, and thus correctly identify themselves.

"The pointing mediums signify to each other by signs what is required, and their silent language is readily obeyed. I saw whole circles formed and placed in their proper order without a word being uttered.

"The dancing mediums are old and young, and of both sexes. Sometimes the dance is performed in a circle of three or four persons, but not always. The movements are very eccentric, yet often exceedingly graceful.

"There was a peculiar feature in this display of spirit-power which arrested my attention. No one who danced desired it, neither could they stop it. They sometimes made an effort [for they were conscious] to sit down or fall down, but they could not do either.

"A lady who had joined the Methodist Church in Cleveland, only two weeks previous, was thrown into a magnetic condition, and called for music, and after she had danced fifteen or twenty minutes was suddenly released and returned home.

"I saw several exhibitions of dancing during my stay in Cleveland, and I have reason to believe that such exercises may be necessary to prepare persons for mediumship. . . .

"Accompanied by Dr. A. Underhill and Mr. H. Camp, I visited Akron. We were cordially received, and met a large circle, convened on short notice at a private house.

"The most remarkable feature of spirit manifestations which I witnessed in Akron was the exercises of Miss R. and a daughter of Mr. Bangs, who had scarcely reached her teens, both of whom were unacquainted with music, yet acted upon by spirits in a way to play the most exquisite tunes upon the piano. I heard a great many pieces, difficult and plain, performed by both in a style that would do credit to the learned in musical science.

"My time being limited I pushed on to Adrian. Here I gave a public lecture, at the request of the Spiritualists, in the evening, and have only to regret that the largest hall in the place was too small for the congregation.

"There are several good mediums in Adrian, and I found them progressing. . . . From Adrian I proceeded to Rome. Here I met a circle at the house of Rev. Robert Wooden. Some four or five mediums met me here, and the number was doubled in twenty-four hours. . . . .

"In Addison I spent two days. A circle was formed, and we enjoyed a very pleasant season.

"Indeed, throughout the State there is scarcely a neighborhood without mediums and friends of the truth.

"In Chicago I tarried two days, met with two or three circles, and delivered a public lecture, which was well attended. In Illinois and Indiana there has been some excitement during the past winter, and I learned that it was constantly increasing. Mr. Eddy, of Chicago, is erecting a hall to accommodate a large congregation. . . . . .

"I next proceeded to Waukegan, by invitation of the several members of the 'Excelsior Society.' Here I gave three public lectures on Spiritualism, and found a great many warm friends of the new philosophy. 'The Excelsiors' number among them the most talented and respectable portion of the city, and they have held meetings twice every Sunday during the past year.

"In the morning a lecture is delivered on such moral or philosophical subjects as the lecturer prefers, and in the afternoon a conference, in which all are permitted to speak who wish.

"On the 3d of July I reached home, and nothing occurred during the whole journey to lessen the conviction that a great reform is contemplated by the spirits among the inhabitants of earth. I saw enough to satisfy me that no human power is competent to arrest or overthrow the work of progress.

"Yours, truly,

"C. HAMMOND."

The circumstances detailed in the following letter are inserted as illustrative of an immense array of facts of a similar character, which were occurring in the experience of the clergy shortly after the first manifestations at Rochester.

It answers the captious inquiry of those who marvel why the "elect and appointed ministers of God" were not favored with the out-pouring of the spirit in the same ratio as laymen. The truth is that hundreds of these reverend pastors of souls *were called* with the same urgency as the one in question, but unlike the Rev. S. B. Britain, R. P. Ambler, William Fishbough, Thomas Benning, and many others [now prominent as spiritual speakers] but few of the reverend body have had the courage or honesty to acknowledge fearlessly the source of their inspiration, or the supra-mundane nature of the power that attempted to deal with them. To "quench the spirit," and, "despise prophecyings," has hitherto been the approved clerical method in treating Spiritualism; hence it is that we select from many cases [some recorded in print, but still more, carefully suppressed, though known to and witnessed by the author] the opinions with which one honest though not very enlightened minister of the gospel viewed the approaches of the spirit in tangible demonstrations.

SPIRITUAL TELEGRAPH, NEW YORK.—A CLERICAL MEDIUM.

"It appears that the Rev. B. S. Hobbs, of Webster, New York, a clergyman of the Universalist denomination, has of late been controlled by spirits in a forcible and irresistible manner. His own account of his experience recently appeared in the *Christian Ambassador* of this city, and has since been copied into the secular journals. We subjoin the concluding portion of his letter:

"'By the request of the friends here I assumed the pastoral duties of this society, and I continued my labors for a period of nearly six months. I had then nearly came to the conclusion that the days of trial were past, and a better and *brighter* future would soon be mine. But the cherished hope was vain. In a moment when I least expected it, the bolt again fell, and I was crushed, in great sorrow, humiliation and anguish, to the dust.

"'It is proper here to say that this exhibition was the most painful, if not the strangest, of any I have experienced. My speech was first controlled while in the solemn act of prayer; and then I again was compelled to speak in a manner that, as before, led me to think it spiritual, and others to think me strangely diseased, if not partially insane. Before, when these more than dreadful trials were mine, the strange influence was of short duration. Not so, however, in the present instance. I was obliged, in spite of all my *efforts* to prevent it, to exhibit the character of the speaking medium in full, by addressing an audience on two different occasions, and going through the strangest ordeals common to the Spiritualism of the present age.

"'Nor did it end here; nor is it my duty now to say, the end is yet apparent. Soon my hand, as often before, was seized by the strange spirit-power and I was obliged to write its prophecies and sayings. This has continued for a few months past and the same work is yet going on, and from Sabbath to Sabbath I am acting, not as a Gospel minister, but as a spirit medium.'

"By this time the reader will inquire, 'Does not the writer believe in the fact of spirit intercourse?' The question shall be answered. I am unable to understand my strange experience in any other manner. It has from the first been my opinion that no derangement of mind could *possibly* do the work with which I have long been acquainted. But the ordeal has been so terrible that I have tried to account for it in some other way than it has ever claimed to originate. . . . . .

"I commend myself into the Father's hands, and to your Christian charity and brotherly love.

"B. S. HOBBS.

"WEBSTER, NEW YORK, *April* 27."

We shall conclude this chapter by a few extracts from the digest of correspondence received by the editors of the *Spiritual Telegraph*.

The cases selected are neither phenomenally strange, nor will our space allow us to insert more than about one per cent. of the number that one year alone could furnish; they are chosen simply for what their title signifies, namely: a "digest of correspondence," also as specimens of the progress of the movement; but above all, they are records, the entire authenticity of which the author is personally cognizant of.

"DIGEST OF CORRESPONDENCE.

"We have received a long communication from G. H. Baker, of Demming, Indiana, detailing some curious spiritual proceedings in that place. We have not room for the communication entire, but the leading facts which it details are, that the writer and others were on one occasion directed by the spirit to meet at a particular house and take a fiddler with them, and they were promised some demonstrations that would astonish them. The assembly having taken place, as soon as the fiddler commenced playing a number of persons became entranced, and commenced dancing in the most graceful manner, though several of them had been brought up Quakers and were entirely unused to that kind of exercise. A young girl of fifteen being also entranced was made to assume the position of moderator; and when some sceptical persons had for sport intruded themselves into the circle of dancers, she would seize them and lead them to the door.

"By mutual consent of the Spiritualists and Methodists a meeting was subsequently called with the understanding that the Methodist clergyman should preach a discourse against Spiritualism, and that Mr. D. Mong, a speaking medium who then happened to be in the place, should reply to him. The evening of the appointed meeting having arrived, the band of dancing mediums, some fifteen or twenty in number, were the first to enter the house. They commenced their gyratory operations to the no-small scandal of the Methodists, one of whom, being the moderator of the church, commanded them to take their seats.

"The only response he received was a blow upon the mouth, inflicted with the palm of the hand by the medium who was the moderator of the dancing circle, and the spirits insisted on taking their own time to finish the dance.

"A long discourse from the clergyman ensued, which was replied to by the spirit, through Mr. Mong; and during the proceedings a Methodist lady, the proprietor of the house where the meeting was holden, came under spiritual influence and bade adieu to the church; and an impression decidedly favorable to the spiritual cause appeared to be left upon the minds of the generality of the audience.

"Upon the question whether these spirits acted an orderly or disorderly part we have nothing to say; but if they were disorderly spirits, and those Methodist friends were really Christians, it does seem strange to us that they had not the power to rebuke them and cast them out—a power which, in the olden times, was considered as one of the necessary marks of true Christian discipleship. [See Mark xvi: 17.—*Ed. Telegraph.*]

"The editor of the Piedmont *Whig*, published at Warrenton, Virginia, who is not a convert to Spiritualism, says, in answer to the cry that the manifestations are all a juggle and humbug:

"'Here are many thousands of 'mediums,' many of them children four or five years old, exhibiting these things daily and nightly in the presence of hundreds of thousands of spectators, many of whom are shrewd, intelligent sceptics. Supposing the thing to be a trick, all these mediums, men, women, and children, must be respectively provided with a set of

Engraved at J.M. Butler's establishment 84 Chestnut St. Philad.a

Robt Hare M.D.

juggling apparatus of the most delicate and complicated character, sufficient to produce results which have all the outward appearance of miracles, but which must nevertheless be so easily managed and understood that a child can operate with it, and yet be so carefully and artfully concealed that thousands of eager, prying eyes cannot find it out. All these thousands of juggling machines in operation, and controlled often by young children, for four or five years, in the presence of hundreds of thousands of spectators, and not one solitary case of detection occurring in all that time! We cannot believe it. It seems to us as great an absurdity as the wildest theories of those who believe in the spirits. And if the thing is not a contrivance—a trick of the mediums—what is it? That's just what we want to know.'

"SPIRITS AND MEDIUMS IN TROY.

"Mr. W. H Vosburgh, of West Troy, writes us concerning some interesting developments which are occurring in that place, the essential particulars of which we condense as follows, not having room for the communication in full: A brother of Mr. Vosburgh, a lad of some sixteen years, becomes possessed by the spirits, who use him for various purposes, and among others for the purpose of diagnosing disease and prescribing its remedies. If while he is under spirit-influence, a stranger enters the room who is in any way diseased, the spirit who controls and speaks through him will detect the disease instantly, without a word being spoken by any person in the form, and will proceed to describe it without failure, proving thus that he has access to a source of knowledge which is beyond the reach of ordinary physicians in the body. Through another medium the spirits are giving lectures upon a variety of high subjects pertaining to natural and spiritual philosophy. The medium's education embraces the knowledge of no language besides the English, and yet his hand has been used to write *different languages*, and further, *both hands have been used at the same time, one writing on one subject and the other on another*.' These latter facts afford a knotty question for sceptics to solve consistently with the denial of spirit presence and influence."—*Telegraph Papers.*

The following is an incident occurring in the mediumship of a very gifted and well-known family of the highest respectability in Washington:

SPIRITUALISM IN WASHINGTON.

"THE RING EXPERIMENT—A GREAT TEST—SPIRIT LIGHTS—NEW YORK SPIRITUAL TELEGRAPH [1853.]

"DEAR SIR,—On Sunday, January 8, the spirits manifested their presence and their power in the following beautiful manner. The phenomenon occurred at the residence of Mr. C. Laurie in broad daylight and in the presence of several persons, among whom was the writer:

"Mr. Laurie's daughter, under spirit-influence, was directed to go to the piano, and place thereon a heavy gold ring. Having done so, her hand was brought up and placed over the ring in such a position that the fingers pointed downward toward it at a distance of about four inches. Presently the ring began to rise. The medium's hand was then moved still higher, and the ring followed it, approaching within some two inches of the tips of the fingers. It then slowly fell down toward the piano; when, having fallen some six inches, it gradually rose to its former position. It soon fell again, in the same gradual manner, but this time to a greater distance, a foot or more. As it once more slowly rose, the medium was made to bend backward, her head being thrown back, while her hand was raised and carried over her head, until the fingers pointed downward to the floor. The ring followed the hand, describing an arc in its passage over the medium's head, and dropped down some six inches from the tips of the fingers behind her, where it hung suspended in air. After remaining in this position a few moments, it dropped nearly to the floor, so slowly and beautifully as to satisfy every one present that *physical magnetism* was not the agent employed in producing its movements. Then it gradually rose again some fourteen inches or more. In this manner it kept rising and falling for some time, as if to convince each beholder that a power outside of and beyond any physical law controlled its motions.

"The hand was next moved slowly back, followed by the ring, and as the medium's body slowly regained its upright position, her hand was carried toward the wall, to which it approached within about three inches. The ring then commenced striking against the wall with a clear, ringing sound, like that of a glass bell. The hand at no time touched the wall, nor came nearer to it than the distance above stated; but the ring would leave the tips of the fingers, dart against the wall, return, and then repeat the act. It then followed the hand while it came back to its first position over the piano, where it again went through with the motions of falling and rising.

"The above beautiful experiment was plainly seen by all in the room, and the circumstances were such as to exclude all possibility of deception, if the medium had been disposed to deceive. But the persons present were only those of her own family, and one other besides myself; and the character of Mr. Laurie and his family would forbid the idea of trickery, even had the circumstances been otherwise.

"On one evening subsequently, the ring experiment was again given, but not quite so perfectly. It rose, however, some feet from the table, and followed the medium's hand again over her head, dropping down from behind her as before. Among the spectators on the latter occasion was the Hon. Joshua R. Giddings. Mr. E. W. Capron and a Senate reporter were also witnesses of the sight.

"In remarking on the above experiment to Mr. Giddings, I observed that it was a most beautiful one. The medium, who was then in a trance, soon after wrote as follows:

"'Well may you say how beautiful is the communion of the spirits with those of the lower sphere! And far more beautiful it will be as the cause progresses. Joy, peace, and Heaven, — all, all, shall be yours, and all connected with you in this holy cause. Glory to God the Most High!

"'BEN. FRANKLIN.'

"The following 'clincher' of a test occurred, I think, on the same day; but I will not be positive as to the precise time. Mr. Laurie, while quietly seated by the fire, was suddenly impressed with the presence and the name of the Rev. Mr. Wardlaw, of Glasgow, Scotland. So strong was the impression that he was forced to speak the name, and say, 'I am here.' In a moment more, on coming to himself, Mr. Laurie recollected that he had not heard of Mr. Wardlaw's death, and so remarked to his family. [Mr. Wardlaw had been an intimate friend of his father, the late Rev. James Laurie, who was long and well known to the people of Washington, and who in early life lived in Scotland.]

"The next week's steamer brought the news of Mr. Wardlaw's death, which had occurred at a date shortly previous to that of the visitation received by Mr. Laurie. Although Mr. Wardlaw was an eminent divine, and well known in Scotland and in this country, no one was further from the thoughts of Mr. Laurie at that particular time than he was, and his death was not then known in this country.

"On Sunday afternoon, January 22d, the little daughter of Mr. Laurie [in the spheres] manifested herself to her parents in the form of a large, bright *star*, which appeared on the wall. It was seen by all the family, and was so luminous as to light the otherwise darkened room to a high degree. It appeared as large as a *saucer* at first, but gradually contracted until it finally disappeared. One of the most remarkable things connected with this manifestation was the outline of a tiny *human form* — resembling the figure of a little girl — which was distinctly seen inside of the radiant star. The *hue* of the star is described by those who saw it to have been apparently like that of the most brilliant colors of the rainbow combined. It was seen by all the family who were present, which fact proves that it was no psychological effect, but a positive presence of spiritual elements and forces, presented in this most beautiful form of manifestation. The curtains were lifted from the windows, and the sunlight allowed to stream into the room and upon the wall where the star was fixed, but the latter still remained, and its "super-solar blaze" paled the ineffectual fires of the god of day. At length, upon the mother's involuntary approach toward the vision with outstretched arms, in an instinctive desire to retain the presence of her child, it vanished altogether.

"Yours, B."

CHAPTER XII.

THE PHENOMENA OF SPIRITUALISM IN THE EASTERN STATES.

"So mightily grew the word of God and prevailed."

"And when they heard these sayings, they were full of wrath, and cried out saying, 'Great is Diana of the Ephesians.'"

DR. ROBERT HARE, HIS METHODS OF INVESTIGATION, CONVERSION AND TESTIMONY — THE AMERICAN SCIENTIFIC ASSOCIATION AND ITS AIMS — DISTINGUISHED OPPONENTS — ROGERS, MAHAN, ELLIOTT, DODDS, AND BEECHER —"DEPRAVITY OF THE TIMES" — RICHMOND AND BRITAIN'S CONTROVERSY.

AMONGST the distinguished savans who became interested in the cause of Spiritualism was Dr. Robert Hare, Professor of Chemistry in the Pennsylvania University, and a gentleman whose successful researches into the occult branches of science had procured a world-wide celebrity for his name.

He first became an investigator in 1853, when, to use his own words, he "felt called upon, as an act of duty to his fellow creatures, to bring whatever influence he possessed to the attempt to stem the tide of "popular madness," which in defiance of reason and science, was fast setting in favor of the *gross delusion* called Spiritualism."

In pursuance of this humanitary impulse, the venerable professor, noticing that the said delusion was running a particularly rampart course in the city of his residence — Philadelphia — and in answer to a scientific inquirer on the subject of electricty, published a scathing letter in which, on "*electrical grounds*, he propounded a theory calculated to destroy even to annihilation the whole phenomena of Spiritualism, ending by the emphatic declaration that he "entirely coincided with Farraday's theory of table-turning." Whether Spiritualism was not in itself based on "electrical grounds," or that it might suffer decapitation a thousand times, and yet cry "I still live," it boots not now to inquire. Certain it is that tables would continue to turn, floors to rap, and ponderable bodies to float in space, though Professor Farraday had demonstrated so clearly that it was not in their nature to do so; and what was yet more remarkable, these sort of performances would keep on increasing in power and number, even after the *American Farraday* had added his dictum to that of his English *confrère* against the legality of these erratic physical proceedings.

To give all possible facility for outworking the Philadelphia professor's humane purpose of restoring bewitched humanity to its senses, the secular press throughout the country republished his letter with triumphant comments of their own; whilst two distinguished divines in New York, several in Boston, Philadelphia, Providence, Buffalo, and various cities of the West, actually made an electrical theory the subject of elaborate Sabbath-day discourses, and for the first time in the history of ecclesiasticism, religion joined issue with science in the pious attempts to prove either that we had no souls at all, or that they were more ignorant and powerless without their bodies than with them. Whilst the whole religious world were rejoicing over the destructive dictum of English and American science, combined in the persons of Farraday and Hare, a quiet under-current of influence was setting in an opposite direction, the result of which proved the glorification of Amer can Christendom to have been somewhat premature. The first action of this counter current will be better understood by the perusal of the following letter, the nature and authorship of which tells its own story:

"SOUTHWICK, MASS., *November* 17, 1853.

"PROF. HARE: *Dear Sir,*— I had the pleasure of a slight acquaintance with you something less than twenty years ago, when I exhibited telescopes in Philadelphia. You will, I trust, excuse the liberty I take in writing to you now. I have seen your letter in the Philadelphia *Inquirer* upon table moving. I never believed it was caused by electricity or galvanism, but is it not as likely to be these as muscular force? You agree with Professor Farraday that the table is moved by the hands that are on it. Now, I know as certainly as I can know anything, that this is not true in general, if it is in any instance. There is as much evidence that tables sometimes move without any person near them, as that they sometimes move with hands upon them. I cannot in this case doubt the evidence of my senses. I have seen tables move and heard tunes beat on them when no person was within several feet of them. This fact is proof positive that the force or power is not muscular. If any further evidence was necessary to set aside Professor Farraday's theory it is found in abundance in the great variety of other facts taking place through the country, such as musical instruments being played upon without any hands touching them, and a great variety of other heavy articles being moved without any visible cause. If tables never moved except when hands were on them, and if table turning constituted *all* instead of the least part of Spiritualism, the case would be different, but as they do move both with and without hands, it is plain that the true cause yet remains to be discovered.

"I wish, sir, you had time and opportunity to witness some other phases of this matter which seem not to have fallen under your notice, and I think you would be satisfied that there is less 'hallucination' and 'self-deception' about it than you have imagined.

"The *intelligence* connected with these movements yet remains to be accounted for.

"If these things can be accounted for on scientific principles, would it not be a great acquisition to science to discover what those principles are? If, however, science cannot discover them, the public are deeply interested in knowing the fact.

"No cause has yet been assigned that does not imply a greater absurdity than even to believe, as many do, that it is caused by spirits either good or bad, or both.

"Yours, respectfully,

"ASA HOLCOMBE."

This letter, which will be found in Professor Hare's elaborate work on "Spiritualism Scientifically Demonstrated," together with other inducements offered by personal friends of the professor's, at length resulted in his visit to a medium, then to another, and still others, until his investigations, stimulated by the fresh marvels that accumulated around him, put to flight all his *scientific* imaginings on the subject, and brought forth the gigantic array of testimony which was afterwards given to the world in the work on "Spiritualism," above alluded to, which was published in 1856.

To a mind like the professor's, imbued with all the principles of that materialistic system, which so many scientists determine *must* cover all mental as well as physical phenomena, the process of convertion was very slow—in fact, a battle in which the learned savant fought over every step of ground which the spirits gained. Besides testing the intelligence of the communicating power through an immense number of media, and in every conceivable form, Professor Hare invented all sorts of machinery through which he proposed to detect "tricky spirits." Even the description of these ingenious contrivances would fill a volume; we must therefore limit ourselves to a brief account which Mr. S. B. Britain published, of one of his "spirit traps," and an extract from the statement of the doctor himself, made to the New York Conference in 1854. Writing of Professor Hare's experiments with prepared machinery, Mr. Britain says:

PLATE I.

PLATE II.

"First, to satisfy himself that the movements were not the works of mortals, he took brass billiard balls, placed them on zinc plates, and placed the hands of the mediums on the balls, and to his very great astonishment the tables *moved.* He next arranged a table to slide backward and forward, to which attachments were made, causing a disc to revolve containing the alphabet, *hidden from the view of the mediums.* The letters were variously arranged, out of their regular consecutive order, and the spirit was required to place them consecutively, or in their regular places. And behold, it was done! Then followed intelligent sentences, which the medium could not see or know the import of till they were told him.

"Again he tried another capital test. The long end of a lever was placed on spiral scales with an index attached, and the weight marked; the medium's hand rested on the short end of the beam, where it was impossible to give pressure downward, but if pressed it would have a contrary effect, and raise the long end; and yet, most *astounding*, the weight was increased several pounds on the scale. These were all novel and very excellent contrivances, and will forever settle this question; and they should be published in every paper in the Union. Proceeding from *such an author*, all little quibblers will of course hide their puny heads forever."

NEW YORK CONFERENCE—SESSION OF SEPTEMBER, 1854.

"The conference assembled at the usual hour, with a pretty full attendance. After the business matters were disposed of, Mr. Partridge stated that as Professor Hare, of the Pennsylvania University, was present, it would, perhaps, be interesting to the assembly, if he would rehearse some of his wonderful experiences in regard to the evidences of spirit presence and power.

"Dr. Hare arose, went forward to the platform, and said, that 'perhaps there was nothing more astonishing in the history of science than that which was presented to the human mind in the fact that the presence of a frail boy or girl supplied the conditions for the exhibition of an invisible power, physical and intelligent, far transcending their normal capacities.' He said, that 'although all men had the power to witness these manifestations, yet there was, undoubtedly, something in the sphere or presence of a rigid sceptic, which interfered with the conditions, and stifled the outcoming of the phenomena.'

"In illustration of this, he stated that he once went into a room appropriated to *séances;* saw an ordinary dining table; examined it thoroughly, and could ascertain nothing unusual or extraordinary about it. A medium was present, and the table was repeatedly moved, without any apparently physical contact, and made to beat time to music.

"He then got upon the table, with his limbs hanging over the side, but without touching the floor, and it was raised repeatedly from the floor, with his superincumbent weight upon it, and made to beat time to a variety of tunes that were sung, the quavers and semi-quavers all being accurately touched off by it, all of which it was impossible for one in the form to accomplish.

"On a subsequent occasion, he took a gentleman—the editor of the *Daily Courier*—to the same place with him, when the phenomena were repeated, the table again beating time to the music with the gentleman upon it, and other equally extraordinary exhibitions of spirit-power. But afterward, he took a Professor of Dickenson College, who was a confirmed sceptic and opposer of the manifestations, to the same medium, and although the external conditions were apparently alike favorable, they failed to get the least manifestation of spirit-power. He told him to call again, and perhaps they would succeed better. After he was gone, the manifestations were produced as usual, and upon asking the spirits why they did not manifest in his presence, they said—'Tell him we could not do so, because he was himself a *counter or antagonist medium*, and that his presence annulled the power of the medium.'

"Subsequently he came again, and brought with him another gentleman, Dr. Bird, who was favorable to Spiritualism, and they all sat down together for the manifestations. The medium was forthwith entranced, and took the hand of Dr. Bird, when the manifestata- were, as usual, produced. The favorable influence of Dr. Bird had evidently countervailed the opposing sphere of the Dickenson Professor. He believed that the spirits had told the truth, when they stated that the sphere of some persons, and especially sceptics, was counter to that of the medium, and destroyed the power of the spirits to operate. Inasmuch as there were degrees of mediumship, it was natural to suppose that they shaded off, until they presented in some persons, and especially sceptics, a positive and antipodal power, which balanced and overcame that of the spirit through the medium.

"A friend of his in Philadelphia had a boy who was an excellent medium. He was often alone with him in his lecture-room, and witnessed a number of most extraordinary test manifestations. On one occasion, the spirit of his brother came and communicated. Said that he had died of dropsy, in intense pain, which was occasioned by the water oozing through the skin. He had died sixty-four years ago. The doctor said he was now seventy-six years of age—had survived all his family, and no one living knew the circumstances of that brother's death but himself.

"On another occasion, a spirit came, moved the spirit-scope, without any physical contact whatever, and spelt out the name of C. H. Hare, and upon being asked who it was, he replied, 'Your cousin from New Brunswick.' This was, in fact, a second-cousin of his, with whom he had but little acquaintance while he resided on earth. He had a basket, filled with a number of small glass and metallic balls, and the spirits would, without any visible contact, throw these balls about the room until the basket was emptied, and then again collect them in the basket. The boy-medium never took any money for his time or the exercise of his mediumship. His father, upon request, consented to let him accompany him on his recent trip to attend the session of the 'American Association for the Advancement of Science,' at Montreal. One evening, on their way to Canada, they were having a *séance*, with the boy for a medium, at Dr. Gray's, of this city. After the usual exhibition of the spirit phenomena, the boy could not find his cap. They searched high and low, through the room and house for it, but without success. The spirits told him to go without his cap; but, not liking to be seen in the streets without it, another was procured for him. After they had gone about a hundred yards from the house, the cap fell upon the table, in the presence of those who remained.

"Next morning, while yet in their state-room on board the boat, they found the door locked, and the key missing. They searched for a long time unsuccessfully, when the spirits said it was in the bottom of the carpet-bag. But the key of the carpet-bag was also gone, when the spirits said it was at the bottom of the trunk, and on taking out the baggage they found it and then found the key of the door at the bottom of the carpet-bag.

"When they arrived at Montreal, and put up at their hotel, he hunted his baggage for his toilet-case, but could not find it. The spirits told him it was under the bolster of his bed. He raised the bolster and searched, but could not find it. He had his eye upon the boy all the time. The spirits told him to look again; and upon raising the bolster again, precisely where he had looked before, he found it. It was impossible, he said, that the boy could have done this, for he stood in the same place all the time, and could not have moved without his seeing him.

"The next evening they went to a large party, at the house of a lady, to hold a circle. They had packed the spirit-scope, balls, and other apparatus in the carpet-bag. There were many sceptics and disagreeable persons present; many counter-mediums, as he supposed. When they came to open the carpet-bag they could not find the key. They went to the table, but could not get any communications. They entered into another room with the boy, and the spirit spelled out, by means of raps, that he would get the key before he got home. Whilst he was riding along the streets of Montreal on his way home, the key came down upon his breast!

"On another occasion, while alone with the boy in their room, and after they had just locked up the balls, spirit-scope, shaving-case, etc., in his carpet-bag, the balls were in some inscrutable way, taken from the carpet-bag, and fell upon him in a shower. Then came the box, razor-strap, etc., all falling, apparently from above, on and around him.

"Upon entering his room one evening, he discovered his spirit-scope, which he had previously locked in his carpet-bag, hanging high upon the frame of the bar of his bedstead. It was so high that the boy could not reach it without procuring something to stand upon much higher than the bed. He then called the chambermaid and interrogated her in regard to it, but she replied that she could not account for it. While they were still together talking about it, the spirit-scope came down beside him on the floor. This, he said, could not have been performed by either the boy or the girl, because he *saw* that they did not do it.

"The doctor related many similar instances of the exhibition of spirit power which took place during his recent journey. He said that he had been engaged in scientific pursuits for upwards of half a century, and his accuracy and precision had never been questioned until he had become a Spiritualist, whilst his integrity as a man had never in his life been assailed until the Harvard Professors fulminated their report against that which he *knew* to be true, and which they did not know to be false."

These meagre details of simple facts by no means constitute the whole or even a tithe of the phenomena with which Professor Hare's experiences abound.

The high reputation of this gentleman for scientific attainment, his invincible love of truth and unimpeachable integrity, no less than the ingenuity which he displayed in his early investigations, and the keen acumen which he brought to bear upon all phenomena of a supra-mundane character, from the trifling facts above narrated to experiments involving the most serious consequences to fortune and reputation, made his accession to the cause of Spiritualism a subject of as much importance to its friends as it was the theme of bitter vituperation, insult, and calumny, from its opponents.

For instance, the Havard Professors, of whom the learned doctor had long been an admired colleague and friend, denounced his "insane adherence to the gigantic humbug" with an insolence which our sense of decency forbids us to reprint; but the culminating point of insult which the venerable gentleman was doomed to experience, because he would persist in recording facts as he found them and defending the truth which he had proved, was dealt by the hands of the body with whom for many years he had been associated, and whom the commonest usages of civilization should have restrained from heaping affronts on the white hairs of him who had heretofore been their shining light and distinguished ornament.

The transaction to which we allude was the impertinent action of one of the members of the "American Scientific Association," sanctioned by the majority of that distinguished body, and subsequently endorsed by *all* of them in their proceedings. In the *Telegraph's* very mild yet significant account of the meeting, no details are given of the coarse and ungentlemanlike tone of the discussion which bullied Professor Hare into silence; still, as the subject of Spiritualism was not deemed a "proper one" for that grave and learned body to discuss, and the *Telegraph* clearly sets forth what, in the same session, *was found to be a proper subject for discussion*, we shall give the report verbatim, leaving the world to judge of the fitness of "the American Scientific Association" to *comprehend*, even if they were willing to discuss the sublime truths of Spiritualism.

TELEGRAPH PAPERS.

"The American Scientific Association has just closed its annual session in this city [Washington, D. C.] The meetings were held in the lecture room of the Smithsonian Institute. Before the close of the session, Professor Hare, of Philadelphia, read to the convention an invitation, made on the part of the Spiritualists of Washington by a committee, to attend the lecture of Rev. T. L. Harris, on Spiritualism, on Saturday evening, April 29th. In the midst of the reading of this paper, Professor Henry entered the hall, and upon hearing the subject of 'Spiritualism' mentioned, he turned red in the face and interrupted Professor Hare by this inquiry: 'I would be glad to know, Mr. President, if *this* subject *is in order?* Professor Hare remarked, that whether the *subject* were in order or not, it was hardly in order to interrupt a member of the convention in that manner before he had finished reading his communication. Professor Henry replied that this was '*a dangerous subject* to be introduced into this convention;' that it had better be *let alone*, and he moved that it be laid upon the table. The invitation was finally laid upon the table.

"It would seem that a subject like this was one which would lie peculiarly within the domain of 'science.' But the 'American Association for the Promotion of Science' decided that it was either unworthy of their attention or dangerous for them to meddle with, and so they voted to put the invitation on the table.

"We cannot omit in this connection to mention that the 'American Association for the Promotion of Science' held a very learned, extended, grave, and profound discussion at the same session, *upon the cause why 'roosters' crow between twelve and one o'clock at night!* Several very ingenious explanations were, we believe, adduced to account for this remarkable phenomenon, which the 'American Association for the Promotion of Science' justly regarded as a question naturally challenging their most serious investigation, and to the task of accounting for which they resolved to bring to bear the combined force of their highest energies. It was finally decided by the association that the important fact that roosters crow at half-past twelve o'clock at night is to be only accounted for on the supposition—strongly sustained, however, by well-ascertained collateral facts in science—that at that particular hour *a wave of electricity* passes over the earth's surface, from north to south, which disturbs the fowls in their slumbers, and being naturally of a *crowing disposition* they all, on being thus wakened and aroused, with one accord set lustily at work a-crowing! We think the 'American Association for the Promotion of Science' have hit the mark at last. They deserve well of their country for having made the above important acquisition to the discoveries of science, and the members who were chiefly instrumental in bringing the subject up and arriving at the conclusion which was adopted should be voted a medallion by Congress. The obverse side of the medal might appropriately bear the image of a barn-yard cock in the attitude of crowing, with the inscription beneath, '*Eureka!*' while the reverse could with propriety represent a cluster of clucking old hens."

One thing was certain, Dr. Robert Hare had become a Spiritualist; and as a lecturer, writer, teacher, and investigator, the youngest soldier in the cause grew tired by his side.

His revered name and the long and brilliant siege which his tenacious opinions endured before he yielded full credence to the spiritual character of his besiegers; the insults which he meekly suffered for the cause of truth, and the rich legacy of spiritual experiences which he has left to the world, render his name a bulwark in "the Spiritual City" and his conversion a memorable era in the history of the cause.

The Rev. Adin Ballou, of the respected ministerial family of that name, had long professed his firm faith in the manifestations, and by writing and public lectures nobly sustained his opinions. The Rev. Allan Putnam, of Roxbury, Massachusetts, and the distinguished poet, scholar, divine, and orator, Rev. John Pierpont, of the same State, also entered the ranks, and performed valuable service for the faith, of which fuller notices will be found in the record of New England Spiritualism; indeed, the shining list of names, great in American annals, if not made prominent with the toy dignities called titles, were extending to a formidable length in every State of the Union.

And now once more let us inquire into the nature of the opposition that was brought to bear against Spiritualism, without, however, in a single instance retarding its progress, or winning back its converts from their faith.

Of the character of the itinerants professing to lecture against it, or give "public demonstrations of the modes in which the raps, etc., *were made*," Messrs. Grimes and Burr form a fair specimen. Trickery, collusion, and a set of dangerous manipulations with the joints, which every physiologist declared could not be continued for three months without developing diseases of the most ruinous character, with a plentiful mixture of libellous falsehoods and defamatory mis-statements, made up the stock in trade of this set of mountebanks.

Still a lower, and more unprincipled class were represented by one Anderson, a professed juggler, who, presuming on the interest which attached to the subject of Spiritualism, attempted to make capital out of it by advertising *immense sums* to be given by way of challenge to the Spiritualists, etc.

All who have ever had the patience to listen to or read the reports of this man's gasconading, will confess that Grimes and Burr were respectable, compared to him. Yet in despair at the lack of better weapons, there have not been wanting those who, when *out* of *the presence of Spiritualists*, and speaking with bated breath, would protest that "*Professor* [?] Anderson had explained all about the raps, and killed Spiritualism right out" Leaving all the small fry of this character to the ignominy which has long since swept over their names, let us glance briefly at the efforts of those whose position in society entitled the world to expect from them something at least worthy of their names.

To commence with those who assume to be the highest literary and scientific authorities on this subject, let us notice the work of Dr. C. C. Rogers, of Boston, who filled a volume with what he called, "The Philosophy of mysterious Agents, Human and Mundane." In strict accordance with the title of his work, Dr. Rogers has favored us with a treatise so eminently *mysterious* that the only comprehensible idea we can glean from it is, that though the manifestations do actually occur, nevertheless they are not the *work of spirits.*

Still, as somebody or something must be answerable for that power which had proceeded from the turning of a table to the turning upside down of an entire continent, the Doctor gravely enunciates a theory which lays the whole burden of the manifestations on the *cerebrum,* which is supposed *somehow* to act somewhat in the way described by one of Dr. Rogers's newspaper eulogists in a criticism on his work which reads as follows: "He said that he thought the revelations were not spiritual, but a cerebral automatic movement, depending for its development upon the idiosyncratic temperament of each individual, inspired through the spinal centres by a mundane process of electrized vitality acting upon every molecule of the system."

As this sentence includes a quotation from Dr. Rogers's book—in fact, claims to be a compendious definition of its meaning—it implies on the part of the writer a condition of lucidity to which few persons besides the Boston editor could arrive after attentively perusing the book. As an example of the effect produced by this *occult* work on less enlightened journalists, we quote a second criticism, which appeared in the columns of the *Cincinnati Commercial,* and which though obviously written in the spirit of satire, is not an inapt description of more learned stuff than that of Dr. Rogers's on the subject of the manifestations.

The extract reads as follows:

> The only true and legitimate manner of accounting for the taps is the physiological defect of the membraneous system. The obtuseness of the abdominal indicator causes the cartilaginous compressor to coagulate into the diaphragm, and depresses the duodenum into the flandango. Now, if the taps were caused by the vogation of the electricity from the extremities, the *tympanum* would also dissolve into spiritual sinctum, and the olfactory ossificator would ferment, and become identical with the pigmentum.
>
> "A friend of ours, who graduated with 'distinguished honors' at one of the Northern universities, says that he must dissent *in toto* from the idea that the 'depression of the duodenum into the flandango' could, by any possibility, cause the 'olfactory ossificator to ferment, and become identical with the pigmentum.' He says the thing cannot be done; and after quoting several learned authorities on the subject, winds up his argument by the remark, that:
>
> "'The vibratory motion communicated to the tunica albugenia by the parturition of the alveola process, effectually disintegrates the cerebellum, and predisposes the patient to preternatural distension of the auricular membraneous orifice; in which case, the rappings become painfully and distinctly audible!'
>
> "Now, whether this is, or is not so, we will not undertake to say, but will leave the whole matter in the hands of the learned savans, in the full confidence that little can be added to the above triumphant and incontrovertible exposition."

As if to compensate for the undue share which Dr. Rogers assigned to the cerebrum in turning the world upside down, Dr. Dodds, another learned philosopher, came to the rescue, with a theory of equal lucidity, which accounted for all the mischief, by the "automatic action of the cerebellum"; both gentlemen agreed that the nerve centres had something to do with it, but the particular way in which they acted, whether in conjunction with the cerebrum or the cerebellum, was precisely what constituted the cream of the *mystery*, and what neither of the learned doctors would or could explain.

Unfortunately for the success of the back-brain theory of Dr. Dodds, just as it was midway in its career, and seemed likely to divide the honors with the front-brain theory of Dr. Rogers, the cerebellum advocate himself became a convert to Spiritualism, and by aid of his accomplished daughter, Miss Jennie Dodds, a medium of fine oratorical capacity, carried into the fold of the spiritual church, a much larger number of converts than his "back-brain" theory had ever found readers.

Soon after the first issue of the *Spiritual Telegraph* in 1852, Dr. Richmond, of Ohio, a gentleman of profound learning and research, commenced a series of papers, which were published in the New York *Tribune*, antagonistic to the claims of Spiritualism.

At the suggestion of Mr. Greeley, chief editor of the *Tribune*, Dr. Richmond consented to engage in a friendly discussion with Mr. S. B. Britain, the arguments, *pro* and *con*, being published in the *Spiritual Telegraph*, and continuing to instruct and entertain a rapidly-increasing circle of readers for over seven months. The learning and ability displayed on both sides by these able disputants not only contributed vastly to the enlightenment of the public, but aided, to a great extent, the circulation of the *Spiritual Telegraph*, in which they were published.

To answer the increasing demand for these valuable articles, they were subsequently reprinted, in pamphlet form, and passed through many editions, every one of which was rapidly exhausted.

The arguments of Mr. Britain were, for the most part, based upon reasons derived from an immense array of pertinent facts; those of Dr. Richmond were chiefly attempts to make the facts fit his peculiar theories. According to these, the manifestations were the production of disease, hysteria, hallucination, excessive excitement, etc. Dr. Richmond brought an immense number of cases forward in illustration of his theories, and concluded a very interesting, though far-fetched *resume* of his arguments, by the following statement: "All intense, long-continued excitement, political, religious, or mental, will induce this state of mind. I pronounce it to be a diseased condition, and *all spirit manifestations* to be the work of spirits in the body."

Not in the spirit of retaliation, but in simple justice to the truths of history, and as a specimen of the kind of warfare through which Spiritualism has marched onward to its present triumphant position, we feel bound to reprint the criticism of the New York *Times* on the Richmond and Britain Discussion pamphlet, which the publishers had courteously forwarded to the office of that journal for review. The first notice which appeared in the New York *Times* was as follows—

"DISCUSSION OF THE FACTS AND PHILOSOPHY OF ANCIENT AND MODERN SPIRITUALISM; by S. B. BRITAIN and Dr. B. W. RICHMOND. New York: Partridge and Britain:

"Appended to the fly-leaf of the copy of this work with which we were honored, was a printed notice from the publishers, drawing our attention especially to the book, and concluding with these words:

"'We are now rapidly extending our list of publications, and shall be pleased to send you, from time to time, the better class of our books, should we learn, from this experiment that you are disposed to treat them fairly.' We are very much obliged to Messrs. Partridge and Britain for their consideration; but could none of their spirits inform them (is not Mr. Britain himself a medium?) that we should certainly treat the present book most unfairly? For, of course, *treating it fairly* means praising the book, the medium, and the spirits.

Now, we can do neither; we have, on the contrary, very harsh things to say of all parties concerned, and the book into the bargain. Messrs. Partridge and Britain will not thank us for our opinion of the 'better class' of their publications, if the present work is to be considered a specimen. They must understand that we look upon the spirit-rapping question as a most detestable swindle; while we believe that many of the mediums are poor, deluded creatures, we are convinced that the projectors and promoters of the affair are knaves, as infamous as ever served out a life sentence in a State-prison.

"Of this particular work, which purports to be the record of a controversy between a believer and a sceptic, we can only say that, if it were not saved from our loathing by its stupidity, the evident collusion between the pretended disputants would disgust us. A more dishonest book has surely never been published in any country. We do not, after this judgment, expect to be favored with any more of Messrs. Partridge and Britain's publications."

On the publication of this audacious article, Mr. Britain addressed the editor of the *Times* in the following letter:

"*Editors of the Times:*

"GENTLEMEN,—My attention has been called to your notice of my recent discussion with Dr. Richmond, of Ohio, wherein I find a simple remark, which must serve to excuse what you might otherwise regard as an unnecessary obtrusion.

"It is not my purpose to controvert your opinions, nor to meddle with the question which involves the facts and philosophy of the present spiritual movement. Respecting the supposed delusion of the media, and the alleged knavery of the prominent Spiritualists, I have nothing whatever to say. Time and the succession of human events will determine whether their claims are well or ill founded.

"The single remark in your criticism, which gives me a claim to your indulgence, in the present instance, is the following:

"'Of this particular work, which purports to be the record of a controversy between a believer and a sceptic, we can only say, that if it were not saved from our loathing by its stupidity, the evident collusion between the pretended disputants would disgust us. A more dishonest book surely never appeared in any country.'

"As the above language charges the respective parties in the aforesaid discussion with manifest collusion and unmitigated dishonesty, I must be allowed to repel the charge, and to insist that the circumstances of the case are utterly irreconcilable with that assumption, in proof of which I submit the following brief statement of facts:

"First, The writer of this *never even heard of Dr. Richmond* until his articles against Spiritualism appeared in the daily papers. Moreover, it is impossible to disguise the fact that the Doctor's letters to the *Tribune* were extensively *copied* and widely *endorsed* by the secular press, as affording a complete refutation of the spiritual theory. At that time, no one doubted Dr. Richmond's disposition, and few, except Spiritualists, questioned his *ability* to demolish the whole fabric of spiritual philosophy.

"Second, The invitation to engage in a critical examination of the facts and philosophy of the manifestations emanated from Dr. Richmond himself, who insisted that he could account for all the phenomena on purely natural principles or physical laws.

"Third, Personally, Dr. Richmond, *even to this very hour*, is a stranger to me. I do not know that we were ever within five hundred miles of each other.

"Fourth, Our mutual correspondence has been limited to the published controversy, and the few brief epistles necessary in the arrangement of preliminaries and the transaction of business.

"Such, gentlemen, are the facts; and your readers will judge whether they afford any evidence of *collusion*, or of the slightest disposition, on our part, to deal unfairly with the public.

"Allow me to add, in conclusion, that while I have hitherto invited no man to a discussion of this subject, I have never shunned a public interview with an intelligent opponent. Any ordeal which recognizes authentic facts and logical deductions as the legitimate means of trial, will still find me ready; and, should you, gentlemen, after the perusal of this letter, be disposed to entertain your first impressions that the discussion already published *was not* entered into and conducted in good faith, and with a view to elicit the truth, perhaps it may be within your province to propose some advocate of the material hypothesis, in whose fidelity and ability you have confidence.

"Should you find it convenient to designate such a man, I shall readily accord to his personal claims, and those of the subject of our inquiry, the respect and attention which they shall seem to require.

"Yours respectfully,

"NEW YORK, *September* 21, 1853. S. B. BRITAIN."

Mr. Brittain goes on to remark :—

"Our accusers did not deem it proper to allow us a hearing in our own defence.

"The foregoing letter was *suppressed* without a word of apology from the editor of the *Times*, whose shameless abandonment of the principles of honorable dealing may be justly inferred from the subjoined editorial remarks, which appeared in their next issue."

"'SPIRIT RAPPINGS.

"'Mr. S. B. Britain, who asserts, we believe, the spiritual nature of the rappings, table movings, etc., about which so much noise has been made, writes to us, denying that there was any 'collusion' between him and Dr. Richmond in their recent controversy upon this subject. He gives sundry reasons in support of his assertion, which, however, is just as good without them as with them. Mr. Britain invites us to designate some person to hold a further controversy with him upon this subject. We do not happen to owe any of our acquaintances so deadly a spite as to lead us to recommend that he should engage in such a task. There are, probably, many ways in which more positive evil may be done, than by studying, writing, or reading upon this subject; but we know none in which time can be more utterly wasted, or from which less good can possibly be derived. It is the easiest thing in the world for a fluent writer to cover reams of paper with interminable disquisitions upon this topic, and it is not very difficult, as things go, to procure their publication. But we can conceive no task more dreary or unprofitable than that of reading them. Every now and then we hear of some poor creature, whose brains have been addled by their devotion to such studies; and the only reason why we do not hear of more is because the majority of those who enter upon such pursuits are either destitute of brains altogether, or else, they are hopelessly addled in advance.

"'We think Mr. Britain would have shown a much stronger faith in his spiritual gymnastics if he had accepted the offer, recently published in our columns, of one hundred dollars to any medium who would move the tables, or answer the questions of the gentleman who made the offer. The money was in our hands, and the offer was repeatedly published in our columns; but as no medium came forward, we were compelled to return the money. If Mr. Britain, however, chooses to accept it now, we presume the offer would be renewed. This would be a much more decisive and satisfactory mode of settling this question than by such a controversy as Mr. B. proposes. What does he say to it?'"

Again Mr. Britain writes:

"To give the *Times* a chance to redeem its credit by some show of moral courage, if any such latent element remained in its nature, we forwarded the following communication to the *Tribune:*

"'READY FOR TRIAL.

"'*To the Editor of the New York Tribune:*

"'SIR,—Some days since, the *Daily Times* charged Messrs. Britain and Richmond, the parties to the late discussion of Spiritualism, with 'evident collusion' and dishonest dealing with the public. Whereupon the writer of this addressed a civil letter to the editors of that journal, denying the charge, and specifying certain facts and reasons which from their nature utterly preclude the existence of such alleged collusion and dishonesty.

"'Instead of publishing the letter, the *Times* renewed its assault in the peculiar spirit which has already given it a mean distinction, and concluded by proposing what it was pleased to regard as a 'decisive and satisfactory mode of settling this question'—the claims of Spiritualism.

"'One of its correspondents had previously offered one hundred dollars for the production of certain phenomena, and the *Times*, to conceal the cowardice of its unprovoked and unprincipled attack on Britain and Richmond, and the leading Spiritualists, who were all characterized as 'knaves as infamous as ever served out a life sentence in a State prison,' calls on the writer to accept the offer of its correspondent.

"'The object of this communication is to signify that the party whose name is subscribed below will accept the challenge, *with or without the accompanying offer of* one hundred dollars, provided the first can be so modified that the *Times* and its correspondent will enter into the following fair and equitable arrangement:

"'First, The undersigned will designate two distinguished citizens of New York, who are known to the public and are above the suspicion of personal or other improper motives; the

Times shall appoint two of like reputation for candor and honesty, and the four thus selected shall name a fifth. The parties so chosen shall constitute a committee to investigate any phenomena that may occur in the presence of such mediums as the undersigned shall select.

"'Second. The committee shall have twelve sittings, or a greater number if the majority of the same shall so decide; and at the close of the investigation it shall report the result.

"'Third. The committee shall be privileged to select the place of meeting, which may be changed, if preferred, at each succeeding session.

"'Fourth. The *Times* and the *Spiritual Telegraph* shall each publish whatever the committee shall be pleased to submit as its report of the essential facts elicited by the proposed investigation.

"'As it does not comport with the illiberal and unjust policy of the *Times* to give publicity to any reply to its unfounded accusations, I am forced to depend on your more liberal and widely-circulated journal, to enable me to reach the general public before which I am accused.

"'Very truly yours,

"'S. B. BRITAIN.

"'NEW YORK, *September*, 23, 1853.'

"How did the *Times* treat this proposition? Why, after the manner which has characterized all of its class—it did not notice it at all. It was silent. We have ever been ready to submit the whole subject of spiritual manifestations to any just ordeal, however severe. We have expressed and otherwise manifested that disposition on numerous occasions, through these columns, before public assemblies, and in social circles.

"When Professor Mattison assailed Spiritualism, and we were sent for to vindicate its claims, we neglected other duties and went to New England to answer the call. The Spiritualists at West Winsted offered to pay Mr. Mattison's expenses and to give him twenty dollars to come back and support his unwarrantable assumption in presence of the writer. But our astronomical friend had already reached his *aphelion*, and owing to the distance of that part of his orbit, he could not return in season.

"The prince of jugglers, Anderson, on one occasion gave a vaunting challenge and offered five hundred dollars to any person in the United States who would produce the spiritual phenomena at Metropolitan Hall. Mr. Charles Partridge presented himself at the hall, and proposed to make an effort to obtain the required results, on condition that Professor Anderson would consent to abide the decision of an impartial committee.

"Notwithstanding Mr. Partridge positively declined to accept the money, in any event, the Professor would not hazard a fair trial. He, however, became greatly excited and abused Mr. Partridge and the mediums. In his confusion he called on the Lord and the New York Volunteers, and, of course, disgusted the sensible portion of his audience.

"Mr. Partridge has elsewere made a similar offer, and on one occasion through the columns of the *Tribune*. The believers in Spiritualism have never declined any fair trial; but how has it been with the opposition? Many of our valiant opposers have kept themselves out of sight, while they have hurled their missiles in the form of challenges and denunciations. They have assumed various disguises that they might stab in secret at the most vital interests of truth and humanity. Whenever we have offered to meet them openly and in a scientific spirit, they have uniformly insisted on imposing unjust conditions and unnatural restraints. They claim that the manifestations, if they occur, must obey the laws of material nature, and insist that they shall be tested by such modes and formula as are alone applicable to the domain of physics.

"When, occasionally, we have driven hypocrisy to its last resort, by proposing terms which sophistry can neither cavil at nor evade, these conscientious opposers became suddenly taciturn.

"Now we desire our readers and the public to observe and remember that *we are in constant readiness for a fair trial;* but our judges must be honorable men.

"We do not propose to go to the *Times* office to turn over the editor's table with or without human hands, and leave him to tell the story, for the reason that we can not depend on the accuracy of his statements. Men who dispute the most obvious facts and principles are in no case the most reliable witnesses, and whoever will falsely accuse and slander even the humblest disciple of the truth, *for nothing*, may not scruple to defame truth itself for '*one hundred dollars*.'"

Such was the conduct of one of the most authoritative of the New York journals, for no other apparent motive than because Dr. Richmond, from whose known ability and personal antagonism to Spiritualism so much had been expected, *failed* signally in overthrowing the arguments of Mr. Britain in the discussion. It is but justice to add that the venomous character of this poison worked its own antidote, calling forth several manly and generous protests from different New York journals against the atrocious conduct of the *Times*. Amongst these, was a frank statement from Mr. Greeley of the *Tribune*, declaring the entire absence of any collusion or even a personal acquaintance between the disputants, concluding as follows:

> "These facts bear their own comment on their face. Whatever may be the truth respecting what is called 'Spiritualism,' we know that Messrs. Partridge and Britain are not scoundrels; that there was no 'collusion' between them and Dr. Richmond; and that the *Times* has acted in these premises exactly like the *Times*."

Besides the agitation which was excited by the narrow-minded selfishness and severity of the pulpit and press, three powers, more just, severe, and authoritative than all the world beside, have been sitting at the bar of judgment to decide on the claims of Spiritualism. These are Time, Progress, and Public Opinion. Their verdict has been rendered in during the twenty years that modern Spiritualism has been on trial before them, and their sentence is, "Spiritualism is a truth, and will live forever."

These same unimpeachable judges have also been dealing with the New York *Times;* and though the opinions of its editors on the subject of Spiritualism now are entirely unknown to the author, the tone of its columns is of such a nature as to justify the belief that its editorship is in the hands of *gentlemen*, who, however they may be personally opposed to the spiritualistic belief, *could not now*, as formerly, be found attacking it with the weapons of falsehood and vulgar abuse.

The next of the valiant crusaders against Spiritualism whom our limits will allow us to notice is a Mr. Charles Elliott.

This gentleman was the author of a book, which he was rash enough to publish in 1852, a period too early to furnish him with much more available material than was to be found in all the then-extant slanders against the Fox family, and the queries as to whether the phenomena claimed by the Rev. Dr. Phelps, of Stratford, to be performed by spirits were not *actually the work of the venerable gentleman himself, or that of some of his family*. Had Mr. Charles Elliott's treatise on "mysteries," or "glimpses of the supernatural," fortunately fallen into the hands of a discerning editor, he might have been spared the expense of publishing a whole volume by the condensation of its material into the following pithy sentences, which will be found to embody all that the author has labored to prove in two hundred pages, namely: *All the manifestations recorded in the Bible are true all others are the work of shallow imposture.*

Next came a volume of about the same size as Elliott's, written by the Rev. H. Mattison, A.M., Professor of Natural Philosophy and Astronomy, and member of the same distinguished body that treated the venerable Dr. Hare with the *courtesies* referred to in the former portion of this chapter.

The title of this book — "Spirit Rapping Unveiled, an *exposé*," etc. — will sufficiently explain the basis of his *argument*. Suffice it to say, that, although his ground, like that of Mr. Elliott's, was wholly occupied with slanderous stories and newspaper libels against the Spiritualists, still, as he wisely took advantage of these three years later for their accumulation, his book possessed that additional claim at least to public notice.

Next comes a book from which the community, whether of spiritual or materialistic tendencies, had a just right to expect some revelations which should help them to unravel the modern "mystery of mysteries." For was it not written by Professor Mahan, President of Cleveland University, and did it not undertake, in nearly five hundred closely-printed pages, to show that it was "modern mysteries explained and exposed?" But alas for the mystery, and still more for the explanation promised! the best that the Professor could do was to deepen the *mystery* past all finding out, and this he accomplished by actually attributing the production of "Nature's Divine Revelations," "The Great Harmonia," "Penetralia," etc., together with all the rappings, tippings, visions, cures, apparitions, disclosures, clairvoyant revelations, spirit lights, floatings, heavings, dancings, writings, and contents generally of twenty or more large journals, and several hundreds of volumes and pamphlets, to the work of odyle.

Wonderful odyle in Professor Mahan's eyes! Unhappily, however, for the credit of the Cleveland University's president, the odylic theory found no favor even with the bitterest antagonists of Spiritualism. The press generally were dissatisfied with the learned gentleman's shallow *addition to the mysticism* of the subject, and even the New York *Times* was ashamed of him, concluding a pathetic lamentation over his failure with admitting that, "We sigh for some means of *explaining the explanation*, and we do not attempt criticism on a book which we find it impossible to understand."

To conclude the list of learned and pious foes who brought their battering-rams to bear against this impregnable fortress, and like the Prince de Condé after his twenty-one days' siege of the Bastile, were forced to retreat, leaving the walls as they found them, "only a little stronger." It but remains for us to record the attack of a certain "theological giant," by whose onslaught it was confidently believed, if never before, the demon of Spiritualism must yield up the ghost. The method of attack in this instance was on this wise: At a regular meeting of the Congregational Association of New York and Brooklyn, the Rev. Charles Beecher was appointed to prepare a report on the spiritual manifestations. This was faithfully executed and read before the association at its session of April, 1853. In his entire treatment of the subject Mr. Beecher certainly maintained, both with the friends and opponents of the cause, the character of a gentleman, a scholar, and a Christian. Mr. Beecher assumed that spirits could only obtain access through prepared odylic conditions; he maintained that "this was the method by which the spirit communicated through the ancient prophets and apostles," and added that "to substitute any other theory cuts up by the roots large portions of the prophetic Scriptures."

> "Whenever," he says, "odylic conditions are right, spirits can no more be repressed from communicating than waters from jetting through the crevices of a dyke." And again:
>
> "Whatever physiological law accounts for odylic phenomena in all ages, will in the end inevitably carry itself through the Bible, where it deals with the phenomena of soul and body as mutually related, acting and reacting. . . . . . If a theory be adopted everywhere else but in the Bible, excluding spiritual intervention by odylic channels *in toto* and accounting for everything physically, *then will the covers of the Bible prove but pasteboard barriers. Such a theory will sweep its way through the Bible and its authority; its plenary inspirations will be annihilated.*"

If Mr. Beecher had rested here, permitted each one to prove the spirits, try them, or, in fact, suffered each one to draw their own conclusions concerning the nature and value of the communications according to the rights of private judgment and conscience, his report would have redeemed the whole ocean of slander, folly, and ignorance that disgraced the age in the language of the opposition; but instead of that, the reverend scholar, finding that his clear perception of fact, science, and reason compelled him to acknowledge the manifestations, and furnished him with a plausible and scientific origin for their production, suddenly became alarmed on the score of his religion. Deeming, possibly, that the new Bible might stand in the way of the old—that a priesthood of laymen, boys, girls, and unconsecrated persons generally, might interfere with the proscriptive rights of the consecrated ones particularly, he changed his tone, and declared that the ancient spirits *did* come "according to the law and the testimony," but the modern ones did not. That the ancient mediums—including, of course, Balaam, Samson, David, Solomon, etc.,—were all *men of God;* whilst the modern—including, of course, A. J. Davis, Kate Fox, Daniel Home, Linton, etc.,—were children of *the other party.* That all the ancient manifestations—including, of course, the destruction of forty and two little children by bears for calling Elisha "bald head," and the sending of a lying spirit into the mouths of Ahab's four hundred prophets, etc.,—were all performed by angels; whilst the modern manifestations—including, of course, the thousands of souls converted to the belief of immortality from atheism and the seventeen hundred marvellous cures of blind, lame, deaf, and otherwise affiicted living persons, reported on unimpeachable authority by Messrs. Partridge and Britain—were all performed by the adversary and his imps; in a word, that the Spiritualism of Judea two thousand years ago was all of God, and the Spiritualism of America, eighteen centuries later, was all of the Devil, and that—because he, the Rev. Charles Beecher, said so.

"Great is Diana of the Ephesians!"

CHAPTER XIII.

THE SPIRITUALISTS' MEMORIAL TO CONGRESS.

"Judas, betrayest thou the Son of Man with a kiss?"

"Speak, Lord, for thy servant heareth."

THE MEMORIAL — GENERAL SHIELDS'S IMMORTAL SPEECH — THE SOCIETY AT 553 BROADWAY, NEW YORK — THE "CHRISTIAN SPIRITUALIST."

IT was in the year 1854, that a memorial was presented to Congress praying that honorable body to appoint a commission of investigation into the subject of modern Spiritualism.

As the grounds of the petitioners' request, and a very fair summary of the aspect of the cause, is presented in the language of the memorial, we shall claim the privilege of placing it on record here, as much for the reasons assigned above as for the propriety of giving that document its legitimate place in these pages.

The memorial was signed by fifteen thousand persons, the name of ex-Governor Tallmadge, of Wisconsin, United States Senator, etc., standing at the head of the list.

Rev. S. B. Britain was intrusted with the difficult task of drawing it up, and at the request of Governor Tallmadge, General Shields, U. S. Senator, agreed to present it, with a view of urging the nomination of a select committee to consider the subject.

"A MEMORIAL.

"*To the honorable, the Members of the Senate and House of Representatives of the United States, in Congress assembled:*

"YOUR Memorialists, citizens of the Republic of the United States of America, most respectfully beg leave to represent before your honorable Body, that certain physical and mental phenomena, of questionable origin and mysterious import, have of late occurred in this country, and in almost all parts of Europe, and that the same are now so prevalent, especially in the Northern, Middle, and Western sections of the Union, as to engross a large share of the public attention. The peculiar nature of the subject to which the Memorialists desire to solicit the attention of your honorable Body, may be inferred from a partial analysis of its phenomenal aspects which are imperfectly comprehended in the following brief generalization:

"First. An occult force exhibited in sliding, raising, arresting, holding, suspending, and otherwise disturbing numerous ponderable bodies, apparently in direct opposition to the acknowledged laws of matter, and altogether transcending the accredited powers of the human mind, is manifested to thousands of intelligent and discriminating persons, while the human senses have hitherto failed to detect to the satisfaction of the public, either the primary or proximate causes of these phenomena.

"Second. Lights of various forms and colors, and of different degrees of intensity, appear in dark rooms, where no substances exist which are liable to develop chemical action or phosphorescent illumination, and in the absence of all the means and instruments whereby electricity is generated or combustion produced.

"Third. Another general class of the phenomenawhich we desire to bring to the notice of your august Body, is presented in the variety of sounds which are now extremely frequent in their occurrence, widely diversified in their character, and more or less significant in their import. These consist, in part, of certain mysterious rappings which appear to indicate the presence of an invisible intelligence; sounds such as are occasioned by the prosecution of several mechanical and other occupations, are often heard; there are others which resemble the hoarse voices of the winds and waves, with which, occasionally, harsh, creaking sounds are mingled, similar to those produced by the masts and rigging of a ship while it is laboring in a rough sea.

"At times powerful concussions occur, not unlike distant thunder or the discharge of artillery, accompanied by an oscillatory movement of surrounding objects, and in some instances by a vibratory or tremulous motion of the floor of the apartment; or it may be, of the whole house wherein the phenomena occur.

"On other occasions harmonic sounds are heard as of human voices, but more frequently resembling the tones of various musical instruments, among which those of the fife, drum, trumpet, guitar, harp and piano have been mysteriously and successfully represented, both with and without the instruments; and in either case, without any apparent human or other visible agency.

"These phenomena appear to depend, so far as regards the process of their production, on the acknowledged principles of acoustics.

"There is obviously a distinction of the sensational medium of the auditory nerves, occasioned by an undulating movement of the air, though by what means these atmospheric undulations are produced does not appear to the satisfaction of acute observers.

"Fourth. All the functions of the human body and mind are often and strangely influenced in what appear to be certain abnormal states of the system, and by causes which are neither adequately defined nor understood. The invisible power frequently interrupts what we are accustomed to denominate the normal operation of the faculties, suspending sensation and the capacity for voluntary motion, checking the circulation of the animal fluids, and reducing the temperature of the limbs and portions of the body to a death-like coldness and rigidity. Indeed, in some instances respiration is entirely suspended for a season — it may be for hours or days together—after which the faculties of the mind and functions of the body are fully restored.

"It is, moreover, confidently asserted that these phenomena have been succeeded, in numerous cases, by permanent mental and physical derangement, and it is positively affirmed and believed that many persons who were suffering from organic defects, or from protracted and apparently incurable diseases, have been suddenly relieved or entirely renovated by the same mysterious agency.

"It may not be improper to observe, in this connection, that two general hypotheses obtain with respect to the origin of these remarkable phenomena.

"The one ascribes them to the power and intelligence of departed spirits, operating on and through the subtile and imponderable elements which pervade and permeate all material forms; and this, it should be observed, accords with the ostensible claims and pretensions of the manifestations themselves.

"Among those who accept this hypothesis will be found a large number of our fellow-citizens who are alike distinguished for their moral worth, intellectual powers and attainments, as well as for their eminent social position and political influence.

"Others, not less distinguished in all the relations of life, reject this conclusion, and entertain the opinion that the acknowledged principles of physics and metaphysics will enable scientific inquirers to account for all the facts in a rational and satisfactory manner. While your memorialists cannot agree on this question, but have honestly arrived at widely different conclusions respecting the probable causes of the phenomena herein described, they beg leave, most respectfully, to assure your honorable Body, they nevertheless most cordially concur in the opinion that the alleged phenomena do really occur, and that their mysterious origin, peculiar nature, and important bearing on the interests of mankind demand for them a patient, thorough, and scientific investigation.

"It cannot reasonably be denied that the various phenomena to which the memorial refers are likely to produce important and lasting results, permanently affecting the physical condition, mental development, and moral character of a large number of the American people.

"It is obvious that these occult powers do influence the essential principles of health and life, of thought and action, and hence they may be destined to modify the conditions of our being, the faith and philosophy of the age, and the government of the world.

"Moreover, deeming it to be intrinsically proper, and at the same time strictly compatible with the cardinal objects and essential spirit of our institutions, to address the representatives of the people, concerning any and every subject which may be fairly presumed to involve the discovery of new principles, which must or may issue in momentous consequences to mankind, we, your fellow-citizens, whose names are appended to this memorial, earnestly desire to be heard on this occasion.

"In pursuance, therefore, of the objects contemplated by the present memorialists, and in view of the facts and reasons herein contained or referred to, your fellow-citizens most respectfully petition your honorable Body for the appointment of a scientific commission to which this subject shall be referred, and for such an appropriation as shall enable the commissioners to prosecute their inquiries to a successful termination. Believing that the progress of science and the true interests of mankind will be greatly promoted by the proposed investigation, the undersigned venture to indulge the hope that their requests will be approved and sanctioned by the wisdom of your honorable Body.

"And to this end the petitioners will ever pray."

General Shields having cheerfully undertaken to comply with Governor Tallmadge's request, proceeded to execute his commission in the following speech, which is a verbatim report from the *National Intelligencer* of Washington, bearing date April, 1854.

Hon. James Shields said:

"'I beg leave to present to the Senate a petition with some fifteen thousand names appended to it upon a very singular and novel subject.

"'The petitioners represent that certain physical and mental phenomena of mysterious import have become so prevalent in this country and Europe as to engross a large share of public attention."

"[General Shields then proceeded to give a summary of the principal features of the memorial, the reiteration of which would be unnecessary in this place. At the conclusion of that portion of his address he proceeded as follows:]

"'I have now given a faithful synopsis of this petition, which, however unprecedented in itself, has been prepared with singular ability, presenting the subject with great delicacy and moderation.

"'I make it a rule to present any petition to the Senate which is respectful in its terms; but having discharged this duty I may be permitted to say that the prevalence of this delusion at this age of the world among any considerable portion of our citizens must originate, in my opinion, in a defective system of education, or in a partial derangement of the mental faculties, produced by a diseased condition of the physical organization. I cannot, therefore, believe that it exists to the extent indicated in this petition.

"'Different ages of the world have had their peculiar delusions. Alchemy occupied the attention of eminent men for several centuries, but there was something sublime in alchemy. The philosopher's stone or the transmutation of metals into gold; the *elixir vitæ* which would preserve youth and beauty, and prevent old age, decay and death, were blessings which poor humanity ardently desired and which alchemy sought to discover by perseverance and piety. Roger Bacon, one of the greatest alchemists and greatest men of the thirteenth century, while searching for the philosopher's stone, discovered the telescope, burning-glasses, and gunpowder.

"'The prosecution of that delusion, therefore, led to a number of useful discoveries. In the sixteenth century flourished Cornelius Agrippa, alchemist, astrologer, and magician, one of the greatest professors of the hermetic philosophy that ever lived. He had all the spirits of the air and demons of the earth under his command.

"'Paulus Jovius says 'that the devil, in the shape of a large black dog, attended Agrippa wherever he went.' Thomas Nash says, at the request of Lord Surrey, Agrippa called up from the grave several of the great philosophers of antiquity, amongst others, Tully, who he caused to re-deliver his celebrated oration for Roscius. To please the Emperor Charles the Fourth, he summoned King David and King Solomon from the tomb, and the Emperor conversed with them long upon the science of government.

"'This was a glorious exhibition of spiritual power compared with the significant manifestations of the present day. I will pass over the celebrated Paracelsus for the purpose of making allusion to an Englishman, with whose veracious history every one ought to make himself acquainted.

"'In the sixteenth century, Dr. Dee made such progress in the talismanic art that he acquired ample power to hold familiar conversation with the spirits and angels, and to learn from them all the secrets of the universe. On one occasion the angel Uriel gave him a black crystal of a convex form, which he had only to gaze on intently, and by a strong effort of will, he could summon any spirit he wished, to reveal to him the secrets of futurity.

"'Dee, in his veracious diary, says, 'that one day while he was sitting with Albertus Laskin, a Polish nobleman, there seemed to come out of the oratory a spiritual creature like a pretty girl of seven or nine years old, with her hair rolled up before and hanging down behind, with a gown of changeable red and green, and a train. She seemed to play in and out of the books and up and down, and as she went, the books displaced themselves to make way for her.

"'This I call spiritual manifestations of the most fascinating kind. Even the books felt the influence of this fascinating creature.

"'Edward Kelly, an Irishman, who was present and witnessed this beautiful apparition, verifies the Doctor's statements therefore it would be unreasonable to doubt a story of which the witness was an Irishman. (Laughter). Doctor Dee was the distinguished favorite of kings and queens—a proof that spiritual science was held in high repute in the days of good Queen Elizabeth.

"'But of all the professors of occult science the Rosicrucians were the most exalted and refined. With them the philosopher's stone implied the possession of health and happiness, command over the service of superior beings, control of the elements, and the most intimate knowledge of all the secrets of the universe. These were objects worth striving for. The Rosicrucians were disgusted with the gross sensual spirits who had communed with man previous to their day, so they decreed their annihilation and substituted in their stead a race of mild, beautiful, and beneficent beings. The spirits of the olden times were malignant and mischievous, but the new generation is mild and benignant.

"'These spirits, as this petition asserts, indulge in the most innocent amusements, as sliding, raising, tipping tables, producing pleasant sounds and variegated lights; sometimes curing diseases; and for the existence of this simple and benignant race, our petitioners are justly indebted to the brethern of the 'Rosy Cross.'

"'Amongst the modern professors of spiritualistic art, Cagliostro was the most celebrated. In Paris his saloons were thronged with the rich and noble, and his charming countess gained immense wealth by granting attending sylphs to such ladies as were rich enough to pay for their service.

"'The 'Biographie des Contempores,' a work which our present mediums ought to consult with care, says, 'there was hardly a fine lady in Paris who would not sup with the shade of Lucretius in the apartments of Cagliostro. There was not a military officer who would not discuss the art of war with Cæsar, nor a counsellor who would not argue points of law with Cicero.'"

"'These were spiritual manifestations worth paying for, and our degenerate mediums would have to hide their diminished heads in the presence of Cagliostro.

"'It would be a curious inquiry to follow this occult science through all its phases of mineral and animal magnetism, etc., until we reach the present and slowest phase of all, spiritual manifestations; but I have said enough to show the truth of Buckles's beautiful aphorism, 'The credulity of dupes is as inexhaustible as the invention of knaves.'

"This speech was received with considerable attention, but was frequently interrupted by laughter.

"Mr. Weller—What does the Senator propose to do with the petition?

"Mr. Petit—Let it be referred to three thousand clergymen. (Laughter.)

"Mr. Weller--I suggest that it be referred to the committee on foreign relations. (Laughter.)

"Mr. Shields--I am willing to agree to the reference.

"Mr. Weller—It may be that we may have to enter into foreign relations with these spirits. (Laughter.) If so, it is a proper subject for the consideration of that committee. It may be necessary for Americans to inquire if they lose their citizenship when they leave this world. It may be expedient that all these grave questions should be considered by the committee on foreign relations, of which I am an humble member. I move its reference to that committee.

"Mr. Mason—I really think it has been made manifest by the honorable Senator who has presented the petition, that he has gone further into the subject than any of us. I would, therefore, suggest that it should either go to a select committee on his motion, or be referred to the military committee, of which he is chairman. Certainly the committee on foreign relations has nothing to do with it. Perhaps it would be better to let the petition lie upon the table.

"Mr. Shields—This is an important subject, and should not be sneered away in this manner. (Loud laughter.) I was willing to agree to the motion of the Senator from California, but I do not wish the petition to go to the committee on foreign relations unless the chairman of that committee is perfectly satisfied that he can do the subject justice. (Laughter.)

"I had thought of proposing to refer the matter to the committee on post offices and post roads, because there may be a possibility of establishing a spiritual telegraph between the material and the spiritual world. (Laughter.)

"Mr. Mason—I move that the petition lie upon the table. Agreed to."

It is almost unnecessary to state that the conduct of General Shields, in following up the memorial which he had undertaken to present by a speech which was calculated to destroy every vestige of interest or importance contained in that document, excited the just indignation of the memorialists, and called forth a scathing protest from Governor Tallmadge. To this General Shields replied by a few lines of defence on the strictly *Congressional* character of his proceedings. Courtesy, honor, sincerity, a love of science or respect for religion, making no part in his conduct on the occasion, of course found no place in his defence; he had acted within *the rules and priv ileges of the Senate*, and so the matter terminated.

The memorial was, as ordered, "laid upon the table;" but according to the law in such cases provided, it is still preserved in the national archives, where it remains as an evidence that in those days there were at least fifteen thousand persons in the land who were better informed on the philosophy of mental science and the high interests of immortality than their elected representatives.

Another movement of important though more local interest to the cause of Spiritualism, was the formation of a society in New York City, which was chartered under the title of "The Society for the Diffusion of Spiritual Knowledge." The members hired a building at 553 Broadway, where they designed to hold circles, conferences, and discussions, and establish a printing press, library, and all the apparatus necessary for the carrying out of the purposes signified in their title.

The list of names appended to the first year's report includes, as will be seen, many of the most distinguished citizens of various States besides New York. It must also be noted that several of the more prominent Spiritualists of that city did not figure in this list at all. For the year 1854, the following officers were appointed:

PRESIDENT.

GOVERNOR NATHANIEL P. TALLMADGE, Wisconsin.

VICE-PRESIDENTS.

Chief Justice JOSEPH WILLIAMS, Iowa.
Judge WILLIE P. FOWLER, Kentucky.
Judge R. P. SPAULDING, Ohio.
Judge CHAS. H. LARRABEE, Wisconsin.
HORACE H. DAY, New York.
Hon. WARREN CHASE, Wisconsin.
Dr. DAVID COREY, Illinois.
Gen. EDWARD F. BULLARD, New York,
Hon. RICHARD D. DAVIS, New York.
Dr. GEORGE T. DEXTER, New York.
Maj. GEORGE W. RAINES, U. S. A.
E. W. BAILEY, Pennsylvania.
PHINEAS E. GAY, Massachusetts.

SECRETARIES.

OWEN. G. WARREN, Architect, New York. CHARLES C. WOODMAN, Editor, New York.
SELAH G. PERKINS, M.D., Vermont.

TREASURER.

NATHANIEL E. WOOD, Chemist, New York.

Besides these officers, Trustees, Advisory, Executive, and Corresponding Committees were formed, including the names of the most prominent and respectable citizens in America. The society inaugurated their commencement by an address, from which the following extracts will serve as examples:

ADDRESS OF THE SOCIETY FOR THE DIFFUSION OF SPIRITUAL KNOWLEDGE TO THE CITIZENS OF THE UNITED STATES.

"But a few short years ago, in an obscure locality, and under circumstances which seemed to warrant the belief in an early termination of the so-called dream, Spiritualism, in its present form, was born. Its few advocates, in the early days of its life, were looked upon as lunatics—were despised for their faith; and men of respectability and standing in society could hardly be found who were willing to examine into the facts connected with the alleged phenomena, for fear of the reproach of the entire unbelieving community. Since that period, Spiritualism has extended with a rapidity unprecedented in the annals of the world, until, to-day, it has become a respectable power in society. Men whose education and genius have fitted them for occupying the highest stations, either in politics or in the church, have sacrificed all positions of earthly aggrandizement for the sake of what they believe to be the enjoyment of high and holy truth.

. . . . "Citizens of the United States, we feel authority for saying that the day for raising the cry of humbug, chicanery, or delusion, has passed away forever. You know, all of you who have reflective minds, that the application of these terms to this subject can no longer produce results; but that rather these invectives, launched at your supposed enemies, will rebound upon yourselves, and cover you with shame. Your professed teachers, your men in high places, the learned of your universities, the eloquent of your pulpits, have dealt in them long enough. And what results have they achieved? The theories which the universities sent forth to account for the alleged phenomena, as they were pleased to term them, have not only rendered their authors, but the universities, ridiculous in the minds of intelligent men.

"Your pulpits—and we mean kindly when we speak of them, for they have a holy office, whether they perform that office or no—your pulpits have launched forth invectives. The cry of delusion and chicanery has been heard all over the land. It produced no effect, except upon the churches themselves; and that course was abandoned. Policy was now adopted; another plan was accepted as the true one for accounting for the spiritual manifestations, and which has been promulgated, not only from the pulpits, but by the religious press of this country—namely, that evil spirits have visited the earth, still further to delude deluded mortals.

"It is very strange, if they believe that evil spirits can come to do evil on this earth, that good spirits will not be permitted by the good God also to come to effect good purposes! We profess to believe both these propositions. We leave you to examine the subject for yourselves, and we tell you, if you will render your minds receptive to the truth, and engage in the investigation of this subject, it will appear that spirits, both good and evil, do come here upon the earth, among their friends and relatives, and teach them good things and bad." . . . . . .

From causes which we deem it unnecessary to discuss here, this society proved but one of numerous illustrations that there is something in the genius of Spiritualism, which up to the present time at least, has proved radically opposed to organization. In various sections of the country *spiritual* organizations had been tried, and uniformly ended in disappointment and failure; these movements will be more particularly noticed hereafter, but in reference to the one under consideration, it is enough to say, its career of a little over three years forms no exception to the rule alluded to. The society at 553 Broadway can scarcely lay claim to have carried out, as a body, any of the propositions with which they started; although some very valuable utilitarian results were achieved, yet it is but justice to say that such results did not proceed from the society, but rather from one of its members, Mr. Horace H. Day, a distinguished merchant of the city, whose name was at the head of the list of the executive committee.

Soon after the opening of the building, it assumed a character entirely different to that which had been anticipated in its inauguration. A feeling of prejudice against the undertaking had been cherished by some of the New York Spiritualists, who found themselves excluded from the initiatory councils, and "after having borne the heat and burden of the day in the early pioneer work of the city," deemed themselves slighted by those who had "come into the vineyard at comparatively the eleventh hour."

These and similar statements were made to the prejudice of the society in its first sessions, but after the usual experimental period had elapsed, and especially after it was proved that as an association the movement could not be considered a success, its promoters and opposers, each alike returned to the fulfilment of the special work their hands found to do, and the undertaking bravely and faithfully sustained, as before hinted, by Mr. Horace H. Day, put into action the following instrumentalities: A paper was started, entitled *The Christian Spiritualist*. A limited subscription list, but a very large gratuitous circulation, enabled this paper for three years to become a missionary for a wide-spread field of usefulness. Miss Kate Fox was engaged at a liberal salary to hold daily *séances* through rapping, writing, and the phases of mediumship peculiar to her, at which the public were admitted free each morning from ten till one.

A library of all the spiritual works, foreign and native, that could be procured was kept for sale and circulation, under the charge of Mr. Munson. A printing office was also established on the premises, and the use of a handsome room was generously presented to Mrs. Emma Hardinge, who had become converted to Spiritualism shortly after her arrival from England, and in zeal for the cause of her new faith had resolved to devote her powers as a test medium, gratuitously to the service of the public.

In this building, then, two test mediums were to be found, at the command of all who sought them, without money or without price. It is not too much to assert that thousands who brought with them guilty consciences, broken hearts, and darkened minds, entered the rooms of Kate Fox and Emma Hardinge to quit them with renewed purposes for good, strengthened and consoled by the ministry of angels, and convinced of the sublime truths of immortality. The fact that this bread of life, too, was dispensed without the usual sordid incentives to action which necessity too often compels the poor spirit medium to resort to, in exchange for time, *which is bread*, made a profound impression on those who thronged these circle rooms, and induced a natural feeling of confidence in the disinterestedness of the source from whence the power came.

It seems here essential to the thread of the history to record a few circumstances in the mediumship of one who has since played a prominent part in the spiritual movement, and therefore as much for the sake of fidelity in history as in response to the repeated solicitations of her friends and fellow-workers, the author will introduce a few extracts from her own life, or "Autobiographical Sketches by Emma Hardinge," spiritual lecturer, and the medium above alluded to.

. . . . "At this juncture [1855], to beguile the tedium and monotony of my life, I suffered myself to be taken to a strange, unheard-of thing or person — I hardly knew which — called a "medium.' I wanted amusement, which was one reason for my investigation; I wanted to carry back to Europe with me subjects for racy articles on America, for the benefit of certain journals to which I was a contributor, and this was a second reason; and nothing I had heard of since my residence in America [all of which I of course deemed could be comprehended in six months of New York experience] struck me as so eminently ridiculous, and illustrative of the technical phrase, 'Yankee notions,' as the daring humbug which pretended to give communications from heaven itself.

"Let any of my readers educated in strict orthodox faith, recall their early theologic opinions concerning ghosts, death, resurrection, heaven, hell, spirits, and angels, and even then they will form but a faint conception of a rather piously-inclined young English girl's horror when informed that souls in bliss descended from their bright abodes to make tables dance; and that angels left 'the throne of God' to say their alphabets to earth, and tell its inhabitants the price of stocks and the best time to buy and sell!

"At first I heard of 'the thing' with unmitigated horror and indignation.

"Becoming familiarized with what they said about 'the spirits,' much of which I heard from some persons with whom I boarded and certain of my professional visitors, I subsided from religious horror into the certainty of its being some gross and clumsy species of *magic* and though I still felt indignant at the pretense of associating this with anything so sacred as an immortal soul, I thought I might learn some characteristics of the people from the so-called Spiritualists, even more daringly impudent in trick and folly than Barnum and his '*What Is It*.'

"It was in such a frame of mind, and with such views as these, that I consented to investigate the subject of Spiritualism.

"Under such a stimulus to search, I accompanied one of my fellow-boarders to the rooms of Mr. J. B. Conklin. A large party was assembled there, every one of whom was—in singular contrast to a similar assemblage of English people—very pale, and, as I deemed, from that circumstance, rather ghost-like.

"This was a good beginning, and suggested ideas of mystics wan and worn with midnight vigils amongst the dead. Presently I heard some of those sitting at the table talking familiarly with *nothing*, and responded to by very rude and clumsy gyrations of the table. Amused at this proceeding, which really looked as if those deluded ones were in earnest, I quietly directed my attention to the table, and, though unable at the time to discover the machinery by which it was moved, I knew it was there. I knew it just as certainly as did Mr. Farraday, Sir David Brewster, and the Harvard Professors, in their investigations with tables, and from the same reliable source, too—a source common to us all—namely, our own insufferable self-conceit and untractable prejudices.

"All passed off well, however, until a sentence was 'spelled out,' which seemed to me to comment irreverently on the Bible. This was enough. I don't know now, even what the sentence was. I did not know then, whether the sentence was true or false. It was sufficient for me, that the 'Holy Word of God' was lightly spoken of in that company of 'ghouls,' and that I impiously sat by to hear it. The next moment I was in the street, and that night, with tearful petitions to Heaven for forgiveness in daring to hear—I did not know what—and solemn promises never again to listen to anything about the Bible but the book itself, I dropped to sleep, fervently resolving never again to visit so blasphemous a place as a 'spirit circle;' a promise I kept for the space of a whole week. And so ends the first chapter in my spiritual experience."

Mrs. Hardinge was already a natural medium, and endowed with the faculties essential to the control of spirits. Her "resolution" was her own, her destiny under the influence of the unseen power that had led her across the ocean, to the Continent of America, and up through the most marvellous vicissitudes of life and fortune to this hour.

Here, then, the hold was not relaxed. An actress at the Broadway Theatre, she became acquainted with Mr. Augustus Fenno, who, like many other members of the theatrical profession, was a warm Spiritualist and an excellent trance and writing medium. At his suggestion, Mrs. Hardinge consented to visit Mrs. Coan, a young married lady, who had lately arrived in New York and established herself as a test, rapping, writing, and clairvoyant medium.

At the time of Mrs. Hardinge's first visit, Mrs. Coan was giving *séances* to the public of New York, and was only introduced to her visitor by Mr. Fenno, as "*Miss* Emma Hardinge [so known in public], from England."

[Here follows a brief description of this *séance*, the insertion of which will illustrate the charcter of what was then known as "test mediumship."]

"My friend Mr. Augustus Fenno, so captivated me with the promise of revelations through 'the raps,' and assurances that spirit-rappings were rarely of a theological character, that I consented to accompany him to visit the now-celebrated Miss Ada Hoyt.*

"Dire were the misgivings with which I set out on this second investigation, and intense the disgust with which the cool indifference of Miss Hoyt's manner inspired me. A medium for departed spirits, I thought, should be, if not saintly, witch-like in appearance; if not ecstatic in gesture and speech, weird-like and fantastic; and so the perfectly plain matter-of-fact characteristics of this live medium threw me fairly *hors du combat*.

"Arrived there, however, I scorned to retreat; and yet if dislike and determined scepticism could have an invariably neutralizing effect on spiritual manifestations, I could not at this day be writing my spiritual experiences.

"I have too often marvelled at the foolish verbosity which induces people to rehearse over the tests they have received, and read whole pages of purely personal communications to others entirely uninterested, to inflict the same penalty on my readers; let it suffice, then, to state that I rose up after a two hours' *séance* with Miss Hoyt, having received all the ordinary tests of name, age, death, etc., from almost every relative and friend I had in the spirit-world. And those obstinate, clear raps came, not only on the table and under it, but on the walls, my chair, following my footsteps around the room, and in every conceivable way that could assure me they were not produced by machinery connected either with the table or the person of the medium. Thus far I was satisfied—that is to say, of the entire

* *Mrs. Coan.* This lady has since been more generally known by her maiden name of Ada Hoyt.

absence of any imposture or delusion. Miss Hoyt, to my inexpressible disgust, assured me that I was myself 'a great medium,' an expression reiterated through the raps by the invisibles; hence, she asserted, the manifestations were more than usually clear and abundant; certain it is that the chief of my questions were unspoken, and, therefore, responded to by some intelligence capable of reading my mind.

"This, together with the number of names and trivial circumstances of identity that were volunteered by the rappers, deprived me of the remotest chance of attributing the communications to the minds of any one present, including my own. This *séance* terminated with instructions for me 'to sit for communications' through myself, a proposition as startling to me as it was embarrassing, since the idea of my putting myself in an attitude of preparation for the performances *of ghosts*, opened up to me a train of probabilities beginning with the Witch of Endor, and concluding with the Devil and Dr. Faustus.

"Returned home, the confession of my second visit to a medium drew from my mother a mild but emphatic declaration that, although she had hitherto followed my erratic footsteps over the wide world, and was still ready to shelter me, even in disgrace, or accompany me, if needs were, to the grave, yet for this horrible and blasphemous subject she had no sympathy, and should I still persist in its investigation, I might prepare to see her depart for England by the next ship; for beneath the roof where such abominations were practiced, she never would consent to stay.

"Finding that I was far more disposed to echo her sentiments than oppose them, my mother next inquired of me the result of the weird interview I had come from. In answer, I read her, without comment, the questions and answers that formed the *séance*, together with the notes, in full, of the whole scene, and then it was that plain common sense triumphed over bigotry and prejudice. The latter amiable qualities with which, I believe, I was liberally endowed, blinded my eyes to the reasonableness of attributing all the mass of intelligence my notes revealed to its true source; but when my unprejudiced, common-sense mother heard precious little sentences read, and tests rehearsed, too clearly identical with her son, husband, father, and dearest relatives, to be by any possibility mistaken for others, and when by plain straight-forward questions she succeeded in eliciting from me a perfect detail of the whole scene, her reason recognized the spiritual truth as the only solution of the problem, and after making me go over and over again the instructions I had received as to sitting at a table for development, she closed this chapter of my spiritual experience by placing a small table before me, and herself and a young lady, at that time visiting us, on the opposite side, with our three pairs of hands solemnly spread out on its surface, and there, in awful silence, we sat 'waiting for the spirits.'"

"For many succeeding days at every available leisure moment we continued this mystical arrangement, sometimes with our simple trio, and occasionally joined by other marvel-seekers of our own stamp. We were 'waiting for the spirits,' and as I imagined the only mode of obtaining spiritual communications was by raps or tips, and neither of these forms were manifested, so I deemed we waited in vain. Meantime I was perplexed and my friends alarmed by the singular effect of these sittings on myself. If the table did not move of itself, it kept up a perpetual St. Vitus's dance in vibration to my own involuntary movements, especially of my resistless, constantly twitching hands, poundings, jerkings, grimacings and all the formulæ of physical development, succeeding each other with such violence and rapidity that I should soon have come to the conclusion that I was completely bewitched, had I not fortunately received a visit from a gentleman well versed in these preliminary mediumistic eccentricities.

"From him I learned that there were many other spiritual gifts besides those I had witnessed, and in a course of exercises which this high priest put me through, he pronounced me to be a fine 'magnetic, psychologic, sympathetic, clairvoyant, clairaudient,' and every other kind of fine subject generally, concluding with the promise to take me to a celebrated public medium, through whose influence, he felt confident, I should be 'developed right away.'

"In proof of the excessive distrust that possessed my mind at this time, I replied to this latter offer, that I would go, provided he would take me then and there, without, as I thought, allowing any time or opportunity for collusion; for, uncertain what the process of 'development' might be, or what fearful changes I might suffer by becoming a medium, I at least resolved to march to the sacrifice with my eyes open. My friend, no doubt apprehending the nature of my very flattering distrust of himself, good-naturedly replied that he would just step over to his store and return at once and fetch me. But I would go with him, and go with him I did, carefully watching him to see that he did not write some secret paper to be slipped into some one's hand with mysterious instructions to do some unknown thing with me; and so carefully did I scrutinize every look, word, and movement, that I could have testified on oath that I never lost sight of my conductor for one single instant, until I stood with him in an upper room in Broadway, where a large party were already gathered together to hold a circle with Mrs. Kellogg, one of the best test mediums I ever had the good fortune to meet, and withal an accomplished and interesting lady."

[The lady here referred to as Mrs. Kellogg was one of the best public mediums in the city. She had rooms in Broadway where visitors were received at stated periods, and from whence sceptics by thousands went away convinced through her inimitable gifts as a clairvoyant, writing, seeing, and speaking medium. Her interview with Emma Hardinge exercised so marked an effect upon the author's subsequent career in the cause of Spiritualism, that it is deemed in place to insert the extract in full from her "Autobiographical Sketches."]

"Let the reader who followed me to the house of this lady, where, according to my friend's promise I was to be 'developed right away,' imagine a person totally ignorant of the meaning of this phrase, finding herself in a room full of strangers, in vague anticipation of some mild kind of surgical operation, by which a rational being in a perfectly natural state of existence was suddenly to be converted into a modern prototype of the woman of Endor. Awaiting my mysterious fate with direful misgivings, I was suddenly addressed by the lady medium — to whom, by my own request, I had no introduction, and from whose notice I had sedulously shrunk away — with the words 'Come here and sit with me; you are a great medium.' Obedient to her commanding gestures, I seated myself at the magic table, when the lady began rubbing my hand with considerable energy, but complaining all the while that I wore a silk dress. Why I should not do so was more than I could divine; but before I could even arrange a question in words to this effect, a strange, misty sensation came over me, which so completely obscured my faculties that an endeavor to recall who I was, and where, only ended in convincing me that I was a highly-respectable old gentleman, in which character I gave what I was afterwards informed were some remarkable personating tests of spirit identity to several strangers in the room. To recapitulate the events and sensations of that evening — the first of my test mediumistic experience — would be neither possible nor profitable. It is enough to record that the touch of Mrs. Kellogg's hand appeared like a magician's wand, illuminating the latent fires of magnetic power, which, once enkindled, ever after burned in the steady light of mediumistic gifts.

"During the three-hours *séance* of that evening, it was found that I could give tests of spirit identity by personations, impressions, writing, and automatic movements of my fingers over the alphabet. All present seemed much more interested in this sudden and unexpeeted development than myself, its subject, who, to confess the truth, was so bewildered with my own marvellous performances, besides being half the time lost in the identity of the spirits who were influencing me, that I was far more disposed to question my own identity than that of any of the spirits I was said to represent.

"The experience of most investigators in the spiritual philosophy has shown that no tests are thoroughly convincing to individual minds, which are not addressed to the individual's own knowledge and reason; hence, all I did by way of convincing others that night would have failed to impress myself with any other belief than that of an unnatural and foreign influence upon me, had not some of the tests been addressed to myself in automatic writing, which, though produced by my own hand—being written upside down, and requiring to be held up to the light for perusal—convinced me my own mind was not the originator of the sentences.

"One of these contained simply these words—'TOM — *Find a great sea-snake!*'

"The name of an only and idolized brother was here written, and with it, the last words I ever heard him utter on earth; namely, a charge that I—a singer—would find for him the words of an old sea-song, of which he was passionately fond, and which he had begged me to learn to sing for his gratification. He spoke this sentence as he was departing on his last earthly voyage, from which he never came back again.

"These utterances of the lost sailor-boy were forgotten, in the whirlwind of grief for his death, far, far, at sea, which swallowed up all minor details, until, after an absence of ten years, what I had been taught to believe the impassable gulf of eternity stood revealed before me, as a bridge, on which stood my beloved and lost, smilingly repeating that sentence,—too trifling to have been preserved in the solemn archives of death-memories, but too surely identical with the precious dead to be repeated by any but his own very self.

"In scornful unbelief of the power I was investigating, I had said to my conductor, before entering the circle room, 'If all you tell me of Spiritualism be true, and they succeed in making me one of these wonderful mediums, I will return to England and make my fortune.'

"Late in the evening, automatic writing, through my own hand, purporting to come from my spirit father, assured me I was a fine medium; that I *must* use my gifts, as such, for the benefit of the world, but—repeating my own careless words—that, so far from using those gifts to make my fortune, I was never to take fee or reward for mediumship, nor would the spirit communicating release me from the strong control in which I was held, until I made pledges before the witnesses then present, first, that I would devote my gifts to the service of others; and next, that I would not take fee or reward for the same. As this was not the custom of my hostess, who was a professional medium—neither was it my own views in the matter—this charge could have been no emanation from either her mind or mine. And, in justice to the many self-sacrificing mediums, who have resigned other and more lucrative employments to give their services to the public in return for fees so modest that they, too often, fail to supply the wants of those who demand them, I must here add that the objection of my spirit friends to taking pay for mediumship was special to my own-case.

"It seemed they perceived in me the capacity to exercise many forms of medumship, all of which they desired should simply be used as means to prepare me for being a lecturer—a destiny which I should then have contemplated with so much disgust that, if apprised of it, I should, in all probability, have ceased my investigations at once. But, though the reasons were not then given me, I have since learned to appreciate the excellence and wisdom of the advice.

"By not becoming a professional medium, I neither felt anxiety to please my sitters nor temptation to impose when the power failed me. Besides this, I passed through many phases too rapidly to be available as a stereotyped test medium for any special gift, and thus I had the happiness of doing good and conferring spiritual light upon those who sought me, beside gaining a vast range of experience and unfettered practice, which has been, and still is, of incalculable use to me as a teacher of the spiritual philosophy.

"All this I can now perceive 'face to face;' though then, I may truly say, I could only 'see as in a glass, darkly.' . . . . .

"[As many contradictory statements have been circulated respecting the first *mediumistic* prophecies of the loss of the ship Pacific, which excited much indignation from the owner when first hazarded, but were as carefully as possible stifled *after* the prophecy was found to be correct, we shall here insert the narrative, as originally recorded by the author:]

"I mentioned in a former paper that I had come to this country in the steamship Pacific, one of the Collins line. Ever since my arrival in America I had maintained a kindly intercourse with some of the officials of the ship, between whom and myself little offices of friendship were exchanged every time she came into port. The ship Pacific was due on the memorable day when I became developed as a medium.

"On Wednesday I went down to the wharf in the hope of receiving a little package that was to be sent me from England in charge of the storekeeper, an officer between whom, my mother, and myself, the most kindly acquaintance had been kept up ever since our landing.

"The ship had not arrived, and no tidings were received of her; but as she was only due some thirty hours [the season rendered it likely that winter storms would occasion the delay of even some days] no anxiety was felt in consequence. I mentioned the circumstance to my mother, but beyond a slight expression of regret, neither of us commented on the matter.

"That evening, just as my mother and myself were about to retire for the night, a sudden and unusual chill crept over me, and an irresistible impression possessed my mind that a spirit had come into our presence. A sensation as if water was streaming over me accompanied the icy chilliness I experienced, and a feeling of indescribable terror possessed my whole being. I begged my mother to light up every lamp we had at hand; then to open the door that the proximity of people in the house outside our room might aid to dissipate the horror that seemed to pervade the very air. At last, at my mother's suggestion, I consented to sit at the table, with the alphabet we had provided turned from me and toward her, so that she could follow the involuntary movements of my finger, which some power seemed to guide in pointing out the letters. In this way was rapidly spelled out, 'Philip Smith: Ship Pacific.'

"As that was the name of the storekeeper for whom I had been only that day inquiring, our curiosity and interest were now considerably excited. For a few moments this mode of manifestation ceased, and to my horror, I distinctly felt an icy cold hand lay hold of my arm; then distinctly, and visibly to my mother's eyes, something pulled my hair, which was hanging in long curls; all the while the coldness of the air increasing so painfully that the apartment seemed pervaded by Arctic breezes. After a while my own convulsed hand was moved tremblingly but very rapidly to spell out, 'My dear Emma, I have come to tell you I am dead. The ship Pacific is lost, and all on board have perished; she and her crew will never be heard from more.'

"I need not remind my readers that this statement, though made within too short a time from the day when she was due, to permit of the least anxiety to be felt on her account, was strictly verified by subsequent results. The ship Pacific and her ill-fated crew were never heard from more; and despite the indignant threats of prosecution that the owners made against the 'impostors' who dared to predict her loss on the faith of spiritual communications, which both myself and others to whom I named the facts did not scruple to repeat, Phillip Smith and some few of his fellow-sufferers, in their messages from the harbor which happily sheltered their enfranchised spirits, were the only revelators that ever lifted the awful veil of doom from their ocean grave. From this time, and during a period of eighteen months, I sat constantly for all who sought my services as a test medium for a great variety of manifestations. These followed in rapid succession, each one practicing my whole frame in a striking and powerful manner. I frequently saw spirits with great distinctness, describing them with accuracy, and conversing with them as I did with my fellow-mortals. I wrote in various ways, automatically and by impression, spoke in various conditions of trance and semi-consciousness; became a psychometrist, partly clairvoyant, and occasionally a physician: in fact, with the exception of boisterous physical manifestations, or that which I coveted beyond all else—the raps—it is impossible to name a phase of mediumship through which I did not pass, and in which I was not fully and powerfully exercised." . .

In the first issues of the new paper—the *Christian Spiritualist*—Professor Toohey was the editor, and it was conducted by him with a talent and ability which secured a high and well-deserved reputation for its pages. On Mr. Toohey's withdrawal, the chief duty of filling its columns with editorial matter and the spiritualistic tidings of the day devolved upon Mr. Munson, Emma Hardinge, and a few voluntary contributors, by whom the work was sustained until its termination.

The building was still publicly associated with the pretentious array of names which constituted "the society," but, with the exception of the persons designated above and Mr. Horace Day, who nobly defrayed from his own private purse the heavy burden attending the publication of the paper, the rent of the building and payment of the officials, the society had viritually ceased to exist.

Still the work that its inauguration accomplished can scarcely be estimated. The office at 553 formed a nucleus where friends and strangers could assemble together, interchange ideas and greetings, read the papers, buy or borrow all the spiritual literature of the day, and attend the circles held in different apartments of the building. During one of the most exciting presidential elections that had marked the country's history, circles were held in that house whose influence went forth and pervaded every State in the Union.

The influence which the spiritual world exerts over the natural can never be properly understood and appreciated until the intimate relations subsisting between them are fully comprehended; meantime, the communion of spirits with mortals discloses the nature and operation of those relations, and in this respect, the revelations that have been made concerning the political destiny of the country, the plans that have been foreshadowed, the prophetic visions that have been mapped out with minutest precision, the predestined scheme of the untried future, and the action that spirits have in some instances required of and through their mediums for the outworking of the Divine plan, would, if it were prudent to reveal it, throw a marvellous and truly supra-mundane illumination over the wild and terrible drama that has been enacted on the American continent during the last ten years, and still more on the events of deep and universal interest that are yet to overrule the destinies of the great New World.

Beyond entailing odium and suspicion on those whose efforts would be most injuriously affected thereby, such revelations would be of comparatively more detriment than benefit. Yet it is essential to the full assertion of the claims of Spiritualism that we should allude to a subject, the purport of

DRAWN & ENGRAVED BY JOHN SARTAIN

JAMES J. MAPES, LL.D.

PRES[t] OF THE MECHANICS' INST[E] ___ VICE PRES[T] OF THE AMERICAN INS[E]

which many of our readers will understand. Many and many are those who know how for long months prior to their public issue, *State documents and Congressional ordinances existed in the secret archives of an unconsidered spirit circle.* Many are the eyes that will glance over these pages, that have seen the wires of the national machinery pulled by invisible hands, and some few there are who *know* that a mightier Congress than that which sits at Washington has helped to lay the foundations of the New World's destiny in the spirit-circle rooms of 553 Broadway.

It was in May, 1857, that the *Spiritual Telegraph* announced the close of the career of the *Christian Spiritualist*, and with it, of the offices and spiritual functions which had been performed in connection with it at 553 Broadway.

The notice which records the termination of this mission is embodied in the following simple sentence:

"CHRISTIAN SPIRITUALIST DISCONTINUED.

"The closing number of the third volume of the *Christian Spiritualist*, published on the 2d inst., comes to us with the announcement that its course is now finished. Its publication, as it states, 'commenced with the Society for the Diffusion of Spiritual Knowledge, and ends with it.' We are sorry that we shall hereafter be deprived of its weekly visits. During the last year more particularly, we have regarded the *Spiritualist* as among the most valuable of our spiritual publications.

"It has been supported chiefly by the munificence of one individual, who, during the last three years, has expended no less than $25,000 upon it and other matters pertaining to the cause, connected with the office of its publication, thus displaying a zeal worthy of all commendation.

"The movement of which this paper was but the least part, has set in motion a living chain of influences which will continue to girdle the western continent until America shall cease to be."

CHAPTER XIV.

SPIRITUALISM IN NEW YORK—CONTINUED.

"How pure in heart and sound in head,
With what divine affections bold,
Should be the man whose thoughts would hold
An hour's communion with the dead."

TENNYSON.

PROFESSOR MAPES AND HIS METHODS OF INVESTIGATION—REVEREND C. H. HARVEY—CLOSE OF THE "SPIRITUAL TELEGRAPH."

As the experiences of remarkable personages form the most instructive of items in spiritual history, we shall here insert a few memoranda supplied to the *Banner of Light* by the late Professor Mapes, a gentleman scarcely less distinguished in the world of science as an agricultural chemist than was Professor Hare in the department of electricity.

Professor Mapes was a friend and contemporary of Dr. Hare's, and like him was strongly in favor of rendering for all phenomena, whether of the visible or invisible universe, a simply material explanation.

The professor's attention having been directed towards the spiritual manifestations, he at first treated them with the scathing rebuke which was so often administered by those who had not investigated the subject; but when he found that many of his associates in science as well as social life were deeply immersed in this "modern magic," he determined to bring his acute mind to bear upon the matter sufficiently to redeem his friends, who, "though otherwise respectable men," were on this point, he declared, "fast running to mental seed and imbecility."

The experiences into which this benevolent purpose led him, would not be sufficiently remarkable to justify their reproduction in these pages, were it not that they present a striking instance of patience and conformity to required conditions in seeking phenomena through the spirit circle. In these respects, a glance at the diary of the learned professor will amply repay the trouble of perusal. The following extracts are taken from the *Banner of Light*, the *Spiritual Telegraph*, and New York Conference, wherein Professor Mapes is reported under the cognomen either of "Phœnix" or "An Old Spiritualist."

The first of his printed articles simply contains a sketch, in the third person, of his sceptical opinions, and materialistic philosophy on the subject of "Spiritualism." The second extract is as follows:

BANNER OF LIGHT.—NEW YORK, MARCH 12, 1859.

AN OLD SPIRITUALIST—NUMBER II.

"In our last article of this series, we gave some account of our friend Phœnix, and now propose to fulfil the promises there made. He had heard of Spiritualism and had attended many circles, in most of which he found persons predisposed to belief; mediums who practiced deceit, and minds so fond of the marvellous as to translate the clumsy dreamings of visionaries into divine aspirations. Night after night passed away without anything having occurred that was calculated to convince him that mediums were controlled by spirits. The manifestations which seem to have been satisfactory to many others were not so to him. Still, occasionally he met friends who recited manifestations, which seemed to be above dispute, of a character far beyond what he himself had witnessed, and thus he was tempted to continue to meet with circles, notwithstanding his own want of success. On one particular evening, however, when seated at the opposite end of the table with a medium and some friends whom he had brought with him, he plainly felt the touch of hands upon his knees and feet. His unexpressed thoughts were answered in the affirmative by three touches of the spirit hand, one touch for no, and five for the alphabet. Upon repeating this inaudibly to the audience, letters were selected by the spirit hand, which, upon being written down by himself, spelt out consecutive sentences containing facts only known to himself and to the supposed communicator. Indeed, on this particular evening every question and answer from all parties present seemed to be consecutive and full of intelligence. He therefore held the following dialogue with the spirits, they answering by raps: *Q.* How shall I be able to satisfy myself as to the truth of Spiritualism? *A.* Form a circle of twelve individuals; employ the best medium you can get, and continue your sittings until you can procure information of a character that will not be distasteful to you. Have six positive and six negative minds. *Q.* What do you mean by positive and negative minds? *A.* Six male and six female minds. *Q.* Do you mean six ladies and six gentlemen? *A.* No; by a positive or male mind we mean such an one as your friend O., who is eccentric, and decides upon the propriety of his own acts without advising with his friends. If he wished to buy a house, he would do so without your approval. If advised by his physician, he would follow such advice only to the extent that he could comprehend it. This is what we call a male or positive mind. A female or negative mind is such as requires the advice of its friends before action of any kind; it is not self-sufficient, is wanting in executive power, and readily swayed by conventionalisms. Both these classes of mind are necessary for an effective circle. When you have met twenty nights, you will have no further difficulty in inducing your friends to continue their sittings.

"Phœnix determined to follow these directions, and as the spirits had told him that the negative minds might be believers or not, just as he chose, he had no difficulty in forming this half of his circle. It was recommended, however, that the positive minds should not be believers, and with these he had much difficulty. The first party to whom he applied was his friend F. Mc.C., who flatly refused, and said, 'You'll disgrace yourself with this nonsense.' Phœnix urged that, to oblige him, he would spend twenty nights in any way, and eventually F. McC. agreed to stand the torture every Monday night for twenty weeks. When O. was applied to he laughed outright, but eventually compromised the affair for the twenty nights, assuring Phœnix that on the twenty-first Monday he should be absent. With great difficulty the six positive minds were found. Mrs. Brown was selected as the medium, and the circle commenced.

"For the first eighteen nights both questions and answers were extremely stupid. The only curious phenomenon was the raps, and with all the theories of snapping of toe and knee joints, rubbing the ball of the toe on the sole of the boot, electricity, and all the other theories which had been from time to time advanced, the six positive minds were divided; but with the negatives it was affirmed there was a marvellous fitness in many of the replies, although the positive minds did not admit it.

"On the nineteenth night the tables were somewhat turned. Phœnix had been lampooned by his associates, and when they came together on this evening, both himself and positive friends agreed that, after one more night of mummery, they would drop the whole affair. The inquiry about the raps had lost its interest, and although the replies had been somewhat consecutive, they had given no indication of talent commensurate with the desire of at least six of the circle. The medium had not yet entered the room, when, in a sort of "lark," five sheets of paper were placed on the floor, and one or two lead-pencils laid on each. The medium entered and took her seat; the circle was organized as usual. In a few moments the pencils were all heard distinctly writing. One of the positive members looked below the table-cloth, and insisted that he saw all the pencils standing upright, and that they fell as soon as he had seen them. The sheets were lifted from the floor, and were found to contain many names, clearly written. The party for whom these names were intended was selected by the spirits, through the raps, and in every case the positive friends were compelled to admit that these names were truly correct as those of their grandfathers, fathers, mothers, etc., who were in the spirit-world. Phœnix was selected by the spirits to ask questions on that evening, and the answers were all pertinent and instructive. On the twentieth evening [the following Monday], every member of the circle had their chairs slightly pulled from the table while sitting on them. Raps occurred everywhere. A guitar placed under the table was played upon, while resting alternately on the knees of every member of the circle. A harmonicon placed under the table, at a point furthest from the medium, was beautifully played, only two of the members knowing it was under the table, they being the first who came into the room, and brought the instrument and placed it there. A tumbler had been placed on the floor at the same time. Late in the evening a handful of coin was thrown on the floor, and then piled up inside the tumbler, without noise. The room was well lighted with gas, and the hands of the circle were placed on the top of the table. Even the positive members agreed to continue their sittings, and the same circle sat for more than four years, once each week."

Manifestations of a far more astounding character than any recorded in this initiatory investigation were afterwards witnessed by Professor Mapes, through a great number of mediums, amongst whom the author has frequently been invited to sit for the learned "savant," and has partaken with him of the most elevating and convincing evidence of the direct presence and control of a vast number and variety of spirits; indeed it seemed as if the noblest minds of the invisible world delighted to answer the appeals of this powerful yet captious investigator with all sorts of convincing methods of proving their presence. Honest, fearless, and unremitting in his search into this wondrous realm of untrodden science, the professor was constantly rewarded by brilliant suggestions which, to his quick apprehension, formed threads leading him into paths of new discovery, both in mental and physical science.

None can bear more grateful testimony to this fact than the author, who was frequently selected by the professor for investigations of a highly occult or scientific character, when the results invariably attested the truth of the homely proverb that "like attracts like;" and whereas his inquiring mind sought for the highest ideality to match his own, he obtained such responses as were worthy the spirit of his inquiry.

The circle alluded to in the preceding extracts continued its session, as we have stated, for several years. Nearly all its members were men of science and public influence; all of them, including Professor Mapes became converts to, and powerful advocates of Spiritualism. Added to this, the wife of Professor Mapes, a lady advanced in life, became suddenly devoloped as a most wonderful drawing medium. Without any previous knowledge of the art, Mrs. Mapes executed, in a marvellously rapid manner, and under circumstances of the most abnormal character, *several thousand* water-color drawings, which, for originality of design and beauty of execution, stand unrivalled as works of art, a gallery in themselves, on which the most fastidious and highly instructed artists of the day have pronounced the verdict of faultless.

Amongst the strange occurrences which gave tokens of the presence and influence of spirits, the following incident may be taken as an illustration of a number of similar cases, transpiring in different parts of the country.

SPIRITUAL ADVERTISER—NEW YORK, SEPTEMBER 12, 1857.

"A strange, and somewhat startling demonstration of spirit power occurred at the Stuyvesant Institute, in this city, on Wednesday evening of last week, at the commencement of an attempt to deliver a lecture by Rev. C. H. Harvey. It should be premised that this is the same Mr. Harvey who, several years ago, wrote a valuable pamphlet, entitled "The Millennial Dawn," in proof of spiritual manifestations, and who, in consequence of his advocacy of spiritualistic views, was much persecuted, and finally suspended from the exercise of his functions as a minister in the Methodist Episcopal Church. Since then, Mr. H. has been quietly pursuing his investigations in the department that was so obnoxious to his former associates, but latterly he has become dissatisfied—very conscientiously, no doubt—with certain theological aspects of the spiritualistic development, and deemed it his duty to propose a series of lectures, which he announced in the following advertisement in the morning papers:

"'A PLEA FOR THE BIBLE. — The Rev. C. H. Harvey will deliver a short series of lectures in defence of the Bible against modern Spiritualism, and in exposition of its phenomena; the first on Wednesday evening, September 2, in Stuyvesant Institute, No. 659 Broadway. Mediums and advocates of Spiritualism are invited to attend, and full liberty will be awarded them to defend their 'new philosophy.'"

At the appointed time, Mr. Harvey appeared at the desk, at the Stuyvesant Institute, with a small audience assembled before him. After offering a prayer, he commenced his discourse, immediatly giving the audience to understand that while his position would be in defence of the Bible, it would be one of general hostility to modern Spiritualism, on account of what was alleged to be its demoniac character.

But while proceeding more fully to defend his position in regard to these points, his utterance became obstructed; he stood for a moment, as if transfixed, and then dropped to the floor, as if smitten down with a heavy bludgeon.

His friends were immediately at his side on the platform. They found him pale and corpse-like. One man, a stranger to those present, who seemed to be a physician, felt for his pulse, and found that it had entirely ceased. Cold water was sprinkled upon his face; brandy was poured down his throat, and every available means of restoration was applied, but without the slightest apparent effect; and the physician, who was *not* a Spiritualist, pronounced him "*dead!*"

But after he had lain in this way for some eight or ten minutes, a gentleman, who was a Spiritualist, and who understood the nature of the attack, got access to him, made a few upward passes over him, when he immediately opened his eyes, and soon was so far recovered as to arise and converse with those surrounding him. He declared that he had never been in better health in his life than he was then; that his attack did not proceed from any physical cause, but that it was from a spirit—from the "Devil," as he termed it—and expressed a wonder that God had not, in this instance, defended him, as he had defended him against similar attacks before.

It was said to be apparent to all persons there, who had any knowledge of philosophy, that Mr. H.'s attack was not of the nature of apoplexy, or a rush of blood to the head—neither faintness, paralysis, nor anything of the kind—but that it was clearly produced by some strange and ultra-physical cause, and was paralleled only by what, in other instances, has been known as adverse spiritual influences.

Quietude being restored, Mr. H. attempted to proceed with his lecture, but his utterance was again mysteriously stopped in the same way, and it was thought by those present that if he had persisted in his efforts, he would again have been smitten down as before. Again he made the attempt, and again failed in like manner; and finally he announced to his auditors that their money would be returned to them if they would apply to the door-keeper, but that it was useless for him to attempt to proceed with his lecture under the circumstances.

But few comments on this remarkable case are necessary. Mr. Harvey had at one time felt the force and beauty of Spiritualism, yet obviously was unable to shake off the trammels of his ancient spirit of sectarian bigotry.

He attempted to vindicate the claims of revealed religion *at the expense of Spiritualism*, without remembering, or perhaps ignorant of the fact, that Spiritualism included in its ranks numbers of believers who were as reverential admirers of the Bible as himself. The crusade implied in his lecture, therefore, was as unnecessary as it was evidently undertaken in a misconception of his subject. How far spirits may have been justified in silencing his erroneous doctrines by using his mediumistic organization in the manner above described, we do not pretend to decide. That a spiritual power inimical to his purposes overshadowed him, there can be no question. His peculiar organism was susceptible to such an influence; and it was obviously exerted to give Mr. Harvey a powerful warning, and the world an evidence that our perversions of Divine truth do not always pass unnoticed by invisible powers.

During the eventful ten years between 1850 and 1860, the Sabbath meetings in New York continued to attract thousands of earnest listeners to the religious phase of Spiritualism.

Fresh and interesting media were being rapidly developed in every grade of society.

The circles held nightly might be numbered by thousands, whilst the press and the pulpit continued to contribute their share of vituperation and denunciation to the notoriety of the subject.

Many changes had necessarily transpired in the external order "of the line of march."

The partnership between Messrs. Partridge and Britain in the *Spiritual Telegraph* had dissolved, and that invaluable and ably-conducted journal had closed its career of usefulness on the appearance of a new paper, edited by A. J. Davis, entitled the *Herald of Progress.*

As the *Spiritual Telegraph* had obtained the first generally wide circulation of any of the numerous journals devoted to the cause, and been sustained for nearly ten years with an ability and liberality which can never be over-estimated, reflecting undying honor on its spirited projector, Mr. Charles Partridge, it is but just that we should insert a few extracts from the valedictory which concludes the last issue of his paper:

"'TIME UP!'—SPIRITUAL TELEGRAPH, NEW YORK, FEBRUARY 25, 1860.

"These ominous words 'Time up!' are not unfamiliar to our patrons. We have written them, from time to time, on the margin of the paper, to signify to our subscribers that the period for which they had paid for the *Telegraph* had expired, and also to signify to them our solicitations for their further remittance and continued support.

"But as time rolls on, human needs and relations change, and the most familiar words even, change their positions, relations, and meaning. So now, instead of writing these words, 'Time up!' on the margin of the paper as an invitation for the renewal of subscriptions, we place them at the head of the editorial columns to signify that the prophecy we made, and the hope we have often expressed, that a man better calculated to unfold this great subject —Spiritualism—and introduce it practically to the people, would ere this appear to take our place, is, we trust, about to be realized.

"The spectre, 'Time up!' and the man, seemingly, has appeared. Mr. Andrew Jackson Davis has commenced the publication of a weekly paper called the *Herald of Progress*, and arrangements between him and ourselves have been made to transfer the *Spiritual Telegraph* to the *Herald of Progress*, which commences its regular weekly issue next Saturday, the 3d of March. . . . . . .

"No pecuniary considerations induced us to commence the publication of the *Spiritual Telegraph*, and no such considerations enter into our present determination to transfer it. In our introductory address in the first issue of this paper, under date of May 8, 1852, may be found the following:

"'I have not undertaken this enterprise with the hope or expectation of pecuniary profit, and I shall be entirely satisfied if it shall meet the wishes of those most deeply interested, and at the same time subserve the great interest of human progress. I shall publish the paper weekly for one year, whether it pays or not.' . . . . . .

"We ought, however, to say that the pecuniary earnings of the *Telegraph* never bore a more favorable relation to its expenses than during the last few months; and it never seemed to be so well appreciated, or to stand so favorably before the public, as at present, which our private letters and the voluntary notices of the press and pulpit abundantly testify. Neither has there ever been a more substantial increase of patronage than of late; and had it not been for a long-cherished hope and a settled determination, as we have often intimated in these columns, to withdraw from our present position of conducting the *Telegraph* at the earliest opportunity which looked promising for a carrying forward by other hands the work we had begun, we should not now have made this transfer. But other business of our own, and the charitable institutions in which we delight to labor, have absorbed nearly all our attention and time in the day, and we have been obliged to do all our writing for this paper while other people have slept, which has, we believe, shortened our life on earth some years, as begins to appear by declining health; and our duty to ourselves, our growing family, our friends, and to humanity, demands that we transfer different branches of our business whenever favorable opportunities occur.

"It seems appropriate that we should say something on this occasion respecting the inception, progress, 'irrepressible conflicts,' and the success, of the *Spiritual Telegraph*.

"First, then, the *Spiritual Telegraph* was projected out of existing spirit manifestations, a knowledge of which was deemed important to the happiness of all mankind; and a paper seemed to be the usual and the best method of disseminating the glad tidings from that world from which it was said and sung that 'no traveller returns.' We did not at first expect to issue more than a few numbers, and these were intended to contain merely statements of the facts which should from time to time appear. Accordingly, a few tracts were issued in the year 1851 and the early part of 1852, entitled 'A New Leaf.'

"But the manifestations of spirits so increased that we found more space and a regular issue would be required to make a record of them. Accordingly, on the 8th of May, 1852, we published the first number of the *Spiritual Telegraph*, and have since continued it regularly each week to the present number, which is but eight copies short of eight complete yearly volumes. . . . . . .

"The *Spiritual Telegraph* has been eminently successful in all the purposes for which it was established. It was designed for a record of the communications and manifestations of spirits, and for an earnest, candid criterion of the same; also as an organ for a respectful and free interchange of experiences and thoughts, *pro* and *con*, on all subjects; and especially those subjects which were new, instructive, and elevating to mankind. In these respects it forms an encyclopedia of new phenomena and of the best thoughts, *pro* and *con*, on the profoundest subjects which ever engaged the minds of men. . . . . . .

"The *Telegraph* was not established for pecuniary gains, and in this also it has been successful, and we have the satisfaction of having contributed the best years of our life, and largely of our means, to so worthy an object; and, finally, we have to say that the *Telegraph* was never so well appreciated, and never exerted a more wide and healthy influence than at present, and never was more successful in all its purposes and interests than at the moment of its change. . . . . . .

"We by no means arrogate to ourselves the credit of all the brilliant successes of the *Telegraph.* Much of this is due to influences which have surrounded us; to the able contributors to its columns, and to Brother Fishbough, who has been our indefatigable co-laborer. We now resign our position to Friend Davis, in hope that he will reap some of the benefits of our labors, and will be able to do more and better for the happiness and elevation of mankind than ourselves."

Believing that all, and far more, of successful and untiring effort than the modesty of the proprietor has permitted him to affirm in these extracts, will be cordially acknowledged in behalf of this invaluable paper by all classes of Spiritualists, we deem this brief tribute to its inestimable service will be found as acceptable to our readers as it is well-merited.

Amongst other changes of a progressive character, the conversion of the Messrs Owen, father and son, to the cause of Spiritualism must not pass unnoticed.

Of Mr. Robert Owen, the elder, the great philanthropist, and originator of a humanitary scheme of socialism, it is needless to speak, except to remark that his obstinate adherence to a purely materialistic belief, and the injury which his influential opinions were supposed to exert on the cause of religion, made his conversion to Spiritualism, through the test mediumship of Mrs. Hayden, of Boston, a subject of wide-spread interest, and universal astonishment.

One of England's most prominent statesmen declared "that Mrs. Hayden deserved a monument, if only for the conversion of Robert Owen."

Meantime the influence of the great socialist leader drew to a careful examination of the subject, hundreds of minds who were ready to follow in the clear footprints of so great a man, although they did not feel strong enough to stand alone, even for the sake of truth and immortality.

About the close of the year 1859, Hon. Robert Dale Owen, late American Minister to Naples, and one of the most esteemed literary and accomplished statesmen of the day, published, in Philadelphia, his popular work, "Footfalls on the Boundary of Another World."

This volume, which is an admirable digest of the Spiritualism of many lands and periods, coming from so authoritative a source, and known to embody much of the author's personal observations, created a new interest in the subject, and increased the demand for Mr. Owen's work almost beyond the publisher's capacity to supply. Another missionary, of equal interest to those who can only receive opinions from high quarters, was the volume of "Life Incidents," indited by the celebrated medium, D. D. Home, whose wonderful spirit *séances* and cordial reception in nearly all the courts of Europe and by the highest magnates, cast a remarkable illumination over the *assumed* "unpopularity" of Spiritualism in the eyes of *unaristocratic* Americans.

By these two volumes alone, Spiritualism, whilst numbering its five millions in America, was discovered to hold its irresistible sway over the minds of princes, potentates, and powers, as well as peoples. Nothing in the history of the movement, however, excites such profound astonishment in retrospection as the silent and mysterious methods of its propagandism.

CHAPTER XV.

SPIRITUALISM IN NEW YORK—CONCLUDED.

"And they were all amazed and marvelled, saying, one to another, 'Behold, are not all these which speak Galileans?'
"Others, mocking, said, 'These men are full of new wine.'"

THE NEW YORK SPIRITUAL ROSTRUM—SPEAKING MEDIUMS—TEST MEDIUMS IN NEW YORK—NEW YORK PROMINENT SPIRITUALISTS—LINTON, THE MEDIUM—THE GREAT TABERNACLE MEETING—INVESTIGATIONS AT THE NEW YORK MECHANICS' INSTITUTE—THE BUFFALO DOCTORS—STEPHEN ALBRO—MISS BROOKS AND CORA SCOTT—BUFFALO SPIRITUALISTS.

FROM the year 1853 the Spiritualists of New York succeeded in establishing regular Sunday meetings, which were held at first in the Stuyvesant Institute, afterwards in Hope Chapel, and finally in Dodworth Hall, where with but little or no interruption, they have continued for above fourteen years. The services consisted generally of select readings, extemporaneous prayers, and a lecture delivered, morning and evening, by the most accomplished speakers that the spiritual ranks could afford.

The musical services, which were interspersed with the readings, were originally organized and conducted by Mrs. Emma Hardinge and a choir of from twenty to thirty volunteer singers.

As the young performers were nearly all mediums, and the anthems, hymns, etc., were composed for them by their directress, the musical exercises formed a highly attractive feature of the meetings. For the most part they were attended by a large and eager throng of listeners, and when the favorite speakers of the spiritual ranks filled the rostrum, the fine hall was invariably crowded to overflowing, and the New York papers vented their usual complement of vituperation and insult by way of satisfaction to the wounded feelings of rival sects and to the manifest increase of the Spiritualists' popularity.

After the establishment of the Spiritualists in Dodworth Hall, the New York Conference held its sittings there on the Sunday afternoons, when strangers were admitted, and though they might possess totally opposite views, were always courteously permitted to share in the discussions.

To give an idea of the meetings that were held in New York about this time, it will be in order to mention the names and characteristics of some of the speakers who officiated, most of whom were engaged by the committee for a course of several successive Sabbaths.

Occupying a deservedly foremost rank in this distinguished array were A. J. Davis, and his amiable and talented wife, Mrs. Mary Davis, who in point of pleasing oratory, was even more acceptable on the rostrum than the great "Poughkeepsie Seer," her husband. S. B. Britain, Charles Partridge, Dr. Hallock, Joel Tiffany, and Rev. William Fishbough, all too well known and appreciated to need description, contributed often, by their talents and eloquence, to the clear exposition of Spiritualism. John Bovee Dodds, formerly one of the distinguished opponents of the cause. was now one of its able advocates on the New York platform.

Rev. R. P. Ambler, and Rev. Thomas L. Harris, were also amongst the most popular of the speakers.

Dr. J. Orton, W. S. Courtney, a highly distinguished lawyer; Rev. Thomas Benning, a most exemplary and accomplished gentleman, formerly a Wesleyan minister; J. H. Toohey, a fine logical speaker, late editor of the *Christian Spiritualist;* Dr. Wellington, a successful medical practitioner; Professor Hare; L. Judd Pardee, a fine trance speaker; Professor Denton- an eminent geologist and admirable lecturer; Hon. Warren Chase, ex-Congressman and one of the most logical and philosophical lecturers in the field; S. J. Finney an inspirational speaker of extraordinary ability; and Thomas Gates Forster, a gentleman of literary talent, whose discourses, for eloquence, power, and wide range of thought, have never been surpassed on any pulpit or platform, formed the chief male portion of the lecturers engaged to discourse to the New York audiences.

Besides these, the array of female talent was equally strong and remarkable. One of the earliest of this class of lecturers was Miss C. M. Beebe, a lady whose written essays form as fine specimens of modern literature as any that the language contains. Deservedly preëminent in spiritual and personal attractions, also, was Mrs. Cora Hatch, a young lady of scarce seventeen summers, but who, after several years of wonderful phenomenal mediumship, was controlled to deliver discourses whose marvellous beauty of diction and style of oratory was their least attraction. Mrs. Hatch lectured on almost every science with equal facility and correctness. Her discourses were always delivered in a profound trance, were most commonly selected by a committee chosen from the audience at the time of their delivery, and were succeeded by the answering of questions propounded on the spot, the apt and felicitous nature of which presented evidence of the highest and most intellectual control that could be brought to bear upon a merely mortal medium. Of a similar character, both in the matter and fascinating manner of delivery, were the trance discourses of Mrs. Emma Jay Bullene, with whom the additional charm of delightful singing was added to her extemporaneous oratory. Miss Sprague, a young lady of scarcely inferior attractions, was another of this gifted band. Mrs. Charlotte Tuttle, a charming and vivacious trance speaker, Mrs. Hattie Huntley, Mrs. Frances Hyzer, and Mrs. M. S. Townsend, were also distinguished favorites of the New York rostrum. The largest and most appreciative audiences that ever sustained with generous sympathy the sensitive natures of those abnormal oratresses, were kindly accorded to Emma Hardinge, the choir leader, who had also, under the control of her spirit guides, become a trance or inspirational speaker; and when to these is added an occasional visit from one or other of the hundreds of speakers who were scattered through various parts of the States, the quality of the spiritual platform at Dodworth Hall, New York, may be fairly estimated.

Besides this meeting, several others were held in different parts of the city; amongst these there was one for many years conducted at Lamartine Hall by the learned Dr. Horace Dresser. In the Bowery, Sixth avenue, Brooklyn, Williamsburgh, and Morrisania, regular Sunday meetings were sustained. Besides the free circles of Miss Laura Edmonds, J. B. Conklin, Kate Fox, and Emma Hardinge, upwards of three hundred private circles were known to be held in New York about this time, at which admirable and accomplished mediums presided.

Amongst the more distinguished professional or public mediums were Mrs. Coan, the excellent test rapping medium; George Redman, a rapping, writing, and test medium of the most astounding physical endowments; Mrs. Cora Brown, Miss Middlebrook, and Miss Sarah Irish, admirable mediums for tests by rapping, seeing, writing, trance, etc.; Mrs. Bradley and Mrs. Townsend, remarkable mediums for the production of spirit drawings; Mrs. Kellog, one of the best clairvoyant, personating, seeing, and writing mediums in the country; Mrs. Harriet Porter, a most wonderful prophetic speaking and seeing test medium; Miss Seabring, an excellent test tipping medium; Miss Mildred Cole, a child scarcely twelve years of age, but whose endowments as a test medium in every variety of development were almost unequalled; and the still famous Mrs. Leah Fish, of the Fox family [afterwards the wife of Mr. Calvin Brown], whose crowded *séances* attested the undiminished force of her wonderful phenomenal powers.

With such facilities for investigating the science, discussing the philosophy, and enjoying the consoling religion of Spiritualism, can it be wondered at that Spiritualists began to number their thousands and tens of thousands in New York, and that, as a science and religion both, it at last compelled respectful recognition from the public. A few more notices of the prominent features of the cause in New York, and our record in that direction must be brought to a close.

Besides opening his house for receptions, circles, conferences, and hospitality of the most profuse and noble kind, Mr. Charles Partridge, in varieties of ways, continued to benefit the cause of Spiritualism with purse, person, and character.

Organizing circles, hiring mediums from distant parts of the country, and bearing his part in the financial and executive departments of the meetings with unsparing liberality, this gentleman's unflagging zeal also carried him on to the rostrum, where his plain, straightforward candor invariably secured for him a respectful and appreciative auditory.

On several occasions he was invited to address the "Young Men's Christian Association" of New York, and in a series of logical yet perfectly plain arguments he brought his strong sense and vast experience to a successful issue in inducing members of that body to investigate the claims of Spiritualism.

Judge Edmonds and Dr. Warner also opened their splendid residences for weekly receptions of Spiritualists, thus promoting a social feeling and kindly interchange of sentiment between different classes of the believers that operated very favorably upon all.

Mrs. Hatch frequently held investigating circles, where the philosophy of the communion was discussed with the most distinguished savans of the country, the spirits controlling the young medium with a display of ability that was acknowledged to be perfectly supra-mundane. Mrs. Brown and Emma Hardinge held investigating circles for the purpose of testing the more rare and occult phenomena by which the physical manifestations were made. These meetings often resulted in the most astonishing displays of spirit-power, and it is to be regretted that their details cannot be given to the public, as they would make the recorded phenomena appear insignificant by their side. Emma Hardinge and two or three of the prominent New York mediums also entered into a set of experiments on mental telegraphy, from which the most interesting results were obtained.

In 1855 "the Society for the Diffusion of Spiritual Knowledge" published a large volume of 530 pages, entitled "The Healing of the Nations." It is a collection of aphorisms on every imaginable subject and condition of life, arranged in short, poetic prose verses, the beauty of which, whether in sentiment, imagery, or purity of diction, makes it a work of unrivalled excellence and spiritual elevation.

The production of this book was due to the mediumship of Mr. Charles Linton, a young man developed into the spiritual ranks from the humble sphere of a blacksmith, where his opportunities for intellectual culture were of course very limited. Notwithstanding this disadvantage, Mr. Linton became a writing medium of such extraordinary capacity that he attracted the attention of Governor Tallmadge, under whose able editorship the "Healing of the Nations" was published.

Governor Tallmadge gives the following account of this work and its origin in his editorial introduction :

"About a year ago Mr. Linton was directed to write no more miscellaneous communications, but to give his attention to writing a book which would be dictated to him through spiritual influence.

"He procured, according to direction, a thick, bound, blank volume, of the largest ruled letter sheet, and in that commenced writing. This book itself is almost a miracle. The chirography is beautiful. The handwriting of the medium herein is entirely different from his own, and can be read as easily as print. It is written with an accuracy and neatness that could not be surpassed by the most expert copyist. There are four hundred and thirty pages in the volume and not a word of importance erased or interlined throughout the whole. A large portion of it has been written in my presence. . . . . . .

"During the time I was with Linton he wrote from five to ten pages a day. He wrote rapidly whilst the influence was on him. . . . . . .

"Many literary and scientific gentlemen have examined the original volume, and pronounce portions of it beyond human conception.

"The style is simply faultless, and adapted to every capacity. The most astute critic cannot strike out a word in a single sentence and substitute another which he can truthfully say will improve it in style or sentiment."

In 1855 an immense spiritual meeting was held in a great building, since pulled down, called "the Tabernacle."

The house, though capable of holding upwards of four thousand persons, was crowded to suffocation and hundreds went away unable to obtain admission.

The following notice of this meeting appears in one of the New York papers.

"GREAT SPIRITUAL MEETING—ADDRESSES BY GOVERNOR TALLMADGE, REV. T. L. HARRIS, AND JUDGE EDMONDS.

"NEW YORK, *February* 24, 1855.

"According to the published notices in the daily papers of this city, a meeting of the Spiritualists was convened at the Broadway Tabernacle, on Friday evening, February 16. Long before the time for the commencement of the services, the house was filled by an immense audience, which must have numbered over five thousand persons.

"The following statement of the *Daily Sun* may be taken as the general estimate:

"'SPIRITUAL MASS MEETING.—The largest meeting of the season was held last evening at the Broadway Tabernacle by the Spiritualists. The galleries and every available spot in the house were densely packed, and the greatest possible interest was kept up during the whole proceedings.

"'The meeting will prove, no doubt, a season long to be remembered, for while it is a significant answer to the assertion that Spiritualism is 'passing away,' the impression left on the minds of those who attended must be the best evidence that Spiritualism was internal and sympathetic as well as external and numerous.

"'If we needed confirmation on the subject of spiritual progress in this city, it would be found in the fact that Spiritualism was allowed a hearing in the Tabernacle, for two years ago, when the Rev. Mr. Madison got up a theological farce in the same place, the friends of Spiritualism wished the use of the Tabernacle to say what 'is and what is not Spiritualism;' but then it could not be had for that purpose. There may have been good reasons for the refusal, but be that as it may, one thing is plain, either Spiritualism is better understood, or else it is more popular—the present meeting being the authority.'

"It would be unnecessary to notice the addresses which were made on the occasion, except to say that they were listened to with deep interest by the secular portion of the audience, and reported in an unusually respectful tone by the press."

Amongst the numerous literary, scientific, and even religious societies that began to realize the growing popularity of Spiritualism and the necessity for investigating its claims, was "the New York Philosophical Society of the Mechanics' Institute."

At three of the meetings of this society, Mrs. Coan, J. B. Conklin, and Mr. Charles Partridge were invited to be present. The investigations through the two first-named mediums consisted of regular *séances*, in which the various members of the association tested the raps and movements of the table in the usual way—writing names of spirit friends, ages, places of death, diseases, and every conceivable token of identity on several slips of paper, and then rolling them up in tight pellets and throwing them pell-mell upon the table.

Each pellet was picked out and arranged by the raps or tips in corresponding series; the questions or tests suggested in them were then all correctly spelled out by the controlling spirits, and as each pellet was opened it was found to correspond, whilst every answer to test questions was given correctly. Many of the questions were propounded in mystic ways, and some in the German language, but the answers to all invariably indicated the personality of the spirit, his or her perfect understanding of the questioner's meaning, besides conveying in many ways an amount of spontaneous intelligence that was not asked for.

The impression produced upon the minds of the shrewd inquisitors was deep and earnest. All agreed in the report which was subsequently issued, namely, that no evidence whatever of fraud or deception could be traced on the part of the medium; that the intelligence rendered was correct, and in view of its supra-mundane character, truly astounding, and could not have been the result of chance, accident, or, in many cases, even psychological impression. On the third evening, Mr. Charles Partridge addressed the meeting in terms so clear and logical that he was listened to with the most profound attention and interest, and the *séances* closed with a unanimous vote of the society to continue their investigations during the ensuing winter session.

It would scarcely be possible to close our notice of Spiritualism in New York without making special reference to the manifestations which have occurred in the extreme western city of the State, Buffalo.

In spiritualistic annals Buffalo has been less celebrated than notorious, as the scene of the famous exposition of the learned "Buffalo Doctors," Messrs. Flint, Lee, and Coventry.

As this transaction stands almost unrivalled for folly and even psychological absurdity, it becomes necessary to assign to it the prominent place which its remarkable features deserve; we shall therefore give the *exposè* in all its details, by inserting the letter written by the said "Buffalo Doctors" to the *Commercial Advertiser*.

It must be stated that the circumstances referred to took place during the visit of the Misses Fox to Buffalo, in 1851. In February of that year, Mrs. Fish and her sister, Margaretta Fox, commenced giving *séances* at the Phelps House, which were thronged with all the *élite* of the city, amongst whom were the Professor of Physiology, the Professor of Materia Medica, and a Professor of the Practice of Medicine, of the University of Buffalo. In virtue, it may be presumed, of the positions occupied by the gentlemen, they deemed that their authority would carry great weight upon any subject coming within the range of their observation; it was doubtless with a full sense, then, of the effects they expected to produce on the public mind, that they penned the following unsought-for communication.

"EXPOSITION OF THE ROCHESTER KNOCKINGS—BUFFALO COMMERCIAL ADVERTISER.

"*To the Editor of the Commercial Advertiser:*

"Curiosity having led us to visit the room at the Phelps House in which two females from Rochester [Mrs. Fish and Miss Fox] profess to exhibit striking manifestations of the spiritual world, by means of which communion may be held with deceased friends, etc., and having arrived at a physiological explanation of the phenomena, the correctness of which has been demonstrated in an instance that has since fallen under observation, we have felt that a public statement is called for, which may perhaps serve to prevent further waste of time, money, and credulity, to say nothing of sentiment and philosophy, in connection with this so long successful imposition.

"The explanation is reached almost by logical necessity, on the application of a method of reasoning much resorted to in the diagnoses of diseases, viz.: reasoning by way of exclusion. It was reached by this method prior to the demonstration which has subsequently occurred.

"It is to be assumed, first, that the manifestations are not to be regarded as spiritual, provided they can be physically or physiologically accounted for. Immaterial agencies are not to be invoked until material agencies fail. We are thus to exclude spiritual causation in this stage of the investigation.

"Next it is to be taken for granted that the rappings are not produced by artificial contrivances about the persons of the females, which may be concealed by the dress. This hypothesis is excluded, because it is understood that the females have been repeatedly and carefully examined by lady committees.

"It is obvious that the rappings are not caused by machinery attached to tables, doors, etc., for they are heard in different rooms, and different parts of the same room, if the females are present, but always near the spot where the females are stationed. This mechanical hypothesis is then to be excluded.

"So much for negative evidence, and now for what positively relates to the subject.

"On carefully observing the countenances of the two females, it was evident that the sounds were due to the agency of the younger sister, and that they involved an effort of the will. She evidently attempted to conceal any indications of voluntary effort, but in this she did not succeed. A voluntary effort was manifest, and it was plain that it could not be continued very long without fatigue.

"Assuming, then, this positive fact, the inquiry arises how can the will be exerted to produce sounds [rappings] without obvious movements of the body? The voluntary muscles are the only organs [save those which belong to the mind itself] over which volition can exert any direct control. But the contractions of the muscles do not, in the muscles themselves, occasion obvious sounds. The muscles, therefore, to develop audible vibrations, must act upon parts with which they are connected. Now, it was sufficiently clear that the rappings were not vocal sounds; these could not be produced without movements of the respiratory muscles, which would at once lead to detection. Hence, excluding vocal sounds, the only possible source of the noises in question, produced, as we have seen they must be, by voluntary muscular contractions, is in one or more of the moveable articulations of the skeleton. From the anatomical connections of the voluntary muscles, this explanation remains as the only alternative.

"By an analysis prosecuted in this manner, we arrive at the conviction that the rappings — assuming that they are not spiritual—are produced by the action of the will, through voluntary muscles, upon the joints.

"Various facts may be cited to show that the motion of joints, under certain circumstances, is adequate to produce the phenomena of the rapping; but we need not now refer to these. By a curious coincidence, after arriving at the above conclusion respecting the source of the sounds, an instance has fallen under our observation which demonstrates the fact that noises precisely identical with the spiritual rappings may be produced in the knee joint.

"A highly respectable lady of this city possesses the ability to develop sounds similar both in character and degree to those professedly elicited by the Rochester impostors from the spiritual world.

"We have witnessed the production of the sounds by the lady referred to, and have been permitted to examine the mechanism by which they are produced. Without entering, at this time, into a very minute anatomical and physiological explanation, it is sufficient to state that the muscles inserted into the upper and inner side of the large bone of the leg [the *tibia*] near the knee joint, are brought into action so as to move the upper surface of the bone just named, laterally upon the lower surface of the thigh bone [the *femur*], giving rise, in fact, to a partial lateral dislocation. This is effected by an act of the will, without any obvious movement of the limb, occasioning a loud noise, and the return of the bone to its place is attended by a second sound. Most of the Rochester rappings are also double. It is practicable, however, to produce a single sound, by moving the bone out of place with the requisite quickness and force, and allowing it to slide slowly back, in which case it is noiseless.

"The visible vibrations of articles in the room situated near the operator, occur if the limb, or any portion of the body, is in contact with them at the time the sounds are produced. The force of the semi-dislocation of the bone is sufficient to occasion distinct jarrings of doors, tables, etc., if in contact. The intensity of the sound may be varied in proportion to the force of the muscular contractions, and this will render the apparent source of the rappings more or less distinct.

"We have witnessed repetitions of experiments in the case just referred to, sufficient to exhibit to us all the phenomena of sounds belonging to the Rochester rappings, and without further explanation at this time, we append our names in testimony of the facts contained in the foregoing hastily-penned exposition.

"AUSTIN FLINT, M.D.
CHARLES A. LEE, M.D.
C. B. COVENTRY, M.D.

"UNIVERSITY OF BUFFALO, *February* 17, 1851."

The publication of this article produced a perfect legion of paper warriors, who did battle on both sides of the question with equal hardihood but doubtful success. Amongst the most interesting results of the *expose*, however, was a letter from the "females" themselves, in which they simply and modestly demanded a more thorough investigation before they would consent to be branded as "impostors" on the faith of a mere anatomical theory.

The challenge thus publicly made could not be evaded.

Another meeting took place, at which the savans were permitted to place the unfortunate sisters in various cramped and painful positions, with a view of rendering the joints "tense" etc.

It would be simply waste of time now to reprint the contradictory, garbled, but almost incomprehensible "stuff" that the learned professors again put forth by way of report on this second meeting, the gist of which was that "when the sounds" were not heard, it was not because there was any suspension of the electric currents necessary to produce them by the cramped position of the mediums, or the neutralizing effect of the antagonistic magnetism of the minds that were watching them like tigers ready to spring upon their prey, "but because they [the doctors] had placed them in such a position that the knee joints could not work." Again when the sounds were produced, it was not attributed to the fact that the scientific clutch was removed or had been partially relaxed, but that they [the females] took sudden advantage of their freedom when the investigators were off their guard, whilst any raps that were heard in parts of the room removed from the mediums, the learned doctors undertook to affirm were not heard there, only appeared to be so heard, and that by listeners who were unacquainted with the law of acoustics, which made some sounds under some circumstances seem to proceed from a distance, when they were in reality made quite near, etc.

Dr. Lee wrote a concise statement of his great discovery for the New York *Tribune*, which was published accordingly, but with an editorial note appended to it, suggesting that as the Buffalo doctors had confessedly prejudged the cause before they had tried it, and determined that the Rochester ladies were humbugging "females" before they saw them, it might have been as well to have intrusted the trial to somewhat more impart al judges.

As usual, the Buffalo University lights only threw a publicity over the subject of the rappings, which resulted in a perfect torrent of investigation, and filled the public prints with reports of *seances* whose highly favorable and often astounding character—witnessed by many of the most distinguished citizens of Buffalo—culminated in the conversion of more investigators to the belief in Spiritualism than had been known in the space of so short a time in any other city of the Union.

Among the investigators provoked into research by the flimsy misrepresentations of the Buffalo doctors, was Mr. Stephen Albro, an old and highly-respectable citizen, whose inquiries into Spiritualism, starting from this simple point, led him into the very thick of the ranks, and procured the powerful advocacy of his pen and purse for the cause, to which for years he lent his aid in Buffalo, besides undertaking the publication of an exceedingly well-written paper, edited by himself, entitled *The Age of Progress*. It is unnecessary to remark further on these transactions except to point to the invaluable results that grew out of the poor medium's martyrdom in the advancement of the cause.

The mere publication of *The Age of Progress*, and the noble championship of its editor, Mr. Stephen Albro, formed a Macedonian phalanx in Spiritualism, for which it owes the Buffalo doctors an incalculable debt of gratitude. Amongst other remakable results of the excitement which followed the visit of the Misses Fox were many new developments of medium power, amongst which we must revert to the case of Miss Sarah Brooks, already alluded to as the wonderful medium for an invisible piano-forte player, and also for a number of philosophical spirits who, through the simple raps, alphabetically spelled out several hundred able lectures, which were each week printed in *The Age of Progress* for more than two years. It was in the city of Buffalo that the Davenport Brothers first became the wonder and astonishment of their time.

Those who have only witnessed their cabinet performances in the midst of a heterogeneous and often bitterly-antagonistic mob, cannot form the slightest conception of the marvellous character of the phenomena which first startled the simple and unsophisticated parents of the two young lads, before either of them had reached his fourteenth year.

Besides the heavy poundings and violent disturbances of the furniture which ordinarily occur with what is called "physical force mediums," spectral figures were frequently seen by the whole family, whilst voices were heard giving them instruction, advice, and encouragement.

Another striking phenomenon of the young Davenports' mediumship was the firing of pistols, rifles, etc., in the dark, against a mark, which, however minute, was always hit with marvellous precision. Very frequently the flash of the piece would disclose apparitions guiding or receiving the bullets, and monstrous arms and hands were constantly seen flashing through the darkness, or even in an obscure light, by members of the family, under the most startling circumstances.

At times the children would be lifted up several feet in the air, and kept suspended there for one or two minutes. The manifestations accompanied them everywhere; in the streets or stores; at their play or in bed, and were always of the wildest and most preternatural character.

As a more extended notice of these wonderful mediums will be given elsewhere, we shall only further add that their residence, like that of Miss Brooks, was continually thronged by eager and astounded witnesses.

Other spiritual manifestations of a far more elevating character were frequently afforded to the earnest seekers for the truth and beauty of Spiritualism, through the joint mediumship of Miss Sarah Brooks and Miss Cora Scott [afterwards Mrs. Hatch, the celebrated lecturer]. These young ladies, both of them mere children in age, shortly after the visit of the Misses Fox, became mediums and frequently held trance *seances*, at which one would be controlled to speak in foreign tongues, whilst the other interpreted the mystic utterances. These, together with the public lectures of Thomas Gales Forster, one of the most eloquent and powerful trance speakers of America, supplied the good people of Buffalo with food for the highest intellectual thought, whilst the more startling phenomena noticed above, fully testified that the work was of a supra-mundane character. Many other mediums of singular power and excellence became prominent in the spiritual uprising of this city. Mrs. Swain, Mr. Sangster, and Mr. Reed, contributed their share to the marvels by the most astounding physical manifestations.

Dr. Griswold commenced, in Buffalo, the publication of *The Sunbeam*, a spiritual paper of an eminently religious tone, and contributed by his remarkable mediumship as a seer, artist, and writer, to the elevation of the mighty cause; in short, no city has been more abundantly blessed with an outpouring of the Pentecostal fire than Buffalo.

Many changes have thinned the ranks and decimated the strength of the spiritual army whose bright phalanx once shone so resplendently in this great Western emporium.

The once-crowded Sabbath meetings have, we believe, languished into occasional gatherings only, whilst the phenomenal men and women who once made the very name of Buffalo synonymous with a Pentecostal outpouring, are scattered far and wide in broader fields of labor.

Stephen Albro, Dr. Griswold, and Mr. A. C. Maynard, three of the most devoted, brave, and unselfish laborers that the spiritual cause has ever numbered, have themselves passed to their spheres of bright and nobly-earned recompense.

But Stephen Albro's *Age of Progress* has not been inaugurated in vain. The mighty flood sweeps on, which his strong hand helped to direct into the channels of human usefulness. The bright little *Sunbeam* which the devotion and self-sacrifice of good Dr. Griswold reflected upon earth's gross darkness, has lighted up the pathway for many and many a pilgrim foot on the highways of immortality, and the ever-open door with which the lavish hospitality of good Mr. Maynard welcomed the spirits and their wayworn mediums, has drawn angel hosts to earth, who will never forsake it more.

The physical forms of the two noble editors, and the well-beloved and generous friend of the medium, have disappeared from the mortal eyes of those amongst whom they so freely broke the bread of immortal life, but we know that their works do follow them; and are gathered up in the light of those sunbeams that will never be quenched in death or forgetfulness, whilst their cherished memory will ever be green in the heart of every true Spiritualist.

Eng.d by A. H. Ritchie

Very truly yours

Cora L. V. Scott

CHAPTER XVI.

SPIRITUALISM IN NEW ENGLAND.—MASSACHUSETTS WITCHCRAFT IN 1849.

"*Dogberry*—Oh that he were here to write me down an ass! But, masters, remember that I am an ass; though it be not written down, yet forget not that I am an ass. . . . Oh that I had been writ down an ass!"
MUCH ADO ABOUT NOTHING.

AN attempt to arrive at the origin of the spiritual movement, proves first, its vast universality, and next, its unbroken continuity with all preceding outpourings of a similar kind.

Even if we were disposed to trace the beginning of New England Spiritualism to Salem Witchcraft, we should find that the victims of that reign of ignorance and superstition inherited their occult gifts in legitimate succession from mediumistic progenitors. In the accounts of special phenomena which we are compelled to reserve for a second volume, will be found the narrative of an apparition whose manifestations by speech, voice, appearance, and direct communion, far transcend any of the other marvels of modern times, yet this occurrence preceded the Rochester knockings by forty-seven years; in fact, although it seems necessary, for the sake of perspicuity, to select a special date for the opening of our history, it is almost impossible to note any period unmarked by spiritual phenomena, which if less prominently heralded forth to the world than the Hydesville disturbances, are still proved to be of a kindred nature, and obviously related to a general and unbroken thread of intercommunion between the natural and spiritual worlds.

The following narrative is strikingly illustrative of these remarks, and had it been more extensively published abroad, would doubtless have been regarded as the true starting point of modern Spiritualism in New England.

About the year 1837, a Dr. Larkin, practicing physician in Wrentham, Massachusetts, became interested in the phenomena evoked by animal magnetism. Observing that it might be made instrumental in the cure of diseases, and finding himself possessed of the requisite power to become an operator, he conducted a series of experiments so successfully as to convince himself of the use of magnetism as a curative agent, also of its value in the development of clairvoyance, which he found to be a very general result of magnetic operations. In 1844 he tried the effect of animal magnetism upon a servant-girl employed in his family, who was afflicted with fits. At first the patient exhibited only a modification in her physical symptoms, but after a time clairvoyance of a most remarkable character supervened; she was enabled during the mystic sleep to describe her own state, and that of numbers of the doctor's patients, of whom she had never heard. When any difficult case was presented to Dr. Larkin, he had only, by a few passes, to place the girl [Mary Jane] in a magnetic sleep, to insure her giving a remarkable diagnosis of the disease he wished to inquire about, and often, in addition, a valuable and effective prescription. Although Dr. Larkin was unable precisely to determine what were the best conditions for the prosecution of his magnetic researches with this clairvoyant, there were certain results growing out of them which were to him—at that time—as unaccountable as they were spontaneous and unlooked-for.

The first of these was the production of loud knockings, which generally seemed to accompany the girl's trances, but in what connection, Dr. Larkin was unable to divine. They seemed to resound on some article of furniture too far removed from the entranced subject to be produced by her, and were never accompanied by any movement of her body which could indicate their source in her volition. Another feature of perplexing novelty to her operator was the constantly-repeated assertion that in these states—which she called "her sleep"—she was attended by a "*fairy*" whom she named "Katy," and whom she described as a female of "rare beauty and exceeding goodness."

Sometimes, she alleged, she was surrounded by "fairies" like Katy, but none of them equalled her in loveliness or power, and Katy it was who described diseases and prescribed for their cure. She said the "fairies" came from Germany and were very good, but "Katy" was her "guardian angel," and when she came the rest were subordinate to her.

It seemed that other influences besides good ones were permitted to manifest themselves in this singular manner.

Under the control of "Katy" and the "fairies" the clairvoyant was gentle, skilful, and sometimes philosophical and exalted, but occasionally an influence seemed to possess her of the most profane and mischievous character. Her entranced lips, as if moved by automatic action over which she had no control, gave utterance to the most blasphemous oaths and rude speeches; at the same time the furniture was often moved about violently by unseen hands, and heavy weights were lifted from place to place. On one occasion, the whole family being assembled round the couch of the magnetized sleeper, and every door being shut, a heavy flat-iron, last seen in the kitchen—quite distant off—was suddenly placed in their midst, and, at the request of Mrs. Larkin, as suddenly disappeared, and was next found in the kitchen, every door of communication having remained closed.

These and many similar manifestations were made, as the girl stated, by "a sailor boy," whom she saw and who compelled her to utter the oaths and profane speeches in which [as he alleged through her lips] he had been wont to indulge on earth. Meantime the power, whatever it might be, seemed locomotive, and followed the doctor occasionally in his professional visits. On one occasion, he was attending a patient whose house was situated alone, on the top of a high hill commanding a view of every object for miles round. During his visit heavy poundings were heard on the front door of the house, but on examining the entrance no one could be seen, and although not the slightest chance for escape or concealment was afforded, the knocking continued as long as the doctor remained.

As some serious misfortunes occurred to the owners of the house shortly afterwards, the mysterious knockings were regarded as "supernatural warnings" of their approach, but from their frequent occurrence in other scenes, Dr. Larkin naturally attributed them to an occult force originating in himself or his surroundings. On another occasion Dr. Larkin attended a public dinner given to himself and several members of the medical profession, about thirty miles distant from his home. On returning late at night, his wife requested him, before retiring, to visit Mary Jane, who was entranced and desirous to see him. On entering her chamber, he was greeted with uproarious laughter from what purported to be the spirit of the sailor boy, who recounted to him all the principal events of the evening, even to his trifling vexation at the salmon being underdone at dinner, and the roast pig being eaten up before his turn came to be helped. Besides Katy and the sailor boy, a number of spirits came through this girl and seemed to take pleasure in rehearsing their histories, giving names, places of birth and death, ages, and many particulars of their lives.

In this way, Dr. Larkin, who was a ready writer, transcribed in a book procured for this purpose, the histories of over two hundred and seventy spirits, many of whose statements he took exceeding pains to prove, and in every instance found the descriptions invariably correct in the minutest details.

In her normal state Mary Jane was exceedingly illiterate and unimaginative, but under the influence of these mysterious beings, her discourse was instructive, and occasionally scientific.

The communicating intelligences varied much in style and tone, but all seemed to urge the doctor to make these remarkable manifestations public, call in witnesses, and challenge from them the most searching investigation. They all prophesied, too, of a coming time, when the intercourse of spirits with mortals should be known and practiced openly all over the world.

About 1846, a most singular and distressing phase of these phenomena was superadded to the rest, under what claimed to be the influence of the profane sailor. The girl's limbs in several directions would be thrown out of joint, and that with apparent ease, in a moment, and without pain. To replace them, however, seemed to be either beyond the power or the will of her invisible tormentor, and Dr. Larkin, though an experienced surgeon, was often obliged to call in the aid of his professional brethren and two or three strong assistants.

On one occasion the knees and wrists of the girl were thrown out of joint twice in a single day. These painful feats were always accompanied by loud laughter, hoarse and profane jokes, and expressions of exultant delight, purporting to come from the spirit sailor, whilst the girl herself seemed wholly unconscious of the danger of her awkward situation. The preternatural feats of agility and strength exhibited on these occasions could scarcely be credited, and the frightfully unnatural contortions of the limbs, with which she became tied up into knots and coils, baffles all physiological explanation, or attempts at description.

One day, a very dangerous dislocation had been effected twice in the same morning, when the medical practitioner whom Dr. Larkin had summoned to his assistance expressed a hope that his services would not be required again, as he was much pressed for time. Uttering the usual fearful oaths that purported to proceed from the spirit of the sailor, the entranced girl bid him stay then, and do his work at once, upon which the limb was again and instantly thrown out of joint, before the eyes of the astonished assistant.

Although Dr. Larkin and his amiable lady had become familiar with these astounding manifestations by their frequency during many succeeding months, they were exceedingly reluctant to comply with the desires of their invisible communicants by making the facts known and courting public investigation. When, however, it became necessary to introduce other practitioners into the house to help in reducing the girl's dislocated limbs, and all the abnormal sights, sounds, and intelligence attendant upon such a case became a matter of notoriety, further concealment was impossible, and the whole country rang with rumors of the weird phenomena transpiring in Dr. Larkin's family. As usual in such cases, the most exaggerated fictions were substituted for realities, but what the current reports lacked in truth, they gained in scandalous misrepresentations; and stories were set afloat, as injurious to the honor of the harassed family as to any scientific value which the manifestations might have had under fair and impartial scrutiny.

In the fall of 1847, nine men, headed by a minister of Wrentham, called on Dr. Larkin; a self-constituted committee to inquire into the evil rumors that were in circulation respecting him. The doctor, without questioning the validity of their claim to intrude into the privacy of his family, quietly narrated to them the circumstances of the case, without offering any other explanation than such as the details suggested.

The committee were not satisfied. They reverted to the outrageous scandals rife in the community, and urged the doctor to plead guilty to the charges. These he indignantly denied, but offered to admit any two or three persons whom the committee or the community at large should select, as inmates of his family for at least one week. He promised to provide them with board free of all expense, entertain them as honored guests, and afford them the most unlimited opportunities for observation, and agreed to abide by their ultimate report, as to the status which he had the right to hold amongst his fellow-men.

Instead of at once accepting his reasonable and candid offer, this committee, and others of the same stamp, insisted upon intruding themselves into the doctor's house at all times and seasons, and made the condition of their reporting to the world in his favor the production of phenomena upon the instant, just as they called for it.

For months the unfortunate girl was tortured with all sorts of absurd and impertinent inquiries and solicitations to call up the spirits, dislocate her limbs, make "furniture jump about," etc.

The quiet of the household was constantly broken into, their occupations disturbed, and their reputation seriously damaged; at last the good, but too-yielding doctor insisted upon a more orderly investigation or none at all, and then his first proposition was accepted, and an orthodox minister of the strictest denomination, with his wife, was invited by the Wrentham select men, magistrates, and ministers to take up their residence for some days in Dr. Larkin's family, for the express purpose of overseeing the doings of the spirits. The choice of the Wrentham magnates was made without consulting the wishes of Dr. Larkin, and fell upon the Rev. Mr. Thatcher and his lady, both of whom it was supposed, from their profession of highly orthodox principles, strict piety, and similar requisites for passing judgment, would prove themselves more than commonly inimical to the deeds of darkness assumed to be transpiring in the possessed house.

The first evening of the Rev. Mr. Thatcher's visit to Dr. Larkin, he proposed to pray by the side of the invalid girl; when in the very middle of his pious invocations, the victim became suddenly entranced, and offered prayers for herself with a fervor and beauty that melted the whole party into sympathetic tears.

Concerning the result of the clerical inquisition it is only necessary to say that both Mr. and Mrs. Thatcher had abundant opportunity for observing and closely scrutinizing all and much more than has been related above, and that both declare themselves "entirely convinced of the sincerity and purity of life and intention of Dr. Larkin and his family, and the veritable nature of the occult phenomena transpiring in the person of the girl."

On one occasion Mr. and Mrs. Thatcher, with Dr. Larkin and his wife, were standing around her bed, where she lay entranced and answering their questions, when the handkerchief which Mr. Thatcher was using was suddenly snatched out of his hand by an invisible power and instantly disappeared, Not a creature in the room had moved, and Mr. Thatcher's eyes were at the time steadily fixed on Mary Jane, so that he could have detected her slightest action.

Remarking that any circumstance, however small, upon which a preternatuıal character could be fixed, would answer the purpose of an investigation as well as more important phenomena, he retired with Dr. Larkin, and left the two ladies to examine the bed, the girl, every inch of her clothing, and the furniture of the room in every conceivable direction.

The girl was then removed by the ladies to another room, and the gentlemen renewed the search, locking the doors and not suffering a pin to escape them. When all was done, they found Mary Jane entranced by the swearing sailor, who roared with delight at their confusion, and protested that he had "carried off the handkerchief to Germany."

They then summoned the spirit Katy, who generally succeeded in regulating the disorders of the house. On questioning her, however, she declared she was unable to help them, and advised that if they really wished for the return of the handkerchief, they should ask it from the spirit sailor.

Curious to pursue the investigation in all its bearings, Mr. Thatcher insisted on following her advice. The sailor was recalled, and after much insolence, promised to return the handkerchief at half-past one o'clock that night. And here it may be remarked that, though this spirit always kept his word and was wonderfully faithful to time, he invariably made his appointments at the most unseasonable hours and inconvenient places possible, seemingly desirous to impose all the trouble he could upon the family.

From the time when this promise was made up to the hour of its fulfilment, the girl was never left alone for one single moment.

Her bed, clothing, and person, were again searched, and either Mr. or Mrs. Thatcher, in company with other persons, were in her presence constantly.

Mr. Thatcher, Dr. Larkin, and their wives, finally disposed themselves to rest, round the bed of the girl, on chairs and couches.

About one in the morning, she spoke under the influence of Katy, and desired that they should all be awakened, as the spirits were preparing to return the handkerchief. The ladies then sat the girl upright in the bed, placed her hands before her on the quilt, and drawing a sheet under her arms, held it firmly so as to prevent her moving a muscle. Mr. and Mrs. Thatcher and Dr. Larkin then ranged themselves around the bed, Mr. Thatcher facing and intently observing her. It was in this position that, as he stretched out his hand to call her attention to a question he was about to put, the missing handkerchief in an instant became visible, crumpled up in his open palm.

The girl then, with a fierce oath, said hoarsely, "There's your old handkerchief for you, d——n you!"

It was the work of an instant. One second, and the hand was empty; the next, with not a movement of a creature within two feet of him, not the motion of a muscle from himself or any other visible being in the brightly-lighted room, the handkerchief was in his hand—how, or from whence, he never knew. The gentlemen looked at their watches—it was half-past one to a second.

Mr. and Mrs. Thatcher quitted Dr. Larkin's house after a week of the most open and thorough investigation, and within a few days afterwards, the reverend gentleman addressed a circular to every brother minister within a circuit of twenty miles, in which he expressed his "entire conviction of the supra-mundane character of the events he had witnessed."

He acquitted all parties concerned of intentional fraud, deception, or connivance; pronounced his belief that the phenomena he had witnessed were worthy of the "most serious and candid investigation;" declared it was the duty of every minister of religion to come to the work of inquiry in an earnest and unprejudiced spirit, and implored his correspondents and their wives to hasten to the scene, and combine in the most serious and practical investigation of the whole subject.

To this letter no attention whatever was paid, but a few days after it was issued, the Rev. Horace James [immortal be his name !], one of the ministers of Wrentham, and an unceasing persecutor and slanderer of Dr. Larkin, summoned three magistrates, who, together with a few persons of the place inimical to the manifestations, constituted a judicial court, before which Dr. Larkin was cited to appear, and on the authority of which the unfortunate sick girl was dragged from her bed and arrested on the charge of "necromancy"!

In this notable trial the Rev. Horace James appeared as complainant, chief witness, and even judge; for when Dr. Larkin tried to address the court, Mr. James rudely interrupted him, and asked the justices if they "were prepared to believe anything that man had to say."

The wise officials, thus prompted, replied, to a man, "Of course not; nobody could believe him."

Dr. Larkin, realizing that spirits lived and could communicate with earth, and perceiving at once that the spirits of Dogberry and Verges had full possession of the Wrentham justices, sat down with the simple remark that "they were wasting time in trying a case which they had prejudged already."

If the details of this unheard-of court of justice should seem to draw too largely on the credulity of nineteenth-century readers; if it seems impossible to believe that in 1849 a poor sick girl could be dragged from her bed on the charge of "necromancy," and a respectable physician hailed before a court of his own neighbors on a charge of sorcery, — let the sequel speak for itself. Mary Jane was convicted on this charge, and actually sentenced to sixty days' imprisonment in solitary confinement in Dedham jail: witness the Dedham jail records in the State of Massachusetts.

As no judicial sentence could be tortured out against Dr. Larkin, a moral one of still more weighty results was pronounced, which doomed him to expulsion from the church of which he was a member and the Rev. Horace James the pastor, unless he made a full and complete acknowledgment and recantation of his unholy participancy in Mary Jane's crime.

In America, where a system of church membership sanctions church tyranny strangely anomalous with the institutions of a so-called "free country," expulsion from church membership, or even an equivocal standing within its awful pale, may be regarded as "anathema maranatha" on all commercial, artistic, or professional interests.

The ban of the church is as potent in a New England town or village, as was the Pope's bull of excommunication in the tenth century. Dr. Larkin loved his church, and had always enjoyed and prided himself upon his good standing within her pale. Of a gentle, kindly, and genial nature, he had maintained for many years the regard and esteem of all his fellow parishioners, and the continuance of these pleasing relations was essential to his peace of mind, no less than to his professional standing and the welfare of his family. But the exigency of his position was in the highest degree embarrassing. He had no errors to recant, no evil practices to acknowledge, and yet the demand to do so was constant and reiterated, and upon his compliance alone, a restoration to his unwittingly-forfeited good standing depended. He determined he would at least endeavor to conciliate his ecclesiastical tyrants, and for this purpose he wrote several letters marked with the most friendly and Christian spirit: but all would not do; nothing short of self-accusations, rife with the grossest folly and falsehood, would satisfy his persecutors. Meanwhile his impending ruin was fast hastening to its consummation. Domestic cares and harassing vexations, thickening around the unfortunate doctor, kept himself and his tortured wife on the rack for more than a year after the conviction of the hapless Mary Jane, when, unable to endure the unequal struggle longer, he bid his persecutors write such a statement as would satisfy them, and he, on his part, promised to sign it. One after the other, he had met his accusers, disposed of and disproved every charge that folly, malice, or slander had brought against him, save the one of "necromancy," which, so far as it included involuntary communications with the so-called "dead," he could not without a gross untruth deny.

Finally, the Rev. Horace James called on him with the report which he deemed would be satisfactory to the church of which he was the pastor. Before appending his name to the document, the doctor read it aloud and found it required of him to declare that he "did not believe that spirits could communicate by signs, sounds, voices, entrancement, or otherwise," and that the whole of the testimony which he — Dr. Larkin — had from time to time given on this subject was false, and hereby declared to be so. As he finished the perusal of this tissue of falsehoods, Dr. Larkin, addressing his reverend visitor; declared in the most emphatic terms *that he did believe in the communion of spirits; did* realize that they could, and had through the organism of the unfortunate Mary Jane again and again communicated with him; that he reiterated and repeated the truth of all he had ever said on the subject; and he then asked if Mr. Horace James, after such a statement, could require of him to append his name to a document which would proclaim him a liar and utterly unworthy of the name of a Christian man? Mr. James coldly replied that his signature to that document was the only condition on which he could be received back into the church; whereupon Dr. Larkin signed his name, handed the report to Mr. James, and declaring that it was the greatest lie that ever was written, and that he [Mr. James], as a Christian minister, ought to be ashamed to admit such a liar into his church, burst into a passion of tears, whilst the Rev. Horace James departed, exulting in his triumph, and proclaiming to all his parishioners that Dr. Larkin was once more a member of his church in good standing! No comment on this transaction is necessary. Its principal details were received by the author from the lips of Dr. Larkin himself, who never made the least attempt to extenuate his own perfidy in the signature of the disgraceful document above alluded to, except by reaffirming the sufferings he had undergone, the ruinous issues to his family if he persisted in refusing, and the impossibility of his believing in his own mind that a Christian minister would degrade his sacred office to push him to the last fearful extremity, and then admit into his church a man who had written himself unworthy of credit in any direction.

The subsequent career of Dr. Larkin, though containing a vast array of deeply-interesting phenomena, does not belong to this history.

It is as much as our space will allow, to advert to the fact that fresh successions of spiritual outpourings rendered the famous report of the Rev. Horace James worthless as testimony against Spiritualism. Dr. Larkin's estimable companion passed away, soon after the last-named events, to the spirit-world; and besides departing in the full and triumphant faith of being cheered in her dying hour by the presence of hosts of the beloved dead, and that the ministry of her spirit relatives sped her parting soul to the bright homes of eternity, this glorified spirit, soon after her transition, commenced a series of manifestations, which brought conviction to numbers of his friends and neighbors that the doctor's wife was with him still, and guided, cheered, and sustained him, through life's rough pilgrimage, during every hour of the passing day and night.

On several occasions of imminent danger this bright spirit saved her husband's life and that of certain others from railway accidents, and finally succeeded in bringing conviction of the immortality of her purified soul, and its continued communion with earth, to many who had formerly been his bitterest and most active persecutors.

These results, however, were not achieved without a system of opposition and superstitious folly, little short of what has already been narrated. The narrow-minded bigots of Wrentham and adjoining villages strove to legislate against the onward sweep of the tide of progress, and dictate laws and boundary lines to the dwellers of the unknown spiritual country. They might as well have passed resolutions against the influx of sunlight or star beams—Spiritualism "broke out" in Boston, and every hamlet, town or city in its vicinity, whilst at least one-third of the inhabitants, including those who had been most active in the crusade against Dr. Larkin and the hapless Mary Jane, contributed to swell the vast and overwhelming armies which now make up the hosts of Spiritualism in New England.

CHAPTER XVII.

SPIRITUALISM IN NEW ENGLAND CONTINUED—BOSTON.

"Oh the spacious grand plantation
Over there,
Shining like a constellation
Over there,
Holy with a consecration
From all tears and tribulation,
From all crime, and grief, and care
To all uses good and fair,
Over there!"

THE SPIRITUAL PHILOSOPHER—MEDIUMS IN BOSTON—REV. ALLEN PUTNAM AND NATTY, A SPIRIT—SPIRIT MANHOOD AND EARTHLY CHILDHOOD EXPLAINED—BANNER OF LIGHT—DR. GARDNER IN CALIFORNIA—HIS "MISSION"—THE BOSTON SPIRITUAL ROSTRUM—MISS BURBANK'S "CIRCLES"—CORRESPONDENCE.

THE public progress of Spiritualism in Boston, "the Athens of America" and centre of New England thought, was far less marked and distinctive in its earlier phases than that of New York. This is due, no doubt, in part to the peculiar reticence of the New England character, since we have abundance of evidence that phenomena were as frequent and powerful in various families in Boston as they were in any other part of the States; yet it is not even now our privilege to speak of many of these manifestations, occurring as they did in great numbers, though entirely within the privacy of the domestic circle.

The first public evidences that were given of "the power" in Boston, came through the mediumship of Mrs. Margaretta Cooper, the daughter of the eminent writer and lecturer, LeRoy Sunderland. Besides his married daughter, Mrs. Cooper, other members of Mr. Sunderland's family were gifted in a remarkable degree with mediumistic powers, and Dr. Larkin, the physician mentioned in the last chapter, together with many other reliable witnesses, affirm that they could obtain satisfactory responses, by raps and movements of a cradle, through the mediumship of Mrs. Cooper's infant, only seven months of age. When Mr. Sunderland first discovered that his family were endowed with these remarkable gifts, his enthusiastic delight knew no bounds. He threw open his house to the public and courted general investigation through his mediums.

In 1850, he commenced the publication of a paper entitled the *Spiritual Philosopher*, from the pages of which the following account of the manifestations in his family may be learned:

"The mysterious sounds have been made in nearly all the rooms of our house, and have been heard at different times by different people. They have been made spontaneously in all parts of the house by day and night. Articles of furniture have been moved often, and at times with considerable force. The spirits have made musical sounds, which we have heard and know were not made by any human power. The members of our family and strangers present have been often touched and handled by the spirits.

"Manifestations have been made by spirits to our sense of sight. The responses to questions are given freely at our table, during meal times, which are thus prolonged often to an hour and a half by conversation with our heavenly visitants. . . . . . .

"They came through Mrs. Margaretta S. Cooper generally, but we have had responses also through our second daughter, Sarah, and also through our grandchild, Mrs. Cooper's babe, when only two months old. . . . . . .

"Communications have been vouchsafed to us, as we believe, from the higher spheres, giving important information relating more or less to the spiritual dispensation now opening to the universe of human beings. . . . . . .

"I can only say my heart is full, and had I ten thousand tongues, it seems to me as if I could use them all in blessing the angelic hosts who have thus taken possession of my earthly sphere. I now enjoy a heaven far more real than any I had ever been taught to anticipate."

Such expressions as these fill up the pages of the *Spiritual Philosopher*, conveying the unmistakable impression to all that perused them that their author was transported beyond the plane of calm and rational observation, and amply preparing the more coldly philosophic for the great reaction which, in Mr. Sunderland's case, as in many others, has followed upon a too-yielding faith, especially in the infallibility of the intelligence communicated.

Despite the claim on the part of the spirits that the telegraphy was "new and very imperfectly understood, even by them," whilst with mortals it was continually being destroyed for lack of proper understanding and requisite conditions, Mr. Sunderland persisted that no mistakes could occur through his medium, etc.; hence it is not surprising that, in addition to inevitable contradictions of this position, supplied by the spirits themselves, Mr. Sunderland had the mortification to fall into a trap prepared for him, which completely annihilated his claim to the establishment of a reliable communion between the two worlds.

His excessive disgust at this one marked failure, seemed to create a revulsion of feeling which prepared the talented editor of the *Spiritual Philosopher* for discomfiture at every turn.

Forgetful of the lessons he had himself inculcated on the effect of predetermined opinions in psychological experiments, he—a most powerful pathologist—brought to the spirit circle feelings of distrust and aversion which his recent failure had awakened.

The result was precisely what the learned lecturer would now teach his scholars to anticipate. His own condition of mind became impressed upon his media, neutralized the magnetism of the spirits, resulted in failure and contradictions, and threw the balance of his prepossessions into the opposite scale, inducing him to write of the once highly-prized communion with spirits in a tone of bitterness only equalled by his former credulity.

The effect upon the community, however, proved the truth of the adage that "in individual failures the world grows wise," and, "in personal experiences, all mankind is experimenting."

The genuine facts evolved by Mrs. Cooper's remarkable mediumship extended far beyond her family circle, and their influence is felt to this day. Various tests of spiritual identity, rendered to total strangers, were published by them in different sections of the country, and though their lack of variety from preceding records does not justify their reproduction in these pages, they are numerous and well-attested enough to have proved the truth of spiritual telegraphy had they existed alone and unsustained by collateral evidence. Good Mr. Sunderland's strong hand and vigorous pen were temporarily borrowed by the spirit-world to set the ball in motion, but it was no more given to him to retard its progress than the Newtonian philosophy was adequate to the production of any cause which could arrest the motion of planets assumed to have received their "primitive impulse" from the hand of the great Creator himself; and thus the excitement produced in the public mind by Mrs. Cooper's mediumship stimulated the community to eager research, promoted the formation of numerous circles, and the development of many very excellent and reliable public mediums; amongst these, we may name Mrs. Helen Leeds, a lady whose gifts in the direction of trance, impression, personation, and clairvoyance were the means of convincing hundreds of sceptics who attended her *séances*.

In the progress of the movement, agreeable social re-unions were held at Mrs. Leeds's residence every week, where the highest order of mind and talent might be found assembled, to interchange kindly greetings, and receive the precious evidences of spiritual presence and communion which were spontaneously rendered by numerous media who attended the meetings, and whose varied powers became thus focalized into a common centre. Mrs. Sisson, a fine clairvoyant physician; Mrs. Hayden, Miss Little, Miss Burbank, Mrs. Langford, and Mrs. A. E. Newton, were also found to be admirable operators for the great spiritual telegraphy which now began to flash its messages of immortal love and wisdom across a net-work of wires inclosing the whole State of Massachusetts. Mr. John M. Spear, a Universalist clergyman distinguished in the temperance, anti-slavery, and other philanthropic movements, became a writing and impressible medium, and by his remarkable methods of procedure — to be hereafter narrated — contributed not a little to the notoriety of the cause.

In 1853 Mr. and Mrs. Newton, now long and favorably known in the spiritualistic ranks for devotion to the cause and brilliant ability in its support, addressed a published statement of their views of spirit communion to the Edwards Street Congregational Church, in Boston, the result of which was their separation therefrom and adherence to the cause of Spiritualism, to which Mrs. Newton devoted her powers as a medium, whilst Mr. Newton became the editor of the *New England Spiritualist*, and subsequently of the *Spiritual Age*, two of the best written and ablest journals which New England has ever contributed to the sum of spiritual literature.

In 1853 the Rev. Allen Putnam, formerly a Unitarian minister, and subsequently a merchant and editor of the *New England Farmer*, gave by invitation a fine scholarly lecture at the Melodeon, in Boston, on the truths of spirit communion, as proved to his mind by a most thorough and searching investigation into the phenomena.

The unimpeachable integrity of Mr. Putnam's character, and his high standing in the community, added force to his calm reasoning and acute logic, and induced a vast number of persons to follow his footsteps in the path of industrious research into Spiritualism.

Mr. Putnam published several excellent pamphlets, some of which were narratives of his exhaustive investigations, others, arguments for the use and divine order manifest in spiritual revelations. One of the works from this valuable source was a little *brochure*, entitled "Natty, a Spirit," in which the author relates his intercourse with a wonderful spirit child who passed into the higher spheres of existence after a brief sojourn of a few days on earth. Natty reported himself to Mr. Putnam through almost every medium with whom he came in contact. He claimed Mr. and Mrs. Putnam as his father and mother on earth by adoption of his own will. He gave convincing and satisfactory proofs of his real parentage and identity; but with a delightful waywardness, bright wit, and yet weird affection, especially manifested towards Mr. and Mrs. Putnam, he insisted on constituting himself a part of their family, joining them at meals, guarding them in danger, prescribing for them in sickness, and by a thousand pretty diverting tricks, innocent yet Puck-like in their singular ingenuity, he constantly manifested his presence in their household and proved the freedom from care or depression enjoyed by the enfranchised spirits of the sphere to which this happy being belonged. Natty succeeded, through a great variety of mediums, and with the aid of Mr. C. L. Fenton, an artist of Boston, in representing himself in a fanciful picture, crowded with allegorical objects, vivid coloring, and all that symbolical form of imagery in which the bright inhabitants of the higher spheres delight to instruct earth's duller intellects through the science of correspondences.

The picture of Natty still in the possession of Mr. Putnam, of Roxbury, represents the youthful spirit as he always appeared to mediums, namely, a curly-headed child of about four years old, with a sweet, wise face, redolent of thought and intellect far in advance of his juvenile form. As the history of "Natty, the Spirit," was the subject of much comment, considerable interest, and the usual amount of ribald insolence directed by the press against the "senile credulity of Mr. Putman," whose talents and standing forbade an attack in any other direction, we shall give an extract from the published accounts of the little *gentleman's* sayings and doings explanatory of his appearance on earth as a child, when according to all the corroborative statements of spirits, the soul grows as surely from infancy to maturity in the spheres as during its tenancy of a mortal body, and as little Natty's earth origin proved him to have been an inhabitant of thirty-five years' standing in spirit land, his juvenile appearance and style of communication was as puzzling to the Spiritualists as it was a subject of scathing ridicule to unbelievers. The following communication, published in the *New England Spiritualist*, was given to Mr. Putman through one of the most reliable test mediums of the city.

"DEAR FATHER,—Do let me call you thus, for you are indeed my spirit father. Towards you first did my spirit experience filial feelings.

"My stay in the body was too short for me to learn on earth what those feelings were. I never knew an earthly father. When first we met at the medium's table" [when Natty was communicating with his brother and Mr. Putnam happened to be present] "your words and tones awakened in me feelings that I had never known before.

"Upon describing those feelings to spirits of more experience than myself, they told me that such were filial emotions—the sentiments which an affectionate child on earth cherishes towards its earthly parent.

"Having first experienced those feelings towards you, you are my father more truly than you had supposed.

"I have come to you as the laughing, playful child, while in reality I am a full-grown spirit; but in earth's ways I am still but a child, and so the child's form becomes me best for the purpose of your recognizing my true state, and the accomplishment of the aims for which I come to earth. . . . . .

"As a spirit, I am full grown; as a child of earth I am little more than an infant, ignorant of earth's experiences and trials. In these, you are my teacher, while in spiritual matters I can help you. . . . . . I need much aid which you can give. . . . . . Strange as it may seem, those who leave the form in early life must return and come in close alliance with the world before they can learn some lessons which are essential to the highest elevation in the spheres.

"None of us can lay the foundation of an all-embracing charity unless we learn by contact with man on earth, his weakness, sorrows, and temptations. . . . . By your example, help, and associations, I can learn best those life lessons which teach charity for all, without which I cannot ascend nearer and ever nearer to the common Father of us all. Spirits in the spheres do not usually learn their need of accurate knowledge of earth-life until they are thirty years old or more. Sympathy, affection for parents, or other motives of attraction, draw the childish spirit back to its home and relatives. But before the age of thirty it seldom returns to study thoroughly human conditions, and learn those lessons of deepest wisdom which are essential to the human soul's highest development. It is for these purposes I now come. . . . . . . In the close connection which you permit between myself and you, I am, as it were, experiencing earth-life — living your life, experiencing your external and internal struggles, and somewhat sorrowing and rejoicing with you. Measurably, my progress is linked with yours; whatever is for your good helps me; your harm is mine also."

Much more to the same effect was given on this occasion, and here it may be remarked that this singular statement is confirmed by a vast array of testimony in similar spiritual communications. Children's spirits, even from the most rudimental periods of life, are always represented as growing to a glorious spiritual maturity, during which, or after its attainment, they are compelled for the purposes of full development, to acquire an intimate knowledge of that life from which they are physically but not spiritually removed. The experiences from which they are cut off by early death are essential, as it would appear, to their spiritual perfection, and hence, have to be acquired through a set of conditions vague and incomprehensible to us, but dimly shadowed forth in the ideas relating to "familiar" and "guardian spirits," also in the philosophy of "medium spirits," of which more will be said in our second volume.

Quite early in the spiritual movement, Mr. Bela Marsh opened a publishing office in Boston, which, up to the day of his departure for a better world, some few months since, continued to be a source of incalculable use to the cause, by putting into circulation a mass of spiritual literature, every page of which has performed its work of missionary labor to the world.

For the last few years, mediumistic *séances*, conferences, and Sunday meetings have been held in the same building with Marsh's book store; so in the quiet seclusion of 14 Bromfield street, the written thoughts and spoken words of this great movement have always found a fitting and continuous representation.

In Boston was, *and still is* published one of the most invaluable missionaries the cause of Spiritualism has ever enjoyed, namely, the *Banner of Light*, acknowledged to be amongst the ablest and most liberally conducted papers in America. As we shall have occasion to make frequent mention of this excellent periodical in the course of our history, of which, indeed, the *Banner of Light* forms an integral part, we shall reserve a detailed description of its origin and status for another occasion.

As the history of Spiritualism in Boston is peculiarly the biography of individuals, it would be as ungrateful as almost impossible to omit mentioning the name of Dr. Gardner, formerly of Springfield, Massachusetts, who was one of the earliest, as he has been one of the bravest and most devoted champions of the cause, from its commencement to its present status.

Within a few months after the Rochester knockings had become a matter of general comment, Dr. Gardner, then a physician in large practice in Springfield and a successful operator in animal magnetism, became interested in the rappings, and in connection with Mr. Rufus Elmer, a highly-respected citizen and now a prominent Spiritualist, held circles for development, at which several of the most astounding phases of the phenomena were witnessed. Floatings in the air—occurring in the mediumship of Messrs. D. D. Home and H. Gordon—raps, clairvoyance, and extraordinary cases of healing, became so common in Springfield that even the usual animosity of the secular press could make no headway against the facts, and the Springfield *Republican*, a local, though very widely-circulated journal, became crowded with records of marvellous and well-attested phenomena. As they do not now present any feature of novelty, it is needless to repeat them; suffice it to say that their effect upon the inhabitants of Springfield was to make thousands of converts in the first five years of the movement, amongst whom was Dr. Gardner. At the urgent solicitation of spirit friends, Dr. Gardner, about 1849, undertook to accompany a relative who sailed his own ship to California.

The exact nature of his "mission" in this voyage, beyond the benefit of his health, he was entirely at a loss to divine, for humanly speaking he had no motive whatever to prompt him, except the urgent appeal of spirits and a concatenation of circumstances which seemed to force him into the undertaking. During the voyage, his benevolent desire to heal the afflicted prompted him to try the effect of magnetism on one of the crew, a poor Chinaman, who lay sick, in mortal agony and danger of immediate dissolution. Dr. Gardner not only succeeded in relieving the sufferer and restoring him to health by magnetic passes, but he also evolved medium powers in his patient, through whose gift of rapping the doctor could communicate freely with his friends in the spirit-world.

By a chain of circumstances seemingly fortuitous, this Chinaman was left ashore at Hong Kong, from whence subsequent accounts brought the tidings that "the rappings had broken out" in that place through a Chinese sailor, and that the "power" was spreading like a contagion, until spirit circles and spirit mediums became as popular and fashionable in the Celestial Empire as opium and souchong.

Landing for a few days at San Francisco, and still unable to discover any other purpose in his long voyage than his restoration to health and the mediumistic development of the Chinese sailor, Dr. Gardner determined to return with his relation in the ship which had brought him out, when, only the day before they were to sail, he was accosted by a total stranger, who met him on the wharf, and with some awkward apology for his intrusion, suddenly, and for no cause that he could assign, addressed him and asked him if he knew anything about these "new spirit rappings."

Astonished as he was at being thus accosted, Dr. Gardner courteously replied in the affirmative, when the stranger acknowledged that he felt impressed beyond his power of resistance to put the question, adding that the rappings and other strange phenomena had transpired in his family, and that himself and friends were much alarmed, yet wholly ignorant of the best methods of procedure.

He added that it had been communicated to them through this mysterious intelligence *that a stranger would shortly arrive at San Francisco, who would direct them how to proceed* and clear up the doubt and uncertainties under which they then labored.

Both Dr. Gardner and his new friend were powerfully impressed with the belief that this meeting was not merely accidental, and accompanying the stranger to his home, Dr. Gardner visited, counselled, and instructed the perplexed mediums, gave them the advantage of his valuable experience, encouraging some, strengthening and magnetizing others, settling many difficulties, and wisely organizing the scattered forces into well-regulated circles. He also distributed amongst them a goodly pile of spiritual literature with which he had supplied himself, and took leave of his grateful new acquaintances happy in the conviction that his mission was now fulfilled in planting Spiritualism on the remote shores of China in the East, and California in the far West. We must here add, we have the best authority for stating that Dr. Gardner's obedience to spiritual monitions has been fruitful of good and blessing in more ways than those detailed above, and besides sowing seeds of immortal light and beauty in distant lands, it has been productive of changes in the good missionary's own condition, essential to the outworking of his momentous life-history. On his return home, Dr. Gardner took up his residence in Boston, where he became the sole and indefatigable *entrepreneur* of the great Sunday gatherings which for twelve years have instructed thousands of astonished and delighted auditors in the sublime and soul-stirring truths of "Natural theology" taught by spirits.

Thomas Gales Forster, Mrs. Henderson, now Mrs. Middlebrook [one of the sweetest and most eloquent trance speakers of the day], Mrs. Cora Hatch, Miss Fannie Davies, Emma Hardinge, and Rosa Amedey, were amongst the first and most popular of the trance speakers who filled the rostrum at the old Melodeon, Boston, where from a thousand to fifteen hundred persons assembled each Sabbath afternoon and evening, to hear their teachings, and listen to the apt and felicitous answers that were rendered, through their entranced lips, to the most difficult questions propounded by strangers in the audience. All the speakers above named were not only extemporaneous, but most commonly gave discourses selected for them by a committee chosen from the audience after they had taken their seats on the platform. Even the bitterest of the opposition accorded to these orations the merit of being unsurpassed in style, diction, and oratory, while they were often profound in logic, learning, historical research, and science. Miss Rosa Amedey, a charming trance speaker, since translated to the bright realms of which she so eloquently discoursed, together with Mr. A. B. Whiting, a young man of fair natural abilities, but marvellous intellectual powers under the spiritual afflatus, generally followed their discourses by poems improvised upon the spot, upon any subject the audience might select through committees. Many other speakers besides those named above were invited to fill the rostrum; all were more or less attractive. The severe New England climate often militated against attendance at the meetings, and the most powerful opposition that ever was levelled against any portion of the spiritual movement was directed against these obnoxious but deeply momentous gatherings. All was in vain, however. They were often thronged to overflowing, whilst the week evening meetings which were always given when Cora Hatch or Emma Hardinge lectured in Boston were literally crowded to suffocation. These gatherings, the admission for which was the trifling charge of one dime, were conducted and sustained with all their fluctuations of occasional financial losses by Dr. Gardner, whose zeal and enterprise in this, as in every other spiritualistic movement, was unflagging and disinterested.

Delightful picnic parties and grove-meetings, often attended by many thousands of persons, were also organized by this gentleman. Conventions, conferences, and debates, ever found him in his place, and being a clear and sensible speaker, his services were frequently in request to fill the desk at various New England meetings.

His championship of this unpopular cause, no less than the fact of his being the noted *entrepreneur* of the principal public meetings held in Boston, frequently brought him into collision with the press, clergy, lyceum, and finally with the *crême de la crême* of science, learning, and religion combined, to wit, the professors of Harvard University, whose position on this globe may be defined as follows: "America is the greatest country of the earth — Boston is the greatest city of America — Cambridge is the brain of Boston — Harvard College is Cambridge, and the Harvard professors are the world!" but as an easier definition than the above is rendered by Bostonians themselves, when they declare that "Boston is the 'Hub' of the universe," so the position of the Harvard professors in reference to the universe may be better understood than expressed. In the following chapter will be found an account of the famous Harvard investigation, in which the professors of that distinguished seat of learning undertook to explain to mankind, now and forevermore, what Spiritualism was not; but as the entrance of these mighty magnates on the scene indicates the commencement of a new act in the living drama of which we write, we shall reserve their experiences for another chapter, and drop the curtain on this by a few extracts from the *Spiritual Telegraph's* correspondence on the status of Spiritualism in Boston from 1850 to 1857.

"'SPIRITUALISM IN BOSTON.'—FROM OUR BOSTON CORRESPONDENT.

"DEAR TELEGRAPH,—The spiritual movement in Boston has some interesting features which your readers may desire to become intimate with. I will therefore endeavor to give them a glimpse of some of the phases the present exhibits, assuring them that at no time since the dawn of the spiritual advent has there been so varied and so intense a devotion here to the investigation of this important subject. Doctors, lawyers, clergymen, merchants, city officers, judges, ect., as well as the 'common people,' who anciently 'heard Jesus gladly,' are all 'with one accord,' engaged in making earnest inquiries as to the truth of Spiritualism, and the facilities for the investigations are now quite numerous and perfect as compared with any former state of the movement, with a good prospect of still greater perfection and usefulness in the future. So you see there is now very little chance of this matter 'dying out,' as some 'wise ones' have flattered themselves, from time to time, would soon be the case."

"SPIRITUAL CIRCLES.

"Our spiritual circles here are quite numerous and very varied. I attended one lately of which Miss Burbank is — humanly speaking — the presiding spirit. Miss B. is a trance medium of the first order, and gives evidence of superior spirit control and inspiration. She holds four circles every week, each of which is different from the others in the specific objects it has in view. One of these circles is called the 'Benevolent Circle,' whose purpose is to elevate persons in the spirit-life who need to come again into contact with earth so as to get such instruction and magnetism as will in some measure compensate for their lack of basic developments in this life. Some time ago I was present at this circle, when idiots, criminals, and others of like condition, presented themselves through the medium, in connection with beings of superior intelligence, and it was very curious to witness the exhibitions of the various degrees of mentality which were made manifest.

"I remember that, on the occasion referred to, Washington Goode, 'One-Eyed Thompson,' and others of the same stamp, were permitted to communicate, which they did in perfect character, abating, of course, anything criminal. Thompson, it seemed, being very much advanced because of a superior intellect and very warm domestic affections, was permitted to have the charge of Goode, for the purpose of raising him to a higher condition. This he could do more readily than those much more elevated, because of his affinity with Goode's condition, which, of course, brought them nearer together and enabled Thompson to work more effectually for the other's welfare. . . . .

"Idiots, too, were brought to this circle for education; and it was very pleasing to see how, as they came, from time to time they were manifestly improved by the communion. At each successive visit they would get some new idea, and gave evidence of decided improvement in mental development. They were always brought by some benevolent spirits, whose delight it was to be thus engaged, and who would have the full charge of unfolding the powers of the previously blank intellect. . . . . .

"STRIKING TESTS.

"Among the many tests of the presence and identity of spirits, perhaps none are more remarkable than those which have lately transpired at the Fountain House, in this city. I recently met a noted medium there, who, I was previously informed, never made a single mistake in his tests. His method of giving tests is for the inquiring party to fix the mind distinctly on some question, without uttering a word, and say to the spirit, in the same *mental* way, 'If the answer be affirmative, please signify it by touching some article in the room; if negative, some other article'—in either case *mentally* naming the article in question. Being previously informed of the method, I sat one day by the medium's side, took his hand, and mentally said, 'If my guiding spirit be present, will he take the medium to a writing which hangs in the room, and touch a certain name, among seven names which are attached to it?' When I had fairly formed this question in my thoughts, the medium suddenly stood upon his feet, led me into the middle of the room, turned quickly round, facing the writing referred to in my mental question, walked up to it without hesitation, and then drew his index finger three times across the name referred to! To me, at least, this was a very fair proof of some ability to read thought. Whether that ability was the man's own mind, or a mind foreign to his, is a legitimate question to ask, and one which should be answered as well by the psychologist as by the Spiritualist. But however this may be, it is certain that the medium was tested in this way several times, and always with similar results.

"Another test medium, much more remarkable, has lately been stopping at the Fountain House, who has given very great satisfaction to all who have met her. I refer to Miss Coggswell, of Vermont. The peculiarity of her mediumship consists in the fact that, in answer to any mental questions, writings are readily made upon her arms and forehead in raised letters, the color of blood! The questioner sits near the medium, in company with several other persons, all in broad daylight, asks any mental questions he chooses, and the answer soon appears as described. These words are raised upon the arm or forehead, and made in somewhat large characters. I had the privilege lately of seeing the words 'Dr. Woodward' standing out in bold relief, and in the color of blood, on the forehead of the medium, in response to a mental question from Dr. Gardner, the present keeper of the Fountain House. The medium was sitting in a circle of several persons at the time, in broad daylight, her hands resting upon her lap, and the party were watching her arms to see the writing appear there; but after looking in that direction some time in vain, some one happened to look into her face, and saw the above name standing out boldly before the eyes of the company. Dr. Woodward—the former superintendent of the Insane Hospital at Worcester, Massachusetts—was, in this life, an intimate friend of Dr. Gardner's and professes now to be his guardian spirit.

"A short time ago some person who had lost a friend by being shot in the heart, desired a test, through this medium, of the presence of that friend. Several persons watched her arms very closely, expecting every minute to see some writing of the name, date of death, age, cause of departure, etc., but much to their disappointment, nothing was seen. After wondering much at this negative result, and regretting it in no small degree, some one took hold of one of the medium's arms, and turned it over, when, strange and most incredible as it may seem, there stood out boldly, raised above the ordinary surface of the arm, the figure of a human heart, clearly defined and painted in blood! But what was most remarkable of all was the very distinct appearance of a wound in the heart, as if made by a bullet! This medium has no disagreeable sensations in the production of these writings; and, if I mistake not, she has no peculiar sensations at all. She is very passive in her temperament and general condition, which no doubt greatly favors the production of these tests. She is truly a wonder to all who have witnessed these unique exhibitions, among whom have been several highly scientific persons of this city, Dr. Bell, of Cambridge, being among the number. Thus the external evidences of Spiritualism accumulate with increasing force, and promise, at no distant day, the conversion of all who need them."

CHAPTER XVIII.

SPRITUALISM IN NEW ENGLAND—BOSTON AND THE HARVARD PROFESSORS.

"Base of heart! They vilely barter
Honor's wreath for worldly place;
Step by step on Heaven's charter
Leaving footprints of disgrace.

. . . .

"Know we not our dead are looking
Downward, with a sad surprise,
All our strife of words rebuking
With their mild and loving eyes."

J. G. WHITTIER.

HARVARD COLLEGE—FREDERICK WILLIS, THE DIVINITY STUDENT—THE TRAP CIRCLE—THE PEOPLE'S TEACHERS—THE "FACULTY" AND SPIRITUALISM—REV. THEODORE HIGGINSON.

TIME has conclusively proved that the action of individuals has had little or no influence on the progress of the vast and ever-onward march of Spiritualism; yet assuming that there may arise very important changes between the then and now, and the now and hereafter, in human opinions, whether of persons or communities, it may be a matter of historical interest to know what were the opinions of the learned professors of Harvard College, on the subject of Spiritualism, in 1857.

The following narrative will be found to contain one of the most marked evidences of this nature that the history of Spiritualism affords.

Numerous instances occur in the experiences of mediums, wherein certain of the Harvard professors have severally and singly investigated the subject, and even become openly avowed advocates of its sublime realities; but in the following incidents the actors assume an amount of representative authority which lays the burden of their conduct on the college, rather than on the individual members thereof, and as it is to the church and lyceum as institutions, that the people have the right to look for teaching and guidance in mooted points of religion and science, it affords us an instructive lesson to contemplate the aspect of the Cambridge University towards Spiritualism in 1857.

It was some time in the fall of 1855 that Mr. Frederick Willis, a divinity student, of Harvard College, became the subject of certain wonderful phenomenal experiences, which ultimately confirmed him and his friends in the belief that he was a "medium" for communion with departed spirits. The power which fell upon Mr. Willis was entirely unsought for and unwelcome, but the phenomena were abundant and wholly spontaneous. They consisted of visions, trances, premonitions, clear sight, impressions, raps and powerful movements of ponderable bodies, and when, at the earnest solicitation of friends, he was induced to sit for manifestations in circles, it was found that musical instruments could be played upon by spirits, direct writing be produced, and extraordinary test revelations communicated through a variety of physical as well as intellectual methods.

Mr. Willis's position procured him access to the first circles in Massachusetts, whilst his wonderful phenomenal endowments and high moral character rendered him an attractive and honored visitor wherever he went.

His exceedingly fragile health, melancholy and studious temperament, and certain religious scruples peculiar to his views and educational prejudices, rendered him conscientiously slow to admit the possibility of spirit communion.

When, at length, his reason and judgment were convinced, his natural reserve and extreme sensitiveness disposed him to shrink with painful reticence from the incessant publicity which the curiosity of his friends drew upon him. A gentle and yielding disposition more than balanced his reserve, and at length forced him into constantly-widening circles, where his astonishing gifts of mediumship became the means of convincing hundreds of the best informed and most influential persons of the State.

In the spring of 1857, and just as Mr. Willis was about to proceed to his "recitations," a lady sought admission to his chamber, announcing herself as Mrs. H——, a person deeply interested in Spiritualism, and a member of a family with whom Mr. Willis had some acquaintance.

Besides her plea of intimacy with mutual friends, and their common faith, Mrs. H. urged her desire to convert her son-in-law, Mr. Eustis, a well-known professor of Harvard College, and, as Mr. Willis was aware, an openly avowed sceptic and bitter opponent of the new spiritualistic movement. Mrs. H. stated that herself and many of her friends, sincerely interested in Spiritualism, were most anxious to secure the services of Mr. Willis at a *séance* with Professor Eustis, whose convictions, however obstinate, they were quite sure "must yield before the astounding proofs of spirit communion which Mr. Willis could afford."

The lady pleaded her cause with almost irresistible logic. Mr. Willis's "high standing, and unimpeachable integrity, his entire disinterestedness and the utter absence of motive for imposture — all this combined with his convincing gifts of mediumship, were precisely the conditions required to affect such a mind as that of Professor Eustis."

The importance of such an adherent to their cause was also urged, and all the motives which could influence the earnest and devout mind of the young divinity student were put into force to second her arguments. Against all this, Mr. Willis had only two causes of objection to urge; the first was an irresistible impression of aversion to the proposed circle, and the other, the prudence which his peculiar circumstances seemed to call for. Not only Mr. Eustis, but several other of the professors as well as the president himself, were known to be inimical to Spiritualism, and Mr. Willis had already reason to fear that his too-ready compliance with the urgent demands that were made upon him for his services as a medium had been injurious to his standing in the college. But to all this, his importunate visitant answered that the present opportunity would be precisely the opening for universal conviction which the circumstances of the case demanded; in fact, under the solemn promise that he [Mr. Willis] should receive "the most candid and courteous treatment" from all parties invited to meet him, he at length consented to hold a *séance* at Mrs. H.'s residence, on an evening appointed for the purpose.

The circle consisted of the lady of the house, Professor Eustis, and some twelve or fourteen persons who were friends or connections of the family.

The company sat, as usual, around a table from which a leaf in the centre had been withdrawn, leaving a space for the avowed purpose of permitting the spirits to hand up any articles that might be placed below.

The room was brilliantly lighted, and the manifestations consisted of loud raps, movements of the furniture, rocking the table, shaking the room, and beating a drum that had been placed beneath the table.

Bells also were rung, and handed up through the open space in the table, and an accordion was played whilst held by one of Mr. Willis's hands only, the other being free and in sight of the whole party. It is proper also to remark that several of the tunes were played on the accordion in answer to *mental requests* of different members of the circle.

When the hour of parting arrived, the whole of the company expressed themselves highly gratified, whilst Professor Eustis, with apparent sincerity, echoed their words.

After this meeting Mr. Willis found his studies so seriously broken in upon and his health so much impaired by the practice of his mediumship, that he resolved to suspend his *séances* until the next vacation. Several weeks elapsed, when he was once more interrupted by a visit from Mrs. H. with an earnest request for another circle. On this occasion Mr. Willis urged his objections more strenuously than ever, and was met by still more irresistible importunities on the part of the lady.

As before, her pertinacity overcame his intense dislike, and with the same emphatic promise of "most courteous and candid treatment," she fairly worried the harassed student into compliance.

The same party, including Professor Eustis, had assembled to meet Mr. Willis, but just as they were about to take seats around the table, Mrs. H. stated that though of course they could not entertain the slightest suspicion of their guests, yet they had all previously agreed, on their own parts, each one to sit with their feet drawn back beneath their chairs; "Would Mr. Willis be so good as to comply with this arrangement?" Mr. Willis replied, with some surprise, that, as he had always sat with and for friends, the idea of imposing conditions upon him had never before been suggested; that the manifestations were invariably of such a character as to preclude the possibility of his interference; nevertheless, if it was their wish, he would certainly comply with the requisition; he only urged, with a smile, that he was then in such a restless and nervous condition of health that in all probability he might forget, and transgress the restriction, but added, still in half-jesting earnestness, that no manifestations had yet been given through him which the position of his feet could affect. Again the party grouped themselves around the table in a room brilliantly illuminated. The instruments, including a small drum and two sticks, several bells, an accordion, a glassichord and its two sticks, were all arranged by the party, under the table, and Mr. Willis, though still entirely devoid of suspicion concerning their motives, observed that they placed them so far from him that, had he been disposed to touch them, it would have been quite impossible to have done so.

The company arranged themselves, and their disposition brought Professor Eustis next to Mr. Willis. For nearly half an hour no manifestations occurred, nor will this surprise any investigator of spiritual phenomena, when they remember that Mr. Willis's extremely sensitive nature was sharpened to agonizing perception by excessive debility, and that he was placed next to one whom subsequent disclosures proved had come there remorselessly bent upon his detection and exposure as an impostor.

Beyond the strange mental suffering which he endured, and which Mr. Willis himself describes as "unspeakable torture," no phenomena of any kind transpired, until the raps gave the signal for the alphabet, and directed that the position of the parties should be so altered as to bring Mr. Willis on one side of the table, a lady of the party next to him, and Professor Eustis at the end of the table, with only a lady intervening between himself and the medium. After this change had been effected, the manifestations proceeded with their usual force and freedom. Amongst other phenomena, let it be remembered that the glassichord and the drum were skilfully played upon with both sticks. On the latter, a certain point of war was executed with great precision and force, upon which one of the ladies present asked, with singular emphasis, whether it was not certain that *both sticks must have been used to produce that effect?*

The whole party seemed to agree in the affirmative, when Mr. Willis felt the accordion, which had been placed far out of the reach of even his extended feet, pressing up against his leg. He intimated this fact to the party, and showed them that to enable the spirits to play the instrument, it became necessary that he should hold it in one hand, with the keys downwards.

This position he accordingly took, placing his left hand on the table fully in sight of the whole party. The accordion resting its whole weight on Mr. Willis's right hand fatigued him, and involuntarily he drew his foot from beneath the chair, and extended his leg for the instrument to rest against.

The action under any circumstances was a natural, even a necessary one, and was executed by Mr. Willis not only upon the customary impulse of such occasions, but also in utter forgetfulness of the charge he had received not to extend his feet.

Free as he had ever been from all intention or necessity to practice imposture, the idea had never entered his head, hence the charge he had received entirely escaped his memory.

"Under any restrictions," says Mr. Willis himself, "it is morally certain that, whether I could have kept the idea of its necessity in mind or not, I never could long have maintained any condition of restraint. Nervous and restless as I always am, the possibility of continuing in any cramped position would be with me a physical impossibility. I could not even at this time undertake to say that I had not changed my position many times unconsciously and involuntarily, but under the natural impulse of supporting the accordion I inevitably drew my foot forward. Had I remembered the restriction I should have called attention to my movement, but it had long since passed from my mind."

Following on this change of position, let it be remembered that several tunes were well played in answer to mental requests by the company, Mr. Willis holding the instrument in one hand, with the other visible to all, reposing on the table.

During the performance of the music Mr. Willis frequently realized a strange touch about his limbs. He had on several occasions been drawn under the table bodily by the spirits and rather roughly handled. Feeling nervously anxious lest such an unpleasant dilemma was now about to befal him, he moved once or twice in his chair, but at length he distinctly felt a foot placed beneath his leg, and raising it up, pinned it to the under side of the table. For a moment he fancied it was, as usual, the vagaries of the spirits who were operating upon him, but the next he was undeceived by Professor Eustis, who, rising from the table, proceeded in the most insulting and violent manner to denounce him as "an impostor," and the whole of the manifestations as the result of the most unmitigated fraud and deception.

At first astonishment rendered Mr. Willis speechless, but when he had sufficiently recovered his composure, he mildly yet firmly expostulated with his accuser, attempted to explain the incident as above stated, and appealed to the nature of all the manifestations produced in evidence of the utter impossibility of his assumed complicity. He cited the skilful performances on the drums and glassichord, clearly requiring for their execution two sticks, whilst his hands were both on the table; the tunes played on the accordion in answer to mental questions whilst one hand was in full view to every one: the obvious and simple explanation of his foot being raised in the endeavor to avoid the manifestations whereby Professor Eustis had been for some time annoying him: all this he calmly urged, and insisted that they proved the absurdity of any attempt to implicate him.

The professor would not even hear him, and his intolerable violence increased in proportion to his victim's agitation. Feeling his strength rapidly failing, Mr. Willis pleaded that he should be allowed an opportunity of proving the genuine character of his manifestations by holding another circle with Professor Eustis, in which he would cheerfully submit to any conditions that might be demanded.

To this the professor only replied by scornfully refusing to "degrade himself by any further intercourse with such an impostor."

At this point the lady of the house interfered, and it being now fully understood that the whole circle and the preconcerted arrangements had been planned with her connivance as a trap for Mr. Willis, she insisted that it was due to herself that Mr. Willis should be allowed a fair opportunity of vindicating himself in a future sitting. As all the rest of the party joined in this requisition, Professor Eustis, with a very bad grace, yielded a reluctant assent, when it was determined that Mr. Willis should call at the professor's rooms the next day at four o'clock, the hour following the students' recitations, and there arrange to hold a circle with Professor Eustis, at such time and place, with such persons, and under such test conditions as should be agreed upon, Mr. Willis only claiming on his behalf that Professor Eustis should suspend his judgment and take no steps, either by word of mouth or pen, to reiterate the still unproved charges of the night until the investigations of the proposed circle should confirm or disprove them.

To these terms also the professor was urged by his friends to accede as being "simple justice" to one against whom none could fail to perceive an accusation, wholly unsustained by the facts of the case, rested.

When these hasty arrangements had been concluded the overstrung nerves of the suffering medium utterly failed him; a constitutional tendency to syncope, induced by an affection of the heart, overcame him, and he remained unconscious and almost lifeless for a considerable time before he could be removed to a carriage and conveyed back to his lodgings.

Fever, delirium, and the most alarming symptoms, supervened. In this state he was found by his classmates in the morning, unable to quit his bed. He retained sufficient memory, however, to think of his appointment with Professor Eustis, and sent one of his fellow-students to report his condition, and assure the professor that he would wait upon him to carry out the proposed arrangement, at the very earliest period his health would permit.

From this point congestion of the brain set in, and in a condition of fever, delirium, and intense suffering, Mr. Willis remained powerless and unable to quit his bed for a fortnight. When at length he became convalescent, and appeared, still enfeebled and greatly broken in health, amongst his classmates again, he heard with equal astonishment and indignation that on the very pay succeeding the circle, though fully informed of the extremely dangerous condition of Mr. Willis's health, Professor Eustis had deliberately violated the terms of their parting agreement by spending the hour that should have been devoted to instructing his class in denouncing Mr. Willis as an impostor, and so violent and unscrupulous had been the language used, that Mr. Willis found himself the common talk and reprobation of the whole college, and the subject of the most injurious newspaper paragraphs. The full force of this dishonorable treatment, however, was not fully realized until the occasion of his next attendance upon recitation, when at the close of the exercises, he was requested by Professor Noyes to remain, and by him was informed that Professor Eustis had preferred against him charges of so grave a nature that it was deemed necessary the Faculty should consider them in an official examination. Mr. Willis replied that the injurious reports which Professor Eustis had circulated had led him to expect this, and in answer to the request of Professor Noyes that he would prepare himself to meet the Faculty, he expressed his entire willingness to do so "at once," when it was resolved that the investigation should take place on the following Friday, namely, March 27, 1857.

On the morning of the appointed day, Mr. Willis received an informal note from Professor Noyes, to the effect that as Professor Eustis had asked the privilege of bringing a "friend" with him to the investigation, he, Mr. Willis, was at liberty to do the same.

Nothing of the function or office which such "friends" were to fill, was, however, suggested.

In this dilemma, Mr. Willis, unable to procure the attendance of the parties he most desired, was advised to solicit the presence of the Rev. H. F. Harrington, a request that was at once cheerfully acceded to by this gentleman, a Unitarian minister of high standing and most estimable character.

On arriving at the appointed place, Mr. Willis — who had at first been informed by the president that his judges would only be the professors with whom he was acquainted — recognized in Professor Eustis's "friend," a Dr. Morrell Wyman, notoriously known to Mr. Willis as an open and bitter antagonist of Spiritualism, and an intimate of one of his own relations, with whom Mr. Willis was unfortunately on very unfriendly terms. Besides these obvious predispositions against him, Mr. Willis was at no loss to perceive that Professor Eustis's "friend" had been wisely selected as exactly the non-professional counsel best qualified to dispose of a case wherein the defendant was a sick, debilitated, and almost friendless invalid.

From the very opening of his case, Mr. Willis felt no hope or expectation of a successful issue. He loved and honored his professors before whom he stood, but the unaccountable bitterness which seemed to possess the mind of his accuser, and the vindictive spirit in which his charge was made, almost determined him to utter no plea or enter into no contest with him.

Still, the statements of Professor Eustis might have carried their own conviction against himself before any tribunal that had not deemed it their duty or predilection to prejudge the case.

Professor Eustis could not avoid mentioning the fact that several tunes were played in answer to mental requests; that the drum and other instruments were manipulated with a skill and power that could only be accomplished by a pair of hands at least, and that one of Mr. Willis's was always in sight during these performances; furthermore, he admitted that when the drum was executing a most vigorous tatoo, and the glassichord was beat by two sticks, with marvellous agility, that both Mr. Willis's hands were not only lying on the table in full view of the party, but that his whole body was in a state of unmoved repose, and not a muscle could be observed in motion. The professors looked puzzled, and once or twice shrewdly questioned how a pair of feet could play such an instrument in such a manner at all, and still more, how they could be in inconceivably violent motion below the table, whilst the rest of the body was in perfect passivity above it. "Did Professor Eustis notice the least movement of Mr. Willis's body at such times?"

The professor could not say he did.

"Granted that the accordion could be skilfully played upon by the feet and the rest of the body maintained in perfect repose—how could the said feet, or the said organism at all, play tunes called for by mental request of certain parties present?"

At this awkward juncture the real use of Dr. Wyman's presence became triumphantly manifest. Rudely breaking in upon the examination, he exclaimed, "Ask Mr. Willis how all that was done; he can tell you." Then turning to the defendant, he cried, in the same rough, authoritative strain, "Come, Mr. Willis, tell us how you did that trick?" Mr. Willis mildly replied, "The Faculty have not yet called upon me for an answer; when they do, I will tell them all I know of the production of the manifestations." "But why not now?" reiterated the friend. "Are you afraid?" Again Mr. Willis replied, he deferred answering only to the Faculty. But the Faculty were silent, and Dr. Wyman was permitted to continue his system of browbeating, until Mr. Harrington interfered, and insisted that Mr. Willis, sick and defenceless as he was, should not be subject to such uncalled-for insults.

Whether the Harvard professors were suddenly moved by the spirit to a sense of their utter incapacity to judge of spiritual things, or the struggle between their consciences and their prejudices was becoming unmanageable, it boots not now to inquire; suffice it to say, the happy thought broke in upon them that they were not "the proper persons to decide upon such a case;" they believed they had "no power to pronounce upon it," etc., and having voted themselves into office as Mr. Willis's judges, they voted themselves out on the same authority, "concluded the case must be referred to a selected committee," and—adjourned *sine die*.

Soon after this meeting, Mr. Willis received a summons to wait upon the president of the college, who, in smooth and courteous phrase, reminded him of the "grave charges" that had been made against him, and that, under all the circumstances, he [the president] deemed it most expedient that Mr. Willis should quietly retire from the college, after which in due course of time a select committee would be appointed to consider his case, when, "after a time, no doubt, all difficulties would be finally cleared away, and no doubt Mr. Willis might be at liberty to resume his studies as usual."

To this specious proposition, Mr. Willis replied that the poorest criminal must be held innocent until his guilt could be proved; that he, Mr. Willis, accused as he was, insisted upon maintaining all the privileges and immunities of innocence, until his guilt had been proved, or declared by a competent tribunal; hence he declined to assume the position of guilt which his voluntary retirement would imply.

The president was urgent, evidently desiring that the case should not occupy an official place in the college records; Mr. Willis, however, was firm, and they parted on the understanding that Mr. Willis should reconsider the president's proposition, and communicate his decision in writing, which was done in the following letter.

"*April 2, 1857.*

"*To the Rev. James Walker, D.D., President of the Faculty of the Cambridge Divinity School:*

"DEAR SIR,—I have given the proposition which you communicated to me on Tuesday as the decision of the Faculty in reference to the charges made against me by Professor Eustis, the most careful and mature consideration; and I respectfully decline to initiate any action tending to establish my innocence, for such a course would be an utter subversion of all moral as well as legal propriety.

"I stand before God and man upon my innocence, until my accusers shall have proved my guilt; and I also respectfully decline to withdraw from the school pending the requisite investigation. I maintain there is nothing in the mere fact that such charges have been preferred, justly to prejudice my character or my position in the school.

"It is the *proof* of misconduct that should be allowed to affect me, and I feel that I may rightly claim as well as anticipate the countenance and support of the Faculty until I shall be thus convicted of imposture.

"I therefore take occasion to inform you that, at the earliest opportunity convenient with my health, I deem it my duty to rejoin my class.

"I am respectfully yours,

"F. L. H. WILLIS."

To this letter Mr. Willis received the following reply:

"CAMBRIDGE, *April* 4, 1857.

"DEAR SIR,—By direction of the Faculty I communicate to you the record of the proceedings in your case.

"At a meeting of the Theological Faculty on Friday, March 27, 1857, a statement of facts alleged to have taken place at two exhibitions of what are called *spiritual manifestations* was made by Professor Eustis, with the understanding that it involved the charge of deception and imposture against Mr. Frederick L. H. Willis, of the Divinity School.

"Mr. Willis was heard in reply and denial of this charge. At an adjourned meeting of the Theological Faculty, on Monday, March 30, the subject under consideration at the last meeting was taken up, none but members of the Faculty being present. After a long and serious deliberation, the Faculty came to the following conclusion:

"First. That Mr. Willis had incurred serious and grave charges coming from a respectable source which, unless he vindicates himself from them, will materially affect his character and usefulness.

"Second. That the hearing of both parties at the last meeting did not amount to an investigation of such a nature as would authorize this Faculty publicly to pronounce upon the truth or falsity of the charges in question.

"Third. That this Faculty must decline the investigation required, on the ground that it would be an unsuitable tribunal for the settlement of the matter in dispute.

"Fourth. That until the question is settled by a competent tribunal, it is proper that Mr. Willis's connection with the Divinity School be suspended.

"Fifth. Whereupon, it was unanimously voted that the president be instructed to communicate to Mr. Willis the above-mentioned results of the deliberation of the Faculty, with the understanding that Mr. Willis be allowed to withdraw from the school of his own accord if he sees fit.

"At a meeting of the Theological Faculty, on Friday, April 3, the president communicated a letter from Mr. Willis, from which it appeared that he declined to withdraw from the school as proposed: whereupon it was voted unanimously, that in conformity with the conclusions arrived at by the Faculty at the last meeting, the connection of Mr. Willis with the Divinity School be suspended until further order of the Board.

"By direction of the Faculty,

"GEORGE R. NOYES, Secretary.

"Mr. F. L. WILLIS."

Let us not be deceived by high-sounding titles, nor even a popular interpretation of their meaning. "The Theological Faculty" of the Divinity School, Cambridge, meant a set of ministers of the gospel of love, charity, and truth—men who were specially qualified by their station and attainments not only to inculcate such principles but to teach and prepare others for their practice.

It meant the highest authority in the land for the enforcement of the divine love which forgives an erring brother seventy times seven times, justifies publicans and sinners, prays for forgiveness to murderers, and teaches men only to expect forgiveness of their trespasses as they forgive each other. To teach such doctrines was what the Cambridge Theological Faculty were supported and paid to do. Yet this was the body of men that branded a young, feeble, friendless man with a stain so infamous in the act of expulsion, that it was calculated to ruin his prospects irretrievably in this world, and perhaps, by the infliction of such a penalty, to drive him into acts of criminality equally fatal to his hopes in the hereafter; and all for what?

By their own resolutions, quoted above, they declare themselves *incompetent* as well as *unauthorized* to pronounce any judgment against Mr. Willis; hence they inflicted their remorseless penalty against one on whom, by their own acknowledgment, *no* verdict of guilt had been found, and in addition to this, every member of that Faculty must have known that the crime alleged by Professor Eustis was an impossible one. No reiteration of the evidence is necessary to justify this assertion, the charge, as made *under the circumstances*, involving simply a set of impossible actions. Thus, on the ground of mere suspicion, the apostolic divines of Cambridge University determined to brand a helpless and unoffending being confided to their care with the doom which almighty justice inflicted upon the first murderer, for it is not too much to say that, in the present state of society, expulsion from such a scene under such peculiar circumstances and notorious publicity, was equivalent to sending Mr. Willis forth to the world as "*an outcast and a vagabond.*"

As Mr. Willis's subsequent career will be found more fully detailed in the biographical notices of our forthcoming volume, it is only necessary to add that his career has not suffered by the tyranny of his ecclesiastical persecutors; on the contrary, that its monstrous injustice produced a reaction in the community which procured for its victim warm and powerful friends, through whose influence, combined with that of the ever-faithful invisible hosts who had their medium in charge, he has been conducted along a pathway of honorable usefullness, every step of which has been an advance in public opinion and private estimation, whilst the immediate consequence of Harvard intolerance and bigotry to the cause of Spiritualism was the publication of floods of evidence in favor of the truth of the phenomena. Our space will only allow us to present three extracts, all of which are pertinent to this case. The first is from the Boston *Traveller* and contains the protest of the distinguished clergyman who accompanied Mr. Willis to the *sham trial* of the Cambridge Faculty, and when it is remembered that the Rev. H. F. Harrington was no Spiritualist, and not even on terms of personal intimacy with Mr. Willis, his testimony becomes the more important.

"PROTEST OF REV. MR. HARRINGTON.

"*To the Reverend Faculty of the Divinity School of Harvard College:*

"GENTLEMEN,—As counsel of Mr. F. L. H. Willis, and in his behalf, I respectfully submit the following in reference to the inquiry before you on Friday evening last.

"I earnestly protest against the use of the 'inquiry' as a basis of judgment upon Mr. Willis in any manner and to any extent whatever, for the following reasons:

"First, It was vitiated throughout by a course of procedure on the part of the accuser and his counsel, eminently partial and unjust. Instead of confining themselves to their proof of the allegations they had made, they shifted the burden upon Mr. Willis's shoulders to substantiate his own innocence. They sharply and perseveringly cross-questioned him, as though he were a witness instead of the accused party, and evidently endeavored to entrap him in his speech. They made many virtual and some positive charges against his honesty of procedure, in connections as to which they had offered no shadow of proof. They brought forward suppositions of possible trickery equally disconnected from any proofs, and boldly assumed these possibilities to be conclusive of fraud. In fine, they took for granted, from beginning to end, the very point in question, to the utter overthrow of the whole inquiry as a fair and reliable ground for judgment. I most pointedly and emphatically exonerate the Faculty from the slightest intentional bias or partiality. But I submit that the position of Mr. Willis was one demanding the most serious consideration; that his character, hitherto unimpeached, should have proved his shield against unsupported imputations; and that the bearing of the investigation on his prospects and his peace, should have secured a restriction of the line of inquiry, and arguments to the points expressly at issue, as defined by the existence of positive testimony. It may be suggested that it was in the power of Mr. Willis to object to the course of procedure at any moment, and that, as he did not avail himself of his opportunity to do so, he cannot now, with propriety, review the proceedings. To this I reply, that under the informal circumstances attending the inquiry — taking also into view the strong bias of the accuser and his counsel — it would have exposed Mr. Willis to severe misapprehension if he had endeavored to narrow down the investigation by insisting on his legal rights. It was emphatically the part of the Faculty to have protected him, had they appreciated the singular one-sidedness of the whole procedure.

"In the second place, I protest against the use of the inquiry of Friday evening as a basis of judgment upon Mr. Willis, because the sole testimony offered on that occasion was that of the accuser, and I impeach that testimony as unworthy of confidence in the premises, on the following grounds:

"First, It may be proved that Professor Eustis has long been noted for an intense and implacable prejudice against the whole subject of Spiritualism, so called; that he has often denounced its alleged phenomena to be deceptions, and its mediums to be impostors, and therefore was utterly precluded from that candor and impartiality of mind which would enable him to investigate, without fatal bias, the *modus operandi* of Mr. Willis on the occasions when the deceptions he charges upon him are alleged to have been practiced.

"Second, It may be proved that in the interval between the time of filing his accusations against Mr. Willis with the Faculty, and the period appointed for a hearing thereupon, Professor Eustis occupied the season of one of his regular lectures before the Scientific School with the subject-matter of the said accusation; that he exultingly declared his preconceived opinions to have been triumphantly vindicated, and that he openly and passionately branded Mr. Willis, by name, as a deceiver and a cheat.

"And I insist that a person who could thus violate the proprieties of his position, as the preferrer of charges yet unproved and uninvestigated, and use the opportunities and influence of his office to pre-occupy public opinion and forestall your decision, has evinced an animosity against the person of Mr. Willis, sufficient to fatally color whatever evidence he might have to offer you.

"At the best, it would be only the assertion of a single person, against which, until it should be corroborated by other evidence, the explanation of Mr. Willis constitutes a complete legal offset. And in view of this extreme bias of feeling it is entirely unworthy to be taken into account.

"I do therefore solemnly and earnestly protest against the acceptance of Mr. Eustis's testimony, unless corroborated, and against the use of the inquiry of Friday evening last as the basis of a judgment upon Mr. Willis. All which is respectfully submitted.

"(Signed) HENRY F. HARRINGTON."

The tone of some of the most respectable portions of the press may be gathered from the following brief extract from the Boston *Traveller*. The article is selected chiefly on account of the prominent position which that journal occupies in the periodical literature of Massachusetts.

"The personal controversy between Professor Eustis and Mr. Willis is of little moment. We have formed no opinion of Mr. Willis's guilt or innocence. Our position, so far as he is concerned, is merely that the charge against him is not sustained by the evidence. On the general question of what is called 'Spiritualism,' we have been led by observation of our own, and by the testimony of others, to the belief that the phenomena called spiritualistic do really occur. We believe that tables and other articles have been moved, and musical instruments played upon, without the agency of any ordinary physical force. We are satisfied that these phenomena have occurred not merely in the dark, but in open daylight, under the eyes of accurate and trustworthy observers, who had no pecuniary or other interest in their production. They have occurred not once or twice, nor twenty times, but in hundreds of thousands of instances, stretching through a series of years, and in the presence, not of professed and mercenary mediums, but in the bosom of respectable households in all parts of the country. They are attested by hundreds of thousands of witnesses, including many persons of the highest character and intelligence, some of whom are themselves 'mediums,' and cannot therefore be the mere dupes of skilful jugglery. In numerous well-authenticated instances the phenomena have occurred under such circumstances that deception or delusion was utterly impossible.

"No satisfactory or conclusive explanation of these phenomena has ever been given. The various theories which have been propounded of 'odic force,' 'new powers in nature,' and the like, are mere conjectures, none of which have borne examination. Our neighbors of the *Courier*, and some of the gentlemen of the University at Cambridge, solve the problem by attributing the manifestations to trickery and juggling. We are certain that this position is entirely untenable, and that to millions of people in this country, it will only render those who hold it objects of contempt and derision. It has been to us, and still is, a cause of regret that gentlemen, in whose reputation for knowledge and sagacity the community has so deep an interest, should have compromised themselves by rashly, without due investigation, taking a position from which they must assuredly, at no distant period, ignominiously retreat."

In the circles of the theological *literati*, no independent clergyman has taken a higher rank than the Rev. Thomas Wentworth Higginson. As a scholar, writer, and orator, this gentleman has long maintained the respect and admiration of the best intellects in New England. It is with peculiar pleasure, then, that we find that the insensate bigotry of the Harvard professors at last attracted the attention of Mr. Higginson and induced him to investigate the subject, and finally to come out of the inquiry in the spirit of the annexed communication, the last which we can select from hundreds of similar statements, to the genuine character of Mr. Willis's mediumship. The extract is taken from one of the Hartford papers, and is as follows:—

"PHENOMENA IN THE PRESENCE OF MR. WILLIS.

"The case of Mr. Willis, the 'suspended' divinity student of Harvard College, is, as we anticipated, attracting much attention in various quarters. We learn from the Worcester *Spy* that the Rev. T. W. Higginson, an independent clergyman of that city, referred to it in his pulpit a Sunday or two since, in connection with a lecture on Spiritualism, and commented, in appropriate terms, on the hasty inferences of Professor Eustis, and the unjust action of the Faculty in the case. We shall probably be able next week to lay before our readers the particulars of this action, when they may look for something for which it would be difficult to find a precedent among the doings of sane men. Rev. Mr. Higginson has also published in the *Spy*, the following affidavit of his own observations in the presence of Mr. Willis:

"'A STATEMENT OF FACTS.

"'TO WHOM IT MAY CONCERN,—The public attention has recently been attracted by the alleged powers, as a 'medium,' of Mr. F. L. H. Willis, of Cambridge, and by the singular proceedings connected with his 'suspension' from the Divinity School of Harvard University. In justice to Mr. Willis, and to an extraordinary class of yet unexplained scientific facts, I wish to state some phenomena, observed by me during two evenings spent with him at a private residence in this city. There were from nine to twelve present, all, except Mr. Willis, being citizens of this place, including one of our most experienced physicians, Dr. Heywood of Worcester, Massachusetts. We sat around a long dining-table. The room was not brilliantly but sufficiently lighted, so that every movement of every person could be distinctly watched; and I, at least, watched them very closely.

"'I shall omit the details of the phenomena, and give only the general heads:

"'First, The musical instruments which had been previously placed by the company beneath the table—a guitar, a small drum, an accordion, and two bells—were moved about from place to place, lifted and knocked against the under side of the table, and repeatedly and loudly played upon. Two were several times played in unison, at opposite ends of the table and entirely beyond the reach of the medium. During this proceeding, the whole table was several times raised, and one slab of it—being an extension table—was lifted altogether from its support, and vibrated in the air without contact of hands.

"'Second, The accordion was raised into Mr. Willis's lap, and being held by him, with one hand, between his knees, was played very skilfully, and executed a variety of tunes selected by us, and even in answer to the mental requests of some of the company. Excellent imitations of the oboe, violoncello, and double-bass were also given. It is well known that the accordion requires, in playing, the use of two hands.

"'Third, Upon our extinguishing the lamp, for the sake of experiment, faint lights appeared upon the table near Mr. Willis, two or three at a time, moving about like glow-worms, which they resembled. Other lights flickered in the air with a more rapid motion, like fire-flies. Upon my obtaining and opening a phial of phosphorus the lights increased in intensity, gradually diminishing, when I re-corked it, to their original amount. Everybody in the room perceived them distinctly.

"'Fourth, The room being still dark, the accordion was held on the table by Mr. Willis, and as it played in the manner before described, faint lights flickered around the keys of the instrument. During the darkness, all the phenomena were more intense, but it seemed very disagreeable to the nerves of Mr. Willis, and he begged to have the lamps restored.

"'Fifth, The room being again lighted, I proceeded to try some closer experiments. Taking the accordion in my own hand, between my knees, and guarding with my feet against the possibility of contact, I found, to my surprise, that the other end was seized by an invisible force, and the different keys audibly handled, producing, at last, musical sounds, but quite imperfectly. Before long, however, it was pulled away from me with very great force, and dropped on the floor. Others afterwards took the instrument, but it was played in no other hands. I may add that I simply held it by the end with one hand, and that I have no knowledge of the instrument; also, that the hands of all the company were upon the table, and that I was beyond the reach of Mr. Willis's person.

"'Sixth, Looking under the table, while the guitar was playing, I saw with perfect distinctness the instrument lying on its back, untouched by any hand, but with faint flickerings of light playing over the strings. I could also see the feet of the persons nearest it, and that they were not in contact with it, while Mr. Willis was out of reach. No other person looked under the table, I believe, nor did I mention these observations till the phenomena had ceased, for I did not wish, at the time, to share my investigations with any one.

"'Seventh, The guitar was moved slowly along by some force, to me inscrutable, and lifted between my knees, the neck resting on my left thigh. At the suggestion of some of the company, I began to sing, first placing myself in such a position as to guard the instrument from possibility of contact. Every song I sang was accompanied accurately and gracefully on the guitar, with a constantly-increasing facility of adaptation. The best accompaniment of all was finely played to a peculiar and rather difficult Portuguese song, probably not known to a dozen persons in America besides myself. I cannot myself play the guitar, but I have heard it played a good deal, and I know that the accompaniment was an extraordinary thing, apart from the mystery of its origin. I know that I was beyond the reach of any part of Mr. Willis's person, and that it was physically impossible for any one to touch the instrument without my detecting it.

"'Eighth, During all these various phenomena, I felt repeatedly a delicate grasp upon my feet, precisely resembling that of a hand with distinct fingers. Upon my slipping off my shoe, it was still more distinct, and was in all cases accompanied by a very peculiar electrical sensation, as when two persons complete the circuit of an electro-magnetic battery. Keeping my own counsel, I heard precisely the same phenomena simultaneously described by persons at the other end of the table. Afterwards, placing my hand beneath the table, I felt the same contact still more distinctly upon that. All the rest of the company held their hands upon the table, and I was beyond the reach of Mr. Willis.

"'I might make these statements still more wonderful by going more into detail, but have probably gone so far already beyond the credulity of my readers that I had better stop. If any refuse to believe these facts on my testimony, I can only say that I should have found it hard to believe them on theirs. Like them, I prefer to verify novel facts by my own observation. I can only say for myself, further, that I have been all my life a student of the natural sciences, and have earned by this time some confidence in the carefulness of my own observations and the accuracy of my own senses.

"'The question of the 'spiritual' origin is not now raised; it is a simple question of fraud or genuineness. If I have not satisfactory evidence of the genuineness of these phenomena which I have just described, then there is no such thing as evidence, and all the fabric of natural science may be a mass of imposture. And when I find, on examination, that facts similar to these have been observed by hundreds of intelligent persons, in various places, for

several years back, I am disposed humbly to remember the maxim attributed to Arago, 'He is a rash man who, outside of pure mathematics, pronounces the word 'impossible.''
"'THOMAS WENTWORTH HIGGINSON.'

"'WORCESTER, SS., *April* 15, 1857.
"'Subscribed and sworn to before me,
"'HENRY CHAPIN, Justice of the Peace.'"

CHAPTER XIX.

SPIRITUALISM IN NEW ENGLAND—THE CAMBRIDGE INVESTIGATION.

"If any old book reached a fiftieth edition,
He could fill forty pages with safe erudition,
He could gauge the old books by the old set of rules,
And his very old nothings pleased very old fools.
But give him a new book fresh out of the heart,
And you put him at sea without compass or chart."

J. R. LOWELL.

THE CONSECRATION OF "CRAFTS"—DR. GARDNER AND THE HARVARD PROFESSORS—THE MEDIUMS AND THE BOSTON PRESS—ANOTHER VIEW OF THE SUBJECT.

WHEN the annals of science can produce recorded proofs that new discoveries generally result from the associative action of schools, colleges, or lyceums; or when they can show that the incipient efforts of genius in the line of discovery have been fostered and sustained by such organizations, we may find a fair excuse for the abject and unreasoning submission with which the great mass of mankind bow down before the dicta of scientific bodies, and assume that the office of a "professor" confers the ability and title to pronounce authoritative judgment, from which there can be no appeal. It was doubtless in this conventional spirit of deference to constituted authority that the Spiritualists of America thought it necessary to memorialize Congress for aid and indorsement from a "scientific commission."

It would seem that the insolence with which Congress had sneered away the Spiritualists' memorial, the humiliating trash put forth by the Buffalo doctors, President Mahan, Dr. Rogers, and others of the "self-wise and prudent," was not yet enough to convince the Spiritualists of Boston that facts spoke louder than the dicta of priests, and truth needed no indorsement from *alma mater*.

The editor of the Boston *Courier* offered a contemptuous challenge of five hundred dollars for the production of certain phenomena under certain conditions, and required that three distinguished scientists of Harvard College should be the umpires on the occasion. The bait of five hundred dollars did not weigh a feather in the scale, but the possibility of inducing the savans of Harvard, to condescend so far as to investigate the despised phenomena of Spiritualism! This indeed was a triumph; and the prospect of indorsement in such a direction, seemed of more moment than the sanction and authority of the supreme spiritual power from which the manifestations originated; and thus came about the production of that remarkable farce, by courtesy entitled the "Cambridge Investigation."

From the best attainable authorities we learn that the challenge above named having appeared in the columns of the Boston *Courier*, Dr. Gardner, as the enterprising conductor of the public meetings in Boston, felt bound to accept it, and agreed to procure the services of some of the best media for spiritual manifestations, to hold *séances* in the presence of the gentlemen selected by the Boston *Courier* editor, who on his part agreed to pay the sum of five hundred dollars, provided that the stipulated phenomena were produced in their presence.

The committee of umpires thus chosen consisted of Professors Pierce, Agassiz, and Horsford, of Harvard University, and Dr. N. B. Gould, of the Albany Observatory, also a resident of Cambridge. The Boston *Courier* was represented by one of its editors, the Hon. George Lunt, whilst Dr. Gardner was sustained by several friends of the cause of Spiritualism, amongst whom were Mr. Alvin Adams, of the express company which bears his name, the Rev. Allen Putnam, and Major Raines, a scientific gentleman of Newburg, New York. At the invitation of Dr. Gardner, one of the editors of the Boston *Traveller* was also present, together with Dr. Bell, late superintendent of the McLean Lunatic Asylum.

Previous to the opening of the meetings, Dr. Gardner had emphatically expressed his determination to waive the award of the five hundred dollars, and only require of the Boston *Courier* to defray expenses, provided the manifestations could be produced as claimed by the Spiritualists. The mediums engaged for the occasion were Mrs. Brown—Leah Fox—her sister, Catherine Fox; Mr. J. V. Mansfield, a writing medium of great celebrity; Mrs. Kendrick, a test, rapping, and writing medium; Mr. George Redman, and the Davenport Brothers. The *seances* were held at the Albion buildings, Tremont street, and occupied a portion of three successive days, namely June 25, 26, and 27, 1857. Now, the result of these meetings, whether we take the acknowledgments of the Spiritualists, or the *pro tem.* report of the professors themselves, was a decided failure.

The manifestations were few, imperfect, and unsatisfactory, and no legitimate claim to the award could have been sustained, even had it been set up, a proceeding which from the first was disavowed by Dr. Gardner, who conducted the affair with the most disinterested liberality, and together with his friends, incurred heavy expenses in procuring the services of the mediums from distant places.

That the best interests of truth may be subserved in a reconsideration of this almost forgotten affair, we shall present such statements as can be fully verified on both sides of the question. The first document which belongs to our subject is the report of the investigating committee, who published the following statement in the Boston papers:

"The committee award that, Dr. Gardner, having failed to produce before them an agent or medium who 'communicated a word imparted to the spirits in an adjoining room,' 'who read a word in English written inside a book or folded sheet of paper,' who answered any question 'which the superior intelligences must be able to answer,' who tilted a piano without touching it, or caused a chair to move a foot;' and having failed to exhibit to the committee any phenomenon which, under the widest latitude of interpretation, could be regarded as equivalent to either of these proposed tests, or any phenomenon which required for its production, or in any manner indicated a force which could technically be denominated 'spiritual,' or which was hitherto unknown to science, or a phenomenon of which the cause was not palpable to the committee, is, therefore, not entitled to claim from the Boston *Courier* the proposed premium of five hundred dollars."

Had the committee confined themselves to the above paragraph, the course of strict justice would have been satisfied with the forfeiture of an award that was not contended for; and though the cause of exact science might require certain explanations for the obvious failures implied above, the professors, either from ignorance of the laws of mental and magnetic science, or predetermination not to comply with such conditions as were requisite, might have found an excuse for the rendition of their unfavorable verdict in the bare facts submitted to them; but what follows not only proves that they wilfully exceeded their functions as scientific investigators, but that they went into the inquiry animated by a spirit of aversion and predetermined hostility, false to the cause of truth, and ruinous to the production of phenomena which depend as much on the mental condition and magnetic influence of the inquirers as on that of the media themselves. When it is remembered that a strong positive will can create or destroy psychological results, and that mediums, the most sensitive of all psychological subjects, are constantly bereft of their powers by the presence of one or more determinately hostile persons, who can wonder at the failure of the delicate and occult phenomena of spirit communion in the presence of four men who entered upon their investigation with the sentiments to which they appended their names, as follows, in the report published in the Boston *Courier:*

"It is the opinion of the committee, derived from observation, that any connection with spiritualistic circles, so called, corrupts the morals and degrades the intellect. They therefore deem it their solemn duty to warn the community against this contaminating influence, which surely tends to lessen the truth of man and the purity of woman.

"The committee will publish a report of their proceedings, together with the results of additional investigations and other evidence, independent of the special case submitted to them, but bearing upon the subject of this stupendous delusion.

"BENJAMIN PIERCE, Chairman,
L. S. AGASSIZ,
B. A. GOULD, JR.,
E. N. HORSFORD.

"CAMBRIDGE, *June* 29, 1857."

Now, besides the effect which the merest tyro in psychology might look for in the presence of investigators holding the above opinions, it is a fact well attested that some of the members of the committee transgressed the rules commonly observed at spirit circles, and notwithstanding their pledge, given in writing to Dr. Gardner and the Rev. Allen Putnam, that they would comply with such conditions as might be deemed requisite for the production of the manifestations, they violated them in several essential particulars; for instance, Mr. Lunt and Professor Agassiz refused at any time to join the circle, though repeatedly requested to do so, and although it was intimated to them through the raps that the spirits could not operate whilst they were standing or restlessly moving about the room. Others of the "investigators" pursuing the same course, the Spiritualists frequently remonstrated with them, to which Professor Agassiz replied that he had "sworn never to sit in a circle," but it seems he had not been sworn to desist from annoying a circle, which he did in many ways, by moving about the table, overlooking the sitters, communicating in suspicious whispers with his colleagues, and in rough and at times insulting speeches with the Spiritualists. We shall here insert a few extracts from the spiritualistic reports, which will at least tend to show that their evidence was not garbled nor the obvious failure of their media misrepresented.

The following quotations are from a printed letter of the Rev. Allen Putnam, who was present at all the *seances*, and in answer to a request from Dr. Gardner, briefly noted down his observations from memory:

"PRELIMINARY ARRANGEMENTS.

"We [Dr. Gardner and the Rev. Allen Putnam] met the four gentlemen at Cambridge, and soon found that they had been named as commissioners, without their own knowledge or consent; and that the first question with them was, whether the services and conditions asked for were such that they could serve. Consequently, a free and prolonged conversation followed.

"Passing from that point, we came to a consideration of those 'natural laws within which we believe spirits are confined in producing the manifestations.' Here Dr. G. turned to myself, and asked for statements from me. My position, taken then, as at other times was, that there is some subtle natural fluid which is essential to the spirits as an instrument, whenever they work here or near the earth's surface; that this fluid can be very easily disturbed and dissipated by the embodied persons present, and this so effectually as to prevent all spirit operations; that lack of quiet and harmonious feelings among the persons present, that intense mental action, the magnetic rays from the human eye, or rays of light, etc., might frustrate its use and prevent its manifestations. Therefore, that it was in the power of the gentlemen there present to make the trial a failure by ejecting certain forces from their own minds and eyes. We stated that it would be best that all should sit in a circle; that all should conform, in the order of sitting, to the wishes of the mediums; that all should avoid intense mental action. Professor Agassiz at once objected to being in the circle under any circumstances, and I think the gentlemen all felt that, when acting as judges, such would not be a desirable position. . . . . . .

"Another point, which required many statements for its elucidation with these gentlemen, as it does with most people who are not familiar with the subject, was the powerlessness of the managers of the arrangements, and also of the media. Even men of science were not free from the influence of the notions that the working powers in spirit manifestation are, on the one hand, subject to man's control, and on the other, that they are almost omniscient and omnipotent, or at least that they can, at any time, overpower man. Professor Agassiz stated that, in all their scientific experiments, if a thing could be done once, it could be repeated twenty times; and, therefore, that they might require the same here. He said this, apparently forgetting that we claimed that the real actor is an individual intelligence, acting according to his or her own will and powers, and not in compliance with our dictation.

"Professor Pierce inquired if we could not ask the spirits whether they would come and manifest themselves at the trial. 'Yes,' was the answer, 'we can ask.' 'And,' said he, 'can you not get an answer?' 'Probably,' we said, 'their reply will be, 'we will try.'' 'Why can't they tell certainly?' he continued. We said, 'Can Mr. Gould now promise certainly that he will examine some particular star in the heavens to-morrow evening at nine o'clock, while as yet he knows not whether there will be clouds or fogs?' 'No,' said Mr. Pierce, 'he can only promise to point the telescope.' 'Very good,' was our answer; 'the spirits can only promise to try, and can, at the time of trial, perform only what the conditions permit.' . . . . . . 'It was proposed to Dr. Gardner that he should be permitted to have his own way in everything, even to the selection of the room, time, and the determination of all the accessory circumstances.' Though this, in their own language, goes somewhat further than what my recollection would lead me to use in indicating my own understanding as to how far the committee promised compliance with every wish the doctor might express as to their own positions and deportment in the room, yet I had no doubt that they then indicated a purpose to give the general subject of Spiritualism free scope and fair play, and not a purpose to act simply as judges, as to whether certain specified acts could be performed in their presence, they remaining inattentive to proper conditions just so far as they chose. . . . . . . In the course of the conversation, Dr. Gardner repeated, in the presence of the company, what he had said to me in reference to the five hundred dollars, and expressed an entire willingness to arrange for the trial, and at its close, report the amount of expenses, and leave it to the option of the *Courier* whether to pay the bills or not, and to thus dispose of the pecuniary point at once and finally. This avowal seemed to give much pleasure to Professor Agassiz in particular, who conveyed the idea that it placed the whole matter before them in a much pleasanter aspect, and would give to them more freedom in the investigation. No dissent from his view was then expressed. . . . . . . From that time—June 13—up to the day of the trial, my belief was unfaltering that the committee would submit the control of every influencing circumstance to Dr. Gardner; that they would be co-operators with him, having ignored the money question; and I was repeatedly heard to express a belief that the learned gentlemen would enter heartily into a courteous and fair investigation, and that palpable and good manifestations would be obtained. Such was my expectation; and it was deduced, and was fairly deducible, from what the members of the committee had themselves said and done, and listened to without dissent, in my presence at least. . . . . . . We met at the Albion. Mrs. Brown and her sister, Miss C. Fox, were present as mediums. A conversation was started which was carried on mostly, but not entirely, by Mr. Lunt, the representative of the *Courier*, and Major Raines, of Newburg, N. Y., a graduate of West Point, once assistant professor there, and who, in connection with Judge Edmonds and others, made a long-continued investigation of spiritual powers scientifically. . . . . . After a time, the mediums and a few others being at the table, raps were heard, mostly on the floor, or rather upon a three or four-inch platform covering the stuffed or deadened floor, while a few gentle ones were felt and heard as if made on the table. Afterward, when Mrs. Brown stood by a large wooden box, and put her first finger and then a common pencil against the box, the raps were heard there as on the box and near her hand. Again, when she stood upon a covered stool, the sounds seemed to be made beneath her on the platform. Again, when the two mediums were both standing on the stuffed seat of a sofa, the persons near them remarked that they heard sounds as from the wood of the sofa, and also from the wall against which the sofa stood.

"Near the close of their sitting, Professor Agassiz stated that the production of such sounds could be referred to known laws, and said, 'Before the investigation is over we will explain to you how they may be produced.'

"When about to separate, Major Raines expressed a wish that all would stop and compare notes, and come to an agreement as to what had actually occurred or been exhibited. A few sentences as to the propriety or importance of this course were exchanged between him and Professor Pierce, when the professor said, with a very ironical and discourteous tone and look, 'We thank you, sir, for your advice,' and bowing, hastily left the room. This occurred while a portion of the company were about leaving the room, while nearly all were standing and ready to go—while promiscuous conversation was going on—and it is not probable that many heard or saw what is here described. I was standing by the side of Major Raines, and saw and heard the whole most distinctly. Mortified and ashamed at the tones and looks of this representative of *alma mater* and of science, when addressed to a gentleman and a man of science, I turned silently away, and was not surprised when, shortly after, Major Raines said to me, 'There seems no occasion for me to remain here because of any knowledge or skill which my experience in such investigations may have given me; there is no attempt—no purpose to have an investigation of the general subject. I had better return home.' And soon he did go, as then proposed.

At the next gathering I asked, privately, and learned from both Professor Pierce and Mr. Gould that they considered the money question as still before them, and that they were but judges and not investigators. From that time my relations to them and to that particular trial became relatively unpleasant. I had little to do or say and nothing to hope for, because of the antagonism in the room.

"At their next sitting Mr. Redman was the medium. Raps and tipping of the table did not come as they usually do with him; yet he asked those at the table to write the names of deceased friends and roll up the slips. Professor Pierce commenced writing in a book. Professor Agassiz, in the meanwhile, was standing near his back, frequently changing his own attitude and position, and looking very intently upon Redman, although he said to Professor Pierce, 'throw that one out,' meaning the slip just written upon. There was the appearance of much mental disturbance in Professor A., as shown by his attitudes, his changes of position, his wild gaze, and his tones when he spoke. No raps came; *nothing* claiming to be spiritual was done by or through Mr. Redman in the public room. At some time during this sitting, Dr. Gardner drew attention to the points of disturbance through strong mental action and intent use of the eyes. Mr. Lunt was understood to say that he had been using both mind and eyes intently and with much effect; but I was on the opposite side of the room from him when he spoke, and may not have taken in the exact import of his words.

"Similar want of success attended the other mediums, at all the subsequent sittings, up to the meeting of the Davenports on the last evening. These boys, or young men, were intrusted almost entirely to the management of the committee, and those of us who were but spectators are not so informed as to make it proper to state in advance of the committee what was attempted or what was the success. We do know that at the close, Professor Agassiz held up a small, short piece of thread, which he said had been '*broken*,' and that was the *test*. Having uttered these words in a very rough tone and emphatic manner, he, in a similar tone said, 'Good night, gentlemen,' and hastily left us.

"Professor Pierce then said to Dr. Gardner, 'I suppose you are through with us.' The doctor replied; 'No; you have promised to show us how the raps were made.' 'Not as a committee,' said Professor Pierce; 'Professor Agassiz made that promise as an individual;' and thus the affair closed—we as much disappointed at the failure of Agassiz to keep his word and unveil the mystery of rapping, as at any one failure during the sittings. . . .

"The investigation, in fact, was a trial of the correctness of the statements made at the preliminary meeting, viz: 'that it was in the power of the gentlemen there present to make the trial a failure by ejecting certain forces from their own mind and eyes!' In this they were successful.

"Two of the gentlemen—Professor Agassiz and Mr. Lunt—omitted throughout all the sessions to comply with invitations to sit in the circle around the table, and there was not in any instance or at any point any opportunity for Dr. Gardner to exercise 'the determination of all the accessory circumstances.' The former gentleman, it seems, was permitted to exercise his own choice as to being in the circle, but not so the latter. Dr. Gardner's friends have been disappointed, and the chief disappointment was at the manners, actions, and mental and emotional states of two of the committee and a representative of the *Courier*. . . . .

"ALLEN PUTNAM.

"ROXBURY, *July* 10, 1857."

The correspondent of the *Tribune*, who was present at all the sessions, thus speaks of them:

"The Cambridge 'investigation' into Spiritualism proved to be, properly speaking, *no investigation* at all. I was present at all the sessions, and took notes of all that occurred. So far as I can see, the matter rests precisely where it did before. Nothing was proved or disproved. The committee, I believe, think differently, and will report in a day or two. Until their report is published, I feel bound to abstain from publishing the details of the sessions. They are entitled to be heard first."

That hearing, however, has never even been claimed by the professors.

Despite the respect due to the public, whom they had undertaken to enlighten on the nature of the "stupendous delusion," weeks, months, and finally years, have elapsed without the production of the promised report, and as far as the Cambridge professors are concerned, "the truth of man and the purity of woman" remains in the same contaminated condition in which they found it. In answer to the numerous appeals for that mysterious report, put forth by the spiritualistic and secular press alike, the only satisfaction that has ever been rendered will be found in the following paragraph, taken from the Boston *Courier*. It appeared several weeks after the "investigation," and is as follows:

"We have already stated that the report of the committee will be *no hurried affair*. The gentlemen of that committee will take their own time to work out the details of the subject. It will be, we venture to say, a calm, dispassionate, unanswerable exposure of this monstrous and wicked fraud; and, although both cheats and dupes may continue to carp at their proceedings, as they have done hitherto, we also venture to predict that all the reasonable minds in our community will rest satisfied with their conclusions."

Fearing that it may take something more than a lifetime to "work out" any details by which the Harvard professors can show Spiritualism to be a "monstrous and wicked fraud," we wait no longer for the promised report.

The world has long since pronounced judgment upon the whole subject, and out of the millions of living believers in Spiritualism who throng the cities of civilization, we doubt if there are ten who know or care what the Harvard professors think or say about it, and, perhaps, not one who has believed or disbelieved in the facts, on the authority of Messrs. Pierce, Agassiz, Horsford, and Gould.

The whole transaction, although it resulted in failure to enlighten the scientists of Harvard [if, indeed, there be anything in heaven above, or earth beneath on which so learned a body could receive enlightenment], is still calculated to read the candid and patient investigator some valuable lessons, not the least important of which is a view of the paralyzing effects which antagonistic psychology and magnetism exert upon every phase of psychical phenomena, whether the influence invoked be of a mundane or supra-mundane character, and next, that we, as mortals subject to the control of beings who are avowedly only in the first rudimental stages of the spiritual telegraphy, must patiently submit to failure until we shall have fully learned and faithfully practiced whatever conditions may be requisite for success whilst the last and most instructive lesson this episode conveys is the reproof and discomfiture which we incur when we attempt to place sublime truth at the mercy of those whose testimony is only valuable because they occupy places of distinction in the community. Great scientific or religious truths have never been intrusted by their Divine originator to the dubious action of conservative or sectarian associations, and we do but seek to pervert the Divine plan when we too-eagerly court the praise or fear the blame of those who have neither been called nor chosen to do the work of reform.

Let time and Supreme Wisdom deal with men. Our part is to accept of the talent confided to us and trust "the truth against the world."

After the last session of the Cambridge investigation, Dr. Gardner, the indefatigable and undaunted champion of "the spirits," proceeded still further in the direction of public investigation, by tendering a general invitation to the members of the Boston press to attend *séances*, for manifestations through the same mediums as had been engaged with the professors.

The gentlemen who responded to this invitation were: Messrs. Carter, Robinson, and Brown, of the Boston *Traveller;* Stockwell, of the *Journal;* Bulger, of the *Post;* Clapp and Shillaber, of the *Gazette;* Marsh, of the *Bee;* Tracy, of the *Herald;* Hill, of the *Ledger*, and the editors of the *Banner of Light* and *New England Spiritualist.* There were also present at a portion of the sittings, Hon. L. V. Bell, A. Putman, Esq., Alvin Adams, Esq., and others. The Boston *Traveller* has the following account of the first session:

"The first session of the committee was held on the forenoon of Wednesday, July 1. Mr. J. A. Redman, of New York, was present as medium. The company were advised to commence by making a thorough inspection of all the appurtenances of the room to satisfy themselves that there was no machinery or hidden apparatus by which the phenomena could be produced. The conditions imposed, simple in their character, only requiring the persons to join hands for a time, and afterwards occasionally to rest their hands in concert upon the table, were cheerfully complied with by all. The result was, that the circle was readily harmonized, and the sounds so well-known by Spiritualists as the 'rappings,' were promptly produced.

"At the request of the medium, each member of the circle wrote the name of one or more of his spirit friends on a small piece of paper, carefully concealed, not only from the medium, but from all others. The papers were then folded, rolled into small pellets—each one performing the operation for himself—and thrown promiscuously together upon the table. Any one present, except the medium, was permitted to mix and confuse them as much as he chose. It was now an acknowledged impossibility for any one to distinguish the paper on which he had written. Hereupon the medium indicated, with the point of his pencil, one after another of the pellets, inquiring of the unseen intelligences if the spirit was present whose name was written upon it. After perhaps a dozen had been passed aside without response, three distinct raps were heard on the table, showing that he had touched the right one. Each person then made the inquiry in turn, 'Is it a friend of mine?' To one of the gentlemen an affirmative was returned. 'Will that spirit write out his name through my hand?' asked the medium, 'Yes.' Mr. Redman's hand was seized by some invisible power, and rapidly wrote the name *Edward.* The pellet was opened and *Edward* found written upon it. A double test will be noticed here; both the name and the person who wrote it were designated before any one in the room could have known either. The spirit was then asked various questions, as to his age, occupation upon earth, number of brothers and sisters, disease of which he died, etc., all of which were answered correctly.

"Other pellets were designated in a similar manner, the names written through the medium's hand, and test questions answered, with unexceptional success. To enter into particulars in reference to these would be but a repetition of the preceding experiments."

A great variety of tests of a similar character, together with very powerful and even astounding physical phenomena, were witnessed in the course of these *seances*, and most of the members of the press who attended them candidly published, in the several journals they represented, fair statements of what they had witnessed and the tests they received.

As these details vary but little from the abundant records already familiar to the reader, we shall only transcribe two more specimen articles, the first of which is copied from the Boston *Post*.

"THE SPIRITUAL QUESTION IN BOSTON.—FURTHER INVESTIGATIONS.

"Notwithstanding the condemnatory report of the 'Spiritual Investigating Committee' appointed by the publishers of the *Courier*, the substance of which report being that all of the committee's four tests had failed of being satisfactorily met, Dr. Gardner invited, yesterday afternoon and evening, to room No. 12 Albion House, representatives from the different newspapers in Boston, for the purpose of exhibiting to them experiments in spiritual manifestations, and placing their practical results before the public. The press was largely represented, and the strictest attention was given to the proceedings.

"Without volunteering any opinion on the subject of Spiritualism, we will give a brief statement of what transpired, as it appeared to our understanding:

"In the afternoon at three o'clock, the mediums, Mrs. Brown and Miss Kate Fox [sisters], were present. At the suggestion of Dr. Gardner, the visitors examined the tables and fixtures in the room. The company, with the mediums, then sat around a large table, and in a short time a very brisk rapping in a variety of tones assailed the ear. A series of questioning of certain spirits now commenced, through the instrumentality of the 'raps,' and under the direction of the lady mediums. The answers were in almost every instance straightforward and satisfactory, and from the system adopted of transferring the questioning from one to another, a suspicion of collusion between the mediums would be difficult to arrive at by even the most sceptical.

"This sitting occupied about an hour and a quarter.

"In the evening, the manifestations were of a different character. Two boys were placed in a box with seats at each end, and the lights put out. It was then desired that 'John' [the spirit] should tie them together, ropes having been placed in the box for that purpose. But 'John' wouldn't do it, and the experiment failed. The boys were then tied together in the most secure manner, with many knots exceedingly intricate, and the lights again put out. The request this time was that the spirit should untie them, and while the investigators held those having charge of the exhibition, the boys were separated amid a great pulling and rubbing noise, like rattling of ropes, and much to the astonishment of all present, who, with the greatest care, were unable to detect any trickery. This transpired within fifteen minutes.

"The next feat was to tie the boys up, which failed before, and it was accomplished in six minutes. They were examined, and the lights were once more extinguished. In accordance with a request, the spirit [and when we say 'John' did this or that, it is only for convenience, based on general supposition] closed the doors of the box and bolted them. A tambourine had been placed on the floor of the box, and upon its top, outside, of course, was a violin. The latter article then fell through, and the two instruments came in contact. In a second they were playing 'Pop goes the Weasel.' The doors were then unbolted and flew open, and almost instantly the room was lighted. The company rushed towards the scene of action, and, wonderful to relate, found the boys as intricately tied as at first.

"The lights were again put out, and the boys untied in two minutes, the shutting and bolting operation being again performed. This was the best experiment of the evening, and the company departed perfectly bewildered at what they had seen.

"We submit the whole matter for what it is worth

"Another meeting will be held this evening."—*Boston Post.*

In one of the Boston evening journals, we find a continuation of the *seances* given, which we shall render in the editor's own words.

"SUBSEQUENT SESSIONS WITH THE DAVENPORTS.

"On the following evening, further experiments were tried through the mediumship of the Davenports, and were continued at three subsequent sessions.

"The results were not dissimilar to those elicited the last evening. On one of these occasions, marline was used in place of clothes-line for securing the mediums, as being smaller and more pliable, and therefore could be tied more closely and firmly. At another time the knots, after completion, were sealed with wax, in order to be sure that the boys did not untie themselves by any means, to perform their feats. The wax was undisturbed; yet a jargon was kept up on the musical instruments which seemed as though several hands were at liberty. Perhaps the most thorough tying was performed on one occasion by Captain Ayling.

"After the process previously described had been completed for securing the boys, he added a small rope about the wrists of one of them, which he wrought into a complicated sailor's knot, of some six or eight inches in length. This knot alone, he said, would require any man fifteen minutes to untie, in the light. But in less time than that not only this knot but all the others were untied, and the rope was formed into a solid ball, called by sailors a 'swab.' A marline spike is always used for making 'swabs' on ship-board; but nothing of the kind could be found in the box, nor about the person of the boys.

"It is proper to state that on several occasions the precaution was taken to pass a cord round the circle, through a button-hole of every person's coat, to prevent collusion with the mediums."

"SESSION WITH MR. MANSFIELD.

"On Monday afternoon, 6th instant, Mr. J. W. Mansfield, and Miss Kendrick, of Chelsea, were the mediums present. As previously agreed upon, each gentleman had prepared a letter, which was to be submitted to Mr. Mansfield, to be answered through his mediumship.

"These were re-inclosed in uniform envelopes, so that no one should know his own. It was hoped that one or more of these would be answered in the presence of the company, but they were not.

"Mr. Mansfield sitting down, pencil in hand, was impelled to write a communication which he passed to Dr. Gardner. It proved to be an answer to a letter left at Mr. Mansfield's office that morning, by a gentleman then stopping at the Fountain House, Dr. A. C. Stiles, of Bridgeport, Connecticut.

"[It may not be out of place here to state that Dr. Stiles called on the writer of this the next morning and brought with him the letter, which he had taken from Mr. Mansfield's room, and the answer written as above mentioned. Dr. S., let it be understood, was a total stranger to Mr. Mansfield. We were permitted to open the letter, which we found inclosed in two separate envelopes, pasted together, and the inside one pasted to the letter, so that it was utterly impossible to get at the writing without destroying the envelopes and considerably mutilating the letter.

"Six questions were asked which were appropriately answered in this communication. We are permitted to copy one of them, with the answer received, the remainder being of a strictly private nature.

"*Q.* Am I in the way of duty? *A.* You ask if you are doing your duty. What says the inward monitor? Let that decide!

"Though this answer contained less of a test than either of the others, yet it is quite sufficient to show it came from an intelligence that perceived the question.]

"As Mr. Mansfield received no further impression to write, it was agreed to seal the letters with wax and permit him to take them to the quiet of his own room, and answer them if possible.

"The next day one of the letters was sent, seal unbroken, with an answer, superscribed to Mr. Brown and signed Stephen C. Phillips. Mr. B.'s letter had been rightly selected and appropriately answered, the name signed by the medium being the one to whom it was addressed.

"Subsequently Mr. Carter had his letter returned, the seal undisturbed, with 'Blank' written on the outside. He had inclosed a blank piece of paper in his envelope. The letter written by Mr. Hill was also returned with an answer containing appropriate replies to eight questions, and signed with a facsimile of the autograph of the person to whom they were addressed.

"This experiment, like the rest at these meetings, was performed under stringent test conditions and witnessed by persons as cool, collected, and far more painstaking than the Harvard professors seemed to have been. Dr. Gardner and the mediums manifested the utmost willingness to afford the widest scope for investigation, and it was evident that the cordial feelings of harmony and good will that prevailed throughout these *séances* measurably affected the occult power by which the marvels were wrought. In fact, it seemed apparent to all present that something of human psychology and magnetism was operating upon the mediums, although this could by no means explain the phenomena, much less the intelligence which [especially in Mr. Mansfield's case] accompanied it. Meantime we retired, not convinced of the spiritual hypothesis, it is true, but still less impressed with the full force of the aggregated wisdom of the Cambridge committee of investi gation."

We should be equally uncandid and unjust were we to fail in remarking upon the noble, courteous, and honorable exception which the chief part of the associated press of Boston afford, in this instance, to the general action of that important body in almost every other city and State in connection with this movement. Whilst fidelity to truth, and the strict demands of historic justice, have compelled us to stain our pages with records equally astonishing to common-sense and degrading to free thought and intellectual manhood, as the general action of the press in relation to Spiritualism, we feel almost compensated for the painful task, by being able to present a few examples from time to time of writers, who dare, in despite of all popular prejudice, or whole colleges of the *Dunciad* School, to take the position which justly belongs to them: namely, as leaders rather than abject followers of public opinion; as teachers rather than pupils of an uninstructed multitude; and as the exponents of new truths rather than the conservators of sacred or scientific fictions.

CHAPTER XX.

SPIRITUALISM IN NEW ENGLAND—CONTINUED.

"'Tis coming now, the glorious time
  Foretold by seers and sung in story,
For which, when thinking was a crime,
  Souls leaped to heaven from scaffolds gory;
They passed—yet see the work they wrought,
  And the high hopes of centuries blossom,
Whilst the live lightning of their thought
  'And daring deeds doth pulse earth's bosom;'
'Tis coming, yes, 'tis coming—the people's advent's coming.'"

GERALD MASSEY.

BIRDS BROUGHT BY SPIRITS—WRITING ON THE ARM—"CUI BONO?"—DR. J. R. NEWTON—TESTIMONY OF PROFESSOR MAPES—PEARLS FROM MANY LANDS—MUSIC OF THE SPHERES—CHURCH THUNDER—T. L. HARRIS, THE SPIRITUALIST.

THOSE who have noticed how invariably the mere fact of notoriety has redounded to the advancement of the cause of Spiritualism, will understand that the results of the Cambridge investigation bore evident relation to the publicity procured for the subject, but none to its implied failure. True it is that some few persons were heard to declare that "Spiritualism had suffered death at the hands of the Harvard professors," but it soon became manifest that it was in a more flourishing condition than ever, and many of its bitterest opponents, provoked into investigation by its unquenchable vitality, became devoted adherents to the cause. In order to meet and counteract the injurious phillipic of the Harvard professors, floods of evidence were poured in upon the public which might else have remained in obscurity, and it is to some of the publications of this kind that the present chapter will be devoted.

A circle had been formed in Boston consisting of thirteen persons, whose harmonious relations with each other seemed to be instrumental in procuring many phases of spirit-power equally interesting and wonderful.

The circle had been named by the presiding spirits, "the Olive Branch of Peace," and as an appropriate token of their invisible friends' interest in their meetings, it was promised that they should be presented with a *white dove*, which would be placed in the hands of the one who was to take care of it for the rest. Minute directions were given as to the arrangement and conduct of the circle in order to secure the necessary conditions; also it was directed that the circle room should be closed and hermetically sealed for twenty-four hours previous to the time appointed for the presentation, and that when opened it should be in presence of all the members, who should enter simultaneously. These conditions having been complied with, and the company being seated in silent expectation for about an hour, one of the mediums in the trance state said, "The dove is now coming," and immediately afterwards, "It is now in Mrs. Vinton's hands." On looking at the party indicated, the entire circle perceived, nestling in her hands, a *white dove* the purest, prettiest, and most gentle creature of the kind they had ever seen.

This mysterious visitant, although docile and intelligent beyond description, was a veritable inhabitant of this mundane sphere, and during many subsequent months, when the circle was in session, held its place in their midst, suffering the caresses which were tenderly lavished upon it, and ruffling its snowy plumage as it rested in their hands, with tokens of reciprocal affection and familiarity. In a highly-enthusiastic account of this singular presentation published in the *New Era*, eleven names from amongst the most respectable inhabitants of the city were signed in witness of the whole scene as above described, and in the strongest terms of asseveration for its genuine character. This was not the only well-authenticated account in which birds were made the appropriate messengers of spiritual remembrance and affection. Mrs. Glover, an aged lady residing at Quincy, Massachusetts, was also favored with the presentation of a dove of singular gentleness and beauty. The precious gift was conveyed in a somewhat similar manner. The family of Mrs. Glover were requested to search a certain apartment thoroughly, and then, in presence of several invited witnesses, to lock and seal the doors and windows for twenty-four hours, at the end of which time the room was opened in the presence of the same witnesses, and found tenanted only by the beautiful bird, which was quietly nestling on the table; and though it turned its bright loving eyes on the party as they entered, it never moved, and unresistingly suffered itself to be taken up by its new mistress and caressed, with all the docility of long acquaintanceship.

The author has frequently had the privilege of caressing this semi-spiritual creature, and received the account of its appearance from those who were present on the occasion of its advent amongst them.

Numerous other instances can be cited in which spirits have manifested their power of influencing birds with a degree of readiness and intelligence as unaccountable as it is interesting.

The somewhat rare phenomena of writing on the arm, produced by spirits, now began to increase and attract unusual attention from its total absence of any circumstances which could account for its origin on mundane principles.

Mr. Colchester and Mr. Charles Foster, of Salem, Massachusetts, have presented remarkable evidences of this singular mediumistic endowment.

Both were favored by the production of all the strongest phases of physical force manifestations, and test intelligence through rapping, writing, clairvoyance, and other phenomenal methods, was frequently given through their organisms; but when total strangers to these mediums beheld, rising up on the surface of the arm, letters of a vivid red hue, resembling a thick cord formed in the cuticle, resolving themselves into the names of deceased friends, or writing intelligent messages, and then as unaccountably fading out before their very eyes, and all this without the contact of a single human finger, conviction of a spiritual origin for such marvels became irresistible, and hundreds of new converts were added to the ranks of Spiritualism by the exhibition of this single phenomenon in the persons of these two highly-gifted mediums.

The readers of the spiritual journals will doubtless remember the accounts published of a young woman residing in the family of Mr. Lewis Burtis, of Rochester, in whose person the remarkable manifestation of spirit writing on the arm was of frequent occurrence.

The following incident, occurring in the experience of the young person above referred to, was communicated to the author by Mr. and Mrs. Burtis themselves, and verified upon the testimony of other eye-witnesses.

A certain celebrated orator and editor of one of the New York State papers was dining at Mr. Burtis's house, and after the meal was ended, sat with his host and family under the shade of their garden trees, whilst the medium was at some distance from the party, engaged in domestic avocations. Being an uneducated person, she could not read clearly the raised letters which from time to time appeared on her arm, and hence she generally applied to one of the family for an interpretation of their meaning. On the present occasion she proceeded coolly to dry her hands, and advancing to the party, addressed Mrs. Burtis aside, asking her to explain the meaning of the figures which had just then appeared on her arm, and which, she added in an undertone, she thought had some reference "to the nigger there," motioning to the visitor, whose nobility of soul and intellectual powers were veiled beneath the sable skin of Africa; in fact, the party referred to, though then holding the position of equality with his host and hostess to which his mental acquirements entitled him, was by birth a negro, and had been a slave.

On examining the young woman's arm, Mrs. Burtis discovered that the red lines corruscated upon it had formed into a distinct and beautifully represented picture of a kneeling man, with a woolly head and African cast of features, a chain round his waist terminating in two balls, which were ingeniously fitted into the veins at the bend of the arm, whilst above the whole was written in fine characters the words, "A POOR OLD SLAVE."

Perhaps a stranger scene could hardly be imagined than that quiet garden arbor presented. The immobile aspect of the medium, gazing indifferently at the mystery wrought in her own organization; the dark-hued stranger regarding with obviously intense emotion this touching memento of the beloved and martyred dead; the tearful faces of the rest of the sympathetic group, and the phantom picture itself, with its deeply significant meaning and an origin in the silent land, where it was vainly supposed the wrong and ruin of many a wretched captive was lost in the mysteries of eternity! And as they gazed, the work of the unknown artist faded from their eyes, dissolving as it had come, leaving behind neither sign nor token—nothing but conjecture to prove that they had been "entertaining an angel unawares;" yet something more thanconjecture that the records of every deed, good and bad, though faded out of earthly sight and memory, are treasured up in the archives of eternity forever!

Amongst the clamoring voices that were carrying the tidings of the spiritual outpouring over the land, one cry now frequently began to make itself prominent above all others, and this was, "What is the use of it?" It seemed as if every day's experience diminished more and more the chances of successfully stemming the flow of the spiritualistic tide, or rendering the charge of delusion and imposture in the least tenable; but this new cry, "What is the use of it?" uttered, as common sense will allow, in total disregard of the beneficent nature of the manifestations or its elevating and cheering effect on human character and feeling, called forth a fresh set of evidences, which, though numerous and abundant beyond the ability of the historian to transcribe, deserve to be represented in a few brief paragraphs, which will illustrate generally the answer which the manifestations themselves supply to the captious propounders of the above-noted query.

Our first example is to the following effect:

Mrs. Kellog, the well-known spirit medium of New York, was one day visited by a gentleman holding a distinguished position as a jurist, and not unknown in the realm of letters. Though a stranger to Mrs. Kellog, she gave him a touching and graphic communication from his spirit mother, who tenderly deplored his one lamentable vice of intemperance, and declared she had influenced him to visit Mrs. Kellog with a view of effecting a cure in his appetite for drink.

The visitor did not attempt to deny the allegation contained in this communication, but quietly awaited the result.

Mrs. Kellog then proceeded to make magnetic passes over him, which produced singularly unpleasant sensations in the digestive organs, but which she assured him [still under influence] would ultimate in his permanent cure. Although for obvious reasons we are not privileged to give the name of this gentleman, the following letter, which he addressed to Mrs. Kellog shortly after the occurrence narrated above, was, by his own request, published in the spiritual papers, that the writer might, thus far, at least, acquit himself of the debt of gratitude which he acknowledged to the "blessed influence of Spiritualism."

"*April* 7, 1857.

"DEAR MADAM,—It is now thirteen days since I met you in New York, and presuming you would like to know something of the result of that experiment, I have concluded to write to you.

"Immediately after leaving your room I felt a disagreeable sensation, almost amounting, to pain, about the pit of the stomach. This continued for some forty-eight hours with but little appetite, when it passed off and such a good appetite supervened as I had not before enjoyed for years; and this continues to the present day, accompanied with an excellent power of digestion. . . . .

"The day I saw you was, as you will recollect, the last of my stay in New York, and according to custom, I was called upon to take at least twenty or thirty 'parting glasses' with friends. But after my interview with you, it was no more possible for me to take a glass of any strong drink than to consume so much aqua fortis. From that hour to this, in fact, I have not realized the slightest desire or inclination to drink any ardent spirits, nor have I felt the want of any such stimulus. It is not that I have any palpable feeling of disgust towards drink, but it does not seem to me as a thing in the least necessary, or even possible; I have not cared for it; do not need, desire, or think about it, except to remember, with the most intense gratitude, my relief from the crushing thaldom of my life, for indeed the demon of intemperance had so tightly wound his folds around me that I scarcely hoped to avoid a doom which I deeply dreaded. But, thank God, I am free! and my fervent prayer is to remain so; meantime, for this blessed result, I need not assure you how unspeakably grateful I am to you; how like a ministering angel you appear, when I reflect upon the awful precipice over which I was rushing, not blindly, but with such despairing speed. May God bless you, as, in the fullness of my soul, I do. May he keep you, is the earnest prayer of your true friend."

And this is but one of numerous instances wherein kind spirit friends, either through clairvoyant prescriptions or magnetic passes, have succeeded in entirely destroying the the taste for intoxicating liquors and tobacco. In the case of the venerable Seth Hinshaw, one of the most distinguished and beloved philanthropists in Indiana, the spirits, after having frequently remonstrated with him on the immoderate use of tobacco, in answer to his half-jesting solicitation that they would remove his appetite for the weed, promised to do so within nine days, and that without any visible means, or the use of drugs, magnetism, or will-power consciously exerted. They kept their word, for at the end of nine days and during the reminder of his beneficent life, a period of some twelve years, the mere presence of tobacco in the room, produced an unendurable and nauseating effect on Mr. Hinshaw.

In other chapters will be found single instances, selected from hundreds of others, in which gamblers have been deterred, and even compelled to withdraw from the gambling table; drunkards cured, libertines restrained, injustice rebuked, lost property found, murders detected, ships guided, travellers directed, and almost every conceivable act of kindness and charity performed which life's pilgrims could require from tender spirit guardians. These acts are neither peculiarly directed towards the believers in Spiritualism, nor are they invariably performed for all who seek and need them. The whole history of Spiritualism makes the fact apparent that the power to act upon human destiny on the part of spirits is limited, and subject to many hindrances inexplicable to us in our mundane sphere.

The sum of our knowledge in this direction simply proves that the purposes of omniscient wisdom seem measurably to use the agency of spiritual beings as instruments, but how far those instruments can shape or modify human affairs, is a mooted point on which experience alone can enable each individual to decide for himself. It is certain that much is done of an eminently beneficent character by kind ministering angels.

The above question of the material uses of Spiritualism receives daily and abundant responses through the beneficent deeds of love and blessing enacted by the "healing medium" alone. The work effected, for example, by Dr. J. R. Newton, of Rhode Island, would form a complete gospel of good use, and evidence of the divine power that operates through mediumistic sources. Dr. J. R. Newton is a gentleman who has received a regular routine education as a medical practitioner; but becoming interested in psychological and magnetic experiments, and finding he possessed wonderful power in these directions, he ultimately abandoned all other modes of practice in favor of the apostolic mode of the laying on of hands. His success in these efforts has been almost unparalleled in the annals of supra-mundane history. The blind, halt, maimed, and miserably afflicted in every shape and form, have entered his presence bowed to the earth beneath their weight of suffering, and left it "leaping and dancing" as of old, physically resurrected with new life. Hundreds of affidavits to the truth of these "miraculous" cures are on record. Thousands of victims who once languished in hopeless misery or were sinking into untimely graves, rise up and call this man 'blessed'; and if the columns of the local journals had not been systematically closed against this kind of testimony, the experience of this one divine instrument alone would have crowded them with answers to the senile question of 'What is the use of Spiritualism?' But when such an example is pressed home upon the notice of determined prejudice, the objection is retorted, that gifts so wholly exceptional do not necessarily belong to the category of 'spiritualistic' endowments.

But we respond, Dr. Newton's gifts are only exceptional in their extraordinary benevolence and singular abundance. Thousands of mediums less distinguished, and of examples less striking than he affords, swell the ranks of Spiritualism; and the reader who will take the trouble to peruse the full details of Dr. Newton's remarkable career, as we shall present it in our second volume's biographical sketches, will find ample reason to justify our claim of a spiritual origin and impulsion for the outworking of his truly divine and Christ-like mission.

In the first article addressed by Phœnix—Professor Mapes—to the *Spiritual Telegraph*, he sums up the uses which he has evolved from Spiritualism in the following brief but pithy sentences:

"The manifestations which are pertinent to the ends required are so conclusive in their character as to establish in my mind certain cardinal points. These are:

"First, That there is a future state of existence, which is but a continuation of our present state of being, devoid of such portions of our organism as are now denominated material. . . . . . .

"Second, That the great aim of nature, as shown through a great variety of spiritual existences, is progression, extending beyond the limits of this mundane sphere.

"Third, That spirits can and do communicate with mortals, and in all cases evince a desire to elevate and advance those they commune with.

"Fourth, That spirits have, in a vast number of well-attested instances, proved their will and ability to ward off dangers, cure sickness, prevent crimes, reform criminals, restore lost property, and communicate many useful, scientific, and some highly-occult and novel ideas to mankind."

The professor then goes on to enumerate, at great length, the curious phases of phenomena which he has witnessed, justly claiming that the extraordinary powers which invisible beings herein display, and the transcendental ability with which they, by means totally unknown to us, manipulate material objects, would of itself form the basis of new revealments in science calculated to revolutionize the entire realm of philosophical knowledge. The same broadly-suggestive operations, he claims, are manifested in relation to mental science, the understanding of which on the part of spirits, puts all our confused attempts at theorizing to the blush. He concludes his treatise on the character of spirit communion in the following unanswerable summary:

"Thousands of erring persons have been reformed by Spiritualism, and many a chilled heart, that had almost ceased to beat in unison with its fellows, has been warmed into human sympathy by communications from loved ones, long since passed from the form.

"Nothing has been so effective in reclaiming the vicious and rendering the family circle a perfect school-house for Christian feeling. It has been the means of educating many a wayward and inconstant heart into prayerful feeling, gentleness towards the creature and reverend aspiration to the Creator."

Continuing this subject, we shall make a few selections from the overwhelming mass of testimony which the records of Spiritualism furnish concerning its peculiarly utilitarian and benevolent character, a few specimen instances of which, are simply illustrative of the thousands that are of daily occurrence in the experience of Spiritualists.

The following incident is taken from the Niagara *Democrat*, Niagara village; the party referred to is well known as an excellent medium, but, for personal reasons, objects to the publication of her name.

"A young woman who resides on Lock street, in this village, who is a reputed 'spirit medium,' in going on her way home passed up Church street, intending to reach Lock by the way of Caledonia street. When she had crossed the latter, she was arrested by some irresistible impulse, or, as she describes it, 'felt some one taking hold of her arm.' Under this invisible and irresistible guidance she quitted her companion, turned on her steps again, and was hurried along until she arrived back on Church street at the railroad crossing. Here she was compelled to hasten along the track to the deep cut west of the transit, when she was almost pushed forward towards something lying on the track, which, on reaching, she found to be a little child lying asleep across one of the rails. The whistle of the approaching cars had already sounded, the train was in sight, and 'the medium' had scarce time to seize the child and jump with it in her arms to the ditch at the side, ere the train of cars dashed past her! The young woman's statement is corroborated by that of the companion whom she so suddenly left, and several witnesses, two of whom actually saw the rescue of the sleeping child before they understood the circumstances that prompted it. Our readers may rely on the accuracy of the entire statement."

In a report of the Boston Convention of 1854, a speech called forth by surrounding circumstances from Dr. Hayden, editor of the Boston *Star-Spangled Banner*, bears rather significantly upon the character of Spiritualism and the habits of Spiritualists, as the following extracts will prove.

Dr. Hayden said:

"Brother Hudson had spoken of hearing profanity from the mouths of some young men on the grounds. He, [Dr. H.] regretted to say, the same blasphemous sounds had floated on the pure air to his own ears, and he wished to say, for the information of any strangers that might be present, that any persons that used profane language in that place were not, could not, be Spiritualists. They were outsiders, attracted hither by curiosity, but did not belong to the meeting. He must here add he had yet to know the first Spiritualist who made use of profanity, or was not opposed to slavery, the rum traffic, capital punishment, and every other physical or mental form of human degradation. . . . . . . Spiritualists have no cloak under which to cover a multitude of sins.

"Mr. Hudson said he hoped he would not be misunderstood, as he did not for one moment suppose the young men he alluded to were Spiritualists. The moment he heard them swear, he knew they might be Christians but could not be Spiritualists."

It would be superfluous to multiply examples of the above character or repeat such testimony as that offered by Professor Mapes on the *cui bono* of Spiritualism.

Purposing to devote a chapter of our second volume to this well-worn subject of *cui bono*, we shall now invite the reader to follow us through a brief summary of the phenomena which was especially rife about this time in the Eastern States.

Amongst other demonstrations of the power with which spirits have favored mortals, that of producing music either through an entranced human organism or automatically from invisible performers themselves, has been one of the most interesting and abundant.

We have already noticed several instances of the production of spirit-music through the mediumship of the Misses Fox, Mrs. Tamlin, Frederick Willis, Mr. D. D. Home, the Davenport Brothers, Miss Brooks, of Buffalo, etc.; but all that we have yet recorded falls short of the marvels wrought through the mediumship of two sisters in the State of Maine, named Annie and Jennie

Lord. These young ladies, both very slight, fragile persons, suffering under the most pitiable conditions of ill-health, and in their normal state unable to play upon any instrument, became mediums for various phases of "the power," requiring the most astounding physical force in execution, in addition to which, spirits, in their presence and in darkened rooms, would play upon a double bass violoncello, guitar, drums, accordion, tambourine, bells, and various small instruments, with the most astonishing skill and power. Sometimes the instruments would be played on singly, at others all together, and not unfrequently the strange concert would conclude by placing the young medium, seated in her invalid chair, silently and in a single instant in the centre of the table, piling up all the instruments around her, and then calling for a light to exhibit their ponderous feats of strength and noiseless agility to the eyes of the astonished circle. The sisters rarely sat together, and though it would be impossible to conceive of any persons more incapable of giving off *physical power* than these two fragile and afflicted girls, yet their manifestations with one alone acting as medium, have surpassed, in feats of vast strength and musical achievements, any that are recorded in the annals of Spiritualism.

With the Sisters Lord, Messrs. Charles Foster Colchester, D. D. Home, H. Gordon, F. L. H. Willis, and at least an hundred of the most highly gifted public test and physical mediums operating throughout the Eastern States, with Dr. Newton, Mrs. Mettler, and a host of admirably-endowed clairvoyants and healers, and while private mediums and circles were to be numbered in each State by the thousand, New England bid fair to outrival New York, Pennsylvania, or even the Western States in the force and multitude of its phenomenal demonstrations. Besides a large corps of variously-gifted mediums at the disposal of the inquring public, Boston was favored by the presence of Mr. J. V. Mansfield, the renowned writing medium, through whom thousands of letters were transmitted from beloved and lamented friends in the "spirit-country" to their mourning relatives on earth.

The office of this great spiritual post-master was constantly crowded with eager investigators, and his *modus operandi* forms not one of the least remarkable demonstrations of spirit-power. Sealed letters, carefully marked and secured, so that it would be impossible to open them without detection, either brought in the hand or sent by investigators, were correctly and often most graphically answered and returned without a single proven case of one ever having been opened. Sometimes the letters of sceptical inquirers were inclosed in plates of metal or curiously interlaced with silk to resist the supposed action of "electricity," the wonderful agent to which so many of the spiritual marvels were attributed. Sometimes they were inclosed in varieties of envelopes, pasted, sealed, and privately marked with every imaginable test for the detection of any attempt to open the inclosed letter. No matter what were the precautions used — excepting in such rare cases as no spirit control being present, when the letter was simply returned — the most conclusive evidences were given in the answers that they had been dictated by spirits, who were fully cognizant of the hidden secrets of the package.

Not only were these replies appropriate and characteristic, but, as if to repel the idea that Mr. Mansfield himself dictated these answers, messages and details were given, not touched on in the querist's letter, whilst names were frequently introduced that were not mentioned or asked for, and not unfrequently the answers were written in German, Spanish, Greek, Arabic, Sanscrit, and even Chinese, whilst all who knew the medium testified to their belief that he was entirely unacquainted with any language but his own.

Reserving further notice of this remarkable medium for a more extended sketch, we call attention to two highly interesting phases of spirit-power, which were manifested in Hartford, Connecticut. The first relates to Mrs. Mettler, the celebrated healing medium. The single testimony to her beneficent power which we can insert in this notice of New England Spiritualism is copied from the *Springfield Republican*, where it is with justice recorded, as—

"SIGNIFICANT TESTIMONY.

"This is to certify that I have been, through the instrumentality of Mrs. Mettler, of Hartford, relieved from blindness which had previously baffled medical science.

"My age is now fifty-three years; my health has always been poor since about my ninth year. During much of this time I had suffered almost everything but death. At my ninth year I received an injury from the fall of a log, since which I have been growing worse, until about eight years ago, when I became blind in my right eye by the formation of a cataract over the sight. For some time, in fact, I could scarcely discern anything with either eye, until I entirely lost my sight in both. I have been attended by physicians of reputed skill and ability; surgical operations have been made, and everything done for me that could be thought of, without affording me the least relief.

"Thus I remained some three years without the hope of ever again beholding a ray of light, when I was advised to go to Mrs. Mettler, at Hartford, and get an examination. I did so, and there for the first time in my life found a person who seemed perfectly to understand my case, tracing out causes which I had long since forgotten. She informed me that the sight of one eye was destroyed, and the other covered with a cataract. She gave me a prescription and I commenced her treatment. At this time my neighbors began to chide me for the course I had taken. But I continued on with the treatment, resolved to get my sight if possible, until I was so persecuted that I was finally obliged to move away to Manchester, and all because I had gone to Mrs. Mettler in the hope of again beholding this beautiful world, a blessing that has been finally vouchsafed to me.

"Some six months ago I began to see a little, and am now able to see to read and do the finest sewing.

"When first I went to Mrs. Mettler my health was so poor that I could scarcely get from one chair to another; now I not only see, but am able to do my work. Just imagine a person so situated as I was, to experience such a relief! It is out of my power to express my deep gratitude to Mrs. Mettler, or to the friend who advised me to consult her. Of my persecutors I can only say, may the light of heaven flow down upon them until the scales of superstition drop from their eyes.

"If by these few lines I may induce some poor sufferer to visit Mrs. Mettler, and obtain from her the blessed relief that I have experienced, then shall I have responded to the highest aspirations of my own soul.

"MRS. DOTIA SPOORE.

"BRISTOL, CONN., *January* 18, 1854."

Our next extract refers to a daughter of the excellent lady referred to above, Miss Catherine Mettler, who, like her mother, was a highly gifted medium, as the following notice from the pen of Professor Britain, written for the *Spiritual Telegraph*, will prove.

"Not long since we gave an account of a remarkable musical performance, in which a grand opera, improvised under spirit influence, was rendered with wonderful effect by a young lady medium from the vicinity of Boston. New England is rich in these musical prodigies, for since that time we have witnessed several still more astonishing musical improvisations from Miss Catherine A. Mettler, whose sudden development and rapid progress as a musical medium has occasioned the deepest surprise. The youthful improvisatrice is the eldest daughter of Dr. G. M. and Semantha Mettler, and is now about sixteen years of age.

"Those who have witnessed Mrs. Mettler's remarkable powers as a clairvoyant and healing medium will readily infer that Catherine inherited a natural title to her inspiration. Previous to her development as a medium, Catherine had taken a few lessons on the piano, and could execute a few rudimentary lessons with tolerable correctness, but had never evinced any remarkable taste for the art, or given promise of ultimate proficiency. One day, whilst laboring to make out the air of a simple song, Miss Mettler's arms were apparently seized by an unknown power, which at once compelled her to commence the most astonishing improvisation, evidencing an extraordinary mastery over the instrument and a thorough knowledge of the science of harmony.

"The medium's hands for some time mechanically obeyed the irresistible impulse of this unseen performer without any volition or mental impression of her own. At length the wonderful sounds issuing from the instrument attracted the attention of other members of the family. Mrs. Mettler, who has an intuitively fine taste for music, whilst engaged in another part of the house, heard and recognized the masterly touch of an unknown performer, and inquired who was in the parlor. She presumed that some very skilful pianist had called on her daughter without her knowledge. To ascertain this fact, she entered the apartment, where, to her amazement, she found no one but Catherine. The young girl was sitting at the instrument, apparently fixed and spell-bound; her hands automatically performing those wondrous symphonies, but her mind locked in the deep unconsciousness of a profound trance. Since this time [some three months ago], Catherine has been daily influenced by spirits whom all skilled musicians recognize by their graphic and peculiar style to be those whom they claim; namely, Mozart, Beethoven, Weber, and others, who each perform with marked and unmistakable indviduality. Sometimes the compositions are wholly original and improvised upon given subjects. Sometimes they are recognized *chef d'œuvres* of celebrated masters, of whom the medium has scarcely ever even heard. These marvellous performances are executed equally well in the dark or the light, and usually occupy several hours of each day. On one occasion, when the spirits had performed a medley of some twenty popular airs, Mrs. Myers, a lady present, mentally desired that some martial music should be given, when the performer, by a skilful modulation, changed the strain she was then executing into a noble march for Liberty, accompanied with some fine variations and closing with a sublime hymn, improvised, as it was claimed, by the spirit of Beethoven.

"One night when the writer, together with several musical *dilettanti*, were present, it was claimed that the spirit of Mozart would perform at the request of the company; whereupon we desired that the medium should be influenced to give his celebrated requiem. After a few minutes devoted to fine modulation, 'Mozart's Requiem' was rendered, as the writer and others acquainted with that composition can testifiy, in the most correct, impressive, and masterly manner. Subsequently 'A Storm at Sea' was played, in which the battle of the elements was illustrated with thrilling effect. The power that holds the winds seemed to have relaxed his grasp, and they shouted aloud for freedom. The angry billows seemed to rise high in the darkened air, and anon, sinking into the fathomless abyss of ocean, to wail like imprisoned spirits. We could hear the booming of the thunder, the plashing of the rain, the rending of the sails, falling of the masts, and signal guns of an invisible ship. The prayers and shrieks of the despairing mariners, then the sobbing of the exhausted storm, sinking into a low wail, a hush! then the transition of the arisen spirits into the land of light and joy was celebrated by triumphant songs splendidly improvised, in a style of the most exalted and artistic excellence, the whole closing with an exquisite and pathetic rendering of the touching ballad, 'Home, Sweet Home.'"

It would be impossible to notice the various developments of individual medium powers that began rapidly to multiply in all the New England States; suffice it to say that they were so marked and numerous that Spiritualism assumed a vast and formidable importance throughout this whole section of country.

In Willimantic, Norwich, Springfield, Chicopee, and other considerable towns and villages regular Sunday meetings were held, at which audiences of from five hundred to a thousand persons constantly attended.

In Worcester, Quincy, Plymouth, and other old colonial towns, the leading minds, both in point of intellect and position, openly avowed their belief in the cause.

The rich and flourishing cities of Providence, Rhode Island; Portland and Bangor, Maine; and Hartford, Connecticut, became perfect strongholds of the faith. Still the lack of variety that attends mediumistic demonstrations, and the limits of our space, oblige us to confine our narrative chiefly to general descriptions of the movement and its progress, hence we must sum up the overwhelming force and abundance of New England Spiritualism by a few closing extracts from the *Telegraph* papers, furnished by their most trusted and reliable correspondents.

The first of these, written by a celebrated trance medium, is as follows:

"PROGRESS OF SPIRITUALISM IN VERMONT.

"PROFESSOR L. B. BRITAIN: *Dear Sir,*—Five years have scarcely elapsed since Modern Spiritualism made its advent in Vermont. At that period, a few daring spirits extended the hand of welcome to the stranger, watching with painful anxiety the result. During the interval since then, zealous churchmen have made themselves jubilant at one time over its persecutions, and indignant at another about its successes.

"Rowdyism and religion have alternated, until the dividing lines between sinners and saints have become obscure, while all the time Spiritualism has reared its temples and planted its groves. . . . . Thus, Spiritualism has advanced whilst the opposition has fallen, until in Vermont above seventy churches—built by all varieties of sects—have been opened for the use of that Spiritualism which, a few years ago, those same sects so furiously denounced. The writer has cause to remember when first an effort was made to open a meeting-house in Vermont for Spiritualism, as that effort was made to allow him, for the first time, to stand before an audience to be influenced by spirits. The attempt failed. A Universalist society held the door fast, even against the wishes of the shareholders and paying members. . . . . . . The writer admits that he can hardly explain the fact why these seventy churches have been opened, unless, indeed, a spiritual key has been used to unlock them; he merely cites the fact and testifies to its truth from personal knowledge. . . . . . .

"In conclusion, we pledge our beloved State to sustain Spiritualism, and, day by day, we see her sons and daughters arise as its advocates, exponents, and adherents, until we believe that she shall become a home of the spirit and a temple of justice, a land where every soul shall rejoice in the glorious light of immortality and the communion with immortals in joy unspeakable. . . . .

"AUSTIN E. SIMMONS.

"WOODSTOCK, VERMONT, 1856."

"TELEGRAPH PAPERS—1856.

"Mr. Isaac Hunt, writing from the conservative old town of Augusta, Maine, states that Spiritualism is just beginning to force its way into notice in that place, met, of course, as usual, with a storm of opposition. There is a young lady in the town, a fine medium, through whom the spirits give some curious demonstrations, manifesting amongst other things the spirit of an old Revolutionary soldier, who, in his unabated opposition to King George of England, refuses to rap time to the tune of 'God Save the King,' but beats time to the air of 'Yankee Doodle' with amazing force and alacrity. Several highly-respectable citizens of the place have recently become developed, as mediums. Among them is a young man who is a seer, and who, by the exercise of his gift of inner-sight, has in several instances found lost and stolen property, and given most interesting descriptions of angelic life and scenery in the spheres. In one instance he stated that preparations were being made in the spirit-world for the reception of several persons still in perfect health. He gave the names of those predestined ones, but was met with no credence. Within a week after this announcement, two of them departed, and we find that a third, from a sudden and fatal accident, is likely to follow."

"TELEGRAPH PAPERS—1867.

"WILLIAM LLOYD GARRISON, who was previously sceptical with regard to Spiritualism, has lately been investigating the subject with Mrs. Leah Fish, of this city. The spirits of Jesse Hutchinson, Isaac T. Hopper, and many other of his friends, manifested their presence in the most satisfactory and convincing manner; and in closing an article in his own paper, on the variety and character of the demonstrations, Mr. Garrison thus expresses himself:

"'How can phenomena like these be accounted for except on the hypothesis of spirit agency? If we cannot positively say that Isaac T. Hopper, and Jesse Hutchinson were actually present on that occasion, we are at least prepared to express our own conviction as well as that of the witnesses who were in our company, that spirits not of this mundane sphere must have performed the demonstrations we have thus briefly narrated to our readers.'"

The following cases have several times been paralleled with similar phenomena, witnessed by scores of persons, of whom the author has frequently been one.

The possibility of rendering the human organism positive to the action of both fire and water by spiritual influence has now been so often proved, in the presence of strong physical mediums and the most trustworthy witnesses, that these instances are not cited for their novelty, but rather in illustration of the class of facts to which they belong; they were published in the *Christian Spiritualist*, Macon, in 1860, in the following extract from correspondence:

"Mrs. Lovejoy, of Cincinnati, being on a visit to this place, brought with her a baby of four months old, who is a remarkable medium. We have been accustomed to sit around the cradle whilst the little one lies asleep, ever since she has been here, and always receive satisfactory responses from our spirit friends, either by raps or rockings of the cradle. If the baby wakes during our circle she never cries, but seems, by the happy smile over her sweet face, and the delight with which she crows along with the raps, to receive some pleasant influence from the power which is operating.

"Last evening [April 3], as we were holding a circle round the cradle, I asked the spirits why the Christians did not give the signs which are promised to the believers in the last chapter of St. Mark? When the spirits rapped out, by the alphabet — 'Because the Christians of this century were believers with their lips, but too many of their hearts were far from God.' They added, 'They would show what belief in the truth of Scripture meant, through that baby, to-morrow, and prove that it was something more than lip service.'

"The next day [this morning], as I returned to dinner, I found my wife and Mrs. Lovejoy sitting on the verandah outside the house. They rose up and went into the parlor with me, also accompanied by Mr. Newman, my overseer, from Mississippi, who was along with me.

"On entering the parlor, we were all four horrified to behold the baby's cradle literally a mass of flames; a spark from the pine fire probably had flown out, and the cradle being incautiously left near the open fireplace, had taken fire, and was now wrapped in flames. I shall never forget the shrieks of the women, or my own feelings of horror at the sight; but Mr. Newman gallantly rushed towards the blazing mass, and, plunging his hands in, snatched the infant from the cradle, and rolled it in its blazing night dress on the matting of the floor, until the fire was extinguished. I seized a bucket of water at the door, brought by Sam for our horses, and hurled it at the cradle, by which the flames were soon put out; but the strange part of the story is that the little one never cried, nor even whimpered, and that, though its night dress was burned to a cinder, not a single scorch can be found on its body, nor the least token of injury; even the bit of hair on its little poll is not singed.

"Mrs. Lovejoy is now in bed, attended by my wife, in a painful condition of hysterical emotion; but the little angel — guarded sign of true Christianity — is merrily crowing in the arms of her nurse, Cherry, on the floor at my feet, as I write.

"MOBILE, *April* 4, 1860. E. HOFFMAN."

"In Macon, Georgia, a colored girl, who was an excellent physical medium, frequently exhibited the feat of thrusting her hand amongst the blazing pine logs, and removing it after some sixty seconds without the least injury. She always insisted, however, that she would only perform this feat when 'Cousin Joe,' whom she called her guardian spirit, was present, and bid her do it.

"At New Orleans, Louisiana, a negro by the name of Tom Jenkins was well known for his power of resisting fire, under what he called the 'fluence of Big Ben,' a boatman, formerly, on the Mississippi river, and who, since his death by drowning, had come and made what Tom called 'magic' for him. On one occasion Mrs. Emma Hardinge and a party of friends paying a visit to Tom, he became entranced, took off his shoes and stockings, rolled up his pantaloons to his knees, and entered the pine wood fire, literally standing in it as it blazed upon the hearth, long enough to repeat in a solemn and impressive manner the 23d, 24th, and 25th verses of the third chapter of Daniel."

The following incident is one which has obtained wide circulation through the press of New England, and relates to a family of high respectability in Vermont. The statement is confirmed by many witnesses, but the official character of the investigation alluded to in the narrative is better warranty than the attestation of private individuals. The relation is copied from the Vermont *Daily Tribune*, bearing date, 1854.

"A STRONG CASE.

"Some few weeks ago the wife of Mr. Henry H. Mitchel, of this city, was controlled by a preternatural influence claiming to be 'spiritual,' under which she wrote a communication purporting to come from Mr. Mitchel's father, who had died in 1816. The 'spirit' stated that at the time he left this mundane sphere, he was entitled to a quarter section of land located in Pike County, Illinois, for military services which he had rendered in the war of 1812; and he requested his son to write to Washington, as the patent had never been issued from the office there; that the land was now valuable, and justly belonged to his heirs. Having but little confidence in the communication, and no knowledge of his father's being entitled to any government land, Mr. Mitchel at first hesitated to write to Washington, but was finally persuaded by some Spiritualists to do so for the sake of the test which it would afford.

"He accordingly wrote to the Honorable James Meacham, one of the members in Congress for Vermont, requesting him to examine the records and ascertain whether there was any truth in the representation.

"A short time afterwards he received from Mr. Meacham his papers and a copy of the record, with the official seal of the Honorable John Wilson, Land Commissioner, showing that his father was entitled to a quarter section of land, that was located and recorded October 16, 1819. The location, as indicated in the documents, was in Pike County, Illinois, just as the spirit had stated."

We have now briefly reviewed the character of the vast and abundant testimony which the annals of Spiritualism afford in answer to the question *cui bono?* pointed to the varied and ever-increasing phenomena with which it is rife, and conclude our notice of the movement in the New England States by selecting one of the numerous examples which the times furnished of the effect which the irresistible progress of the cause produced upon professing Christians. The following extract from the records of the day will prove for itself the desperate methods by which the afflicted shepherds of souls sought to hinder their flocks from participating in the new light, which all other efforts had failed to extinguish. It is taken from the columns of the *Spiritual Age*, the editor of which prefaces its introduction with these remarks:

"We have received the following circular with a request that we would give it, through our columns, a more extended circulation than would be secured to it by sending one copy to each family in the Baptist Church at Ballston Spa, New York.

"We comply with this request very cheerfully, and, moreover, call the attention of our readers to so truly orthodox a production without the least fear that the effect of its perusal will damage our own subscription list. — *Editor Spiritual Age.*

"'CIRCULAR.

"'*To the members of the Baptist Church, Ballston Spa:*

"'*Whereas,* The theory and practices of Spiritualism, or necromancy, are believed by us to be directly contrary to the teachings of the Bible, by which it is expressly condemned as an abomination in the sight of God; and,

"'*Whereas,* We discover from experience that its practice leads directly to gross infidelity and the subversion of Christian character and reputation, and thus involves a great reproach to the cause of Christ; therefore,

"'*Resolved,* That we affectionately request all brethren and sisters to desist and invariably refrain from all connection with the thing, and from all countenance of it, whether by word or deed.

"'*And resolved,* That the clerk be instructed to print the above resolutions, and send one copy to each family in the church.

"'Done in church-meeting at Ballston Spa, February 4, 1854.

"'CHARLES T. HARRIS, Church Clerk.

"'*Saratoga Republican.*'"

The same paper from which the above circular is copied publishes a discourse of the Rev. T. L. Harris, *at that time* a full believer and indefatigable advocate of the truths of Spiritualism.

Although this discourse, entitled "the New Ministry," by no means expresses in its fullness the length, breadth, or beauty of Spiritualism, its appearance coincident with that of the Ballston Spa circular, charging on Spiritualism the act of bringing "a great reproach on the cause of Christ," is, to say the least of it, significant, and requires that the two documents should be perused by every candid reader side by side; and before Christian brethren and sisters determine to refrain from "the thing" on the charge of the Baptist shepherd's view of it, let the said "thing" speak for itself concerning its own relation to Christian life and character.

The following extracts from Mr. Harris's discourse are sufficiently indicative of the whole:

"But there is an argument still more grave than any to which I have hitherto alluded. It is said that persons in the interior state are hostile to the Christian revelation. To this I answer that I for one will never admit that the influxes flowing through a spiritual seer are necessarily hostile to revelation. . . . .

"All the prophets were interior and illuminated men. Through them came not any sort of denial of religion, but the very revelations that confirm religion.

"All the apostles were interior and illuminated men, and we are indebted to them for Christianity itself in its documentary and historical form.

"Like seeks like; if there is a sublime Christianity in heaven it must flow down to man. I can conceive of no form of Christian ministry more grand than a ministry of Christ-like men, in sympathy with humanity and *en rapport* with the skies.

"This or that medium may be influenced by the peculiarities of his organization, by the tendencies of his intellect, by his associations in the body, and by his impressions from the spiritual world, to take ground against some revelations in the past. This I do not deny, but I maintain that if religion be true, our strongest allies are in the world beyond the grave. . . . .

"Christianity needs not the sanction of authority; it courts investigation. It sits in the sun, and says to all men, 'Prove all things; hold fast that which is good.' . . . .

"It may be objected that we are to try the spirits, and believe only those that teach that Christ has come in the flesh. To this I reply:

"This passage in St. John has no certainty as a test. I believed it in my early experience as a medium, and acted on it. However valued it may have been in the period for which it was written, it is useless now.

"I prefer to try spirits by their works. We cannot gather grapes of thorns, nor figs of thistles. 'Not they that say 'Lord, Lord,' inherit the kingdom, but they that know the will of the Father AND DO IT.'"

CHAPTER XXI.

SPIRITUAL MOVEMENTS—"MOUNTAIN COVE."

. . . . "This man is the great power of God."

ACTS OF THE APOSTLES.

"Who is this that darkeneth counsel by words without knowledge?"

JOB, xxxvii.—2.

HOW THE APOSTOLIC BROTHERHOOD GREW FROM A CIRCUMFERENCE BACK TO A CENTRE—HOW THE CENTRE BURST AND VANISHED INTO THIN AIR—HOW IT GATHERED ITSELF UP AGAIN, AND GREW BEYOND ITS OWN CENTRE AND CIRCUMFERENCE, AND SOARED AWAY BEYOND ITSELF—HOW MR. CHARLES PARTRIDGE BROUGHT IT BACK TO EARTH AGAIN UNTIL IT FOUND ITS LEVEL.

IT now becomes the duty of a faithful scribe to record some of those darker shades of the spiritualistic history, which, doubtless, in the providential plan, as on the canvas of the artist, are essential features in the landscapes of human destiny. In fulfilling this part of our mission, let it be understood that we write with no unkind intent toward the individuals whose experiences we detail. Doubtless their acts, if stimulated somewhat more by mundane than supra-mundane psychology, were still measurably influenced by the magnetic contagion of the time. One marked result of spirit influence has been to externalize character, and develop into sudden prominence the hidden traits, perhaps scarcely known to their possessors.

In accordance with the testimony adduced, even in the last chapter, it will be seen that vicious persons, hitherto deemed irreclaimable, have been led into the paths of virtue and goodness by the angelic ministrations of guardian spirits; on the other hand it is certain that latent evil tendencies are not uufrequently matured into ugly prominence by the effects of magnetism, especially in its indiscriminate use or in heterogeneous circles. Let these remarks be borne in mind, and due weight be attached to the original idiosyncracies of individual characters, ere we proceed to charge upon Spiritualism the onus of the follies and fanaticisms which become revealed in the history of the various movements which deform the sacred name of Spiritualism, under the pretence of "reforms," an example of which we now propose to record, in the notorious "Mountain Cove" movement.

This remarkable transaction originated about 1850, at which time spiritual manifestations had taken strong hold of many enthusiastic minds in the town of Auburn, New York. Here, in consequence of its proximity to the scene of the first demonstrations at Hydesville, and the number of the mediumistic gifts called forth by investigation, Spiritualism had a fair chance of exhibiting its tendency to externalize latent specialties in human character. The egotist became inflated by "the power" into a belief of direct communion with the highest heavens, and especial gifts from heavenly personages. Obscure fanactics suddenly announced themselves authorized by some high apostolic dignatary to undertake "missions," the least of which was destined to move the world, and subvert all its present existing institutions.

"The Holy Ghost," was the favorite authority with this class of inspired ones, and no one under the rank of an apostle—except now and then a Jewish prophet, or patriarch—was deemed worthy to hold communication with these "highly favored of the Lord."

Meantime, the immediate personal advent of the "Messiah" was declared to be the aim of the manifestations, whilst the self-elected saints of the dispensation were every one the particular "John Baptists" of the second coming. The great body of Spiritualists, who happily represented the majority as well as the common-sense of the movement, were contented to seek for the facts of identity which proved them to be in communion with the spirits of recognized friends and kindred. Such tests were striking and abundant, and with them communications were often made from spirits who were once highly distinguished on earth, and who represented themselves as engaged in the task of missionary labor, for some special season or purpose; but few, if any, whose communications brought with them internal evidence of their claims to respect and credence, attempted to dictate to mortals, or impose upon them any other authority than such as they would have exercised over others legitimately on earth.

The leaders of the "Auburn Apostolic Circle" were originally a few persons, who, notwithstanding their high and pretentious claim to communicate with no spirit born out of Judea, or after the year 1 of the Christian era, still failed to secure adherents outside "the faithful," or to induce the sinful

Semantha Mettler

world to purchase the tracts, wherein the wisdom of Solomon appeared clothed in very bad grammar, and the theology of St. Paul came forth masked in orthography quite too hard for modern well-bred Peters to swallow. But though it was at last discovered that the blind made but a poor hand of leading the blind, the usual resort of getting on the blind side of the strong, and pampering to the weakness of the ambitious, in this as in other cases, proved successful. "In the fulness of time" the "Apostolic circles" were directed by their archangelic leaders, through Mrs. Benedict's rapping, to summon to the work the two "chosen vessels" before alluded to, namely, the Rev. J. L. Scott, a Baptist preacher, and the Rev. Thomas L. Harris, an Universalist, both of New York City.

Shortly after the accession of these two "great lights," a paper superior in tone and orthography to anything that the apostolic band had hitherto put forth, appeared, under the caption of "Disclosures from the Interior, and Superior Care fór Mortals." If the grammar and style of this publication had risen with its new editors, its authoritative claims kept ample pace with its improvements; for whilst its columns were, humanly speaking, chiefly indited by the twin "Reverends," Scott and Harris, their words, they informed their readers, were wholly dictated or inspired by a circle of prophets and apostles, who derived, in their turn, plenary inspiration from the "Lord Supreme himself."

Besides the strongest affirmations of the duty and deference which the whole world owed to the "Apostolic Circle" in general, and Scott and Harris in particular, it was claimed through Mr. Harris that his interior revelations were dictated by Paul, John, Daniel, and other distinguished Biblical personages, whilst the poetry which enlivened the columns of the "Disclosures," was the spiritual lucubrations of none less than Coleridge, Shelley, Pollock, and a few of the higher geniuses of modern times, to whom Mr. Harris thought proper to assign prominent positions in the celestial realms, of which he alleged himself to be a frequent and privileged visitor.

The authority maintained by Scott and Harris over the credulity of their followers would be amusing enough to read of, were it not for the monstrous assumption of their pretensions and the degradation of such intellects as could submit to their claims. After the society had maintained its place amongst the people of Auburn until forbearance appeared to be no longer a virtue, and they received pretty emphatic hints that their holinesses might find their longer residence in that profane city disagreeable, Mr. Scott had a timely vision, which suggested a "change of base," whereupon "the faithful" removed to Mountain Cove, Fayette County, Virginia, and under the leadership of Scott, were guided to that particular spot, which the inspired ones of the band informed the rest was inhabited by no less a personage than the spirit of Isaiah the Prophet! Here, in the company of about one hundred persons, who had been induced to join him and throw in "all things in common," including in some instances very considerable worldly possessions, Mr. Scott became elevated to a height where no other atom of frail mortality could follow him, much less comprehend or question the edicts which he, in a supernal condition of inspiration, enunciated. In short, Mr. Scott claimed to be "divinely inspired," and having soared away above even the circle of prophets and apostles who formerly attended him, and attained even "unto the counsels of the Most High," he henceforward claimed supreme and unquestionable authority in all matters, whether social, religious, temporal, eternal, or *financial*, that concerned those who were privileged with him to share the joys of "the holy mountain." If a question should arise as to whether one man, in this nineteenth century, could enunciate such blasphe mous pretensions and find rational human beings who could submit to them, let the sceptical reader satisfy himself by perusing the statements of one who had the most peculiar facilities, not only for becoming acquainted with the interior arrangements of the Mountain Cove New Jerusalem, but who preserved in published form many of the literal utterances upon which the great Prophets of the Mountain founded their claims: we refer to Mr. E. W. Capron, from whose admirable work on the facts and fanaticisms of modern Spiritualism, we present the following account of this remarkable movement.

"I have endeavored from every source to obtain accurate information and give an impartial history of this singular movement. From an acquaintance who was induced to join the movement and spent a long time at the Cove, I have received a statement of which the following is the substance:

"Mr. Scott and others arrived in Fayette County, Virginia, in the month of October, 1851, for the purpose of establishing the community of true believers in Spiritualism, with Scott at the head. It was stated and understood, before any of the company left Auburn, that the land, when purchased, would be sold in small quantities to all who wished to settle with them, and those unable to purchase house and land would be furnished by the association.

"They also were promised business, such as each were able to perform; each family to be their own regulator, as fully as out of the association. The labor performed was to be paid for at a fair remuneration. Schools were to be established, and different branches of business instituted. . . . .

"It was also understood that there was to be no dictation in the movement; but the whole was to be under the direction of 'the spirits,' and that all things should be governed on the principles of brotherhood, unity, and equality. On the 2d of December, 1851 [the day on which my informant arrived at Mountain Cove], himself and some sixty others were told by Scott, who had somehow been given, or taken the title of '*Doctor*,' that he was receiving communications from the Deity. Scott declared that he received these communications, standing 'face to face with God!' and strange as it may appear, most of the people there believed this story.

"Soon after this, Scott informed the people that he had been appointed, by high spiritual power, *medium absolute*, and that nothing but truth would or could henceforth be given through him, and that whatever was given through him must not be doubted, all doubting being rank heresy. Soon after this, Scott informed Mr. H.—[my informant] that there had been a serious quarrel among them before he [Mr. H.] arrived.

"To the question as to what was the cause of the quarrel, Scott replied that a certain individual had slandered his character, and alleged that he had been guilty of licentiousness and adultery.

"Mr. H. replied that the matter ought to be investigated at once.

"A meeting was accordingly called, professedly for that purpose. There were but few persons present, and as soon as it was organized, Scott professed to pass into the 'superior or clairvoyant state,' and said, 'We'—himself and his particular friends—'must stand firm, and say nothing unless the enemy makes the attack.'

"And thus ended the investigation into the charges of licentiousness against Mr. Scott. Those who had first made the charge continued it, but no other 'investigation' was ever instituted.

"Strife and dissension continued from that time to distract the 'harmonious mount.' In February, 1852, the plantation originally purchased was returned to the person from whom it was bought, as the payments on it could not be met. At this time several families left the place on account of the contention and want of confidence that prevailed in the movement. In this emergency a meeting was called, and Scott passing into the 'superior state,' gave the following communication: 'James must go to New York to seek new minds to carry on the Lord's work.' The 'James,' of course, was himself.

"In accordance with his own direction, he went to the city of New York, and with the aid of Rev. Thomas L. Harris, succeeded in inducing several persons of property to engage in the enterprise. Being thus provided with funds, Scott returned and re-purchased the Cove property, which they had surrendered in February. About the first of May, 1852, Thomas L. Harris and family, and several other families, arrived at the 'New Jerusalem.' It should be mentioned, that as soon as Scott returned from New York, he resumed all his tone of unlimited and arbitrary authority, declaring that 'the people should work to the line and plummet,' and those that did not sympathize with his views should leave the place.

"This latter command was carried out, and the persons obnoxious to him were sent away. On the arrival of Mr. Harris, a new era in the spiritual affairs of the community commenced.

"It was announced that Scott and Harris were 'the chosen mediums,' through which 'the Lord would communicate to man on earth,' and that all other mediums would be silenced, or become the channels of communication for deceptive and lying spirits. Thus, they claimed for themselves infallibility and 'truth absolute, direct from heaven."

"In proof of this, a letter was sent to the still-confiding circle of believers at Auburn, from which the following passages may be taken as illustrative of the enormous claims set up by these 'divinely-inspired mediums of the Lord.' After detailing in the usual inflated style the growth and procedure of the 'Apostolic Circle' in its initial steps, the pastoral epistle goes on to say:

"'In these, our dictated and recognized records,* James L. Scott and Thomas L. Harris are styled 'vehicles of inspiration,' provided for the transmission of truth from heaven to the external world. It is also written therein that these vehicles were specially provided and prepared for this end, and that the apostles, martyrs, and confessors, together with the prophets, patriarchs, and seers, lifted supplication for inspiration to pervade the chosen vehicles; that their prayers received response loud from the angelic messengers; that the glory of God filled the sanctuary, and that the voice of the Lord Creator was audible therein and gave answer favoring the supplication.

"'Thus be it known, a further commission was given unto the mortals aforesaid, constituting them in unity as the organ of inspired communication from the celestial sphere. In order that this their work might be accomplished, their minds were blended by supernatural influence, and thus made one adapted vehicle for transmission of truth absolute, and light, in confirmation and exposition of truth previously revealed from heaven to man.'"

[A vast deal more of a similar nature follows, which it would be equally repulsive and unnecessary to reprint. The message ends thus.]

"Having thus guided the vehicles of communication to the place directed by His most holy will and united them thereupon, the spirit who desireth and establisheth the redeeming procedure, issueth commandment unto us, His messengers, to resume 'the Disclosures' of his truth without delay, that His name may thereby be glorified, His people instructed and comforted, and His compassionate and loving kindness, in accordance with the purpose in the consummation of His procedure, be manifest unto the earth and the inhabitants thereof."

Of the communications whereby "the Lord's people" were to be so specially "instructed and comforted," the following sentences, spoken, of course, in the "interior condition," by Scott, may be taken as a specimen.

"I read written in letters of fire, 'Dost thou believe? and what dost thou believe? Who, thinkest thou, called thee here? Who inspireth? Not an angel, for he is led; not a seraph, for he is controlled; not created existence, for that is inspired. Who, then, thinkest thou, called thee to the mountain? Who but God inspireth. . . . . . . I am that I am now inquireth of thee; and prepare to answer thou me. . . . . . . None other than God, thy Redeemer, calleth for thee. None other than He who hath the keys of death and hell addresseth you through one of your members." . . . . . .

And in pursuance of this claim — to which, as the reader will perceive, Moses' claim of direct personal intercourse with the Jewish Jehovah was humility itself — Mr. Scott soon after called upon his followers to yield up all pecuniary interest in their own possessions to him, which command he issued in a general address "to Spiritualists everywhere," of which the following is an extract:

* "Disclosures from the Interior."

"But while spirits operate from the interior, man in clay demandeth external benefit, and God supplieth, by laws operating externally and external means conducted by external stewards, chosen for external purposes. He hath therefore aforetime committed to your charge, as his stewards, the means designed to be employed while conducting the external in the manifestation unto its consummation. And lo! now he cometh and calleth upon you, and requireth the charge committed with its improvement. [To wit, principal and interest. —AUTHOR.] Who so hath and now consecrateth to this great work, to him shall be given, and he shall have more in abundance. To him who holdeth in his hands the gifts of God, and hath not occupied for His glory, and is wanting in disposition to render back to the author of all blessing, from him shall be taken even that which he hath; for the earth and the substance thereof is the Lord's, and in the redemption He establishes therein His kingdom; hence his will shall be done on earth, as by angels in heaven. Come, then, to the mountain with thy substance; give it to the Lord, who calleth for thee! for he now provideth a feast of fat things which shall be unto all people, and proceedeth to remove, by the immortalizing procedure, the veil of mortality, cast through sin over all nations."

Among other specimens of this movement put forth by the leaders, we have in our possession a paper called the *Mountain Cove Journal*, but as its columns are simply reiterations of the claims alleged above, sermons to the same purpose by Harris, and bulletins issued direct from the high empyrean courts of Heaven, by Scott, it would be simply a repetition of an already disgusting theme to reprint them. We conclude our notice of the Mountain Cove drama by a further quotation from Mr. Capron's informant, and one of the participators in the scenes he so graphically describes. Mr. H. says:

"Mr. Harris frequently declared that the house which he and Scott inhabited was *the house of God*, while Mountain Cove was *the gate of Heaven;* that the redemption of man on earth would commence there, and all who opposed them, "the two perfect prophets," would be driven from the mountain, from which there would be no redemption. Some time during the summer of 1852, it was declared that the spirits, through Scott and Harris, had announced to "the faithful" that a certain piece of land within a boundary which contained the Cove buildings must be leased to the Lord as his heritage. Accordingly, "the faithful" assembled, and the spirits, through the two prophets, directed the lease to be made out in their names, as the "Lord's chosen vessels," a command that was obeyed accordingly.

The Lord and his chosen ones being secured in their lease, a series of persecutions were commenced against all who in any way rebelled from the authority of the "two perfect mediums." Slander, discord, and contention were rife, and peace and harmony were unknown among the chosen people.

In the fall of 1852, Scott and Harris had proclaimed that they were the two witnesses named in the tenth chapter of Revelations, and that they possessed the powers, to their fullest extent, spoken of therein. Strange as it may appear, they found adherents and firm believers in this declaration; persons who were kept in awe by these self-appointed saints and their constant assertion of their own divine authority. In one of his prayers, uttered about this time, Harris said: "*Oh Lord, thou knowest we do not wish to destroy man with fire from our mouths!*" etc.

The state of discord continuing to increase into a perfect pandemonium, and one after another becoming more and more disgusted with the arbitrary assumption of divine power and holiness on the part of the dictators, many departed and left the Cove to the most fanatical, but finally the whole movement entirely dispersed. . . . . This history adds another to the wild and numerous schemes conceived in the spirit of religious fanaticism, and born of the spiritual excitement, which was made a convenient hobby for men who graduated through the old forms of theological mysticism, until there was nothing new in the field to feed their ambition but a pretence to special calls and special inspiration."

Thus ended the "Mountain Cove movement," but unfortunately the spirit that gave it birth was still in active existence.

The love of rule and the insane desire for spiritual distinction seem to surpass in greed all other forms of human ambition. Whether it be that men really deem the divine government, whose empire they audaciously assume, is strictly impersonal, or too far off to interfere with them, or that they can actually psychologize themselves into a belief in the reality of the claims they arrogate, it would be difficult to decide, but certain it is that the demon of ambition which had vented its arrogance at Mountain Cove could not be laid by a single failure.

Mr. Thomas L. Harris returned to the world to run a mingled career of supra-mundane usefulness and sub-mundane folly, which the spirits that held sway at Mountain Cove, alone could have been the authors of. For two or three years after the above episode, the disgrace which it entailed on the name of Spiritualism was temporarily obliterated by the brilliant evidences of spirit-power which Mr. Harris manifested in the improvisation of his wonderful poems, "A Lyric of the Golden Age," "An Epic of the Starry Heavens," "The Morning Land," etc.

In these, as in other minor poetical productions, Mr. Harris claimed that the spirits of Byron, Keats, Shelley, Coleridge, Pollock, and other celebrated poets were his inspiring genii. He not only cited their names and assigned various portions of his works to their authorship, but compelled from the grudging pen of his critics unqualified admissions of the striking similarity of style observed in the poems to their renowned spiritual authors, while many acknowledgments were made that these magnificent poetical marvels were fully worthy of any names, however illustrious, or any authorship, however honored.

Meantime these efforts of genius were poured forth, wholly impromptu, in the presence of many witnesses and under circumstances that could leave no doubt of their supra-mundane origin.

Besides these tokens of spiritual control, Mr. Harris frequently acted as a test medium, giving communications to strangers, and describing spirits with an accuracy which left no doubt of their identity.

And yet, after thus lending himself to the propagation of the spiritual faith with unwearied assiduity and an amount of mediumistic power which amply qualified him for a successful propagandist, we find him again assuming the airs of apostolic leadership. Separating himself from the Society of Spiritualists meeting at Dodworth's Hall, New York, by whom he had been often acceptably employed as a speaker, when they would not avail themselves of his services as their permanent ruler, Mr. Harris proceeded to draft off a few attached followers into what he called a "New Brotherhood," a "Sacred Family," etc.; titles by which he dignified certain little gatherings of persons devoted to his opinions, whom he attempted to control on the Mountain Cove plan.

Mr. Harris's fine mediumship, wonderful poetical improvisations, and former devoted advocacy of the cause of Spiritualism, unquestionably identified him at one time with that faith and its adherents in America; hence the belief still exists among many persons, especially in Europe, that he yet represents the Spiritualism of America, and that his somewhat eccentric proceedings are due to the peculiarities of that faith. In justice to the cause of truth, it is proper to state that when Mr. Harris found that the Spiritualists meeting at Dodworth's Hall, New York, repudiated his pretensions to leadership, and his attempt to usurp authority was met by a public rebuke from an honored member of the committee who employed him, he immediately felt the necessity of severing his connection with that "profane" and "infidelic" body, and bitterly denouncing the "falses" of their faith; whereupon he gathered together a little handful of "the faithful," to whom, in his own exclusive meetings, he proceeded to pour forth torrents of abuse against the society in whose behalf he had before been a zealous worker.

This separation occurred in the winter of 1858–9, shortly after which Mr. Harris, now the professed champion of "Christianity" versus "Spiritualistic Pantheism," published a poem called the "Song of Satan," an epic of so shocking and repulsive a character that even many of his best friends were obliged to credit its inspiration to the source which the title so candidly claimed for it. In this truly Satanic production, the author assumes that all the spirits that come to earth to communicate to men save only the celestials who visit the "Sacred Family" and their leader, are "demons" in the worst sense of the word. These "demons" he represents as personating the spirit of the poets, whom he formerly claimed had inspired his charming epics.

Thus, the name of the honored dead, no less than others too sacred to be mentioned in such a connection, are mixed up in his dark and evil imaginings until he scruples not to represent himself, in the only really honorable and useful portion of his career, as the agent or medium of "infernals," for the sake of stigmatizing every other spirit medium in the same detestable category. All these preceedings he brought to a climax by announcing to his very little flock at New York that he had been "intromitted" into some supernal degree, which obliged him to visit England, in which place he poured out to the astonished ears of the English Spiritualists, not thoroughly informed on the politics and personages of American Spiritualism, such a tide of abuse against his former associates, occupations, and spirit-guides, that the prejudice thus raised in a position where it could not be met and conquered, has never been fully eradicated from the minds of the Anglican Spiritualists. The chief advantage resulting from this *coup d'etat* of the great self-appointed apostle, may be found in the simple, manly, and to this day, incontrovertable statement wherewith Mr. Charles Partridge met and answered the ex-spirit-medium's charges against American Spiritualism and American Spiritualists.

We shall quote Mr. Partridge's paper verbatim, as it gives an interior view of a strange and anomalous life, the darker hues of which the world has unscrupulously attributed to the influence of Spiritualism. Perhaps a careful perusal of the following article may reverse the picture, and show how much the noble cause of Spiritualism has to endure, from the "demonic" characteristics of man, when he is impelled by his own human promptings to use that cause as a hobby to move the chariot of his own ambitious cravings for spiritual leadership and distinction.

SPIRITUAL TELEGRAPH—NEW YORK, FEBRUARY 18, 1860.

"If all persons who have heard or may hear Brother Harris, and if those who have read the above article,* and others of like character which may be published, knew the peculiarities of Mr. H. as well as those do who have been most intimate with him during the last fifteen years, it would be unnecessary to make any reply to his unsparing denunciation of all

* Mr. Harris' sermon, preached in London, England, on American Spiritualism, republished in the *Spiritual Telegraph*, New York.

those who do not accept him as their oracle, and labor to help him magnify his assumed office. But those unfamiliar with him, do not know his weaknesses; besides, he goes out from us to a foreign land under the insignia of a *Reverend*, and to the brethren and friends of the same general cause, denounces by wholesale the great body of Spiritualists in America as 'Pantheists,' rejecting alike the ideas of Scripture as a divine revelation, and the existence of God, and as gross sensualists, and immoral in their conduct in all relations of life. These are grave charges; and it is not to be supposed that a brother would prefer them in a foreign land without a cause. What then is the cause?

"If the charges were true even, it is contrary to the genius of the new dispensation to magnify human delinquencies to the neighbor and much more to do this in a foreign land, where there is little or no opportunity for the accused to be heard in defence. But the great body of Spiritualists in America deny severally and singly the charges preferred against them by Mr. Harris.

"Each one claims for himself the same right to investigate and determine whether the Scriptures are partial or plenary revelations of Divine truth, which Mr. Harris has exercised for himself; but they do not recognize Mr. Harris's right to dictate for their acceptance his peculiar views of Divine truth, and here is the rock of offence, and the sole ground of his charges.

"The Spiritualists' creed, if they have any, respecting the Divine rights and duties of man as to faith, knowledge, and conduct, is that each person shall be permitted to observe, experience, reflect, reason, and judge for himself.

"Truth, rather than man, is their oracle. We can conceive of no objection to this, save by those aspiring to be oracles.

"Spiritualists of America have no inquisition to try men's faith and conduct by; but each person who claims to believe that spirits communicate with mortals is by common consent a Spiritualist. Consequently there may be Spiritualists who are Pantheists and sensualists, and so, perhaps there may be some persons who do not believe in Divine revelation exactly as Brother Harris teaches; but what authority does a man derive from these facts to denounce the great body of Spiritualists in America as Pantheists, sensualists, and rejectors of Divine revelation?

"The great body of Spiritualists in America has many members, some of whom saw great lights and heard spirit voices whilst persecuting the faith. The balm of the new dispensation has done much for the restoration of wounded minds and consciences, and if it has not yet had time to make them all perfect, it is hopeful to accomplish much in the way of doing so. But Brother Harris's accusations against Spiritualists are but a duplicate of those he preferred against the Universalist denomination, to which he is indebted for the insignia of 'Reverend,' which he now uses to sanctify his denunciations of both faiths.

"While Brother Harris was settled over the Universalist Society in Elizabeth street, in this city, some fourteen years ago, he became infatuated with the revelations which were just then being given through Andrew Jackson Davis, and when these were published under the title of 'Nature's Divine Revelations,' Mr. Harris asked leave of his society to go to Europe for his health, which being generously granted by the society, Mr. Harris, instead of going to Europe, went to this and other western States lecturing, not for the 'Divine Revelations' of the Bible, but for those of Andrew Jackson Davis. The society continued their leave of absence, settling Rev. E. H. Chapin in place of Mr. Harris. After a time, the latter relinquished his ardor for 'Nature's Divine Revelations,' and has since denounced its author as cordially as he did the Universalists and Spiritualists.

"Brother Harris subsequently tried to build up a society to sustain his preaching in this city. He preached in the Socialists and afterwards preached them out; and his erratic preaching caused a constant change of hearers, and the meetings were not sustained.

"He subsequently commenced preaching in the Stuyvesant Institute, and while laboring there endeavored to show the possibility of spirit intercourse. During this time one Dr. Scott, a Baptist minister, discovering that singular phenomena occurred in the presence of a Mrs. Benedict, of Auburn, New York, concluded that he had evidence that St. Paul communicated through her rappings.

"The idea that St. Paul would and could condescend to speak through a mortal much excited Mr. Harris, and arrangements were made for Mrs. Benedict and Dr. Scott to come to Mr. Harris's boarding-place at Brooklyn, and deliver the oracles of St. Paul to twelve chosen persons, and if possible develop or remodel Mr. Harris, so that henceforth he should be Paul's oracle to the world. Dr. Scott also became infatuated with the ambition of being a medium for some of the apostles, and fancied that he was accepted by St. John, and henceforth they supposed that St. Paul and St. John communicated through them.

"It would make this article too lengthy to give the minutiæ of the dramatic performances to which these men subjected themselves to secure these mediatorial offices.

"It is sufficient to say that they worked themselves into the persuasion that they had been chosen by God, Christ, and the Apostles, as the mediums of their oracles to mankind, and, under the flattering unction of this persuasion, they set about gathering the elect, and travelling westward to a land sufficiently pure for the influx and efflux of Divine wisdom.

"They induced a small company to take up their beds and follow them to Mountain Cove, Virginia, where they made purchases and settled.*

"Here they established the Mountain Cove *Journal*, and through its columns they gave, as they supposed, supernal wisdom of 'God, Christ, and the Apostles' to the world; and it was very generally conceded that it might be 'supernal wisdom,' since no mortal could comprehend it. In about two years, we believe, this community broke up in great confusion, amidst the criminations and recriminations which have generally attended the various changes of Brother Harris's visions and enterprises.

"Mr. Harris then returned to New York, and the Spiritualists received him as it becomes a father to receive a prodigal son, and invited him to lecture for them in Medical Hall, which they procured for that purpose. Here Brother Harris delivered some of the most scorching discourses on the Scriptures as a Divine revelation, and the Christian Church generally, that we have ever listened to. They were even too strong for those whom he now denounces as rejecting the Scriptures as a divine revelation. Nevertheless, we heard him gladly, not as an oracle, and not for his censoriousness, but for his acknowledged eloquence and zeal in what he appeared to think right.

"After a few months had elapsed, and the mortification of his Mountain Cove apostolic failure had subsided, he seemed to come more and more to himself, and preached some excellent discourses to the Spiritualists at Dodworth's Hall. Finally, his prevailing ambition to have a church began to pester him, and grew into an open demand, to which the Spiritualists did not accede, when the Mountain Cove spirit again took control of him, and he concluded that the love and wisdom of God and Christ were not permitted to penetrate the cloud of evil spirits, and flow down, even through him, to the reprobate minds, as he alleged them to be, which congregated to hear him in that place.

"This he said to them, in some of his last discourses, in the plainest terms, and at the same time he called upon the few pure minds to go out, follow him, and help to build up the kingdom of God. Brother Harris and some others then separated themselves from the main body of Spiritualists in this city, and they afterward met in the chapel of the University, under the assumed insignia of the Swedenborgians, namely, "The New Church;" and in his teachings he even out-Swedenborgd Swedenborg himself, much to the annoyance of many of his disciples, who feigned to know something of the philosophy of the Swedish seer before. He continued to speak here to a small company of admirers, until he became persuaded—and so said—that he had been developed above their plane of comprehension, and that the Lord had prepared a man to receive the mantle of that plane of teaching, and that he had been instructed to soar aloft, go to Europe, and disseminate 'supernal wisdom' there.

"Subsequent to the time when he withdrew himself from Dodworth's Academy, he formed the persuasion that the higher spirits were constantly trying to ward off the evil ones, and that they were trying to develop him into a higher plane, for which purpose it was necessary that he should keep his bed.

"This he did, eating but little, and in bed he wrote, or rather dictated to his amanuensis, what appeared in his publications. He was persuaded that he acted in accordance with the dictates of the apostles, Christ, and God, and only got up when he thought they so impressed him, which was only on Sundays to preach.

"Thus we have with pain and sorrow responded to the demands of the article in the London *Critic*, in giving a very brief history of Mr. Harris, during fifteen years.

"We have not done this to injure him, far from it, but in the defence of truth, and as an illustration of a prevalent psychical phenomenon which is often mistaken for spirit influence, and to call Brother Harris's attention to the changes which have come over his mind, to the end that he may be less positive in his opinion as to the divinity of his persuasion, and, above all, to be less censorious of the brethren who are not willing to follow him in his sudden changes, and chimerical enterprises.

"If also this narrative shall suggest to his friends the injury they do him by falling into his persuasion, and thus binding him more strongly in psychical chains, we shall be thankful. CHARLES PARTRIDGE."

* In the *Spiritual Telegraph* of October 16, 1852, will be found a long article from the pen of Mr. T. S. Hyatt, one of the Mountain Cove brethren, and editor of one of the earliest periodicals issued by the "Apostolic Circle" at Auburn. Mr. Hyatt states his case with much frankness, and assigns reasons very similar to those supplied by Mr. Capron for his secession from the "Holy Mountain;" indeed Mr. Hyatt was Mr. Capron's "informant" concerning the details of the movement, and supplied the account which Mr. Capron abridged, and from which we have made extracts.

With Mr. Partridge's admirable analysis of a case whose disorderly psychical states refer to many others besides Mr. Harris, we close our account of one of the earliest, most prominent and persistent slurs that the white standard of Spiritualism has endured from the hands of its own legionaries.

CHAPTER XXII.

"THE NEW MOTIVE POWER."

> "Speak of me as I am. Nothing extenuate;
> Nor aught set down in malice."
>
> OTHELLO.

VERY early in the publication of the Boston *New Era*, numerous notices appeared in its columns calling attention to the writings, lectures, and propagandism generally effected through the mediumship of a Mr. John M. Spear, a Universalist minister, whose philanthropic life had procured for him the title of the "prisoner's friend." Mr. Spear had distinguished himself in nearly all the benevolent but unpopular reforms of the day. He had labored bravely in the Anti-Slavery, Peace, and Temperance movements; and the desire to benefit his fellow-creatures was so obvious in all his public efforts, that this fearless disregard of popular opinion and faithful adherence to what his own heart dictated to him as right, must be borne in mind by those who would judge fairly of a very remarkable, but ill-understood, character.

Mr. Spear was stated to have became a medium for the exercise of various spiritual gifts, about March, 1852, from which time he devoted himself with characteristic zeal to the use of the powers which he possessed, and to the dissemination of the doctrines which he claimed to have received from circles of "high and distinguished spirits."

A book entitled "Messages from the Superior State," affirmed to have been dictated to Mr. Spear by the spirit of John Murray, the founder of the sect of Universalism, was his first public appearance before the world as a medium. His next step was the announcement that, under the direction of a council of "highly-exalted spirits," he was to deliver a series of public lectures, amongst which were a number of essays on various parts of the human organism, purporting to originate with the spirit of the celebrated Dr. Rush. As these, like the rest of Mr. Spear's published books, are already before the world, our history would have little or nothing to do with them beyond a passing notice, were it not for the fact that their author became prominent in several movements whose bearing upon the progress of Spiritualism have been too marked and important to be passed over.

The first of these which challenges notice was the presentation to the world of what its originator called a "new motive power." It requires some familiarity with Mr. Spear's peculiar style and idiosyncracies, to appreciate the history of this extraordinary claim; moreover, as this gentleman's early public career illustrates in a remarkable degree the results which grew up under the hot-house process of strong magnetic influence, and shows how the marvel of open spirit communion developed the latent specialties of exceptional natures, we shall antedate our notice of the "Spear movements" by presenting some characteristic illustrations of their originator, drawn from the published matter already before the world concerning him.

Mr. Spear was in the habit of journeying over the country as the spirit moved him, or, as he himself affirmed, at the command or direction of spirits, to whom he professed himself willing to render a childlike and unquestioning obedience. In thus narrating the acts of individuals who have figured in the wonderful drama of which we write, we must neither be understood to endorse, nor yet to criticize them, and when we use the term "the spirits" in connection with the affirmation of human mediums who profess to be acting wholly under their influence, we do so in deference to the faith of the parties themselves, rather than to any disposition to label everything as "spiritual" which claims such an origin.

That Mr. Spear honestly believed in a spiritual origin for the various "missions" he undertook, and the remarkable part which he played, none who have ever come into personal relations with him can question. The unwavering fidelity with which he adhered to his purposes, and the patience with which he endured reproach and odium for their execution, would attest his sincerity, were other evidence wanting.

Mr. Spear alleged that in the prosecution of these said "missions," he could not always at first discern their object; nevertheless, he firmly believed they were "instigated by the highest wisdom," and "designed for the most beneficent ends."

Like many of his compeers, Mr. Spear lived by faith, trusting for direction and also for financial resources to the invisible world, and maintaining that the providential dispensations of the hour had never failed him. His numerous imitators have rarely been equally fortunate, and not a few of them have procured for themselves, by a too faithful copy of their remarkable exemplar, the harsh title of "vagrants" and "spiritual mountebanks." In his various itinerant progresses, Mr. Spear frequently gave satisfactory testimony of spirit control, by ministering successfully to the sick, and effecting cures either by the laying on of hands or prescribing for different forms of disease.

In several instances he alleged that he had been sent by a spiritual command to the houses of total strangers residing in unknown and distant places, where he became impressed to lay his hands on the afflicted, for whose benefit he had been thus "spiritually led." He was also gifted with strong psychometric power, and delineated character with singular accuracy. Amongst other revelations which this gentleman alleged to have recieved from "on high," was that of the existence of divers societies in the upper spheres, whose names and functions he was especially instructed to make known to mankind. In connection with this charge he undertook, whithersoever his wanderings led him, to "consecrate" to the service of these heavenly societies sundry mortal assistants, upon whom he bestowed names, whose very number and originality was not the least curious feature of his mediumistic career.

The earnestness and good faith with which these strange "missions" were achieved, and the not less memorable character of the missionaries whom he gathered around him, would, in any movement less broad and cosmopolitan than Spiritualism, have placed Mr. Spear and his followers in the position of a new sect, whose eccentricity of names, language, and opinions would have furnished all the elements required to separate them from the rest of mankind. In order to give the most faithful possible representation of this singular personage and the relations which he alleged to exist between himself and the dwellers of the spirit couutry, we shall here quote some of his own correspondence addressed to the Boston *New Era.*

In July, 1853, Mr. Spear writes from Utica, New York, as follows:

"NEW SPIRIT ASSOCIATIONS.

"BROTHER HEWITT,—We arrived in this place on our journey homeward yesterday. By spirit direction we visited Niagara Falls and Rochester; at both these places our spirit friends made important declarations. At Rochester, through friend Hammond and myself, it was declared that the following associations had been recently formed by spirits:

"First. An association called the Association of Electrizers.

"Second. An association called the Association of Healthfulizers.

"Third. An association called the Association of Educationizers.

"Fourth. An association called the Association of Agriculturalizers.

"Fifth. An association of Elementizers.

"Sixth. An association of Governmentizers.

"The above associations will co-operate with the Association of Beneficents, which was organized some months since, and has begun its labors.

"It was declared that these newly-formed associations would soon select their agents to execute their schemes. In this place an agent has been selected by the Association of 'Agriculturalizers,' and the selection shows great wisdom. He was given the name of the 'Explorer,' and in connection with him was a Decorator. It was also declared that Brother Hammond would be much employed by these associations, and that he was now the best mediumistic writer upon the face of the earth. He was given the name of The Writer. It was, moreover, said that the Associations of Governmentizers and Educationizers would be selected from amongst the 'feminines.'

"Such were some of the new things declared at Rochester. Your readers will quietly wait, I trust, for the fulfilment of these things, and will do their part as they may be selected to aid the newly-formed associations.

"Yours truly, JOHN M. SPEAR."

Whether Mr. Spear's followers lacked the zeal and enthusiasm which animated their leader, or that he himself lived, talked, saw, and felt before his time, He who reads the secrets of human hearts, alone can decide; certain it is that though promises of the kind above cited, and "missions" of various use and spiritual co-operation were freely dealt out wherever Mr. Spear's indefatigable and earnest purposes led him, his followers have observed no part of his charge so faithfully as that of "waiting quietly" for the fulfilment of the things that were to come.

We should be unfaithful to the truth, which we are pledged to record in this history, did we omit a description of those numerous "consecrations" which Mr. Spear felt impressed to bestow on various individuals, who, whether they realized any subsequent spiritual unfoldings from such ceremonials or not, generally acknowledged an effect at the time something akin to the passionate emotions of a great revival season.

The particular instance to which we call attention occurred with the celebrated clairvoyant and physician, Mrs. Semantha Mettler, to whom Mr. Spear, yielding as usual to the impressions of the hour, paid a visit, when the following scene is reported in the *New Era* to have transpired:

"Passing into the superior state, Mr. Spear enunciated these words:

"'How fondly, how constantly, how widely, is this one [Mrs. Mettler] beloved! How beautiful is the influence this woman exerts! Wherever she is she attracts! In this particular she possesses a most remarkable character. Her friends know no bounds to their affections for this one; and there is nothing which they would leave undone to gratify her. There passes from this woman a very marked influence. It is not precisely the religious influence; it is not precisely the moral influence; it is not precisely the practical influence; but it is, so to speak, a compost of all; and these are charmingly intermingled, imparting a most adhesive influence.

"'This medium [Mr. Spear] has been commissioned to wisely instruct this woman for a high purpose. There is before this woman a new and beautiful labor. At ten o'clock to-morrow the purpose of his mission to this place will be unfolded. Let this woman be in the region of the tranquillities at that hour.'"

The report of the *New Era* further goes on to state, that, at ten o'clock the succeeding morning, Mr. Spear, "descending upon bended knee, pronounced these words:

"'Father of Fathers, and Deity of Deities; Thy wills be done on the earths, as they are done in the heaven of heavens. This fondly loved one [Mrs. Mettler] shall be consecrated to the charities. Thou shalt henceforth be called Charity.

"'Receive now this blessed power.' Here Mrs. M.'s hand was closed and breathed upon, and when it was opened, it was said,—

"'This hand shall be unfolded to dispense blessings,' etc.

"'It is done.'"

That these scenes were deemed to be pregnant with high spiritual import is proved by the fact that they were recorded in some of the spiritual journals of the time as matter of solemn interest, and commented upon by the actors therein, with terms of such enthusiastic reverence as significantly testifies to their sincerity.

Let us here state, once for all, that Mr. Spear's peculiar tone, language, and views were not accepted or sympathized in by any large class of American Spiritualists; nevertheless, they are representative of a certain number of his especial admirers, and their illustration, after their own fashion, is absolutely necessary to the full comprehension of the results which followed, in what has been called "the new motive power" movement. Considered as an isolated fact, what we are about to narrate may seem to excuse the opprobrious epithets with which its founder and his sympathizers were assailed; but regarded as the production of a mind whose marked idiosyncracies became powerfully developed by the afflatus of a great revival season, and whose high aspirations and really reformatory aims were stimulated by the influence of sanguine minds of kindred nature in the spheres, the history of the "new motive power" may be regarded as precisely the sequence to be expected from the temperament of its human originator. We must add that Mr. Spear's mind had evidently been exercised on the subject of combining mineral with vital electricity as a means of developing the latent powers of mediumship, and he had on more than one occasion subjected himself to the most scathing ridicule from his contemporaries by seeking to promote the influence and control of spirits, through the aid of copper and zinc batteries, so arranged about the person as to form an armor, from which he expected the most extrordinary phenomenal results. An experiment of this nature, tried at St. Louis, proved, so far as external effects were concerned, a complete failure; hence it was denounced as "the most preposterous presumption and absurd fanaticism."

Had any manifestly successful effects followed this attempt, the historian would have had a different record to make. Mr. Spear would have been pronounced by the Spiritualists "inspired," and by the materialists a "shrewd scientist."

Success and failure are the real touchstones of public opinion; yet who can say whether we are not more indebted to the bold adventurer, who is willing to incur the risk and odium of failure for the sake of possible success, than to the cautious idler who waits upon the results of others' experiments to determine whether he shall condemn or applaud? After many consecrations, announcements, and premonitory symptoms of some great and momentous crisis to follow Mr. Spear's remarkable design, the one event in the spiritual movement, in fact, with which his name is most prominently associated, namely, the birth of a "new motive power," was heralded forth to the world in the columns of the *New Era*, in a tone, the very nature of which will explain why the whole subject, instead of commanding the attention of the scientific, only incurred unmixed scorn and reprobation from all but its immediate friends and projectors.

Mr. Spear, as will hereafter be seen, had long indulged the idea of embodying in some tangible form the crude conceptions of certain minds [not limited to the earth spheres alone], who have labored to discover and scientifically control the mystery of the life principle. The medium and his invisible counsellors deemed they had made this stupendous discovery, and the result upon his own mind and that of his human coadjutors, was a tone of jubilant and premature triumph, which even from the first arrayed the great majority of calm, dispassionate thinkers against the whole transaction.

The editor of the *New Era*, a gentleman apparently in strong sympathy with Mr. Spear, announced in the columns of his journal that the association of the "Electrizers" in the spheres, were preparing to reveal to mankind a "new motive power," "God's last, best gift to man;" a work that was "destined to revolutionize the whole world" and "infuse new life and vitality into all things, animate and inanimate;" in a word, the glowing language in which the "great discovery" was heralded forth stimulated expectation to fever heat, and left little room to doubt that a modern Frankenstein had arisen, who, like Mrs. Shelley's famous student, was prepared to show a living organism, created at the hand of its fellow-man, only that the new "monster" was a being of metal and wood, instead of flesh and blood like its German prototype.

From time to time, mysterious hints had been dropped in the columns of the *New Era* concerning "this thing" which was to "awaken the world to wonder," and at length it was announced, in the terms above quoted, that "high spiritual intelligences" had, through the organism of Mr. John M. Spear, given directions for the construction of a living machine, whose properties were summed up, in language the most exalted and triumphant, as "a new motor." In connection with the existence of this remarkable work, reports of the most singular, and, it must be confessed, revolting nature, were circulated. A well-known Boston medium, a lady of amiable character and unsullied reputation, was named as the mother of the "new motor," and the most shocking, though absurd and impossible stories were bruited about concerning the practices by which "the life principle" had been infused into its organism.

To the truly scientific, the only question was, whether the life principle was actually there, not how it got there; but the prurient mind, stimulated by the awkward and most injudicious claims of a human parentage for a material machine, indulged in scandalous and even atrocious rumors, whose effect have marked the parties concerned so injuriously that it requires the most unprejudiced consideration of the real facts of the case to disrobe it of its dark and obnoxious features. As our part is that of a faithful as well as impartial historian, and as we propose neither to set up a defence of, or attack upon, the motives of the parties concerned, we shall confine our narrative chiefly to the most authentic published statements which we can find on this subject, especially to such as represent, with equal candor, opposite views of the question. The following paragraphs announcing the birth of the "electrical infant," are taken from the columns of the *New Era*, and represent the editor's methods of gratulation on the great event.

"IMPORTANT ANNOUNCEMENT.

"THE NEW MOTIVE POWER, OR ELECTRICAL MOTOR, OTHERWISE CALLED 'PERPETUAL MOTION'—THE GREAT SPIRITUAL REVELATION OF THE AGE.

"It is with no ordinary feelings of satisfaction that we now announce to our readers for the first time the result of some peculiar labors under spirit direction, in which, in addition to those incident upon the editorship of this journal, we have been engaged during the last nine months. . . . . . . But now, after about nine months of almost incessant labor, oftentimes under the greatest difficulties, we are prepared to announce to the world,—

"First. That spirits have revealed a wholly new motive power, to take the place of all other motive powers.

"Second. That this revelation has been embodied in a model machine by human cooperation with the powers above.

"Third. That results are thus far satisfactory to its warmest friends.

"THE THING MOVES.

"We may also say that we have the birth of a new science, a new philosophy, and a new life. The time of deliverance has come at last, and henceforward the career of humanity is upward and onward—a mighty, a noble, and a Godlike career. All the revelations of Spiritualism heretofore, all the control of spirits over mortals, and the instruction and discipline they have given us, have only paved the way, as it were, for the advent of a great practical movement, such as the world little dreams of, though it has long deeply yearned for it and agonized and groaned away its life because it did not come sooner. And this new motive power is to lead the way in the great speedily-coming salvation. It is to be the physical Saviour of the race. The history of its inception, its various stages of progress, and its completion, will show the world a most beautiful and significant analogy to the advent of Jesus as the spiritual Saviour of the race. . . . . . . Hence we most confidently assert that the advent of the science of all sciences, the philosophy of all philosophies, and the art of all arts has now fairly commenced. The child is born; not long hence he will go alone. Then he will dispute with the doctors in the temples of science and then ——"

Here even the size of the editor's capitals failed him, language faded into insignificance, and nothing could be given further beyond vague hints of what was to follow the awful "then" which broke off breathless at the contemplation of its own inexpressible possibilities. Besides the lectures—two hundred in number—through which Mr. Spear had given directions for the construction of the "new motor," this indefatigable revelator had projected plans for the building of a "circular city" or "perfect earthly home." Houses of "symmetry and peace," temples of art, science, and worship, were mapped out, and elaborate diagrams planned, all of which were carefully described and engraved in the *New Era*, where these designs were spiritually built, inhabited, and handed down to such portions of posterity as may yet peruse the columns of a paper excellent in intent, faithful and self-sacrificing in execution, but, like the minds which dictated it, far too much bent upon the starry idealities of a spiritual existence to realize the obstacles of a material one, and too much concerned in the possibilities of the future to perceive the impossibilities of the present.

Immediately after the announcement of the birth of the "electric motor," the columns of the *New Era* were filled with descriptions of the mechanism, which, it seemed, was designed to correspond to the human organism and perform the functions of a living being. In the midst of the intense excitement which the subject created in Boston, and as if to counteract the jubilant tone of the New England spiritual organ, a surly growl made itself heard from the New York *Spiritual Telegraph*, which, as representing the dubious frame of mind in which the great majority of the spiritualistic ranks regarded the enthusiastic perorations of the *New Era*, we shall here insert:

"BOSTON AND THE EAST.

"THE NEW·MOTIVE POWER—RATHER PREMATURE.

"In the *New Era* of the 12th inst. is announced by Brother Hewitt, the editor, the partial success of the new motive power, or electrical motor, otherwise called perpetual motion, which is said to have been constructed by the aid of spirits, through Brother John M. Spear and others as mediums, and which is to take the place of all other power, at least very largely for driving ships, cars, and all the endless whirl of mechanical machinery. The terms of enthusiasm in which Brother Hewitt announces it, might beget the faith in its ultimate and *complete* success. 'The Thing Moves!' Yes: but it should be distinctly stated that this refers to some little balls connected with the machine, which for some months have given evidence of motion. But the grand revolver—that which answers to the main wheel of a factory, and upon which *all* the executive power is made dependent—has *never* moved. It has not started one bit. What *may* take place, we presume not to say. We are ready for great improvements in the mechanic arts as well as in theology, and it is reasonable to suppose that some of them may take place by the revelations of spirits. But, at present, we believe there is no such thing as can be really called a new motive *power*, of the character described in the *New Era*. It is there—all but the power! Even the motion of the main revolver is not yet, and it is hardly in reason, we should think, to proclaim the advent of the 'physical Saviour of the race.' And yet it is announced in capitals, that 'The advent of the science of all sciences—the philosophy of all philosophies, and the art of all arts, has now fairly commenced. The child is born—not long hence he will go alone.' That remains to be proved. In the meantime, we cannot lift the exhortation, 'Be not faithless, but believing.' It is sufficient to say that a great deal of money and labor have been expended, and the machine, whether it goes or not, exhibits a good deal of philosophical principle and considerable evidence that spirits have had something to do with it. We believe the earthly parties engaged in it could not have thought of such a thing. It is sincerely to be hoped that its main Thing *will* move, and move to some purpose."

After an immense amount of curiosity, doubt, hope, fear, triumph, and editorial sparring, and whilst very little of the real character of the subject of all this agitation was known, a renewal of hostilities was provoked upon more assured ground, after the following account of the new motor machine had been extensively circulated through the columns of the spiritual press, from the pen of Andrew Jackson Davis. We shall only quote such passages as tend to throw light upon this mysterious subject, and at the same time prove the estimation in which the amiable writer held the much-abused authors of the strange machine.

"THE NEW MOTIVE POWER—A. J. DAVIS AT HIGH-ROCK COTTAGE.—TELEGRAPH PAPERS.

"BOSTON, *June* 1, 1854.

"*To the Editors of the Telegraph:*

"Yesterday I visited High-Rock Tower. . . . . . . The object of my visit was to investigate the 'new motive power,' as developed through the mediumship of John M. Spear, assisted by the willing heart and hands of S. Crosby Hewitt,* who, I understand, is not a practical medium, but rather a friend and doer of whatsoever the former is impressed to dictate, especially in reference to the 'new motor,' which is now denominated 'the great spriritual revelation of the age.'

"Many persons of most excellent and truth-loving attributes of mind really accept this mechanism as the best, dearest gift of God to mankind. . . . . . .

"They invest the very materialism of the mechanism with principles of interpretation which give out an emanation of religious feeling altogether new in the development of scientific truth. Each wire is precious, sacred, as a spiritual verse. Each plate of zinc and copper is clothed with symbolized meanings, corresponding throughout with the principles and parts involved in the living human organism. The philosophy given through Mr. Spear, upon which the mechanism is predicated, is this:

"'First. That there is a universal electricity.

"'Second. That this electricity has never been naturally incorporated with mineral and other forms of matter.

* The editor of the *New Era*.

"'Third. That the human organism is the most superior, natural, efficient type of mechanism known on the earth.

"'Fourth. That all merely scientific developments of electricity as a motive power are superficial, and therefore useless or impracticable.

"'Fifth. That the construction of a mechanism on the laws of man's material physiology, and fed by atmospheric electricity obtained by absorption and condensation, and not by friction or galvanic action, will constitute a new revelation of scientific and spiritual truths, because the plan is wholly dissimilar to every human use of electricity.'

"With some of these positions, if not with all, the intelligent, unprejudiced mind will agree. These propositions, with numerous collateral affirmations, characterize the scientific discourses of the medium, Mr. Spear. And whoever has come into friendly relations with this man needs no assurance from me that he is intellectually disqualified for the development of absolute science. . . . . . . He is naturally a religious, spiritually-minded, plain, direct, believing, confiding, simple, honest, philanthropic man, doing good with all his guileless heart, and standing fearlessly out in unpopular reforms; all this, and more, even at the risk of incurring the displeasure of helping friends, and bringing himself and family to the very brink of destitution.

"His religious nature and former ministerial profession color all his discourses; they therefore look spiritual and hierophantic. His extremely beautiful simplicity, his teachable and therefore receptive nature, without the exercise of a vigilant reason and practical estimation of psychological laws, subject him to the terrible misfortune of being easily imposed upon by his own impulses, his own desires and secret tendencies, mistaking them at least two-thirds of the time for 'impressions' from higher intelligences.

"No one can for a moment believe but that this medium, John M. Spear, is phrenologically incapable of the original propositions that rest at the basis of this mechanism. But with all the secondary propositions which legitimately grow out of the primary ones, I think no one can fail to perceive a mingling of the mental peculiarities of the medium. Consequently, on this head, I have come to these conclusions:

"First. That the beginnings of these scientific discourses, if they may be so styled, were imparted to the mind of the medium from the world of spirits.

"Second. That then his own mind, receiving, each time he enters the state, the essence of the new thoughts and a sort of momentum, continues the sayings in a style and spirit corresponding to the inceptive impressions. . . . . . .

"A few months ago, I visited this peculiar construction, and then, by observing the progress made, the principles involved, I could not but encourage the addition of at least another part, in order, if possible, to procure the best results. And it was, as I have said, with the desire to obtain the realities, the merits and demerits, of this new motive power, that I made this last visit. And having received into my mind what I conceive to be satisfactory conclusions, I hereby proceed to give them public utterance, being replies to questions repeatedly put to me respecting it:

"First. That the various parts of this mechanism, both the wood work and the metallic, are extremely accurate, and so mathematically arranged with reference to some ulterior result or effect, that no one can fail to see the design of some intelligence superior in mechanical contrivance to these faculties in the head of John M. Spear.

"Second. The medium, in giving directions for this and that part to be added, never used 'rule and compass,' as would seem to have been the case, because the parts are precise as to measurement, and, according to his directions, artistically put together.

"Third. Theoretically, the laws of positive and negative electricity are strictly followed.

"Fourth. The mechanism is, in my estimation, a demonstration that spirits have communicated to mankind. I think we can find nowhere any better evidence.

"These are the merits of the matter; on the other hand, the demerits are:

"First. That the progressive construction, the private history, so to speak, of this mechanism, the manner pursued, by which, from time to time, one part has been added after and to another, proves the whole work to be essentially experimental, conducted very honestly, and at Friend Spear's expense, by several persons in the other world, who, doubtless, have the correct philosophy of the development of the new motive power, but who are deficient in the practical knowledge of the means to consummate its actualization.

"Second. Another demerit is, that although the positive and negative, the male and female, laws of nature are very truthfully divulged and prescribed, theoretically, as the only 'rule of faith and practice' in the elaboration of this mechanism, yet, practically, as every student of nature will perceive, the adjustment of the poles, magnets, zinc, and copper plates, etc., are by no means in physical harmony with these laws.

"Third. Another demerit is, that the 'motion' said to have appeared in the small extremities or pulses of the mechanism was merely phenomenal and temporary, owing, simply, to the centrifugal escape of electricity from the rapidly-oxidizing surfaces.

"Fourth. And there has been an attempt to infuse human vitality into the mineral substances, on the religious theory of the 'miraculous conception,' for which, however, the spirits have divulged what is considered a natural explanation.

"Fifth. Another demerit is, that, supposing the maximum 'motion' obtained, even then — no matter how gigantic in size the mechanism might be — it would not move any additional weight, nor drive the wheels of a carriage or a mill.

"Sixth. It has already cost nearly two thousand dollars, occupying the time and attention, and at times severely trying the faith of Messrs. Spear and Hewitt, as well as others, who might have done more good in many other ways, more to the gratification of their fellow-men. . . . . . .

"In another department of this strange category of psychological and spiritual developments there is an experience — a very peculiar and delicate experience — to which I am now obliged to refer.

"I speak of Mrs. ——, of Boston, whose recent connection with this mechanism has added fresh interest, not to say additional perplexity, to it. I have conversed with her. I have examined her condition, and have traced, at least to my own satisfaction, the causes of her apparently extraordinary experience. This experience, according to a report that has gone abroad, is this:

"That by means of a spiritual overshadowing, *a la* Virgin Mary, the maternal functions were brought into active operation; a few of the usual physiological symptoms followed; the crisis arrived; and being in presence of the mechanism, the first living motion was communicated to it; in other words, that then the new motive power was born, which was therefore regarded as 'heaven's best, last gift to man.' . . . . . .

"In regard to Mrs. ——, I observed that she and her quiet and beautiful psychological experiences have been sadly misunderstood and exaggerated. In the second place, I observed that no one, except with sensibilities truly delicate and tender, can appreciate her state enough to do her experience even common justice. In considering her condition, I came to three conclusions:

"First. That her nature is sufficiently impressible to render her mind extremely psychological — by which I mean, that she is organically susceptible to the influence of minds both in and out of the body.

"Second. That her former religious experience has been deep — has left many of its symbols [I mean the forms of her early religious ideas] fixed upon her understanding — upon her affections not less, although the old ideas themselves have perhaps permanently departed, giving place to newer and higher conceptions of life and immortality.

"By considering well these primary facts in her condition, you will readily perceive that Mrs. —— could not only receive the sphere of the impressions emanating from and actuating Friend Spear, but, in addition to this, that her own sensitive yet resolute spirit, operating in conjunction with congenial spirits actuating his, would easily produce the physiological effects which have really occurred. You will please understand me, Mr. Editor, when I affirm that the maternal functions were simply excited — not to perform any natural office, but merely, through the nervous forces, to impart the ordinary sensations of maternity. The symptoms were very good imitations and were psychologically produced.

"In regard to the use of the mechanism, let me add, that if the object to be gained is a demonstration of the fact of spiritual intercourse, then, in my mind, they have accomplished that object, by presenting a construction superior to the mechanical information of the medium. But if the object is to prove that spirits [who were once men] can overstep the boundaries of human intuition and reason, and give us light which we cannot obtain by the proper means and extent of investigation, then, in my mind, they can never more successfully discover their mistake and its impossibility. Spirits can prove the immortality of the human soul — nothing else with certainty. When disappointed, some mediums say, 'These are evil spirits.' Others, when provoked with mistakes and failures, say, 'There, I will give the whole thing up as a humbug.' Now, Mr. Editor, I know that such mediums are not philosophical. . . . . . .

"It is with deep and deepening sorrow, Mr. Editor, that I recognize a species of unreasoning faith — I may say, a frightful and pernicious tendency to fanaticism, among the true and faithful and teachable friends of spiritual intercourse. There are getting to be multitudes of Spiritualists. When shall we look for a beautiful crop of harmonial philosophers? If the spirits have led you into trouble [simply by their own ignorance of mundane forces and circumstances], you ask, 'What shall we say? What shall we do?' I reply, 'Why not step when and where you see the path?' If spirits tell you to do this or that, my advice is, follow them only when you can give the world a philosophical reason for the faith you possess. Or, if you can socially and pecuniarily afford it, give the spirits a fair chance, in order to test their skill and wisdom. But never allow yourself to pay too high for a little good, practical common sense. I say this because many persons give much time and money to learn a lesson which a well-balanced mind would impart for the asking. . . . . . . If I were to leave the world this hour, never more to speak or write to my fellow-men, I should say to each, 'Be yourself; follow the truth you see; do not faint or be discouraged in well-doing, though your ways may not be as the methods of

"'Your spirit brother,

"'ANDREW JACKSON DAVIS.'"

The publication of this letter called forth, as may be supposed, much argument and mutual recrimination from both the partisans and opponents of the "new motor." Mr. S. C. Hewitt defended his position and sustained the faith of the adherents with marked ability. A still more timely article appeared from the pen of an anonymous writer, who was understood to be the talented and highly-esteemed husband of the lady who has been referred to as Mrs. ——, of Boston. Calmly stripping from the story the gross and impure mask of absurdity and shocking impossibility which the prurient fancy of common report had woven around it, this writer proceeded to show that Mrs. —— had been made the subject of a set of most remarkable psychological experiences and prophetic visions, at or about the same time as Mr. Spear was engaged in directing the construction of the machinery at High Rock; that neither of these parties seemed to have the least intimation of any relation existing, or designed to exist between their several experiences, until a certain period arrived, when Mr. Spear was instructed to summon the lady to visit the machine. On this occasion a crisis was said to have been reached, in which all parties concerned recognized their correlation to each other and the singular piece of mechanism. To the latter, it was affimed, an actual *living principle* was then communicated, and subsequently maintained, through certain mediumistic processes, until the machine, in virtue of some electric pulsations which appeared in a part of its organism, was pronounced by its friends to have become "a thing of life."

Divested of the repulsive features which ignorance and prejudice throw around it, there was, and ever will remain, something singularly mysterious and suggestive in the dual experiences of persons whose psychological action, from whatever cause it originated, was powerful enough to induce physiological results of a marked and indisputable nature. From whence originated these inexplicable manifestations? and what class of mind, embodied or disembodied, could have projected experiments demonstrating, on the one hand, so much intelligence and mechanical skill, and, on the other, such a total lack of adaptation in the means employed as to convert the whole transaction into a deplorable failure, will in all probability forever remain a mystery. It is enough for our present purpose, that we represent fairly the whole transaction; and as a large majority of the Spiritualists indignantly protested against associating the history of the "new motor" with themselves or their cause, we shall insert some extracts from the pen of another correspondent, who, whilst claiming to belong to the ranks of Spiritualism, obviously desires to disclaim the application of any *side issues* to his belief. The letter from which the following quotations are taken is written by a well-known and respected Spiritualist of Massachusetts, Mr. J. H. Robinson; and though he does not wield quite as gentle a pen as the "harmonial philosopher," A. J. Davis, the plain homely truths he writes represent such a large majority of the opinions which prevailed concerning the "electric child," that it is but justice to give them a place in this history. In the *Spiritual Telegraph* of June, 1854, Mr. Robinson says:

"BOSTON, *June* 4, 1854.

"MR. EDITOR,—It is probably true that every individual owes some duty to his fellow-beings; and, impelled by a sense of such obligation, I solicit the use of your columns through which to express my honest convictions upon a subject of much interest. It is generally known that I believe in the possibility of intelligible communications with those who have been the subjects of physical death. The simple declaration of such a belief is equivalent, in the estimation of two-thirds of the community, to an admission of a greater portion of those absurdities and fallacies, of daily occurrence under the broad and indefinite name of 'Spiritualism,'—a concession which I am by no means willing to make. . . . . .

"There is a pseudo-Spiritualism, much over-grown by over-feeding, who has got on his 'seven-leagued' fanatical boots and goes fast for one who carries weight—of absurdity. But his course is erratic: first this way and then that, no fixed object in view; feeds on excitement and thirsts for wonders. I believe that seventy-five per cent. of the *prevailing* Spiritualism is spurious or useless, or both. Many well-meaning persons are expecting mighty revolutions, sudden changes in governments, and a speedy overthrow of the present order of things. We have 'Governmentizers, Electrizers, Educationizers,' and all kind of *izers* you can mention, which do not affect the great questions of the age in the smallest possible degree. They are simple follies, which will die out, leaving only regretful remembrances behind, coupled with some wonder that such things should have been. . . . .

"Common magnetic phenomena are often mistaken for spiritual exhibitions, and I suspect that the inhabitants of the next sphere are unjustly held responsible for much inane drivelling, as incomprehensible to them as to us.

"You have heard of the 'new motor,' so styled by its friends. Having some knowledge of this wonderful 'infant,' I am constrained to say that it lives, moves, and has its being only in the imagination. There is no such thing as an electrical motor in existence. A motor is a moving power; but no man whose sympathies are not largely enlisted, and whose judgment is nor to some extent warped, can claim for that curious combination of metals any such characteristic. The part of the machine intended for the application of power has not performed a *single revolution;* the mere 'throbbing' of a few balls suspended by wires is no marvel at all, especially where there are electrical currents; but it is a marvel that such incidental, nay, inevitable, oscillations should be hailed as a motive power —'the physical Saviour of the race, bearing a beautiful and significant analogy to the advent of Jesus!'

"This is much to say of an agglomeration of zinc, steel, and copper, possessing no practical value. It is said to correspond to the human body—has a brain, heart, lungs, etc.; but such analogies are solely factitious and amount to nothing, because there can be no just comparison between inert matter and the living human organism.

"I regret that this 'new motive power'—which cannot turn a coffee-mill—should have been compared to one whose whole life was severely practical. It is vain to talk of conception, gestation, the birth of motion, lactation, etc.; they are at best sublime follies, unworthy serious consideration.

"It may be said, perhaps, that I know but little of the history of this 'new Messiah.' I am conversant with enough of its history to regret its premature announcement as a 'motor.' . . . .

"If spirits have had anything to do with it, they are obviously fanatical, experimenting ones, devoid of that wisdom which ought to characterize the minds they profess to represent, and without that elevation of thought that lends dignity to the wise and good of every sphere. So far as 'science' is concerned, the results do not bear evidence to any marked display of that acquirement.

"Let the machine stand at High Rock as a lasting evidence of human credulity; and let no one hereafter surrender his judgment to the dictation of beings, visible or invisible, without seeing perfectly, step by step, the practical application of a reasonable, comprehensible principle. Jesus of Nazareth has not yet made his second advent in zinc and copper at Lynn, nor do I ever expect to recognize him in such 'questionable form.'

"I believe in the presence and assistance of invisible guardians; but there is a limit to my belief: I cannot accredit everything that comes in the garb of 'Spiritualism.'

"Yours for the truth, J. H. ROBINSON."

There is but one more act which we feel called upon to record in this remarkable drama, and that we are unwilling to present in the scathing and vituperative tone in which we find it mentioned in most of the periodicals of the time, whether spiritual or secular, save in one instance; and as that contains the historical portion of the record, divested of the bitterness which partisan feeling has infused into other accounts, we trust we shall be excused for citing Mr. Spear's own statement, published in the *New Era*, of the final destruction of the hapless "new motor" machine at the hands of an infuriated and insensate mob, who, under the impulse of very angry and, in some respects, wholly delusive feelings, broke in upon the cradle slumbers of the *wonderful infant* and ruthlessly tore it to pieces.

The wanton destruction of property, the outrageous abuse of the liberty of the individual, and the superstitious folly which prompted the attack, cannot be sufficiently deprecated; the only excuse that could be urged in extenuation of such a deed is the publicity as well as perversion of the private portion of the history, already hinted at, as including the experiences of the Mrs. ——, to whom frequent reference has been made. Those who best know this person and her peculiar temperament and disposition, will acquit her of aught that could merit censure or provoke the insulting and ribald remarks that were levelled against her. That peculiar and ill-understood psychological experiences prompted her to the incomprehensible part she seems to have played in this singular drama, is the utmost that any one can allege with justice. Beyond this, what mortal is, in his own life and conduct, unimpeachable enough to decide upon the secret and unexplained acts of another? Or what mind is sufficiently intuitive to be able to understand, much less to analyze and judge of those mysterious springs of action that are hidden in the mystic recesses of a sensitive human soul, and have only been interpreted on the external, by the harsh tongue of rumor.

And yet, on this baseless and unintelligible ground, a rude mob, stimulated by the coarse and ribald remarks of the public journals, persuaded themselves they were doing good service to the cause of religion and morals by tearing a harmless piece of mechanism apart, and uttering threats of similar treatment against the obnoxious parties who had most injudiciously set up, or at least sanctioned, the monstrous claim of its *human parentage!*

Unable, as we have above stated, to find any published report of this transaction free from the bitter and vituperative spirit of partisanship, we shall close our narrative by giving the much-abused inventor the benefit of his own statement respecting the destruction of his property, and we do this the more cheerfully as the following letter is one of the most consistent and rational documents that we can find in print over the signature of John M. Spear.

"THE ELECTRIC MOTOR MOBBED.

"MESSRS. EDITORS,—From the hour when it became publicly known that the Association of Electrizers had undertaken to introduce to the inhabitants of this earth a new motive power, the press and the pulpit have assailed, ridiculed, and misrepresented it, until a public sentiment has been generated which encouraged the mob to assail and destroy it.

"It was moved, as you know, to Randolph, New York, that it might have the advantage of that lofty electrical position. A temporary building was erected to shelter it. Into that, under cover of the night, the mob entered, tore out the heart of the mechanism, trampled it beneath their feet, and scattered it to the four winds.

"I know that the friends who were engaged in constructing this mechanism, and those who cheerfully gave of their means to promote the work, will mourn that the world has not yet arrived at a condition when it could welcome a philanthropic effort of this kind; but thus it is. It did not wish the effort to succeed, and it determined it should not.

"The course pursued by the avowed enemies of Spiritualism, and also by some of its professed friends, in relation to this effort, has caused me much pain and not a little surprise. From the hour that I became fully convinced that a new, truthful, and direct communication was opened between the earth-life and the spirit-world, I determined to give my time, my strength, my reputation, my all, to a work which I deemed so important. As I had in former years devoted myself to the elevation of the inebriate, to the promotion of peace, to the emancipation of the slave, and to the aid of the destitute prisoner, so I resolved to aid in this new movement, the grandest and the most comprehensive that has ever been commenced.

"Sometimes when I have been made acquainted with the comprehensive views and the philanthropic plans which persons in the more perfected conditions desire to unfold, I have thought that perhaps they were somewhat too sanguine; that the hour had not yet come when the world could receive them, and that on that account they might fail of accomplishing all the good they wished to do; but I have desired to cheerfully co-operate with them, and to give them a fair chance to try.

"From the hour that the Electrizers expressed a desire to unfold to the inhabitants of this earth more perfectfy a knowledge of electrical, magnetic, and ethereal laws, that a new motive power might be exhibited, I said to them, 'Friends, my time, my strength, my means, my influence, to aid a work so important and so beneficent, are at your disposal.' Aided by several philanthropic and highly-intelligent gentlemen, to whom their plan was unfolded and the model exhibited, labors were commenced, some two hundred highly scientific and very philosophic discourses were communicated; and at precisely the time designated, and at the point expected, motion appeared corresponding to embryotic life.

"But the mob has done its work. The little mechanism has been assailed, torn asunder, and trampled beneath the feet of man. But if this effort to use electricity as a motive power fails at this time, I am persuaded that in the coming future, when man becomes more intelligent and more fully unfolded, he will be able to command this element with greater ease and with more economy than he now does steam. Thank God, the principles which have been presented, and the philosophy which has been communicated, are beyond the reach of the mob, and can not be harmed by the slanders of the pulpit or the misrepresentations of the press!

"'Truth crushed to earth, shall rise again:
The eternal years of God are hers.'

"Garrison has been mobbed, Birney's press was thrown into the river, Lovejoy was murdered; yet anti-slavery still lives, and the oppressed shall yet be free. So shall it ever be with all truths which have been communicated to man. They are immortal and can not be destroyed. . . . . .

"Yours, for the aid of the common humanity,

"JOHN M. SPEAR."

CHAPTER XXIII.

THE KIANTONE MOVEMENT.

"To-day abhorred, to-morrow adored—
So round and round we run;
And ever the truth comes uppermost,
And ever is justice done."

KIANTONE—THE MAGNETIC SPRING—THE NEW COMMUNISTS—"THE SACRED ORDER OF UNIONISTS."

ALTHOUGH the personal history of Mr. John M. Spear, like that of most other individuals who have taken a prominent part in Spiritualism, includes the progress of the cause itself, press of matter in other directions prevents our entering further into the details of his remarkable mediumistic career, save to give a brief notice of a movement which has very generally, but somewhat invidiously, been identified with his name alone. The "Kiantone movement," as the subject of our present narrative is usually termed, includes the experiences of many individuals beside Mr. Spear; and though it has obtained an unenviable distinction for the attempt on the part of its participators to establish a highly unpopular system of communism, it has also been remarkable for some phenomenal features of interest, to which we shall devote a few pages of impartial notice.

It was generally believed by the early settlers of Chautauque County, New York, that salt existed in great abundance in the valley of the Connewango or Kiantone, and that this and other mineral treasures had been discovered by the aboriginal Indians, who sedulously concealed the knowledge from the whites. The final discovery of mineral waters in this region is briefly detailed in the following extracts from a letter addressed to Dr. Gray, of New York, by Dr. Greaves, of Milwaukee. This gentleman was requested to make a visit to Kiantone for the purpose of testing the waters, and the result of his investigations will be found in the columns of the *Spiritual Telegraph* of 1853:—

"MILWAUKEE, *January* 24, 1853.

"J. F. GRAY, M.D.:—*Dear Sir*,—I avail myself of the present opportunity to fulfil a promise I made you, while sojourning in New York, to give you the result of my observations and personal inquiries in relation to the remarkable mineral spring alleged to have been discovered, near Carroll, Chautauque County, New York, by spirit agency.

"Having listened to the account given by our friend, Sheldon, when he brought the water to New York for analyzation, I resolved to turn aside from my homeward journey, and examine the whole matter for myself. . . . . . .

"Fortunately I found the owner of the Spring at Carroll, who took me immediately to his house, which is located about half a mile over the line in Pennsylvania. His name is John Chase. From early youth he has been a resident of that region, pursuing his trade as a blacksmith, until three or four years since, when he removed to the farm on which he now resides. . . . . . .

"About fifteen years ago, while Mr. Chase was residing at Carroll, following his trade, his wife made a visit to a neighboring town, where there was a 'fortune teller' who was considered an 'oracle' by those who consulted her. Mrs. Chase, from mere curiosity, visited her, and during the consultation she was informed that since she had left home her husband had bought a farm; that on it was a great treasure, and that he must never part with it. Mrs. Chase ridiculed the idea, expressing her unbelief in the strongest terms, and gave as a reason that they were so poor her husband had no means of paying for one. When she arrived home she immediately asked her husband if he had bought a farm. He replied that he had, but said no one knew it except himself, the seller, and a witness, and he wished to know how she had heard of it. She informed him of the interview with the fortune teller. . . . . . . Having bought the tract for the purpose of using a small water power on it for propelling machinery for the manufacture of wagons in company with another individual, and that project having failed, Mr. Chase repeatedly offered the tract for sale, placing no confidence in the sayings of the seeress, and not being able to pay for it. He could get no offer, and was obliged to keep it until about four years ago, when he bought forty acres adjoining, which came to a highway, to enable him to sell the whole tract more readily.

"Still he got no offers, when, about three years ago, William Brittingham, who was a magnetizer in the neighborhood, learned through a clairvoyant that there was a great treasure on John Chase's farm, and besides, a valuable salt spring, and that he must not sell it. This was subsequently confirmed through other mediums and clairvoyants, until Chase was constrained to act in the matter, and resolved to follow directions and dig for the reported treasure.

"Accordingly, he took a good clairvoyant on to the ground some time last spring, who located the precise spot, where they afterwards dug with signal success.

"Subsequent trials with other mediums corroborated the statement of the first clairvoyant. On the strength of the above, he bargained with Mr. Brittingham to dig the pit, for a certain interest in the investment, and early last summer the work was commenced. They were directed to sink a pit, then to bore to a certain specified depth, when they would come to the spring. The distances they were directed to dig and to bore corresponded exactly with the account of the digging. . . . . At this point they commenced boring in the same soil for ten feet further, and struck the rock, which was very hard for the distance of six inches, when it became porous, and through it the water began to flow. At the depth of three feet they again struck the hard portion, and ceased boring. Not finding it in sufficient quantities, they were directed by the spirits to bore in the centre of the pit, which they did, and struck a full supply, flowing at the rate of about five hundred gallons per hour. They were then directed to commence boring on the north side of the pit, and they would strike the salt water. After boring through the hard clay and gravel they struck the rock — red sandstone — into which they bored to the depth of four or five feet, and came to strong salt water, flowing at the rate of about seven hundred and fifty gallons per hour, which they were directed to plug up; they did so, but not doing it effectually, the plug escaped during their absence, and the water filled the whole pit and flowed over the surface of the ground. With much labor for five days, they succeeded in emptying the pit and stopping the flow. They were then directed to insert a tube in the hole bored in the centre of the pit, reaching to the surface of the ground, which they did, when the water flowed to the height of twelve feet above the surface of the earth. The water obtained from this spring flows turbid all of the time, containing a large amount of sediment of earthy matter, of an unctuous character to the touch, emitting a peculiar odor, and the taste strongly alkaline. Experiments were made by mixing the water with flour, which showed its alkaline properties by raising bread and biscuit very light. You have, doubtless, ere this received from Chilton the chemical analysis, but as I have heard nothing from that source, I am unable to say what are its chemical constituents.

"The work was completed about the first of September last, when they were directed to commence testing, under spirit direction, the efficacy of the water in the cure of diseases. I will not detail to you the cases treated, but simply enumerate a few of the diseases in which, according to the testimony of numbers in that vicinity, the use of the water had been effectual. Various kinds of fevers, dyspepsia, pneumonia, rheumatism, inflammations of the throat, burns and scalds, erysipelas, scarlatina, etc. The details as given to me are exceedingly interesting and almost incredible; and I think the whole matter is worth a thorough investigation. It is directed to be used in various ways. The water from the spring is used internally and by bathing.

"An ointment is also made for external application for all inflammations, and the results of its use are truly remarkable. . . . . .

"Two well-marked cases of felon yielded in a few hours to the application of the ointment. In one case, where the lady had not slept for two nights preceding, and was suffering so severely that she could hardly keep from groaning in my presence, the pain left in half an hour; in twelve hours the tumefaction had almost disappeared, and she is now well, without any aggravation. The other case was characterized by a gradual subsidence of the suffering in the course of six hours, together with the swelling, and the result was a final and complete cure. . . . Similar results have followed in a severe case of croup, and in obstinate cough. . . . . .

"In conclusion I would say that the main facts above narrated are fully corroborated by friend and foe in that vicinity. Indeed, there is no doubt left upon the minds of any in that neighborhood who have known anything on the subject, that the discovery was made under the circumstances narrated above.

"The parties concerned have been subjected to an amount of obloquy and ridicule truly disgraceful, and it is wonderful that their moral courage should have so long sustained them under such trials. . . . . .

"Yours truly,

"JAMES P. GREAVES."

Immediately after this discovery the mediums to whom the waters of the spring were sent, or those who chanced to visit the place, became enthusiastic about its curative properties and the valuable results which were to accrue to mankind from its use.

In 1853, a gentleman who had become much interested in the spring, and sanguine concerning the effects of its discovery, sent a portion of the sediment obtained from the water to Mr. John M. Spear for psychometrical examination.

Mr. Spear's report confirmed the testimony of other clairvoyants, but the effect produced upon his own mind was so great as to induce him, in company with several of his friends, or, we might almost say, followers, since they were persons especially in sympathy with his peculiar opinions, to visit the spring for the purpose of establishing in its vicinage a community whose views would be in harmonious relations with each other.

Impressed with the perfect fitness of the place for the designs they contemplated, Mr. Spear and his friends entered into an agreement with Messrs Chase and Brittingham to pursue their explorations, settle upon certain portions of the land, and possess themselves of an appropriate share of the wealth they expected to realize; but when the astounded proprietors of the district heard of the magnificent prospective views mapped out by the enthusiastic clairvoyants, they began to believe that the untold mines of wealth which their new neighbors designed to realize were just as well reserved in their own hands; hence they curtly "backed out" of the arrangement, and left the baffled seers to pursue their researches elsewhere.

Besides Mr. Spear and Dr. Abel Underhill, himself a most excellent clairvoyant, there were several other mediums in the spiritualistic party. Among these were seers who no sooner found themselves shut off from the Chase and Brittingham estate than they at once perceived torrents, floods, and even oceans of underground wealth in other directions.

The whole character of the district testifies to the abundance of mineral wealth in the form of springs and subterranean deposits, with which the earth there is teeming; hence it only required the exercise of the natural eye to perceive the possibilities with which the region abounded, and the uses to which it could be turned under judicious management.

At the suggestion of Dr. Underhill, it was agreed to purchase a farm on land adjoining the Chase property, where it was affirmed that a spring known as "the great deer lick" would be found to possess all the valuable qualities attributed to the waters already becoming so renowned. Notwithstanding the fact that the resources of the place were in reality as great as the enthusiasm of the clairvoyants alleged them to be, several circumstances combined to retard the useful developments which were so confidently anticipated from its possession. Among these was lack of the capital necessary to pursue the explorations, or work the ground to utilitarian purposes. A still greater obstacle was the determined hostility of Mr. Chase to the new settlers, and the culminating cause of grief arose from internal discord amongst themselves, paralyzing their associative efforts, neutralizing their attempts at harmonious combination, and finally giving rise to current reports whose very scandalous nature it is unnecessary to repeat, except to notice that they seemed to justify the determinaton of Messrs. Chase and Brittingham to oppose the establishment of the contemplated little "kingdom of heaven" on their land.

In fact it has become a matter of too much public notoriety to veil or gloss over, that some of the inspired party who had assembled at Kiantone Springs, claimed to be the organs or human mouthpieces not only for spirits of an adventurous and scientific turn of mind, but also for others who proposed to establish a new social order upon earth, in which the marriage obligations were not treated with any great amount of reverence or conventional respect.

As may be anticipated, the enunciation of these startling propositions was received with as much abhorrence by the opposition as they were stoutly maintained by their advocates. Both parties were in sincere earnest, and here justice, no less to individuals than to the great body of Spiritualists in general, compels us to offer a few remarks on a controversy which, properly speaking, has no reference whatever to Spiritualism; nevertheless the unfounded affirmations of certain Spiritualists, and the malevolence of those who have made their views a subject of scandal and reproach to the entire body of believers, render it necessary that we should take the notorious experiences of Kiantone as an illustration of the position which we insist upon our right to claim for Spiritualism.

It is a well-known fact, that long before the advent of modern Spiritualism, many communities existed in America, the members of which maintained opinions on the marriage question which procured for them the title of "Free Lovers."

Many individuals of high social standing, talent, and influence in American society professed opinions of a similar character, without, however, enrolling themselves as members of a separated community; in fact, the doctrine of "free love" in all its ramifications permeated the country, even to the point of world-wide notoriety, years before the advent of the *Rochester knockings.*

That the believers in these doctrines sustained themselves on some points which they conceived to be "right," none who have ever observed the sacrifices they made for opinion's sake, can question. Odious as their views are in the eyes of a moral and orderly community, they were just as ready to endure social martyrdom in their defence as if they had been advocating the noblest truths and highest degree of purity; hence none can refuse to accord to them the merit of sincerity and a realizing sense of some worth in their individual opinions, however abhorrent these may have been to the good sense and pure feeling of their opponents.

Now, when it is remembered that a belief in spirit communion may be and most generally is, based upon the evidence of sensuous facts, and that its intellectual acceptance is just as rational to the robber and murderer as to the saint and sage, it can be no matter of surprise that persons who profess the broadest license on the marriage question should have accepted the demonstrations of spirit communion as well as those who believed in the strictest views of the conjugal relation, or even advocated the asceticism of celibacy. Still the mere fact that certain individuals who professed "free love" doctrines became convinced of the truths of spirit communion was quite sufficient, when all other causes of offence failed, to give a handle for antagonism to fasten this obnoxious and totally irrelevant opinion upon the entire body of Spiritualists, until malice, grown desperate for lack of more available weapons, continued to aim the shaft of "free love" against Spiritualism, and labor to make the two words appear to be of synonymous meaning.

An effort so palpably false and shallow must have failed as signally as all other antagonistic warfare has done, had not a few individuals, who desired to make the broad white standard of Spiritualism float over all the little hobbies which they thought proper to harness to its triumphant car, given out as veritable communications from "archangelic spheres," "*spirit messages*," endorsing, nay, enjoining, the practices and doctrines of "free love." The world has forgotten, in its eagerness to find real matter for offence against Spiritualism, that the most celebrated as well as the earliest professors of spiritual gifts upon the American continent have been *Mormons* and *Shakers*, the antipodal points from which "Free Love" starts and departs. It would have been as easy to prove that all the ghastly lists of crime that disgrace our daily police reports are chargeable upon Christianity, as to show that "free love" had anything to do with Spiritualism, had not the presumption of certain Spiritualists chosen to father their practices in this respect upon the authority of "the spirits."

It is evident that if Joseph Smith's spirits taught polygamy, and Anne Lee's insisted upon celibacy, there must be a very wide diversity of opinions in the spirit-world, and the generic term of "the spirits" would not have been sufficient authority to account for all the vagaries in which mankind chose to indulge, on the plea of a supra-mundane command, had it not furnished the weapon for which the opposition had so long waited. Finding it at length, they proceeded to use it with such good effect that for a long time the pernicious report gained ground, and was sanctioned by the most injurious illustrations, that free-loveism was the professed doctrine of Spiritualism.

To no point do we trace this most baseless allegation more clearly than to the Kiantone community. It would be unfit to assert that all the Spiritualists who were there assembled, professed, or even favored these opinions, but it would be equally false to truth and the cause of Spiritualism to deny, that from this place, and at the time of the settlement narrated above, the propagandism of these opinions became most mischievously associated with Spiritualism, bringing a scandal and reproach on the heads of thousands of innocent persons, who loathed and repudiated the doctrine, and causing thousands of others to shrink back from the investigation of a belief which was so strangely associated with the most repulsive features of communism.

The proof of the practices at Kiantone, their public opposition, attack and defence, are all to be found in the eighth volume of the *Spiritual Telegraph;* it is needless, therefore, for us to burden our pages further with the details of this movement, which eventually broke up in mutual recrimination and failure. The facts of the case may be briefly summed up thus: Amongst the Kiantone community the piercing eye of the spirit discovered in the first instance the mineral treasures that lay hidden in the mystery of time and matter, waiting for the utilitarian hand of man to appropriate and convert them into blessings for humanity. The association of a number of persons of different views and purposes developed the special idiosyncracies of all, and called forth the special ideas of some to an extent which, however injurious for the time being to the progress of Spiritualism, ultimately produced separations in its ranks which have been equally healthful and necessary. By temporarily fastening an obnoxious reputation upon the noble cause of Spiritualism, the "Kiantone movement" called forth discussions and eliminated questions of the highest import, which have been of incalculable benefit, and have ended in the sifting process which sooner or later was essential to free Spiritualism from all other claims and pretensions than the sublime purposes of proving the soul's immortality, the unity of spirit, and individual responsibility. All other side issues are fungi, springing up from the corruption of undeveloped natures, and, like the morals of Kiantone, must ultimately be shaken off from the divine body, on which they are a simple excrescence.

With the breaking up of the little community at Kiantone, Mr. Spear once more became a "missionary at large." He gave to the world a volume called the "Educator," containing some highly suggestive and valuable essays. Several attempts at associative action also owe a fleeting success to his sanguine and enthusiastic genius, few of which are of sufficient moment to claim further notice.

Whilst writing on the subject of "movements," however, and the temporary influence such combinations exercised on the progress of Spiritualism, we must not omit to notice one more attempt, which nothing less than the inherent strength of "the cause" could have transformed from an instrument of suicidal ruin into a page of salutary warning.

It was about the spring of 1862 that a rumor went abroad concerning a new movement permeating the ranks of Spiritualism which had already enlisted in its interests some of the wealthiest and most distinguished citizens of the New England States. About this time a trance speaker, whom we shall designate as Mrs. E., came to Boston to deliver a course of lectures under the auspices of the Spiritualists.

Mrs. E. had already been apprised of some of the initiatory features of the new movement, and from sources both mundane and supra-mundane, had been warned that it contained the seeds of irrevocable mischief, if not ruin, to the cause of Spiritualism. Other mediumistic predictions tallied with these dark premonitions. It was affirmed that "a monster would be born in Massachusetts, whose demoniac nature would threaten the overthrow of the entire fabric of strength and beauty that spirits had been for years laboring to uprear." In various communications from spirit friends, the part which Mrs. E. was required to perform in the coming struggle was clearly pointed out to her, and her arrival in Boston soon confirmed the statements made as to what was expected of her.

Boston had been selected, it would appear, as the headquarters of the mystics; and as Mrs. E. was one who could command the ear of very large audicences in her public ministrations, she soon began to be plied with earnest solicitations to throw whatever power and influence she possessed into the scale of "the great new movement." All that could successfully influence a female heart — the most flattering prospects of temporal and spiritual distinction as well as appeals on the higher score of angelic authority — were urged upon the medium to secure her adherence to the movement. But angels had already preoccupied the sphere of her mind, and made their appeals to her judgment; hence these importunate human solicitations only the more conclusively proved to Mrs. E. that the hour of active decision already predicted was at hand. The association was not in actual operation at the time of which we speak, yet its preliminary arrangements had a startling magnitude.

One thing struck Mrs. E. with peculiar significance; it was the fact that although this movement seemed to include a wider field of action than had ever yet been canvassed, and a greater number of prominent persons than had ever before seemed disposed to combine in a spiritualistic association, yet the leaders and principal officials were unknown, or so veiled in mysterious reserve that it was by a seemingly fortuitous circumstance only that Mrs. E. learned who the central sun and immediate satellites of the system really were. Acting under the stimulus of this knowledge, and aided by interior guidance, Mrs. E. deferred all direct communication with the agents, who strove to wind their web around her with singular pertinacity, until the second Sunday of her ministrations in Boston, when a discourse of the most marked and obvious character was delivered through her lips, the purport of which could not be mistaken. The subject was the pernicious and retrogressive character of secret societies, contrasted with the purity, integrity, and progressive tendency of modern Spiritualism. Scathing rebukes were administered to those who sought to usurp the holy and beneficent name of Spiritualism to veil their assumptions of authority, and mask in mystery and darkness the world-wide and sun-like revelations from the realms of immortality.

All organizations that would not bear the scrutiny of light, the tests of science, or the analysis of practical religion, were denounced as effete, worthy only of the days of priestly domination, and subversive of the broad, comprehensive, and truly practical bearings of Spiritualism. . . . .

This lecture, delivered to an immense and attentive audience, was most indignantly received by the partisans of the new movement, who were assembled in the hall, expecting to hear an address of a very different character. One of their number, addressing Mrs. E. as she was quitting the rostrum, assured her, in fiercely-impassioned tones that, "as she had used her great gifts to war against a mighty and heaven-born movement, so she would yet repent that night's oration in dust and ashes!" The members of the association were in terrible earnest: this now openly-avowed antagonist not less so. An attempt at compromise, made on the following day by parties who wished well to both, entirely failed.

The association avowedly consisted of an esoteric as well as an exoteric circle. Mrs. E. charged some of the "order" with revolving around certain persons and principles veiled in the supposed mystery of the esoteric adytum, and the announcement was received with confused denial by the members of the interior, and indignant astonishment by those of the exterior circles; obviously, they did not enjoy a perfect understanding, and some good reason for the mystery of a "secret society" within an open one, began to dawn upon the minds of the unenlightened. Although it was not consistent with the principles of the opposition to accept of office or enter into the secrets of initiation for purposes of treachery, the few hints which, as above stated, glanced at the veiled mystery of the secret portion of the order, manifestly began to affect the faith of those who had allied themselves with the exterior circle, in the belief that it was based simply on the highest affirmations of the highest Spiritualism.

The external and popular operations of the association were of so attractive a character, and so broadly humanitary in their views, that however transcendental some of their propositions might seem, few could take exception to them. The society was called the "Sacred Order of Unionists," and the following excerpts are selected from a small tract which they put forth in exposition of the exoteric branch.

"THE SACRED ORDER OF UNIONISTS—'THAT THEY MAY ALL BE ONE.'

"This order is a voluntary association of men and women, instituted for the following general purposes:

"First. To unite man to man, nation to nation, planet to planet.

"Second. To abolish war in all its forms, and to promote universal peace.

"Third. To organize various co-operative and beneficent institutions, which, without injuring the rich, shall greatly aid and help to educate the poor and the improvident classes.

"Fourth. To establish such religious institutions and observances as are in harmony with man's nature, and shall tend to his highest culture. . . . . . .

"As collateral objects the order will seek:

"First. To promote among men exact justice to all.

"Second. To establish universal freedom.

"Third. To fraternize all races of men.

"Fourth. To encourage all good works.

"Fifth. To ameliorate and banish human suffering, etc.

"Sixth. To inaugurate a state in which there shall be one head, one heart, one language, and one interest, etc. . . . . . .

"For a season, and for the sake of greater efficiency and security in its incipient labors, this order will be veiled from the public eye; that is, its specific operations and its membership will be known only to the initiated; but in due time the injunction of secrecy will be removed, and the world will be permitted to behold its glory and to feel its power. Its work of social reconstruction thus follows the natural or divine method in the formation of the human organism, beginning in secret and proceeding in an orderly manner from centre to circumference. The centre or heart of the new social order is the church, the divine in man, from whose vital pulsations all other parts proceed.

"It has one supreme head, and an assembly consisting of twelve members; which assembly will organize its various branches under distinct heads. . . . . . .

"The methods of action proposed by the order, while comprehensive in their purpose, are, in its incipient stages, of a very simple character. It has at its head a single mind, who receives suggestions from all sources—from the heavens above, as well as from the earth beneath."

But despite of the united action of the interior and exterior circles, nothing could fully restore the confidence which had been shaken by the antagonistic efforts which were silently, but surely, working against them. Still the issue, if left to man alone, might have been doubtful. The veil of mystery which inclosed the hierophantic centre might be pierced by the shrewd eye of speculation, or the keener glance of clairvoyance, but would never have been shorn of its mystic pretences, had not some power, whose agency has never been fully disclosed, moved two of the fully initiated, even the hierophants of the most interior mysteries, to recede from them, in what they emphatically called "disgust," and boldly to come before the world with the offer to expose them to any ears that would open to receive them. Upon this, ensued a scene which probably was then enacted for the first and last time in the spiritual ranks. As the promised revelations immediately affected the characters of many persons who had committed themselves to the association without a very clear understanding of what their connection with its mysteries might involve, it was determined to call together as many of those interested as possible, and then resolve, according to the nature of the revelations they should receive, whether their further adherence was consistent with their views of propriety or not.

The judges and jury who were to constitute the first court of inquiry ever held in the annals of modern Spiritualism, assembled in the ante-chambers of Lyceum Hall, Boston, in the month of May, 1862, and hastily extemporized themselves into something of a judicial form.

The names of those present, or the full details of what transpired, are no longer of essential moment in the annals of the time. The history of the spiritualistic movement imperatively demands a record of the causes, however remote or indirect, which became influential upon its external character and progress, hence we are prepared to notice the succession of every important event, as it occurred; but when we are required to connect those events with individuals to whom the record may attach censure or misunderstanding, we must remember that in the great upheaval which society endured by the advent of so wonderful and unprecedented a stimulus to new thought as Spiritualism, many violent extremisms, temporary exaggerations, and excessive revulsions in newly-awakened habits of old thought, might be naturally expected. Such were the causes which unquestionably conspired to produce the fanaticism of the "new motor movement."

Restless reformers, keenly apprehensive of the real evils which afflict society in uncongenial family relations, sapping the very foundations of life with the curse of inherited wrongs, rashly rushed into excessive extremism, and uttered their unconsidered protestations against the ancient *régime* by originating a new and far more dangerous one at Kiantone. A remnant of the broken ranks, which incurred failure in these and many other similar undertakings, seemed determined to make one final rally in the Boston movement now under consideration, but with their purposes marred by fanatical zeal and ill-digested views of reform, they once more failed, or, as they themselves doubtless believed, started their undertaking in advance of their time. The accusations preferred by the hierophants consisted of what they claimed to be "immoral practices, teachings, and tendencies," and proved by citations from communications, sanctioning these courses, alleged to have been received from the spirit-world by certain mediums connected with the order.

The defence set up was that the said mediums represented their own individuality rather than the will or aim of the association, and when their authoritative position therein was urged, a still more exculpatory tone was attempted by the application of the well-worn adage that "to the pure all things are pure."

It were needless to pursue this subject further. The real details are but little known to the world. Had they been so, they would have furnished the press with so many grains of ugly truth that they might have been spared a whole world of invention, and filled their columns with fresh editorials, and interminable variations of the story from that time to the present. The real animus of Spiritualists and Spiritualism, however, may be judged from the fact that though the most repulsive features of the case were only known to themselves, that though they had in reality nothing to fear from the world, and as yet suffered no discredit in their own persons, no sooner was the real character of the "secret society" known than the tree was uprooted by some of the very hands that had been foremost to assist in its planting.

The great body of the Spiritualists did not wait to see good fruit springing forth from a plant which they perceived carried the seeds of corruption in its heart. From the very moment when they deemed the elements of good sense and pure feeling were lacking at the root, they laid the axe to the tree, and it fell ere it had begun to put forth leaves or branches.

The mysterious association affected to drag on an effete existence for some time after the memorable trial above noted, but in reality it virtually ceased to be, from that hour.

But though the life of the order [in this generation at least] terminated, the results which sprang from its fleeting existence were more enduring.

A meeting was convened by several of the prominent Spiritualists of Boston, and a committee appointed to draft a plan for a "declaration of principles," whereby the Spiritualists then and there assembled might be known and understood for what they really were, and their professions of belief no more be confounded with the disorders of "free-loveism," or the vagaries of fanatics, or one-idea reformers, who, speculating on the credulity of their fellow-mortals, planned schemes for elevating thenselves into positions of leadership.

At the next adjourned meeting of the Boston Spiritualists above referred to, the plan of the committee was unanimously accepted, printed, and widely circulated, as the "Declaration of Principles of the Lyceum Church."

With the exigencies of the time, the effects of both poison and antidote have ceased to be publicly felt, though the warning conveyed in the one, and the stern protestations of the other, have doubtless carried their results silently forward into the tides of life in which the characteristics of new generations are formed.

The broken ranks of the "Sacred Order," after having made great pecuniary and personal sacrifices for its advancement, have lived to realize either that the force of public opinion, or the unseen but still more potential forces of spiritual influence were against them; and having endured some self-imposed martyrdoms in behalf of their cause, they have silently returned to the well-beaten paths of ordinary life, in which they have doubtless found both safety and usefulness. And thus, over obstacles far more real and portentous than any which the shadowy realms of falsehood and the petty arm of malice could invent, Spiritualism has marched to its triumphs over the legions of its own slain. Suffering infinitely more at the hands of its professed friends than its avowed enemies, nothing but the inherent strength and potent divinity of this mighty movement, could have made head against the combined forces of persecution from without and corruption from within.

In this, as in other religious movements, persons calling themselves "Spiritualists" seem to have labored to overwhelm their cause with all the folly and selfish purposes of their own natures, as if for the express purpose of shaking down the magnificent temple, even though, Samson-like, they should perish beneath the ruins they create.

True it is that experience proves, and observation shows, that the wrongs, falses, and evils of society have not been originated, only prominently exhibited by Spiritualism; and when Spiritualists remember that the few fanatical episodes our space has allowed us to notice can be matched by twice-told ten thousand far more formidable evils, which the hypocrites of society are ever striving to cover with the white mantle of religion, they may feel encouraged to affirm that folly and corruption are not the peculiar attributes of Spiritualism alone; and if that movement can survive the shocks administered to it by its friends, its vitality is unquenchable enough to overcome all the attacks of its enemies.

CHAPTER XXIV.

SPIRITUALISM AND SPIRITUAL MOUNTEBANKS.

"Not serve two masters?
Here's a youth will try it:
Would fain serve God, yet give the Devil his due;
Says grace before he does a deed of villainy,
And utters prayers devoutly when 'tis acted"
OLD PLAY.

"To be, or not to be: that is the question."
SHAKSPEARE.

THE SPIRITUAL MOUNTEBANK SYSTEM — BLY—VON VLECK — PAINE — MR. COLES AT THE NEW YORK CONFERENCE — RANDOLPH AND HIS RECANTATION — THE NEW YORK PATHFINDER AND SWEDENBORG — MISS VINSON — GEORGE WALCUTT AND HIS SPIRITUAL GUARDIANS — PROFESSOR AND MRS. SPENCE, ON NON-IMMORTALITY.

WHEN it is remembered that Spiritualism numbers one-fourth at least of the population of the United States in its ranks, it can be no matter of surprise to find many persons associated with it, whose character and actions are calculated to inflict far more damage on the cause than the most bitter antagonism or sectarian opposition. Amongst those, none have been so active for mischief as "spiritual mountebanks" and dishonest mediums.

They consist for the most part of persons endowed with genuine mediumstic gifts, but who, not possessing sufficient ability to insure financial success, use these gifts as a means of pandering either to the marvel-seeker or the opposition, whichever chances, for the time being, to pay the best.

This class of fungi generally spring up when Spiritualism is at its maximum point of excitement, and after operating on both sides of the question, strike the balance in favor of the most popular, which is of course the most profitable likewise. The dishonest medium is scarcely less unprincipled than the mountebank; for the temptation to imposition only arises from the fact that all mediumship is unreliable, and the desire to procure the reward or credit of devices which cannot be legitimately rendered is the stimulus to imposition. Even the medium who occasionally practices deception, betrays the most holy of causes and the most sacred impulses of the heart, and such acts of cheating are as much the result of avarice or ambition as the acts of the professional trickster. We might be excused from pointing to these blurs on the fair face of our cause, on the ground that such proceedings are *not Spiritualism* and therefore do not belong to our narrative, but as they measurably produced their effect on the progress of Spiritualism, they have their place in this record, and form a necessary feature in a chronicle which bases its claim to acceptance on the immutable principles of truth. The period from 1858 to 1862 was particularly rife with the action of "spiritual mountebanks." Up to that time such persons had been simply "trying their hand" at Spiritualism, and feeling, perhaps, a little uncertain of the power with which they were dealing, feared to tamper with it. No sooner did they begin to understand the really human character of the once-mysterious world of spirits, than with cool assurance they proceeded to deal with it on strictly human principles, and discovering on which side of the movement the financial successes lay, they shaped their action accordingly; and since Spiritualism proper would not pay, they proceeded to make capital out of popular prejudice against it by "recanting their faith," "exposing its fallacies," and proclaiming all mediums cheats and all Spiritualists knaves or fools, because they were willing to brand themselves in the same category. It would be almost impossible to say who led the van in this respectable crusade, as none of the parties have attained sufficient celebrity to distinguish them in their high calling. As they appeared like wasps in the feverish heat of summer, or noxious living things born of the undue excitement which reacts in corruption, it is difficult to select individuals from the generic mass. Amongst the most notorious of the fraternity, however, a few stand out more prominently than the rest, foremost of whom in paramount impudence may be mentioned one *Bly*, who whether mediumistically moved to advertise Spiritualism, or a mere *chevalier d'industriê* laboring in any vocation that he thought would pay, it matters not now to inquire; suffice it to say, that at special points in the progress of the spiritual movement, and just when a certain amount of antagonistic stimulus became necessary, Bly appeared, now acting as a medium- and now going about from place to place recounting his own treachery, demanding credit for his own assertions of being an unmitigated cheat, and acting as a self-appointed detector-general, for "humbugs" of the same class as himself. At first his pretentions were so bold and assuming that some of the Spiritualists actually responded in good faith to his daring tone of challenge, and allowed themselves to appear in public discussious or paper controversies with him. It was soon found, however, that his principal aim was to procure notoriety and full audiences; that his tricks were so shallow, his impudence so unscrupulous, and, even with the opposition, his whole procedure so offensive, that to notice him at all, was to concede his point, and discredit any name or person associated with him. Another of the exposers was one Von Vleck, a little man, whose hardihood was displayed in continual alternations between his assumption of genuine mediumship and his audacious acknowledgment of deception.

Both these worthies assumed the title of "doctor," and one of them actually exhibited his tricks at Barnum's Museum for a "consideration."

After these, appeared a certain "Melville Fay," who, though repeatedly detected and openly exposed by the Spiritualists themselves, insisted upon palming himself off as a medium until he was literally chased out of the field, when he, too, hired public halls to exhibit his own tricks as specimens of all mediumship. The chief injury effected by this member of the mountebank fraternity was the fact of his bearing the name of "Fay," hence causing him to be sometimes mistaken for Mr. William Fay, an excellent medium, who travelled in Europe with the Davenport Brothers and was deservedly celebrated for remarkable phenomenal gifts.

It was about the year 1858 that another "bogus medium" was added to this choice list in the person of a Mr. Paine, of Worcester, Mass. This man had actually succeeded in carrying on a systematic course of deception for some years, by the aid of machinery the nature of which was reported in the *Spiritual Telegraph* by Mr. J. F. Coles, who sums up the mode of detecting the imposture in the following words:

"Up to Sunday evening, the 4th instant, the *plan* was undiscovered. On that occasion, in a circle of ten persons, there happened to be three Spiritualists who were very sceptical, viz., Mr. Henry Smith, the well-known 'Razor-strop Man;' Mr. C. B. J. Waters, of Worcester; and the writer of this article. At the conclusion of the 'manifestations,' all appeared satisfied save the three *sceptics*, who determined not to leave the house until the carpet was taken up and the floor examined. The result of this sceptical determination was a clear unravelling of the mystery, and there is now one less humbug in the spiritual field. . . . . . .

JOHN F. COLES."

Now, the discovery of machinery in the case of Mr. Paine was not so very astounding after all. Up to the time of the *exposé*, Paine's "manifestations" had never been remarkable for intelligence, and had always been given in his own house, circumstances which did not conform to the genius of the spiritual phenomena, whose chief characteristics were the tests of identity, which proved the presence of individual spirits, and the fact that they could be produced anywhere, that is, in any locality, whether in field or forest, private houses, the dwelling of friends or strangers, as well as in those of the mediums themselves. The imposition practiced by Paine, therefore, was only remarkable for the length of time during which it had remained undiscovered and the extraordinary reasons which he assigned for his conduct.

The Spiritualists in general have held for their motto, "The truth, the whole truth, and nothing but the truth;" hence, with characteristic frankness, they were accustomed to discuss at their conferences any subject that related to their belief, whether of a disparaging nature or otherwise. At the New York Conference this spirit of candor led them to invite strangers to take part in their discussions, and on one occasion, Mr. Paine, the "bogus medium," being present, and requesting permission "to define his position" in reference to the late exposure of his practices, he was permitted to make the following statement, which we copy from the *Spiritual Telegraph:*

"Mr. Paine said, he felt himself alive to the delicacy of his position; but if the thing were to do over again, he would not vary his programme in the least. He is a Spiritualist. He believes there have been, and may be yet extant, a few honest mediums, and occasionally a veritable spiritual manifestation; but a large proportion of the reputed mediums are cheats and the manifestations shams. He does not ask for the pity of the conference, for he does not feel himself to be the subject of pity.

"He stands commended in this matter to his own conscience; he has resorted to deception in order to meet deception and ultimately to expose it. He thinks the end justifies the means, in this case at least, whatever doubt there might be about it as a principle of ethics. [Here Mr. Paine held up a bit of what appeared to be No. 2 wire as the mighty instrument with which he set out to rid the world of humbug.] But he counts this as amongst his treasures in heaven. He has never charged anybody. Somebody gave his wife six chairs, and small presents may have flowed into his earthly coffers from time to time; but it was a labor of love on his part—love of the cause—a self-sacrificing devotion to truth. . . . . . .

"Having arrived in New York, he commenced operations with the expectation of getting the indorsement of the Spiritualists to his mediumship, and then he intended to visit the benighted cities of Boston and Philadelphia, where it was fondly believed a like success would crown his efforts.

"From this vantage ground of spiritualistic indorsement, it was fully his intention to rescue the cities aforesaid and the cause generally from the thraldom of cheating mediums, by issuing to each and every one of them a private mandate to vacate the field, or be publicly denounced as cheats. He has no faith in Spiritualism founded upon spiritual manifestations. His aim is to lift the soul from all such grovelling evidences as address themselves to us through the senses. . . . . And it may be permitted the reporter to remark that inasmuch as Mr. Paine has been the first martyr to his own pious fraud, he will retire into private life with a thorough disgust for his machine."

Considering that Mr. Paine had actually been practicing on the public for five years and never attempted to put into action his philanthropic purpose of saving the world from the tricks of mediums, until after his own had been detected, his very candid admissions did not seem to produce much effect upon the conference; but it may not be amiss, in this connection, to quote a few pages illustrative of the opinions of those who listened to him. The following sentences spoken by the Rev. J. S. Loveland, form a pretty fair expression of the general sentiment respecting Mr. Paine:

"Mr. Loveland said: It might be profitable to consider whether or not Mr. Paine, who has felt himself impressed to cheat his fellow-creatures for God's sake, and Mr. Coles, who has exposed him, are not, themselves, slightly tinctured with fallacy in concluding, as they seem to do, from the deception proved and confessed, that cheating is universal. This is strange logic. It is an imputation at once repelled by every mind that feels itself to be honest. The logical inference arising from the fact that there are perhaps thirty thousand mediums, embracing every variety, as to age, condition, etc., is that honesty is the *rule* and cheating the *exception.*

"Coolly to insinuate, as Messrs. Coles and Paine seem to do, that these are mostly, if not all cheats, is a libel on human nature and common intelligence. The very fact of Paine's silly imitation or counterfeit presupposes an original and genuine. Whence the original? What expert in deception first started the idea that spirits could rap and move ponderable bodies?

"Mr. Coles could not well have originated that idea, for, in common with the whole Christian church, he disbelieves that spirits can communicate at all in any tangible way. It could not have been Mr. Paine, for his stupid hoax proves that he has not sense enough."

For the benefit of those who may not have an opportunity of acquainting themselves with the fact, it may be well to state that after this memorable failure to sweep physical manifestations out of America with a bit of No. 2 wire, Mr. Paine, of Worcester, did retire into private life, from whence, up to the date of going to press, no further tidings of that illustrious individual have reached us.

It was in the year 1858 that a great jubilee was proclaimed in Boston by the societies of Christendom, who make that city their headquarters, on account of the public "recantation" of an individual known as P. B. Randolph, a Spiritualist and a trance speaker. Randolph, it was acknowledged, had not been very well sustained in his career amongst the Spiritualists, and it was suggested that some of their number neither desired to sustain him nor retain his services in connection with the cause; hence, no very great alarm for its future was experienced when he came out in the form of a "recantation," throwing himself at the same time into the arms of a certain sect of Christians in Boston, by whom he was most cordially received, formally baptized, and greatly patronized and prayed over. Even while in the full tide of his popularity amongst his new brethren he was induced, for a "consideration," to appear on the Spiritualists' platform at the Melodeon under the management of Dr. Gardner, for the sake of making his "recantation" more public and proclaiming it in the very heart of the spiritualistic ranks. Many of the sterner believers in the faith highly censured Dr. Gardner for parading this unworthy subject on the spiritual platform, and various motives have been assigned for the doctor's conduct. Some declared that he only desired to fill the hall; others that he was just then destitute of a sensation, and was glad to accept of anything short of negro minstrelsy. Some thought it was an act of bravado intended to show the sectarian who had so eagerly snatched at this precious morsel how utterly unimportant such "recantations" were, and others there were who shrewdly suspected what we believe to be the real truth, namely, that the doctor was desirous of publicly exhibiting the true character of the loss sustained by Spiritualism and the gain of Christianity. In this as in any similar object aimed at, all parties were foiled; for after having made some rambling and utterly inapplicable remarks about Spiritualism, interspersed with evidently sensational attempts to show that he was still "under the influence" and compelled occasionally to break off from his written lecture and return to his old style of improvisation, the whole affair concluded by the said Dr. Randolph's speedy return to the ranks of Spiritualism, in which he has been practicing on and off ever since. And yet this petty attempt on the part of a single individual to drag himself into notoriety, even at the expense of character and reputation, was another of the popular weapons which the press and pulpit eagerly seized upon to wield against Spiritualism.

Amongst the more respectable and intelligent class of the community it becomes difficult to find any one stirred with the special motives which could induce a "recantation" from the scientific facts and reasonable philosophy of Spiritualism; nevertheless, and in order to give every phase of the movement in its most protean shape, and with all available candor, we present the only instance we can find of an intelligent and apparently reasonable mind's revolt from the once accepted faith of Spiritualism. We shall offer the plain facts of the case, without comment, or attempt to extenuate the motives of the party involved, or to explain away whatever of shadow in Spiritualism he affirms he perceived. We refer to the case of Mr. Whitney, the editor of the New York *Pathfinder*, a gentleman, who having, as he himself claimed, "thoroughly investigated Spiritualism," and even become a medium for its influence, finally arrived at the conclusion that spirits are only allowed by the Almighty to come to the earth for the purpose of leading mankind on to ruin and eternal perdition.

Strangely enough, in the same articles which contain his rambling disquisitions on the Swedenborgian theory that spirit communion with mortals is "disorderly and perilous," he gives some of his experiences during the years in which he had deemed himself "blessed and happy" in that intercourse. As Mr. Charles Partridge has condensed Mr. Whitney's experiences, and the deductions he draws from them of *demoniac influences*, from that gentleman's own words, printed in the columns of the *Pathfinder*, we shall republish them in a verbatim extract from the *Spiritual Telegraph.*

PERSONAL EXPERIENCES OF MR. WHITNEY.

(From the Spiritual Telegraph.)

"Having been once or twice to a tipping and writing medium, we were only desirous of proving the identity of a dear departed one, and drew up a series of questions which we intended to propound to the spirit. The questions referred to were written on a letter sheet of paper, and covered the whole four pages in a small and closely-written hand.

"These questions were written by ourself, when entirely alone and locked in our sanctum free from mortal sight. Having finished the document, we placed it in an envelope, sealed it, and then placed it inside of our coat breast-pocket.

"We went directly from our office to the room of the medium, holding no conversation with any individual until the following took place while seated with the medium at his table in company with three other persons, entire strangers to us.

"We had sat probably fifteen minutes at the table, when the medium turned to us and remarked that we could inquire if there were any spirit that desired to communicate with us. The response came immediately—'Yes.' After putting two or three questions of minor importance, we concluded we would not produce the written questions, but defer it for another time, when the medium's hand was controlled and the following message was written out:

"'My dear, why do you not ask the questions you have prepared?'

"This was signed with the given name of the spirit to whom our written questions were addressed.

"It may well be supposed that it created a surprise in us, that we can little describe, knowing, as we did, that the name of the spirit had not been mentioned, or that any one present knew the spirit we were seeking.

"While under this surprise, a gentleman who sat opposite to us, like us, come to investigate, said, 'Now, before anything is spoken, let us get a test out of this. Will the spirit state whether the gentleman has any questions prepared, and if so, will they indicate it, and write out through the medium's hand the first question written?'

"'Yes,' was the reply, 'he has questions prepared,' and then the medium's hand wrote out a question. We immediately drew out the letter, opened it, and read to those present the first question on our list, which proved to be an exact copy of the one the medium had written.

"The spirit again wrote: 'I will now answer your questions; ask them mentally.' We held the paper in front of us, using care that the medium or any one present should not overlook us.

"We then read, mentally, the questions, and, at the end of each question, the spirits responded, either by tips or through the mediums' hand, correctly and satisfactorily.

"Had the spirit been present in the body, it could not have done it more correctly.

"We left the circle in a state of thought that no one can conceive of who has not passed through a similar scene."

"RELIGIOUS INSTRUCTIONS FROM THE SPIRITS.—It so happened that most of our family became firm believers with us, with the exception of the mother, who looked upon the manifestations as we do now, she being a professor of religion and member of a Presbyterian church; hence she did all she could to persuade us we were under the influence of evil, and predicted that no good would come from it. She begged, entreated, nay, implored her children to denounce and give it up.

"So far were her feelings concerned that she even refused to remain with us in the house, and demanded that the younger part of her family should go with her. Whilst in that state of mind, one of her family present was observed on a certain occasion to be peculiarly affected; a paleness came over his face, and, with tears streaming from his eyes, he called for a pencil and wrote the following sentiment, remarking, after he had finished it, that it was for her—the mother—and was from the spirit of Christ, as nearly as his spirit could approach the earth:

"'Let the voice of truth and reason ever guide you in all your acts. Keep heaven ever in your view, as the great idol of your soul and the pole-star which shall guide you to happiness and a glorious immortality.

"'Let love and unity entwine around your hearts a garland of pure affection, which God in his goodness has decreed to all who shall desire to receive it. Be calm, modest, unassuming, trusting in that blessed promise of Jesus which says, Where I am, there ye shall be also.'

"She immediately rose from her chair and exclaimed, 'I am a believer in Spiritualism; for whilst sitting here, I uttered a fervent prayer to Jesus that if these things were true he would reveal it to me by a communication from himself. I am satisfied that my prayer was heard and this is the answer.' From that hour she became a believer, and has continued so to the present time; and more, she became developed as a medium."

"SAVED HIM FROM THE FLOOD.—Happening to visit a well-known medium one evening, while sitting outside of the circle that was gathered round the table, not seeking or expecting a communication from the spirits, the medium wrote the following: 'My dear Son, on your return home, look well to your house. ABIGAIL.'

"The medium inquired who was present that had a mother in the spirit-world of that name. We said nothing, none responded, and finally the medium asked, 'Is it for this one?' pointing to each one in turn in the room, until it came to us, when the spirit responded 'Yes.'

"We acknowledged that we had a mother deceased by that name, took the communication, and returned home. We naturally took a look about the house, but could not discover anything that required more than usual vigilance, until our attention was directed to a 'scuttle' or trap-door in the roof, which had been blown open by the wind. Having closed this trap-door our attention was called to the flues, which we found in a precarious condition.

"Suffice it to say, that had not our attention been directed in the channel it was by the spirits, we should have had a large part of our household effects destroyed by soot and water, as in the night one of the most violent rain-storms came up that we ever remember.

"Now these are facts, and to our own mind are understood to be communications from disembodied spirits; and the reader will naturally exclaim, 'We see no evil in all that, but simply a desire on the part of the spirits to prove their identity, and promote your worldly comforts and interests.' We grant it, and can only say, in the language of another, that 'Whom the gods would destroy, they first make mad;' and we, from observation of the fruits of modern Spiritualism, are fully satisfied that whom the devil wishes to control, he first makes happy."

Now it may be naturally supposed that having given an experience which must commend itself to every candid mind as presenting naught but good, we should be equally frank in revealing the nature of the shoals and reefs on which Mr. Whitney's faith was ultimately wrecked, and his confidence in Spiritualism destroyed, but we are obliged to confess that on searching the columns of the *Pathfinder*, we are unable to fix upon a single fact detailed, which would warrant any conclusion of a diabolical agency in the spiritual movement, and no other philosophy for such an idea, than the passage above quoted, namely, that "whom the devil would control, he first makes happy," and certain remarks from the writings of Swedenborg, the most apposite of which is quoted by Mr. Whitney, as follows:

"When spirits begin to speak with man, he must beware lest he believe them in anything, for they say almost anything; things are fabricated by them, and they lie; for if they were permitted to relate what heaven is, and how things are in the heavens, they would tell so many lies, and indeed with such solemn affirmations, that man would be astonished; wherefore, when spirits were speaking I was not permitted to have any faith in the things which they related. . . . . . .

"On this account, the state of speaking with spirits on this earth is most perilous unless one is in the true faith. They induce so strong a persuasion that it is the Lord himself who speaks and who commands, that man cannot but believe and obey." . . . . . .

And thus, upon the one-sided representations of a philosopher who claimed the Divine privilege of spiritual sight and communion for himself, but denied it to others on the peril of mysterious and wholly incomprehensible possibilities of danger, Mr. Whitney was contented to renounce the intercourse whose truth and blessed ministry his own statements bore witness of, and brand the experiences of millions of his fellow-mortals as disorderly, if not absolutely diabolical.

We shall take but one more glance at the dark features of Spiritualism, which just about the time of which we are writing threatened to overcloud the bright sky whose sunshine had so long gladdened the hearts of the believers, and even involve the whole cause in the night of a terrible and materialistic reaction. The case in question refers once more to the injurious frauds which were just about this period perpetrated in the name of Spiritualism.

The narrative is taken from one of the local Ohio papers, and reads as follows:

"PRETENTIOUS SPIRITUALISM.

"According to a statement in the *Daily City Facts*, printed in Columbus, Ohio, it seems that Dr. Ensign, an elderly man, formerly a Methodist preacher, with a Miss Vinson, both of Cardington, Ohio, advertised to give exhibitions of Spiritualism in Mechanic's Hall. The lady claims to be a medium for some remarkable manifestations by the spirit of one 'King.'

"On Wednesday and Thursday evenings large audiences attended, at an admittance of twenty-five cents each. The entertainment consisted in seeing strung up before the audience, drums, tambourines, and other instruments, and of a brief, illogical, chopped-up speech from the minister, in explanation of the kind of Spiritualism they were about to exhibit. Then the hall was made perfectly dark, and a person whom they had engaged commenced playing lively tunes on the violin, and it was said that the spirit 'King' and his associates accompanied the music by playing the drums and tambourines. During the exhibition on the third evening, two persons in different parts of the hall suddenly and simultaneously opened on them the glare from dark-lanterns which disclosed the fact that the players on the drums and tambourines were none other than the Methodist preacher and the young girl.

"The meeting of course broke up in confusion."

There are two facts connected with this case which did not come under the notice of the Columbus journalist. The first is, that one of the parties who sprang a light on the impostors was a well-known Spiritualist of the city, confirming by practical proof our assertion that the Spiritualists have nothing to fear for the real facts of their belief, and never seek to build them up with the corrupt material of fraud or error. The second incident is of a more private nature and involves a curious evidence of the guardianship and ministry of spirits.

At an exibition of Miss Vinson's pretended power as a medium, and previous to the *exposé*, Mr. George Walcutt, of Columbus, was present, and became strongly impressed with the deceptive character of what he witnessed. At the following *séance*, which he also attended, he resolved, for the sake of the sublime truths which he acknowledged in Spiritualism, that he would test the reality of his impressions, and if there was falsehood in the matter, expose it.

Mr. Walcutt, it may be remembered, was one of the far-famed artists through whose wonderful mediumship hundreds of portraits of deceased persons have been painted with marvellous fidelity, although executed only from spirit originals, under spirit influence, and often in the dark, or blindfolded. Besides his remarkable gifts in this direction, Mr. Walcutt was a fine clairvoyant and clairaudient. By aid of his spiritual sight, he distinctly, in the dark, perceived Miss Vinson—who was supposed to be quietly seated in her chair—arise up just after the light had been extinguished, and commence manipulating the instruments which were assumed to be in the hands of the spirits. Indignant at such a fraud, Mr. Walcutt—himself one of the most truthful of men—resolved that he would detect and expose the imposture; for this purpose he was determined to rise noiselessly from his seat, and grasp the arm of the operator as she was swinging the instruments about in the darkness. His further course he had not resolved on, but to seize her in the very act of trickery was his fixed purpose. Just as he was about to rise, he felt the grasp of a strong spirit hand on his shoulder, and a voice, which he recognized as a beloved guardian's, whispered in his ear, "Sit still for your life." For a few moments Mr. Walcutt obeyed the injunction, paralyzed beneath the grasp of the spirit hand, but just as it relaxed its hold, a light was sprung from two distant parts of the hall at once, discovering the "medium" and her asso ciate on the floor and in the very act of manipulating the instruments.

The audience was large and highly incensed at the discovery. Miss Vin son was permitted to make her escape quietly enough, but her male companion was subjected to some very rough usage, and nothing but the vigorous interference of the police saved him from the retributive hands of "Judge Lynch."

Mr. Walcutt, as a well-known spirit medium, was particularly obnoxious to some of the "roughs" of the city, consequently he was aware that had he carried out his intention of stepping forward to seize the arm of Miss Vinson, at the moment when the lights were struck, he would have been revealed by her side, and apparently in the act of aiding her deception.

No explanation of his motives or appearance in such a situation would have availed in that excited assembly, and hence Mr. Walcutt truly and gratefully inferred that the interference of his kind and judicious guardian spirit saved him from a most equivocal and dangerous situation, and perhaps was the means of preserving his life.

The most severe blows that Spiritualism has sustained have been those aimed by unprincipled and avaricious mediums, who, when the manifestations failed to come as freely as the circumstances required, practiced imposition to supply the deficiency. The detection of this lamentable species of fraud gave occasion for the opposition to charge an universal system of trickery upon the spiritual ranks, while not a few of the most staunch believers themselves alleged that nearly all the mediums might be taxed with similarly dishonest practices.

In respect to these statements it must be recollected that the mediums in America count by thousands, whilst those engaged before the public alone number several hundreds.

The gifts of mediumship fall upon all ranks of society, and all grades of moral and intellectual development alike. The most careful observation of this power and its exercise, at present, only reveals the fact that it is a physical peculiarity of certain organizations, but that it is by no means dependent on moral or intellectual endowments. Hence the idea that the gift of mediumship implies or creates a tendency to deception is wholly unphilosophical, and without foundation. Some of the most estimable and some of the most unscrupulous natures have become the subjects of this remarkable power.

Highly refined and tenderly conscientious minds are to be found in the mediumstic ranks, whilst persons of unmistakably vicious proclivities are equally susceptable of the spiritual afflatus. We can but record the fact, without at present attempting to theorize upon its character. The whole difficulty which it presents to the mind of the observer ceases, however, when we banish our preconceived and utterly erroneous opinions of what a medium between the two worlds ought to be, and simply acknowledge that which seems patent to the communion, namely, that it depends upon some electrical properties evolved from the physical organizations of favorably-endowed individuals. We must all admit that special temptations to practice deception, at times, overshadow the position of a medium. The scornful incredulity which defies them to produce phenomena; the intense and sometimes painfully *exigéant* desire of others to witness it. Their own professional pride or the necessity which urges them to render the service promised; all these, together with other sources of influence peculiar to the position of a medium, are amply sufficient to account for fraud, without resorting to the far-fetched and wholly undemonstrated theory that "tricky spirits" prompt the imposition. We believe that no one well-proven case of this kind has ever occurred, whilst it is proper to add that, from a wide and carefully-trodden field of observation, the author is justified in the assertion that cases of deception, on the part of genuine mediums, are very few, although their industrious circulation by the interested world gives them vast notoriety, and multiplies their number *ad infinitum.*

It was from this cause that an opinion unfavorable to the genuine character of all the manifestations at one time gained ground amongst the high minded portion of the Spiritualists, producing a most painful revulsion in their feelings, and giving fair occasion for the jubilant cry of the opposition, "Whom the gods would destroy, they first make mad."

In the New York Conference, the tone in which the various exposures and "recantations" were discussed grew serious, especially when Mr. John F. Coles, above alluded to, a gentleman who had enjoyed a wide experience in Spiritualism, and been himself the subject of certain mediumistic influences, declared in unmeasured terms, his belief, that all mediums were either deluded or deluders, and that the whole movement was little better than a wide-spread humbug, or gigantic hallucination.

To the candid and unprejudiced reader, satisfactory reasons enough could be assigned, why mediums should be fallible, yet spirit communion true; why counterfeits should abound, yet real coin exist. In looking down calmly from the hill-tops of time, we may marvel that a faith founded upon well-tried and constantly-recurring facts, should be disturbed by the discovery that a few mediums, out of many thousands, should be found subject to the ordinary failings of humanity.

Still the faint-hearted consoled themselves by saying, that even if the phenomena were unreliable, the philosophy was all-sufficient; appealing, as it did, to their sense of right, reason and justice, and carrying with it internal evidence of its sublime realities. But even here, as if the "enemy" had had license to sift the revelating angel like wheat, and bright, beautiful, much-loved Spiritualism was destined to undergo every ordeal that human perversity could put upon it, a fresh blow was levelled from the very centre of its own ranks, which threatened to destroy even its foundation and corner-stone, the cherished philosophy on which its religious superstructure was based.

This *coup d'etat* originated with a Professor and Mrs. Spence, both distinguished members of the spiritual ranks, and persons whose influence was marked and diffusive. Mrs. Spence, as Mrs. Britt, of St. Louis, had greatly contributed to the success of the cause in its early stages, by her trance lectures. After her union with Prof. Spence, a gentleman of marked ability as a physician, this lady became a highly popular and influential travelling lecturer.

About the time when "zeal waxed cold," and the "faith of many was shaken" from the causes above detailed, Mrs. Spence and her talented husband promulgated the strange theory that a large proportion of the human race did not attain to the glory of immortality, and that only certain souls, under conditions which seemed terribly vague and unsatisfactory, survived the shock of death as individualized entities; their spiritual essence being either absorbed in the great ocean of being, or reincarnated in some subsequent state of higher development, etc. It is needless in this place to consider the theories on which Mr. and Mrs. Spence based their opinions of non-immortality for a large portion of the human family: it is enough to state that, in view of the influence they exerted, their doctrines were received with profound dismay, and in some instances with agonizing despair; in fact, the promulgation of this most repulsive theory from a moderately authoritative source, would have excited much painful discussion at any time, but coming as it did, just when the cherished facts on which the whole spiritual superstructure was founded had to undergo the severe ordeal which a tide of recantations and exposures necessarily put upon it, it seemed to fill the cup of feverish doubt and incertitude to the very brim, and it might with truth be asserted that in those days Spiritualism was "weighed in the balance;" but whether, like Belshazzar of old, it "was found wanting" or not, let the next chapter decide.

CHAPTER XXV.

SPIRITUALISM ON TRIAL.

"Those tones, that halting sound, to you,
Are not the tones I hear,
But voices of the loved and lost,
That meet my longing ear.
I hear my mother's angel voice,—
Those were the notes she sung;
I hear my brother's well-known tones,
As once on earth they rung."
MRS. H. B. STOWE.

COUNTERFEIT AND GENUINE COIN—"EMMA HARDINGE'S CONFESSION"—UNSOLVED PROBLEMS FOR SCIENTISTS—MR. ALBRO ON "THE RECANTERS"—LIVING SPIRITS—IMMORTALITY *vs.* ANNIHILATION.

IT is now our part to consider the effect which the various "revelations," "exposures," new versions of Spiritualism, etc., etc., produced upon the community at large, and the progress of the spiritualistic cause. We have noted the fact that jubilant voices were heard from the ranks of the opposition proclaiming the inevitable death of "the great heresy" at the hands of its partisans; also, that feelings of deep despondency and lack of confidence prevailed in the ranks of Spiritualism. When we remember that the cardinal points on which Spiritualism is founded are its facts, and that its whole aim has been the discovery and application of demonstrable truths, it seems strange to find one class of persons rejoicing and another lamenting over the threatened destruction of propositions, which, if true, could not be shaken, and if simply theoretical, were not worth maintaining.

This was the ground which the author took some eight years ago, when, in answer to an immense flood of correspondence which was poured in upon her, soliciting, as a public teacher, her opinion concerning the genuine character of the movement, she responded simply by a reference to that class of facts which are beyond the reach of humanity to produce or tamper with.

Having in the lapse of time, since then, seen no occasion to change her views concerning the superior value of this kind of testimony over all others, and by way of illustrating the tone of the discussions which arose at this juncture, we shall republish some communications, addressed by the author to her numerous correspondents through the pages of the spiritual journals. The first of these relates to Mr. Coles's sweeping assertion, made at the New York Conference, to the effect that "all spirit mediums were either deluded or deluders." In imitation of the popular tone of the times, the letter is styled

"EMMA HARDINGE'S CONFESSION."

It is addressed to the editor of the *Spiritual Age*, and is as follows:

"DEAR SIR,—Since confessions are the fashion of the day, and a confiding public has been voted into the office of Father Confessor, I solicit the medium of your columns to tender my 'confession,' in addition to the general sum of spiritual light, which conscience, or a panic in the market of anti-spiritual jugglery, is diffusing over the world.

"I have no very startling disclosures to make; but, as I understand that modern Spiritualism is summoned to the bar of justice, to be tried for life and death, so I, as one of the accessories to the fact of its wilful murder upon the body of infidelity, beg to yield myself up as 'State's evidence' for cross-examination.

"Our friend, the *Banner of Light*, has recently undertaken to enlighten the world upon some of my antecedents, and as that sketch was as ample as the occasion demanded, I need not inflict further personal details upon your readers.* Suffice it to say that my career in America has been mainly enacted in some public capacity. In one way or the other, the whole of my time has been passed in a crowd; and with so many eager witch-finders on all hands, and so many qualified witnesses to my good or bad behavior, the world need have no fear but that I shall soon be detected if, in this, my 'confession,' I am caught fibbing.

"The first point upon which I desire to be heard, and in turn demand that the pastors of the nineteenth century will enlighten my darkened understanding, is the dealing which I had in the very outset of my career with that form of the 'imposture,' called 'physical-force mediumship.' To show you, Judge World, that I had all the pious proclivities that were necessary to defend me from infidelic tendencies, I may state that when I first visited a test medium in New York, I refused to sit at his table because I heard a sentence spelled out which I fancied was somehow not in exact conformity with the Bible.

"For many weeks after this, I heard of the 'spirit rappings' with a horror so pious that nothing but the hope that my excessive shrewdness would enable me to find out what was a mystery to thousands of my better-informed fellow-mortals, would have induced me to inquire further. 'For the sake of the cause of truth,' and with a fixed determination to 'expose this infidelic fraud,' I accompanied Mr. Augustus Fenno, the well-known comedian, to the house of Mrs. Coan, the 'rapping medium.'

"The first act of the farce I there witnessed consisted of loud rappings, a phenomenon which, being performed on the table, I concluded could not have been produced by Mrs. Coan's ankle-joints, which were quietly reposing beneath it.

"My part in the drama was to turn the table suddenly over, examine its under side for springs, which failing to detect, I impertinently transferred my scrutiny to Mrs. Coan's hands, during which vain process the raps began vibrating beneath my own feet. Whilst engaged in a rigid search for the 'springs' concealed in the carpet, the pertinacious raps knocked the idea of floor machinery out of my mind by drumming on the wall quite six feet from any of our party.

"We were but three of us; and fairly aghast at the evident absence of human agency in the production of these locomotive sounds, I sank into a chair, from which I was instantly aroused by vigorous poundings on the back rail, close against my very shoulders. All this while, Mrs. Coan and Mr. Fenno, instead of being covertly engaged in working hidden machinery, were coolly talking to each other without evidencing the least interest in my unquiet investigations. Being informed that the raps would obey my mental request and sound anywhere I wished, I silently desired that they might be produced in a distant corner of the room. An instant compliance with this unspoken thought dissipated all my preconceived theories of 'ankle-joints,' 'carpet-machinery,' or 'table-springs.' Besides, there was intelligence here — intelligence that could read and answer my mind.

"That mind could not, of course, begin to aspire to the sublime heights attained by a Faraday or Agassiz, but having just wit enough to put two and two together, it at once perceived that these great men's theories did not quite fit the case at issue. The next act of the rapping humbug was to hold intelligible conversation through a sort of telegraphy, by which, as it seemed, my friend Mr. Fenno was informed that I was a 'fine medium' — an announcement I received with the most intense disgust. Hereupon Mrs. Coan handed me an alphabet, and having shown me how to point to the various letters, whilst the knocks would indicate the special one required, I found spelled out, to my astonishment, not the names of any of the near and dear relatives of whom in such a scene I was most

* Emma Hardinge's Biography, by Dr. A. B. Child. —*Banner of Light.*

naturally thinking, but the Christian and surname of an acquaintance who had not even entered my head.

"Whose mind was read in this instance I am unable to say, save and except that it was not mine, whilst neither of my companions had ever heard of such a person before. In the absence of any visible agent for this intelligence, I was fain to conclude that the atmosphere was the delinquent, and it is in the earnest hope that some of the learned professors who *know* 'Spiritualism is all humbug,' and the recanters and exposers who say ditto, will enlighten me, that I have ventured to detail what would appear far too peurile to notice did it not so happen that neither 'ankle joints,' 'machinery,' nor 'mind reading,' will cover this very trivial case. Where is the theory that will? Echo answers, 'Where?'

"I could detail thousands of more remarkable manifestations, and thousands of investigators could exceed me in marvellous relations, but I purposely confine myself to facts, no matter how simple they may be, for which, as yet, no explanation has been offered, and which no theory, as yet promulgated, can cover. And yet I have a soul to be saved. Will no divine professor of logic, or doctor of humbug, show me how to account for exactly such a case as this? No side isuses will do. I can prove the truth of what I narrate, and the explanation must cover the truth or it wont suffice.

"I pass over many months of similar experiences closely followed up, and beg to select, out of hundreds of far more startling occurrences, a transaction with Dr. Redman, equally out of the pale of popular explanations.

"At a circle with sixteen persons, all living, producible, and reliable witnesses, all entire strangers to myself and Dr. Redman, himself a stranger to me, I, with others, wrote names of spirit friends on some dozen slips of paper, and then rolled them up into pellets so tightly that if my life had depended on it I could not have told one from the other. When all the party had made similar pellets, we threw them, by the direction of Dr. Redman, into a large confused heap, together, on the table. The number of pellets thus indiscriminately piled up must have amounted to over a hundred. These Dr. Redman gathered up into his hand, and then rolled them upon my hand, rolling away one after another until there only remained between our two hands one pellet; this, he informed me, was mine, and in proof thereof he desired me to put it aside. I did so, when the raps spelled out by the alphabet a name which I recognized as one I had written. On opening my pellet in presence of the whole company, there was my own handwriting, and the name just spelled out by the rapping imposture aforesaid.

"This is another case for which my waiting soul demands an exact explanation, especially as it is one which fits the case of thousands of other deluded ones besides myself. Passing over manifold similarly unexplained problems occurring in my daily experience of Spiritualism, I proceed to notice some of the 'tricks' practiced upon me by Mrs. Brown, of the Fox family. I shall only notice the least of this lady's performances, hoping that a clue once afforded to the 'small impositions,' the large ones, like the large impostors of the day, will collapse, of their own accord, of spontaneous combustion.

"For many Sunday evenings I was in the habit of forming one of a friendly circle at Mrs. Brown's house. We had tea; tea-table raps, and nothing to pay; and as the ordinary motive to imposition in the world's eyes, namely, gain, was out of the question — nay, as pastime, rather than any kind of business was the order of the day, I must presume that Mrs. Brown's 'trickery' on such occasions, being entirely gratuitous, proceeded from an irresistible and chronic tendency in her to trick. On one of these same 'evenings at home,' we all sat after tea singing, whilst the 'imposture' rapped, sometimes in one place, sometimes in another, sometimes five or six 'ankle joints' all going at once, in tones, too, so various, that Mrs. Brown's ankles must have been a perfect orchestra in themselves.

"At last the signal was given for the alphabet, when a single knocker, in tones as loud as those produced by a carpenter's hammer, spelled out the request that we should darken the room: we obeyed by extinguishing the gas, but still the fire gave sufficient light to reveal every form in the room and disclose the whole party with all their hands joined and spread out before them on the table; and then it was that I felt a large and heavy hand on my shoulder, evidently placed there from some one behind me. The room was small, the door fast; Mrs. Brown's hands held by myself and another person, and my other neighbor's hand in mine and his neighbor's. The space behind me was empty; but in order to try if there was intelligence directing that invisible grasp, I mentally requested that the hand should stroke my head, when instantly a warm, soft, though large hand gently patted my forehead and stroked each side of my face. Gideon-like, requiring a still further test, I again mentally requested that the hand should touch my mother, who was sitting at the further end of our long table. 'Good heavens! there is a hand laid upon my head,' uttered by mamma the very moment after framing this unspoken wish, convinced me that if ankle joints were the originators of the Rochester knockings, their action in the persons of the Fox family were, of all the world's phenonmena, the most marvellous, omnipresent, locomotive, independent, and intelligent. I am not going to weary your readers, Mr. Editor, by recounting details with which every visitor to Mrs. Leah Brown must be familiar. I have simply noticed one of the as yet undetected and unaccounted-for 'tricks,' which are so frequently enacted in her presence, and hereby give notice that there are a very large number of still more cunning 'Fox tricks' to be accounted for, before I, for one, am prepared to sign a full recantation of my spiritualistic faith in that family.

"With a long hiatus in my experience filled up with tremendous hard nuts for science to crack, I beg to suggest another subject for the philanthropic labors of the exposing mediums of the day, and one which has also remained untouched save by the rather illogical argument of senseless abuse. I speak of Mr. J. V. Mansfield's faculty of answering sealed letters. True it is, that I have been told upon the highly creditable authority of Professor Felton, of Harvard College, that he knows—without the least proof of the fact, great savan as he is!—that Mr. Mansfield first 'opens all the letters he answers, and then cunningly seals them up again;' whilst others, who have seen the spirit postmaster answer letters correctly which have never even passed out of the investigator's hands, know upon authority equally good as Professor Felton's that the said postmaster answers the said letters all by aid of clairvoyance; 'first clairvoyantly reading them and then answering them out of his own mind.' Without stopping to consider whether clairvoyance is not as wonderful a phenomenon as any fact claimed in Spiritualism, I must inquire of the last set of sages, how it happened that Mr. Mansfield made so egregious a blunder in my case as to answer a letter, which I addressed to my father in the spirit-world, in the name of a sister whom I had not asked for or even mentioned in the letter? As the said letter never passed out of my hands, and Mr. Mansfield answered it whilst I held it, Professor Felton's theory fails; whilst the fact of my being an entire stranger to Mr. Mansfield, and above all, my sister's name neither being mentioned in the letter or at the time in my mind, militates rather awkwardly against the clairvoyant theory; besides, this wonderful 'clairvoyant' has been known to mention scores of names that have never been asked for in sealed letters; to write moreover in German, Spanish, Italian, Arabic, Greek, Hebrew, and even Chinese, and that without, as his most intimate friends can testify, the slightest knowledge of any other language than his own. Come, noble army of recanters! bring up your rear guard of tricks, to account for these ugly facts! . . . As my inquiry from the beginning to the end of my career has been for 'the truth, the whole truth, and nothing but the truth,' I have spelt out my lesson with almost every medium of the day, and could enumerate a thousand problems which the poor short-sighted exposers have never even touched, did time and space permit; but as these are limited, I must confine myself to the consideration of one more case, which common justice requires should receive its share of illumination with the rest, and that, Mr. Editor, is my unworthy self.

"Mr. Coles is represented in the *Spiritual Telegraph* as having said at the New York Conference that every trance medium is an impostor, and every other kind of medium something of the same order. Mr. Coles is a gentleman with whom I enjoy a very agreeable acquaintance; but if he means to say that all persons who communicate an intelligence beyond their own knowledge are 'impostors,' then I, as one of that class, affirm that Mr. Coles tells an untruth.

"At the very earliest stage of my investigations, I found I was, and always had been a 'spirit medium;' that is, that I could communicate, by various methods, intelligence I had not learned, and give tests of the presence of spirits [unknown to me] to strangers.

"My spirit friends, or the imposture that calls itself spirits, affectionately charged upon me their wish, that I should sit for the public, and give tests freely to all who sought me; yet [for reasons which were satisfactory to my judgment, the chief of which was that I had other means of living besides my mediumship] that I should never receive fee or reward for my services in this direction. They wished me to make a profession of my lectures, but considered that my mediumship in other respects was uncertain, and only necessary to prepare me for becoming a lecturer. With this understanding I set to work, and that so successfully, that with no other contrivance of my own than mere passivity, and waiting for some unknown and invisible 'impostor' to dictate what I should say, see, or write, I managed to convince hundreds of strangers, who flocked to my circle room at 553 Broadway, of the presence and identity of their spirit friends. The evidences of this nature, as they were given by writing, seeing, and pantomimic action, are all out of the reach of 'ankle-joints' or 'machinery' theories, but although I am unwilling to enter into personal details, I give notice that there are hundreds of living and producible witnesses to my asseverations, and that sooner than consent to be unjustly branded as an 'impostor,' I shall compel a retraction of such an assertion at the risk of being deemed egotistical, by taking advantage of the many grateful offers that pour in upon me, to bear testimony to the genuine character of my mediumship. Amongst an immense variety of tests given, as I have stated, to hundreds of producible witnesses, I shall cite but one in illustration of the spontaneity of spiritual influence, and the impossibility of sneering away its facts on the baseless charge of universal deception. During my last visit to Boston, my friends observing my passionate love for flowers, kindly adorned my platform with sweet floral offerings, which I as regularly transferred to the dear friend I was visiting, in order that she might carry them to the grave of a sweet little girl who had passed away in the spring, and after whose earthly form the poor mother's eyes still yearned. One night I returned from my lecture at the Melodeon with a lovely wreath and a large bouquet. The arrangement of the flowers was somewhat injured in the carriage, and I gave them, as usual, to my dear hostess, to carry to the cemetery. The next day, when the mother was about to depart with her prize, she sent her maid into the garden to gather two large dahlias which she placed in the wreath, and a very small one with which she renovated the bouquet. I had never visited the grave myself, and had no idea how the flowers were to be placed. The next evening I was dressing to lecture at the Music Hall, when, just as I was about to quit my room, the bright spirit of the child stood in my path and besought me in her sweet, winning way to give a message to her mother.

"I have seen spirits from my earliest childhood, had often before seen this fair little apparition, and did not question but that her mother would place perfect reliance on my report; but as the message contained no particular test, and it has always been my custom to require tests both for myself and others I said, 'You must tell me something, Nannie, that will convince your mother you have really appeared to me.' 'You shall have such a sweet nosegay to-night at your lecture, Emma,' said the fair spirit, 'and that shall be a test.' 'Not enough Nannie,' I replied; 'I often have bouquets; that will be no test.'

"'Tell mother,' answered the bright spirit, 'I saw the angel she put on my grave, whose wings fan away evil spirits; also tell her, the two large flowers she put into the wreath yesterday from her garden are gone, but the small one is still there, in the bouquet —now remember.'

"I hastened to my lecture, on to the rostrum, and there lay test the first, a 'sweet nosegay.' The reporter of the Boston *Courier*, in a critique on my lecture more honorable to his gallantry as a gentleman than philosophical as a scientist, remarked, with some humorous attempts to account for my 'inspiration,' that I 'looked lovingly at the splendid bouquet.' Well I might! Ah, Monsieur Boston *Courier!* could you have known the happy thoughts that those flowers called forth, you would not have wondered at my loving look. I thought of the poor mother, whose faith that her darling was not sleeping in the cold ground might be strengthened through the intelligence connected with those flowers. I thought too of the rest of that mysterious little communication, but as I thought and wondered if it would prove true, no effort upon my part could shut out from my mind a memory of my old calling, the stage, and the oft-quoted phrase of the Danish Hamlet, 'My life upon the ghost!' The next day, when the bouquet which I had presented to my friend was about to be transferred by her once more to the cemetery, I rather hesitatingly told her I thought she might possibly find some disturbance amongst the flowers. Being urgently pressed for an explanation, I recounted to her the vision above narrated, when my friend responded, 'On my way to the cemetery yesterday, I bought and placed on the grave a little china image of an angel, with wings extended, which seemed to be hovering, to my morbid fancy, over the hallowed dust of my child. As to the flowers, I know all about the disturbance; for when arranging them on the grave I thought the large, flaunting dahlias looked out of place, so I took them out of the wreath myself. The smaller one, being less intrusive in the bouquet, I suffered to remain. It is all true; and, Emma, I now know my child must have seen me, for not another living creature could be aware of either circumstance.'

"And now, if I may seem very puerile in making the casual arrangement of a bouquet, and the appearance of a little paltry china image, evidences for the immortality of a precious human soul, why then I am willing to plead guilty to the charge; but as I know china images cannot come to describe themselves to me, and bouquets do not arrange themselves or come and tell me when they are disarranged, I conclude I am no wiser nor yet much more foolish than Isaac Newton was, when he made an insignificant apple the corner-stone of the world's grandest philosophy. . . . . . .

"One word more, and with it my final apologies for this long detail. I have never avowed myself a trance speaker, because I am not entirely unconscious; and yet, when questioned what definition I should give to my ability to speak upon any subject committees may choose for me, without a moment's premeditation, I should be absolutely dishonest if I did not acknowledge that the whole of my lectures are obviously, to myself, uttered without thought or volition of my own, and clearly prompted by some attendant intelligences, who, also, to myself as well as to the eyes of many of the most reliable seers, present the unmistakable characteristics of a risen, spiritual, and glorified humanity.

"Besides this, I have seen, conversed with, and described hundreds of spirits whose identity and continued existence was thus clearly proved to their mourning relatives.

"There is, moreover, a voice ever present with me, cheering me in sorrow, prescribing for me in sickness, encouraging me on long, weary journeys, advising me in all my engagements, revealing hidden characters, and counselling me in nearly all and every emergency of life.

"This voice has warned me in danger, brought me news of absent friends, and rebuked me when I deserved it, not the least frequent manifestation, by the by, of my 'demon's' presence. To one of the most popular of the New York ministers, who informed me that Spiritualism was 'a most dangerous delusion,' I stated my case, and earnestly implored him to point out the nature of the danger; but though the reverend divine was a minister to the people, and I reminded him that I was one of the people, and one too that was leading away many souls to my way of thinking, he left me with the cold assurance that it was not in his way to deal with 'the thing,' and that it was none of his business—he only warned me, etc., Just so with my friends, the 'recanters.' The divine exposed his own unchristian neglect of duty, but convicted me of—nothing.

"The 'recanters' prove themselves to be rogues and cheats, but touch nobody else's case; whilst for my own part, I can truly say I have tested this matter in every form and shape; and, let it come from whence it may, I own, with grateful thanks to God for its manifestations, that it has made me a better and a happier woman than I have ever been before.

"If money or public applause were my object, I have two professions,—the stage and music,—in either of which I am a proficient, and could treble my present earnings, besides exchanging celebrity for notoriety, ease for fatigue, and adulation for ribaldry, scorn and persecution; but as all the world's gifts would fail to replace, to my mind, the full cup of joy and compensation which I have tasted in Spiritualism, I must await personal conviction, derived from facts as stubborn as those upon which my faith is founded, before I am prepared to admit as error that which personal experience has assured me to be invincible TRUTH.

"I am, dear Mr. Editor, yours very truly,

"A soul waiting to be saved,

"EMMA HARDINGE."

Amongst the numerous letters, essays, and other forms of affirmative philosophy which the "recantation movement" called forth in vast abundance from the noblest minds in the spiritual ranks, we select the only additional one which our space will allow us to print, from the pen of Stephen Albro, Esq., the highly-respected editor of the Buffalo *Age of Progress.*

Mr. Albro's letter is addressed to a gentleman whose faith had been rudely shaken, it would seem, by the discovery of a great deception in the cause so near to his heart — Spiritualism. In the doubt and incertitude of mind thus awakened, he wisely came to the conclusion to take advantage of the long experience and highly philosophical opinions of Mr. Albro, than whom no more truthful, candid, or enlightened adviser could be found in any emergency, especially in the one under consideration, as the reader will be able to determine from a perusal of the following extracts of Mr. Albro's correspondence, as published in the *Age of Progress:*

"*To Mr. Simmons, of New York:*

"ESTEEMED FRIEND AND BROTHER, — I am both pained and gratified by that portion of your letter which refers to an unfortunate class of professing Spiritualists.

"It pains me to hear that the eternal truths of the spiritual Gospel that the angels have brought us are not sufficiently established in your mind to prevent its being swayed to and fro by the fitful puffs of inharmony which issue from the lungs of unsuccessful traffickers in the spiritual philosophy. . . . .

"Before proceeding any further, I will give you a direct answer as to the effect upon my mind which has been produced by the 'exposures' you refer to.

"They have admonished me that Spiritualism has more to fear from unsound advocates than from the most rabid of its opponents; and even from these there is nothing to apprehend as regards the final sweep of the spiritual philosophy throughout the world, only they are stumbling-blocks in the way of honest but timid investigation, and tend somewhat to retard the spread of celestial truth in the realm of terrestrial intelligence.

"Your mind has been disturbed by the croaking voices who attribute the loss of their faith to frauds committed by pedlers of pretended spiritual manifestations. You have heard of 'exposures' and 'recantations' from those who publish their own shame by showing how they themselves practiced the frauds which they are exposing, and you are at a loss to decide for yourself whether they were greater rogues and liars when they committed the frauds or when they confessed them. The safe position in such a case is to give them credit for what they really and continually report themselves to have been on the occasions alluded to in their confessions.

"I shall not pretend to deny, nay, I know, that there are many itinerant mountebanks who perambulate the country under the pretence of being spiritual media, for the purpose of defrauding the unwary of their dimes. And what does this fact amount to? Nothing but the evidence that every genuine and valuable product of nature, art, or science, is counteracted for the purpose of administering to the insatiable spirit of avarice.

"Those physical manifestations which our spirit friends have found it expedient to practice, for the purpose of startling scepticism and awakening conviction of their presence, have become so interesting and attractive that they have naturally suggested to the unprincipled the practicability of making capital out of their imitation. Hence the many performances of mock manifestations by which the country is infested, and hence the evidences adduced by 'recanters' to prove that there are no genuine manifestations. . . . .

"There is one phase of spiritual phenomena which is peculiarly favorable to the success of mountebank imitations; these are the physical operations by spirits which cannot be performed in lighted rooms because the light is an absorbent or disturber of those electrical forces which are essential for the production of the manifestations in question. . . . . It has been observed that when heavy bodies have been suspended in the air, or moved about with immense force in the dark, the introduction of light instantly stops the operation, often causing the floating mass to fall to the floor in a second. . . . . And these circumstances, as above hinted, have opened up a wide field for the operations of those unprincipled tricksters who feed upon the unwary and those who are too ingenuous themselves to suspect treachery in others. And in many instances adventurers in this ignoble field of enterprise have associated with them genuine mediums as unscrupulous and immoral as themselves; knaves, who are ready, for hire, to enter into a league with knaves and prostitute God's noblest gift to man for the sake of unhallowed gain.

"And besides these there are not a few veritable mediums who might render invaluable service to the cause of truth and demonstrate by their high gifts the glorious fact of immortality, yet who, being themselves destitute of all conscientious scruples, when conditions will not allow spirits to manifest through them — as must often be the case with all mediums — do not hesitate to carry out the advertised or expected programme by fraudulent devices of their own, held by them in reserve for such occasions, and performed with such art as to render detection difficult. . . . . And the most despicable of all apologies by which such impious tricksters attempt to excuse their guilt is the disavowal, when detected, of any fraudulent design on their own part, and the crimination of a spirit; stoutly and persistently averring that the deception was practiced under spirit influence and control.* . . . . Every 'exposer' of whom I have had personal knowledge, has been for years past a professed propagandist of the spiritual philosophy, and a practical speculator in the phenomena. Think you these recanters would have become such at this day if their labors in the service of ministering angels had met the pecuniary returns which prompted that service!

"I tell you nay; for the whole genus 'speculator,' by common instinct, will think well of and endeavor by every means to protect that traffic by which the greater amount of gain can be made. And thus it happens that most of the present exposers of the 'spiritual humbug' are persons who have failed to make its advocacy a paying vocation, and are now endeavoring to mend their fortunes by exhibiting to the scoffers at Spiritualism the manner in which they formerly practiced and imposed upon the public with 'bogus' manifestations.

"Marryat, in one of his novels, tells of a gin-drinking mother who took fire and was reduced to cinders by inhaling the flame of a candle; and he also tells of the son of that mother, who gathered together her charred remains, and exhibited them to the public for a penny a sight, recounting at each exhibition the cause and manner of his mother's decease. Which is the most respectable, think you, Marryat's hero, or the charlatan who peddles counterfeit imitations of communion with the spirits of the dead, and then exposes his own villany for a dime? If you find the question difficult to decide, I confess my inability to help you. . . . . . My course of investigation has resulted in the following conclusions. As respects mediums in general, and spiritual communications in their present status, I confess there is much to complain of, regret, and wonder at; but still more to stimulate us to further inquiry, rejoice over, and thank God for. . . . . . But those who look more deeply into the philosophy of Spiritualism are not surprised at this. They see at once that the mundane and supra-mundane spirits are congenial in their natures, and equal in development.

The undeveloped mortal attracts to himself associates from the spirit-world of a like nature, and these are as capable of mastering the science of the communion as those of superior mental and moral characteristics. But even in the darkest features of this case there is light, and some good resulting even from the communications of false and untruthful spirits. No one will deny that a man is a man because he tells a falsehood, neither can he deny that a spirit is such because he wilfully or ignorantly perverts the truth. And again; the falsehood of the communicating spirits proves the great philosophical truth that death makes little or no change in the soul, and that the spirit, whether of the false or true, was and is *the real man*.

"That there are many mediums of most estimable character, and manifestations in abundance which can be relied on, all industrious investigators will affirm; but whether all communications are equally true or not is another question, and one which only long experience and careful observation can decide. . . . . Good and truthful spirits often disagree, and contradict each other in their opinions, just as surely as do spirits still incarnate in mortality; and for this disagreement in spirit communications, the true remedy is the exercise of human reason and the sovereignty of individual judgments."

After pursuing the above line of argument at great length, and illustrating his affirmations by the recital of numerous excellent tests of spirit identity,

* The author apologizes for some liberties used in shearing superfluous phrases from the talented editor's original letter, for the sake of brevity.

Mr. Albro sums up with several highly interesting narratives of interviews with spirits. Our limits will only permit us to cite one of these, which occurred through the mediumship of Dr. Redman, and is related by Mr. Albro, as follows:

"A gentleman who resides in this city [Buffalo], but who has not authorized me to give his name, called at Mr. Redman's room last Sunday for the purpose of introducing a friend who was visiting him. Besides this friend, a brother of the gentleman first named was present.

"This brother was an inveterate sceptic, and decidedly opposed to Spiritualism. He called with the others for curiosity, but refused to sit at the table for investigation.

"The spirits, however, requested 'all present' to be seated at the table. The sceptic at length complied, when the spirit of a deceased brother who had departed this life in England at the age of seventeen years, addressed him, writing through the hand of the medium backwards, giving many proofs of his identity and signing his name in fnll.

"The sceptical gentleman then asked the spirit if he could tell the manner of his death, to which the spirit answered by affirmative raps, when the hand of the medium was immediately used to make numerical characters, as follows:

"9 23 1 19 19 13 15 20 8 5 18 5 4 9 14 20 8 5 5 1 18 20 8 4 5 1 18 2 18 15 20 8 5 18.

"What the meaning of these figures could be no one present could divine, till direction was given by the spirit through the raps to place numericals over the letters of the alphabet thus: $\overset{1}{\text{A}}, \overset{2}{\text{B}}, \overset{3}{\text{C}},$ and so on, up to $\overset{26}{\text{Z}}$ when the figures read: 'I was smothered in the earth, dear brother.'

"The fact thus uniquely represented was strictly true, the two brothers stating that he, the spirit, and another lad were at play in a sand-hole, the projecting bank of which caved in and suffocated him before he could be extricated.

"This test proved too strong for the sceptic, whose tears bore witness to the strength of his conviction.

"Truly and fraternally yours, S. ALBRO."

It will be remembered that we mentioned the promulgation, by Prof. and Mrs. Spence, of the non-immortality theory for a large proportion of the race. During the numerous discussions which ensued upon the enunciation of this very startling doctrine, some of its opponents pressed strenuously for a definition of such conditions as the promulgators assumed to be necessary for continued existence, when, being driven to some extremity, and compelled to make their propositions as clear as the dark features of the belief would permit, they suggested an opinion that few, if any, souls maintained their individuality after death, unless they lived out their rudimental existence in the earth-form, for at least seventy years.

Considering that the average rate of all human life upon this globe is estimated by the most accomplished philosophers to range at about forty years, the prospect of a very abundant crop of souls in the spirit spheres became, under this hypothesis, remarkably slender, and as this theory cut at the very root of the tree of hope for bereaved parents, nine-tenths of whom the same general calculations assume must see their brightest blossoms untimely nipped in the bud, the promulgation of such a doctrine became, in the spiritual ranks, tantamount to the dissemination of the principles advocated by the French encyclopedists of 1793.

The most remarkable feature of the discussions evoked by this kind of teaching was the universal resort to the old-fashioned method of proving religious problems: namely, by theoretical philosophy.

In such a warfare then, as in all former times, nothing was proved, and everything became assertion merely, or opinions utterly valueless, because based upon theories undemonstrated by the facts which form the very cornerstone of the truly spiritual philosophy. Weary alike of the hair-splitting verbiage, which crowded the spiritual journals, and the pathetic appeals which poured in upon the mediums from bereaved parents, whose newly-born hopes of eternal life and unbroken progress, this remorseless theory crushed into annihiliation, the author brought all the influence she possessed amongst her spiritual friends, to bear upon her own customary method of "proving all things" before holding fast aught that could be called "good." To do this, she reminded her friends that Spiritualism afforded a field of operative facts, occupying three millions of square miles, and involving the experiences of from five to seven millions of persons; and as such methods of dealing with the hitherto shadowy propositions of religious belief must eventually supersede all others, it may not be amiss to reprint one of the communications in advocacy of this course, addressed by the author to the *Banner of Light* towards the conclusion of the "non-immortality" discussion. It was styled:

"EMMA HARDINGE ON LIVING SPIRITS AND DYING SPIRITUALISM.

"MESSRS. EDITORS,—Observing a general feeling of antipathy towards the repulsive subject of non-immortality, as recently discussed in your paper, I should not intrude any further remarks upon your readers concerning a theme so unacceptable, had I not noticed the singular absence of that peculiar kind of testimony which is more calculated to rebut groundless theories than all that reason and logic can adduce, namely, *facts*. When it is remembered that in this nineteenth century, thousands of the noblest minds of the age were professed materialists, and that within ten years a few stubborn facts alone have brought to them a conviction of the soul's immortality, which not all the theoretical teachings of religion could produce, it seems somewhat remarkable that your numerous correspondents should waste their time, and your readers' patience over columns of theory, which one single well-attested fact would confirm or disprove *in toto*.

"Did we desire to learn aught concerning the Arctic or Antarctic regions, the centre of Africa, or the Steppes of Siberia, from whom would your correspondent expect to obtain the most reliable information—the fire-side philosophers who sit at home, and do all their geography, geology, and natural history on paper, covered with theories of what they deem those unknown realms ought to be, or the bold adventurers who have penetrated into the heart of the mystery, and taken living cognizance of the scenes they describe?

"And why do we not apply these self-evident propositions to the dwellers in the spirit country, and the theorists who pretend to determine the nature of that *terra incognita* out of their own imaginings. . . . . . . With such evidences of total failure in merely theoretical beliefs as the present day affords us, it seems to me astonishing that the simply theoretical principles of this hideous 'non-immortality' doctrine should engage the attention of Spiritualists to the total exclusion of those facts upon the strength of which they have become Spiritualists at all. If I can put faith in any of my senses, they assure me as conclusively of the truth of spirit communion as of the existence of any ordinary objects of sense; and if I believe in one class of facts ranging under the general appellation of spirit communion, how am I to separate them from another class, equally rife with proof and demonstration of the existence of all, instead of a part of the race? For example, if I have the conclusive evidence that I am communing, now with my grandsire of eighty years, and now with my child of eight, upon what hypothesis am I to believe that the grandfather lives and the child is a myth, or that the one communication is true and the other—conditions being exactly similar—is false?

"By way of illustration, I shall select a few cases, which are about as well attested as any that the spiritualistic movement can offer:

"In Greensboro', Henry County, Indiana, lives a noble and venerable gentleman, well known throughout the country as Mr. Seth Hinshaw. In his house are a large collection of portraits of deceased persons drawn by Mr. George Walcutt, a spirit artist of Columbus,

Ohio, who, himself an entire stranger to my respected friend Mr. Hinshaw, executed them with a fidelity so marvellous, that they are recognized by the whole family and every neighbor who chanced to be acquainted with the originals. Most of these pictures were drawn blindfolded; some of them before Mr. Hinshaw sent to request them, and all contain special tokens of personal identity which cannot be mistaken.

"A very interesting account of these portraits—nineteen in number—is to be found in a recent issue of the *Spiritual Telegraph*, written from Mr. Hinshaw's residence by Mr. Giles Stebbins. Now, amongst the pictures are not only a wife, young daughter, sons, and other household jewels, whose beloved and well-remembered features are inimitably preserved, but there are also a pair of twins represented in the pride of youthful adolescence, but who never showed signs of life, and in giving birth to whom the mother died. If the mother's semblance is so perfect, and the stranger artist could give the test evidence of the birth at all of those twins, where is the proof that their representation as living immortal dwellers in the spheres is a falsehood or mistake *

"Those who deny the existence of these children, their appearance to a total stranger for sittings, their correspondence—as growing girls—in age to what they might have been had they lived on earth, must also invalidate the manifestation of the spirit mother herself, who appeared to the same artist with them, and whose portrait, then and there executed, is pronounced to be a 'most faithful likeness' by all who knew her.

"Mr. Stebbins's record goes on to say:

"Also three sons of present wife, Abigail Hinshaw, one still-born, etc.

"And these are no mere phantoms, or dead, 'imperfect' infants, good people, who are so anxious to snuff out other people's children—your own, of course, being in the full glory of immortality—but real, living, growing boys and girls of different ages, all and each being just at the stage of maturity which might be expected from them.

"Besides these, there is a goodly array of sweet young grandchildren, removed at different periods of extreme youth, but obstinately persisting in living, although not seventy years of age, and retaining a family likeness to their parents and to each other, and proving that, though by virtue of the said 'non-immortality' theory, they ought by this time to be little puffs of hydrogen or nitrogen gas, or used up perhaps, according to the French reincarnation theory, in the material of somebody else's 'progressed' baby—yet in God's good providence, that they are still themselves, and that the glorious function of individualized being, however rudimental, having been once achieved, retrogression is impossible, and the germ soul ultimates its Creator's highest design here or hereafter, but never mars or breaks the plan by that loss of individuality which implies annihilation.

"One of my earliest experiences as a test medium in New York was to present to a lady who called upon me, a perfect sceptic, descriptions and tests of the identity of two deceased relatives, in such striking and vivid characters that conviction became irresistible.

"Just as the lady was taking leave of me in considerable agitation of mind, I became impelled to write her a communication purporting to come from a daughter, who, unlike the other spirits, gave no name.

"Mrs. B. replied, there must be some mistake, as she had never had a daughter. Still the spirit insisted, and finally reminded the mother of the birth of a still-born female child, with whom she identified herself by stating accurately, dates and certain remarkable circumstances, which proved to the lady even more astonishing tests than any which had preceded them.

"On another occasion a spirit, appearing as a girl of about eighteen, and beautiful as a seraph, manifested her presence and claimed to be the daughter of a lady for whom I was then sitting, but who denied having had any such child until the fair spirit reminded her

* The author has herself inspected these portraits; heard their history from the lips of the venerable Seth Hinshaw, now a dweller in the bright homes of immortality, and received from his amiable daughter two of the pencil sketches, namely, Hannah, first wife of Seth Hinshaw, and one of the above-named daughters.

that she had only lived on earth a few hours, and in the little box in which the poor remains had been put away, was a certain piece of delicate muslin wrapped around the form, which the spirit described most graphically. This manifestation is strongly imprinted on my mind; first, from the beauty of the fair apparition, and next from the regret she expressed that the cold mother felt no interest in a child whose birth she acknowledged, but whom, as she said, she 'had never known, and therefore could not possibly feel any love for.' . . . .

"I could go on enumerating scores of instances in which young infants, and sometimes even embryotic births, were declared by spirits manifesting, under the strongest test conditions, to be the germ of their own individualized and unquenchable immortality. Enough for me to add that quite two-thirds of my experiences as a test medium included communications from spirits who had left the form under twenty years of age; in fact, in our present imperfect understanding of the laws of health, it is evident that the chief of the soul freight that crosses the 'beautiful river,' are the youngest and fairest of earth's blossoms, and if these are changed, even to annihilation, then is creation a failure and spirit-land a desert to which the blooming, child-peopled villages of earth are, in comparison, Edens of love and beauty. A shrewd Yankee, commenting on the 'non-immortality' theory to me lately, observed 'that if it were true, the Lord was a poor trader, and would never grow rich in souls, so long as he created such an awful waste of raw material.' . . . . .

"I shall close these few fragmentary illustrations from a page which I am sure any of our reliable test mediums might swell into a volume, by narrating a case which has very recently come under my observation, and which is well known to most of the mediums who visit Rhode Island.

"Being the guest of a most estimable Quaker lady of unimpeachable character and veracity, my hostess said to me one day, 'How can I help being a Spiritualist when I remember the facts of my conversion?'

"I cannot continue to quote my friend's words, but the sum of her narrative is as follows:

"Mrs. C. had at one time in her service, a girl who proved to be a fine rapping and physical force medium. Her mistress and friends held frequent sittings with her, thus obtaining numerous communications from dear departed ones.

"On one occasion the spirit of a young man reported himself, claiming to be the lady's son. 'She had no son in the spirit-world,' she said; 'there must be some mistake.' But the spirit persisted, and, to deepen the mystery, spoke of a beautiful sister he had with him, whose existence was equally unknown to Mrs. C. until he reminded her that some twenty years previous, she had given birth to a pair of twins, in whom not even a sign of life was manifest. The occasion was brought vividly to her mind by the recital of many attendant circumstances, of which spirit guardians, it seems, always instruct the spirits of embryotic births, for the purpose of identification.

"And so the communication went on to say that the young spirits, carefully matured, unfolded, and fully ripened, in the more perfect spheres of spiritual existence, were now brought to the parents' home to establish the natural relationship which eternally subsists between the root and branches of humanity. The delighted mother's conviction, strengthened by the numerous tests which the spirit gave her concerning family details, only stumbled at the fact that she had not even given a name to these unknown offspring, not deeming at the time of their birth that they possessed any spiritual individuality. To this the spirits rapped out: 'That is true, mother; thee gave us no names, so the angels call me Love and my sister Beauty. Wilt thou name us now, mother?' Mrs. C. replied that she would endeavor to think of appropriate names for them against the next meeting, which was appointed at a circle for the following evening. During the ensuing night, the mother pondered long on the interview with her 'angel-born,' and mentally decided on the names she would call them, though she carefully kept this decision to herself. The next day, whilst pursuing her household avocations in company with her maid, loud raps arrested their attention. It was some hours before the appointed circle was to take place, hence the expected interview with her spirit children was not in Mrs. C.'s mind. Calling the alphabet, however, the young spirit son rapped out: 'Mother we like the names thou hast thought of very much.' Knowing that these names had never crossed her lips, and that they could not even be dreamed of by her totally uneducated medium, Mrs. C. requested the spirit to give them through the raps, which immediately responded by spelling correctly the mother's anticipated names of 'Angela' and 'Angelo.' . . . . .

"My venerable friend Seth Hinshaw, and my respected hostess, to whom the above little narrative relates, your eyes will undoubtedly meet these lines, and if they should grow very wide with astonishment at the liberty I have taken with these portions of your family history, forgive me for the sake of the happiness which your highly respected testimony may bring to the heart of some bereaved mother whose wounds have been torn open afresh by the horrid and groundless theory that blank annihilation can ever be the doom of the divine spark that is enshrined even in the most imperfect human organism, and marks itself in characters as immortal as the Designer from whence it came, on the unfinished but not wasted framework meant to enclose life, when in the fulness of time in this sphere, or some other equally rudimentary, the design should be perfected to that point of consciousness which is in itself immortality. . . . . .

"EMMA HARDINGE.

"OSWEGO, N. Y., *July* 10, 1860."

Of the final result of the teachings communicated by Prof. and Mrs. Spence, we are unable to give any definite account; their progress and growth — if they effected any — having been lost sight of in the stupendous successes achieved by the proven facts of Spiritualism.

If however, "faith be the substance of things unseen," and the "non-immortality" theorists have a sufficient supply of that quality, they may possibly have a large influence in directions unknown to, as well as unseen by, the rest of mankind.

CHAPTER XXVI.

SPIRITUALISM IN NEW ENGLAND (CONCLUDED).

"So let it be, in God's own might
We gird us for the coming fight,
And strong in him whose cause is ours,
In conflict with unholy powers
We grasp the weapons he has given,
The light, and truth, and love of Heaven."

J. G. WHITTIER.

EFFECTS OF THE RECANTATION MOVEMENT—REV. THOS. HIGGINSON'S CHALLENGE — THE TEN THOUSAND DOLLAR CHALLENGE — LETTERS FROM TALLMADGE, DANSKIN, CHASE, AND OTHERS— MORE TESTIMONY FOR IMMORTALITY— THE BOSTON POST ON PHYSICAL MEDIUMSHIP—THE BOSTON SPIRIT-ROOM — SINGULAR CASE OF HEALING — CORRESPONDENCE — CIRCLES — EXORCISM — WARREN CHASE ON WORK AND WAGES — STATISTICS OF SPIRITUALISM IN 1860.

IT would be almost impossible to give an idea of the mass of evidence in favor of genuine Spiritualism and reliable mediumship which the "recantation movement" called forth. True Spiritualists, instead of lamenting over the defalcations of the worthless, were compelled to acknowledge their indebtedness to them for undertaking that sifting process in their own behalf, which the rapid spread of the cause and the heterogeneous character of its believers so imperatively required.

In describing the various phases of deception, trickery, and fanaticism, which from time to time have deformed the movement, we have wandered far from the actual limits of the New England States, whose Spiritualism it was the business of the last few chapters to describe; but the wide-spread influence exerted by the manifestations, renders it almost impossible to narrow down our observations to any particular section of country.

The influence of Messrs Harris and Scott, for instance, though originating in New York and Virginia, spread over the whole country in its effects, and the same may be said of the Spear movements, although they first started in Boston and Kiantone. To draw up the status of the spiritualistic cause east of the Alleghanies up to 1860, we must traverse a much wider space than that occupied by the New England States alone. Commencing with these again, however, we find that the communications called forth by the sifting process described in the preceding chapters, exerted a marked and healthful influence on the dissemination of the highest and purest form of Spiritualism. Amongst other distinguished speakers, Reverends John Pierpont, Thomas W. Higginson, and Adin Ballou preached on the late exposures in terms of high congratulation, and felicitated their hearers on the healthful action which such a course must inevitably produce.

The Worcester *Spy*, a paper generally sufficiently violent in its declamations against Spiritualism, gives the following synopsis of a discourse given by the Rev. T. W. Higginson, appropriate to the occasion of the late exposures:

"Rev. Thomas W. Higginson lectured at Dodworth's Academy, New York, last Sunday.

"The following is a brief sketch of his discourse. Mr. Higginson said that he could imagine no general class or modes of spiritual intercourse, which was not represented in Spiritualism. He rejoiced that it had been scrutinized by so many hard-headed and sceptical scientific men. After hundreds of thousands of facts, extending over eight years, during which time three out of every four who had investigated it had become converts, he had the right to claim that the burden of proof rested on the other side.

"During this time at least twenty thousand mediums have been continually tested by sceptics.

"It was easy for them to be deceived in some things; natural to expect that some deception, voluntary and involuntary, must exist in such vast operations. But if the whole thing was deception, then there were twenty thousand persons in the country who were guilty of the blackest species of fraud. And who were these deceivers? Our brothers, sisters, mothers, fathers, children, and most intimate friends and kindred! What could be the purpose of such a wide-spread deception?

"Of the many thousands of mediums in the country, how many had made money by it?

"For every one that had, he could venture to say there were at least ten who had lost money, reputation, friends, and worldly advantage of all kinds—setting aside the possibility of gain. Then, was vice so intrinsically attractive that human beings would wilfully sacrifice their honor and fortune for the sole purpose of establishing an unpopular falsehood? . . . . He would give his hundred dollars to any one who would sustain fifteen minutes' conversation by trick or machinery in precisely the same manner as that practiced by the mediums. . . . . . It was, he knew, of little use to detail facts; we should all see for ourselves: still, what could the exposers make of such facts as these?

"He had seen a guitar play in broad daylight, without any human hands upon it or any human being within three feet of it. The widow of 'honest John Davis,' late Governor of Massachusetts [herself the sister of America's most eminent historian], had told him, that while sitting in her own parlor, with two other ladies and a medium, she and they saw a pencil rise up on a centre-table in the room of itself, and while no human being was within several feet of it, write an intelligent communication addressed to herself. And yet, this is but one of thousands and thousands of facts, some greater and some less, which are daily transpiring in the world, and which have only been hailed by the jeers and sneers of academies and lyceums. . . . . .

"Mr. Higginson closed a long and earnest address with prayer.

The brief synopsis above quoted was particularly noted in the secular papers for the offer of "one hundred dollars" to any trickster who could simulate precisely the practices of genuine mediumship. This offer appeared to excite the peculiar merriment of the press, as if the thing could only by possibility mean one of the fictions in which clerical gentlemen sometimes indulge. Presuming that the railing world had already forgotten the numerous challenges of a similar kind issued by Messrs. Partridge and Britain, the author added to Mr. Higginson's offer five hundred dollars to any trickster who could, by machinery or trick, give such test facts of intelligence as were daily revealed through certain specified mediums; such tests to be given under precisely similar conditions to those employed by the mediums. This offer was immediately doubled by Mr. Miltenberger, of St. Louis, and added to by similar offers all over the States, until it amounted to the sum of ten thousand dollars. But as no competitor for this prize has ever yet appeared, it is presumed that the "tricksters" did not happen to see the various papers in which the offers were advertised, or that, like Mr. Paine, of Worcester, "they never performed for money." Out of the floods of testimony that soon began to pour in from all quarters concerning the rapid advance of the cause, we shall select a few items from well-known and reliable correspondents. The first whom we shall cite is Governor Tallmadge, who, in describing an incident connected with the decease of an old friend and near neighbor of his family's, writes to the *Spiritual Telegraph* as follows:

"HON. J. B. MACY LOST FROM THE NIAGARA.

"FOND DU LAC, WISCONSIN.

"*Messrs. Partridge and Britain:*

"You have, no doubt, seen in the public papers the melancholy fate of our friend Hon. John B. Macy, by the burning of the steamer 'Niagara' near Port Washington, on Lake Michigan. He, with several others, was precipitated from the small boat into the water, whilst it was being let down at the stern of the steamer. . . . . . . He was unsurpassed in his energy, enterprise, and public spirit, and was withal a devoted Spiritualist. . . . . . . His noble widow entertains the same belief, and the greatest consolation she has in this sudden bereavement is the assurance that her husband, as a blessed ministering spirit, can still communicate with her. . . . . . .

"Mr. Macy was drowned on the 24th instant, about four o'clock, P.M. On the morning of the next day, and before any rumor of his fate could possibly have reached us, my daughter saw shadows flitting across her room, which she mentioned to the family as a presage of bad news. Mr. Macy, who had been our near neighbor, had started for Lake Superior, and was not expected home for several days.

"In the night, after the family had retired to rest, my daughter discovered a bright light in the sitting-room opening into hers, and the same shadow, which she had indistinctly noticed in the morning, now appeared in the shape and exact semblance of Mr. Macy. She informed her mother of the apparition, immediately adding, under impression, 'Mr. Macy is drowned.' Another daughter, who is also a medium, sleeping in a different part of the house, saw the same light and the shadowy form of Mr. Macy as he appeared to her sister, upon which she was influenced to write 'Niagara—drowned by the upsetting of the small-boat.' The next day, and for the first time, the news of the catastrophe, and the manner of Mr. Macy's death, reached our village.

"Incidents small as these being of such frequent occurrence amongst us, do more in their totality to convince the community that spirits live, and do communicate with earth, than all the action of cheats and vagabonds can avail to shake that belief. Still I believe even these poor tools are doing a good work for the cause of truth, for they stimulate inquiry, and serve as a check to that excessive credulity which necessarily results from such an abundance of phenomena.

. . . . . . "Circles are numerous here, investigations keen, and the phenomena more striking and abundant than ever.

"Yours, very truly,

"N. P. TALLMADGE."

Colonel Danskin, of Baltimore, wrote to the same effect in the succeeding paragraphs, copied from the *Banner of Light* of 1860:

"We hear no more now of the insanity of the Spiritualists. The cry of 'humbug' is dying out, and the denunciations of the pulpit in this section of country are waxing feeble. Even the sneers of the secular press are subsiding, and the pity which some good people have expressed for the 'deluded Spiritualists,' has been transmuted into admiration for the wonderfully intellectual power displayed upon our rostrum. . . . . . .

"Some ten years ago, when my attention was first drawn to the subject, that wonderful medium, the poetic Harris, was advertised to lecture in Carroll Hall. I thought it worth an hour's attention to learn what could be said upon so strange a subject. The hall was crowded by a throng of curiosity-hunters, some of whom had come to sneer, and a few to learn whether there was really a communion between the two worlds. I listened with wonder and delight. The very thoughts which had been flitting through my brain for years were here embodied in compact and logical propositions.

"The absolute necessity of the intercommunion of men and angels was clearly proven. The facts upon which the claims of that communion were based were distinctly stated, and the philosophy deducible from those facts was so eloquently presented that I saw a new world unfolding before me that my soul had long yearned to behold, but for which theology had forbidden me to search.

"Since that time many spiritual speakers have visited our city,—the inspired Ambler, the modest, yet earnest, Achsah Sprague. Here Cora Hatch was for months made the mouthpiece of the angels, who poured through her finely organized brain the melodies of the higher spheres. Then came the logical and eloquent Thomas Gales Forster, sowing the seeds of truth, which have since germinated and brought forth such good fruit; Emma Hardinge, the dashing, brilliant, and forcible Emma, who took her hearers by storm, and won the applause even of those who were not morally strong enough to cast aside entirely the creeds in which their infant minds had been swaddled; Lizzie Doten spoke a short season for us, and it was during this brief visit that exquisite poem, 'The Streets of Baltimore,' was given by the spirit of Edgar Poe, who has often used her mediumship for the outpouring of his rhythmical sermons. Since October last, Mrs. Hyzer has been our principal speaker, and delighted audiences have continued to fill our hall, listening to the sublime utterances which fall in living light from her lips. . . . . . .

"WASHINGTON A. DANSKIN."

Deeming that the likenesses of deceased persons, given under marvellous test conditions by Messrs. Rogers, Walcutt, Anderson, and others, would furnish undeniable proofs of spirit intercourse, many anxious inquirers, whose faith had been shaken by recent occurrences, appealed to these mediums for the proofs they sought. The services of the spirit artists were in unusual demand at that period, therefore, and the success of their mediumistic efforts became almost fabulous.

From an immense mass of testimony incidental to the time, our limits will only permit us to select one case, which we insert because it gives the experience of a well-known citizen of Newburyport, and is communicated and vouched for by one of the most prominent and reliable of the advocates of Spiritualism, namely, Hon. Warren Chase.

"QUERY—BANNER OF LIGHT.—1860.

"Would the hole in the carpet, wire in the floor and table of Mrs. Paine, account for the following? or, is this one of the tougher kind of manifestations that requires the devil theory of Beecher and Co.? Mr. R. Sherman, overseer in one of the factories of Newburyport, has a wife who has been many years an inhabitant of the spirit-world. His second and present wife is a medium, through whom the other often communicates with him, mostly in writing. Some months ago, Mr. Sherman requested his spirit companion to try and get for him her likeness, and soon after she informed him that she would try to do so; promising to visit the room of Mr. Walcutt, spirit artist, of Columbus, Ohio, naming a day and hour for that purpose, and requesting him to inform Mr. W. of the appointment.

Engraved by J.C. Buttre from a Daguerreotype

N. P. Tallmadge

"That there should be as perfect a test given as possible, Mr. Sherman got a friend who had no interest in the matter to write for him to Mr. Walcutt, as follows:

"'DEAR SIR,—I have made arrangenents with a spirit to visit your room at —— [naming day and hour]. Please forward the result by mail.' etc.

"Mr. Walcutt was sick in bed at the receipt of this letter, but, bolstered up, he drew the likeness of a spirit who appeared at the time appointed, and sent it to Newburyport. On being examined, it was instantly recognized to be Mr. Sherman's first wife as she appeared in her last days, with her hair cut short as it was only a few days before her death, and a peculiar curl on one side, just as she wore it. The hand was placed at the side of her face, which was a constant habit with her, and the whole picture contained unmistakable proofs of her identity. Mr. Sherman even was surprised to see her hair cut short, but the spirit said she was so represented, to make the test more complete.

"This is only one of many similar and equally good tests that daily come under my observation, and which may help to furnish our enemies with fresh subjects to account for.

"I am sure there is no science in old Harvard that explains this one fact alone, away, but those who have a devil to charge such occurrences to, have the start of me, and are ahead of my time.

"WARREN CHASE."

The following extracts are from an essay on immortality published in the *Sunbeam*, New York, by Professor Whipple, a gentleman of unimpeachable veracity, and scientific attainments, who had resigned the chances of worldly distinction to which his education and position entitled him, for the sake of becoming an itinerant in the cause of Spiritualism. Mr. Whipple's cases, although not very remarkable either for originality or marvel, were highly applicable to the time, and are illustrative of a subject which will ever continue to interest mankind, namely, whether the apparitions of deceased persons are produced by unknown forces in the atmosphere, mental images, or the actual living spirits of the departed. In the settlement of such questions the proofs of intelligence as well as identity communicated by Mr. Whipple, are exceedingly valuable, and being recited moreover with extreme directness and simplicity, they commend themselves to the attention of every reader.

"PROFESSOR WHIPPLE TO THE BANNER OF LIGHT.

. . . . . "Eight years ago I was travelling in Medina County, in this State.

"I put up over Sunday with a family in the town of Brunswick. In the family were two rapping mediums. They and myself held a circle during the day, when we were seated round a large dining table. I propounded many questions to my deceased relatives, all of which were correctly answered through the raps.

"After I had concluded questioning, the mediums rose and took a position by the window six or eight feet from the table, which, whilst they sang a hymn, kept time by raising itself directly from the floor, without the slightest physical contact, or the approach of a human being within six feet of it. I introduce this fact to call attention to the intelligent agency manifested independent of the medium.

"Last spring I attended a circle at the residence of Mr. Tuttle, father of Hudson Tuttle. It was the first time I had ever been at their house. Mr. Tuttle became clairvoyant, and corectly described the spirits of my mother, two sisters, and a twin brother. She was entranced and spoke to me of events only known to my spirit mother and myself.

"Whilst lecturing in Morrow County this last winter, I attended a circle one evening composed of about twenty persons, and there, for the first time, met a young man, a medium, who had no acquaintance with me and knew nothing of my history. He was controlled to give tests to different individuals.

"At length he turned his attention to me; said he saw a young man, a spirit, by my side, whom he described very particularly.

"The description answered exactly to my brother. He compared his features with mine; said we greatly resembled each other, and that he appeared to bear the relation of brother to me. 'Now,' said he, I will see if I can tell how old he is.' He paused a moment and then exclaimed, 'Why, he says he is neither older nor younger than you.' 'Very true,' I answered, 'for he is my twin brother.' . . . . .

"A short time before my brother departed this life, while he lay sick in Minnesota, I went to Mr. Durkee, a spirit physician residing in Middlefield, Ohio, who, I understood, could examine diseases at a distance, without being informed of the symptoms of the patient. He examined my brother correctly, described his symptoms and their complication, and said he was incurable. He told the medicines he had taken, the effect produced by them, and a marked change then occurring in his symptoms. All this I noted down, and found to be correct on my arrival in Minnesota.

"My brother lived but a few days after my return. Last September, at the Spiritualists' convention, in Ashtabula County, Ohio, whilst on the speaker's stand in the public hall, a Mrs. Shaw, a trance medium, described to me my twin brother, correctly delineating his appearance and character in every respect; yet she never saw him in the earth form, or had the slightest idea that I had a brother. I might relate numerous instances of the same kind, did space permit. . . . . . Rogers, while on earth, painted hundreds of portraits of individuals he never saw. He would sometimes have a portrait finished for months before it was recognized and claimed by its appropriate owner.

"Rogers was a tailor by trade, with only an ordinary education, and mediocre talent, without the least knowledge of the art. Eschew his own explanation of the production of his pictures, namely, that one spirit appeared to him, and another entranced and used his organism to paint the likeness of the apparition, and what account could be given of his otherwise miraculous gift?

"At the early age of sixteen, Hudson Tuttle, a farmer's boy, with a very common school education, commenced under spirit influence to paint a geological panorama.* He painted correctly the different geological systems, and characteristic fossils, occupying eight hundred feet of canvas.

"At that time, he had no practical knowledge of geology; yet many eminent professors have pronounced the painting scientifically correct, and a remarkable exhibition of skill. . . . . . And thus, I might go on *ad infinitum*, introducing facts, some of which absolutely demonstrate that the soul lives beyond the tomb, and others bearing equally conclusive evidence of the influence which the immortal world, exercises over the mortal."

The New York Conference, at which so much publicity had been given to the doings of the "tricksters," of course became the scene of many earnest expressions of counter opinions. The following is a specimen of the tone the discussions assumed, subsequent to the exposures. The report dates a few weeks later than the Paine confession:

"At the conference of last week, the question under discussion was whether all so-called spiritual communications cannot be accounted for by the theory of clairvoyance. Dr. Gray was of the opinion that clairvoyance covered the whole ground, but as a salvo, made clairvoyance a spiritual state, into which none could enter without first coming into rapport with a spirit. . . . . . . The session of the conference to which I allude was rich in facts. Mr. Conklin related the following:

"Last week two Baptist clergymen from Brooklyn, called on him, the one being a Spiritualist, the other openly acknowledging his frank belief that the whole thing was 'a humbug. Mr. Conklin, without the least feeling of annoyance at such an introduction to the *séance*, directed the sceptic to write names and questions away from the table; and when he was quite sure that he, Mr. C., could not have seen them, the names, together with most appropriate answers, were written out by his hand. The sceptic was astonished; and, after spending an hour in asking questions and receiving the most satisfactory tests in answer, he avowed his belief that he must have been conversing with the world of spirits, since the knowledge communicated could have come from no other source.

"The other reverend gentleman stated that on a certain occasion, when it had been previously announced to him, through Mr. Conklin, that George Fox, the celebrated Quaker founder, would preach through him a sermon on immortality, he found himself unable to follow his notes: his congregation seemed to fade from his sight, and whilst but partially conscious of his surroundings, he found himself most pleasingly impelled to pronounce a discourse, which his congregation subsequently declared to have been 'the grandest sermon he had ever preached.' He added that, at midnight on a recent occasion, the fear of burglars became so powerfully impressed upon his mind that he could neither sleep nor lie still. At length he was compelled to rise and search the house, when, on entering his dining-room he found the stove red hot, and a horse of clothes, which had been left standing around it, upset by some means upon the stove. Just as he entered, the clothes had ignited; a moment later, and they would have been in a blaze: the result must have been destruction if

* Hudson Tuttle has also given, under the same control, two of the finest works on the "Arcana of Nature," which the literature of the present day supplies.

not of the lives, at least of the property of the family, had not this timely impression sent him there in season to extinguish the flames. Shortly after, the spirit sister of this gentleman informed him at a circle that she was the controlling power on this occasion. She perceived the danger, and finding it impossible to impress him with the true nature of the case, succeeded in exciting his mind to the fear of robbers. Mr. Conklin also related a well known instance of spirit telegraphy, which was the more interesting as all the parties concerned in it were present to verify his statement.

"Mr. Conklin was at Washington. One of his children was taken ill, and attended by Dr. Gray, who considered the case so critical, that he advised the family to telegraph for Mr. Conklin. The party charged with this mission, on his way to the magnetic telegraph office, stepped instead, into the office of the *Christian Spiritualist*, at 553 Broadway, where a public circle was then in session. Mr. John F. Coles was one of the persons present, and hearing the report of the messenger, asked if there was any spirit then present who would take the message in advance of the telegraph. 'Black Hawk,' the Indian chief announced himself, and volunteered to do so. The message was given and the spirit purported to depart on his errand.

"Meanwhile, Mr. Conklin was in his room at Washington, and being fatigued with the labors of the forenoon, was reposing upon a sofa, when he felt suddenly impelled to get up and go to his table. There the influence came upon him, and immediately wrote through his hand: 'Go right home—your little boy Sammy, is very sick. Black Hawk.' Mr. Conklin at once telegraphed home, and after receiving a confirmation of his message, followed himself in person.

"N. B.—Mr. Coles, who was concerned in the delivery of this spirit telegraph, and present when Mr. Conklin repeated the narrative, was quite willing to except this case from the list of impositions. No general rule without an exception, then, it seems. [*Reporter*.]"

The following narrative was furnished by a correspondent of the Boston *Post*, from whose volumes it is now reprinted. It was published about the time when the majority of the secular papers were writing voluminous obituaries on Spiritualism, slain, as they alleged, at the hands of the camp-followers who ever hang on the rear of the armies of progression. Besides the interest derived from the narrative itself, its record by one of the most respectable journals in New England, the editor of whom vouches for its authenticity, renders its testimony peculiarly valuable. It is only necessary to add that the *séance* took place in the house of one of the most distinguished merchants of Boston, and that the medium, Mr. Rollin Squire, was a gentleman whose standing and position rendered all idea of interested motive or deception impossible. On this head, moreover, the nature of the occurrences will be ample witness of their supra-mundane origin.

"*To the Editor of the Boston Post:*

"It was about ten minutes past seven, on Friday evening, December 7, 1855, that a party of ten were admitted into the house of Mr. ——, the much respected merchant, of Boston, for the purpose of witnessing the strange phenomena alleged to occur there. The medium in this case was a young gentleman under twenty years of age.

"In the chamber to which we were shown were chairs, a sofa, bed, wardrobe, looking-glasses, etc., etc. The room was about ten feet high. In the centre was a round table weighing about fifty pounds. Around this we became seated. The medium took a gold watch, suspended it by the chain from his his right hand, closely enveloped that hand in a handkerchief to prevent the play of a single joint, and requested the spirits to open the watch, remove the cap, shut it again, and notify by raps when it was completed. All this was done. Also, the cap was taken in a similar way from a silver watch of one of the party, and could not be found, until it dropped on the table, at our request. The watches were passed from hand to hand under the table many times.

"The room was now darkened, when the following phenomena occurred: The table was forcibly drawn up to the ceiling, leaving the dents of its legs on the ceiling; it then came down, having adhered to the ceiling with such force as to drag down the plaster-dust with it. It was raised some twelve or fourteen inches from the floor whilst the whole party had their hands on its upper surface. Whilst six of our party strove to hold it by main force, it was wrenched from our grasp and thrown some six or eight feet upon the bed. The medium was lifted bodily from the floor at various distances, whilst we held him by either hand.

He was lifted from the floor and placed, standing, on the centre of the table, and again stretched upon his back thereon. Being seated in his chair, himself, chair and all, was elevated several inches, and hopped about the room like a frog. Suddenly it was lifted, medium and all, into the centre of the table. Again it was drawn up so high that the medium's head knocked against the ceiling; and finally the medium was thrown out of it upon the bed, whilst the chair was hurled upon the floor. A leg of the table, being slightly loose, was wrenched off, and a still heavier table—one weighing ninety pounds—was substituted. This table was gently raised, turned in the air topsy-turvy, and then lightly laid, legs upwards, on our heads, resting there as lightly as a feather pillow.

"This table was also tossed about, pitched over, and floated hither and thither with the same ease, apparently, as the lighter one.

"Pillows were thrown, and every one of us was touched and pinched, whilst we all joined hands. We were fanned as by a cool current of air, and something like a heavy arm or leg floated by us, brushing our hair aside.

"One of the party received a smart slap on the forehead, with what felt to be a human hand—the tips of the fingers slanting downward, as if from some one above us. Others also were slapped and touched by a small delicate hand, but coming from the same direction. . . . . . . About ten o'clock we broke up our sitting; but ere we departed, we were invited into the parlor, when the medium, standing on the floor, played several tunes on the piano—a very heavy one—which rose and fell in excellent time to the music. The æolian pedal, too, was pressed down by an invisible performer, whilst the medium's two feet were resting as he stood, on the ground, at full arm's length from the piano. Then, whilst he pressed the keys as before, the instrument became mute, and whilst he still played the sound was resumed. Finally, each party was bid "good-night," his name being rapped out on the piano case, and we left the house at a quarter past ten.

"All this was done promptly, and to the entire satisfaction of all present. Not a single request was refused. No hesitancy was evinced; not an error was committed.

"It was a private residence; no fee of admittance, and of the ten persons present, besides the medium and the gentleman of the house, eight were sceptical when they entered. They left the mansion fully convinced. The whole of these marvels were executed within three hours. We leave comments to the reader. We state sober facts. W."

In Boston, a spirit room similar to the one established by Jonathan Koons, in Ohio, was fitted up by a gentleman by the name of Barnard, who opened it free to the public. The arrangements consisted only of an ordinary table, chairs, and a platform on which the instruments were placed.

Everything in the room, including even its floorings and walls were repeatedly searched, to detect imposture, if any had been possible.

The first circles held in the Boston spirit room are described by Mr. Barnard in the following communication to the *Spiritual Telegraph:*

"MR. EDITOR,—I have recently instituted a 'spirit room,' with apparatus similar in some respects to that of Mr. Koons in Ohio, and which, like his, is free to the public. We have had but three sittings as yet, and last night the spirits called through a writing medium for a vial of pure water. This was procured for them from the office of Dr. Pinkerton, our neighbor. They then requested the room to be darkened a while; and after it was, at their request, lit up again, we found the vial contained pure sweet wine, of a dark red color.

"They also played upon the instruments, drums, tambourine, and bells, most powerfully; produced many spirit lights, and gave general satisfaction to the whole company, twenty-eight in number. Amongst others who were present and will certify to the above, were Rev. Allen Putnam, of Roxbury; Rufus Elmer and wife, of Springfield; John Orvis, of Boston; Luther Parks, of Boston; and Jonathan Buffum, of Lynn.

"Yours for the cause of truth,

"GEORGE L. BARNARD.

"13 AUBURN COURT, BOSTON."

Far more wonderful phenomena than are here described soon ensued in the "spirit room" in Boston, besides which many other circles of equal interest were held in the city in every rank of life and phase of spiritual power.

About this time—from 1855 to 1866—physical manifestations of the most astounding character, were given at Providence, Rhode Island, through the mediumship of Mrs. Wilbur, an invalid lady, who was chiefly confined to her bed; also in Portland, Maine, through a little girl, the daughter of a distinguished lawyer of the city. Writings produced by the spirits with their own hands, under the most stringent test conditions, were given through these mediums, and contained exact fac-similes of the handwriting of numerous deceased persons, descriptions of the spheres, and philosophical essays. Other non-professional mediums, variously endowed, were reported from different parts of the New England States, furnishing an incontrovertible mass of testimony in favor of genuine mediumship, and the total absence of any possible motive for deception or fraud. Amongst the innumerable cases of healing which were daily flooding the spiritual journals from all sections of the country, we select—as the only one which our space will here permit us to insert—a singularly curious and interesting instance of spirit beneficence, vouched for upon the authority of unimpeachable witnesses, and furnished by Mr. Charles Partridge, who was personally acquainted with all the parties. Mr. Partridge reports the circumstances in the *Spiritual Telegraph*, in the following terms:

"SINGULAR SPIRITUAL VISITATION AND EXTRAORDINAY CURE OF CONSUMPTION.

"While the writer was on a visit to Brunswick, Maine, a few days since, the interesting facts recorded in this connection were communicated to him by the lady and her friends, for whom the spirits exercised their extraordinary powers.

Mrs. D. P. Newman, of Brunswick, belongs to a family in which consumption is a congenital disease, one sister and eight members of her father's family having been removed from earth by this insidious destroyer. The health of Mrs. N. had been failing for some years, owing to her consumptive tendencies, when a sudden cold had the effect to prostrate her system and reduce her to the condition of incurable suffering. Confined to her bed, she continued to fail rapidly. Her cough was incessant and every fresh paroxysm of pain was succeeded by increasing and hopeless debility. One day, when Mrs. Newman had been confined to her couch of pain for five weeks, a singular circumstance occurred in Vassalboro, which is some forty miles from Brunswick, the residence of the patient. Mrs. Norcross, widely known in the eastern portion of New England as an excellent clairvoyant and healing medium, was seated alone in her apartment.

The time was early evening, and nothing occurred to disturb the silence of the room until the door suddenly opened, and Mrs. Norcross beheld entering what appeared to be a human figure concealed by loose drapery. Presuming it to be a boy belonging to the family who had assumed this disguise for the childish purpose of affrighting her, Mrs. Norcross spoke, addressing the boy by name.

"Thereupon the covering seemed to fall from one side of the figure, disclosing, to her great surprise, a beautiful female form, with a face glowing with earnest purpose and remarkable tenderness of feeling. This lovely apparition Mrs. Norcross did not recognize as any one she had ever seen before. After a moment's pause the mysterious visitant said: 'My name is Jordan, and I have brought my dear sister to have you heal her by the power which you possess.' As she spoke the covering fell from the other side, disclosing a pale invalid, who reclined upon the arm of the radiant stranger. Mrs. Norcross at once recognized in the invalid the shadowy appearance of Mrs. Newman, of Brunswick, and it subsequently appeared that the fair unknown was a sister of the name of Jordan, who had long been an inhabitant of the spirit-world.

"Before the figures vanished Mrs. Norcross had a distinct perception of the patient's dangerous condition in all its details; but with it she also received a prescription, which, by direction, she immediately forwarded to Mrs. Newman. Four days later the seeress visited Brunswick, learned that Mrs. Newman had followed her prescription, and already a marked and beneficial change had succeeded. Other prescriptions, given under spirit influence, followed, and the patient, whose case had seemed utterly hopeless, began gradually to recover, until, at the expiration of eight weeks, every distressing symptom had disappeared, the consumptive resumed all her domestic duties, and is now freed from the debility and suffering that has afflicted her for ten years, and in the enjoyment of perfect health. The writer has given this narrative substantially as he received it from Mrs. Newman and her friends a few days since. Mrs. Newman cannot now refer to the subject of her mysterious treatment and providential recovery without intense emotion, and whilst making this record was compelled to leave the room to regain her self-possession.

"When she returned she gratefully acknowledged that she had become a medium, and was often entranced by the beautiful spirit sister, whose angelic ministrations had restored her to life and earthly usefulness."

A fair specimen of the methods which may be successfully adopted to cultivate spiritual communion, as well as an evidence of the spontaneity of the influence, wherever conditions are favorable, will be found in the following simple sketch, recently communicated to the *Banner of Light* by a highly-respected and prominent citizen of Greenfield, Massachusetts:

"*Editors of the Banner of Light:*

"Within a few months, from various circumstances, an interest in the subject of Spiritualism has sprung up in the minds of a few of the citizens of this place—Greenfield, Massachusetts.

"Some persons, each of whom have enjoyed good educational advantages, mutually agreed to meet together regularly, for the purpose of critically examining the curious phenomena which each had either witnessed or heard of from sources calculated to arrest their attention. These persons were all acquainted with each other, were of irreproachable standing in society, and were all satisfied of the entire integrity of each others' intentions. In forming this circle they mutually agreed to lay aside all preconceived prejudices, and selfish purposes; in short, to investigate patiently, and simply with the honest purpose of discovering if any new and valuable truth could be brought to light.

"During the first few sittings, the phenomena of table-tipping and movements occurred. By these, questions were asked and answered correctly, through the alphabet and the movements of the table at the right letters, in the usual manner. After a while this form of manifestation discontinued, and was succeeded by the following: One of the circle was influenced to give long-continued, steady and forcible blows of the hand upon the table; blows which must ordinarily have caused severe pain and swelling, but though sometimes prolonged for hours, caused no inconvenience, unless violently restrained.

"After this, the hand was moved as if in the act of writing. At first the words were illegible, but after a time became distinct, and frequently wrote out, 'Have patience.' The writing was purely automatic, and seemed to be facilitated by the accompaniment of music, which was called for by pantomime. . . . . . .

"Shortly after the writing became legible, entrancement supervened, and while in this state a complete transformation seemed to come over the appearance of the medium. The predominant expression was that of drollery, and hearty merriment. By signs, music was called for, and accompanied, on the part of the medium, by dancing, sometimes deft and graceful, at others very energetic. Occasionally striking personations of deceased persons were given and recognized. The information communicated by writing, was to the effect that a circle of spirits were earnestly engaged in the development of our medium.

"We were reminded in our impatience that there were laws and conditions in spirit-life as stringent as those on earth; that these were imperative, and often hindered their coming to us as we expected or desired, and that, moreover, we frequently marred their attempts by our ignorantly breaking the conditions of their manifestation.

"After a time the development of our medium became characterized by the regular appearance of three successive influences, each of which is marked and distinct from the other. First appears the merry influence already described, who dances and talks gaily. The second is grave, earnest, and instructive, delivering a well-arranged discourse, and inviting us to discussion. . . . The third influence is that of an Indian, of apparently majestic mien, and highly characteristic manner and language. . . . .

"Music is demanded by signs, and sometimes an Indian song or dance is performed. . . . . Under this influence the medium returns to his normal state. It is a fact worthy of notice that the medium's health has materially improved since the commencement of these sittings. . . . . The first, or merry spirit, it is claimed, professes to come for the purpose of preparing for the second, who is our teacher and guide, instructing us in wise philosophy and pure religious feeling. The third, or Indian influence, professes to come for the purpose of restoring our medium to his normal condition. By the second, or superior intelligence, we are assured that all which is now mysterious to us in this matter shall be ultimately explained and made clear to all mankind. . . . . This article is written at the request of our spirit-teacher, who desired thereby to offer an inducement to other thoughtful and earnest souls, who might be encouraged to organize circles amongst themselves, and thus open the door for spirit visitants who were everywhere waiting for such opportunities to bring the truths of spirit communion to their friends on earth.

"ONE OF THE CIRCLE."

A correspondent of the *Spiritual Telegraph* writes from Lawrence, Massachusetts, concerning the origin and progress of the cause in that place. He says:

"The first public manifestations occurred about 1857. Those, and subsequent ones, provoked much investigation, and honest inquirers 'have not failed to receive their portion of ridicule.'

"Nevertheless, the truth continues to spread, and the friends there have secured a hall, and hold two meetings every Sabbath, besides many circles during the week. At a convention held there during the last winter, a certain sceptic, attending with the full purpose of converting all the infidel Spiritualists from 'the evil of their ways,' became suddenly entranced by the spirits, compelled to deliver an admirable address in favor of the cause, and since then has become, under the same influence, one of its most efficient advocates."

The following letter refers to a new, though, as it will be perceived, ineffective method of attempting to stay the "spiritualistic delusion.' It is one of many recorded similar efforts, and is given as a specimen of all the results hitherto achieved in such directions:

"EXORCISM BY HOLY WATER A FAILURE.

"NEW YORK, *September* 18, 1859.

"*Editors of the Spiritual Telegraph:*

"In your paper of the 7th inst. I notice that you intimate that the Right Rev. Bishop of Albany purposes to 'exorcise spirits,' or, in other words, 'to cast out devils.' It may be of interest to the reverend gentleman, and the balance of the Catholic clergy, to know that the thing has been tried and proved a failure. The case which proves this is as follows:

"Four silly, badly-educated girls, of ages ranging from fifteen to twenty, having gathered together at a friend's house to 'have a time with the spirits,' or, in other words, to trifle with spiritual manifestations, seated themselves around a table, and after asking all manner of foolish questions, requested the spirits to take hold of them.

"The spirits at once complied; seized them, treated them in the roughest manner, and shaking them, caused them to use the most violent actions and outrageous language, etc. In this strait one of the dignitaries of the mother church was sent for in haste, to 'expel the obsessing demons.' After the priest had arrived at the scene of disorder, he put on his robes, got ready the holy water, and approached the possessed girls in the due formulæ proper to such occasions. After many sallies with the holy fluid, and a vast number of incantations, none of which produced the slightest effect, the mediums at length charged upon him with such irresistible power, and such capacity of finger-nails, that the worthy *padre* fled precipitately, leaving the field in possession of the 'demons' and the spectators, who had gathered together to witness the 'exorcism.' The girls still continued to be used roughly by the discordant spirits they had invoked, until the arrival of some of their spiritualistic friends, by whose judicious passes and gentle remonstrances with the spirits they were instantly relieved. This is not the only case where 'holy water' and holy incantations have failed in cases of obsession, and, did time and space permit, I could cite many other instances to prove it. The Boston *Pilot* said some time ago, 'that a few hearty prayers and a plentiful supply of holy water would soon put down the humbug.'

"Now I will agree to produce a hundred mediums, whose manifestations the whole Catholic Church cannot affect. I know of one upon whom they may commence experimenting immediately, and though they may collect oceans of holy water, and perform their most imposing orgies, if they can stop the manifestations through that medium I will agree to raise money enough to build, at least, one small-sized church.

"Yours, etc., SPIRITUS."

The writer's name and address were furnished to the editor in full verification of the genuine character of his offer; but, as yet, the "small-sized church" has not been demanded.

An old and highly-respected correspondent of the *Spiritual Telegraph* furnishes the following illustration of the fallacy of attempting to explain the spiritual manifestations upon the principes of animal magnetism.

"A BIOLOGIST DEPRIVED OF HIS POWER.—TELEGRAPH PAPERS.

"MORETOWN, VERMONT, *January* 20, 1854.

"MESSRS. EDITORS,—The cause of Spiritualism is making rapid progress in this vicinity.

"We have healing, writing, speaking, and physical mediums, yet not enough of either to satisfy the demands of inquirers.

"There was a curious case of spiritual prophecy last fall at Montpelier, in which a great biologist by the name of Stone was told that all his power was given him from God to prepare the way for spiritual manifestations, and that he would soon have his power taken from him if he continued to use it against Spiritualism. Whilst he was lecturing at Montpelier, he called on two mediums in that place, and declaring that all the marvels reported of them could be explained by animal magnetism, requested the privilege of magnetizing them, having previously promised his friends that he would 'show them up.' The permission to try his power was readily granted, and as long a time as he pleased allowed for the experiment, which, however, utterly failed.

"He could do nothing with them, but after the trial the spirits influenced them and again warned him that he would have his power taken from him, unless he determined to use it for Spiritualism.

"Disregarding the prediction, he continued his former course; but at his next lecture his usual experiments over *his own subjects* utterly failed. He at once proceeded to Northcote, and a similar failure there ensued; and we learn that after experimenting with other subjects, and in other places, his power seems to be utterly gone, and latterly we have ceased to hear of Stone, 'the great biologist.'

"Here is an important fact illustrated; namely, that whilst the influence which controls the spirit medium and biological subject is the same, yet the former, coming from a higher and purer source, is so much the stronger that between the two it establishes a difference great enough to make the spirit the controlling power over the biologist.

"ROSWELL CHILD."

To attempt following further the progress of Spiritualism in New England would be simply to enumerate its cities, towns, and villages, and to say that one or all of the representative facts we have named is as rife in one district as another; or to number up at least one-third of its principal citizens, and affirm that they were either openly or covertly known to be Spiritualists.

Amongst our notices of mediums, journals, spiritual literature, associative movements, etc., New England will still be found to occupy a prominent place. To these special records we must refer our readers for further information, and conclude our notice of Spiritualism in the East up to 1860 by presenting two pieces of statistical matter, both of which deserve to be perused with attention. The first is a summary of the receipts which a first-class lecturer obtains through his itinerating system of spiritual propaganda, to which several hundreds of persons are devoted, many of whom are endowed with talents which would procure for them a field of honorable and remunerative labor in various other directions. As Hon. Warren Chase, whose report we quote, is one of the oldest and amongst the most popular of the spiritual speakers, his case forms a fair illustration of the average receipts of most of his co-workers, and a very sufficient answer, moreover, to the allegations of those who, knowing nothing of the genius of Spiritualism or Spiritualists, determine that the immense number of the latter must, judged by their own standard, enter upon their missions for the purpose of gain.

The following paragraph will, we think, furnish its own comments on such a belief or assertion. Mr. Chase's statement is prefaced by the succeeding remarks from the editor of the *Banner of Light*.

"WARREN CHASE—WORK AND WAGES.

"The cry is often raised, 'Lecturers are getting rich.' . . . Warren Chase has made his yearly report and there seems from it little danger of his retiring to live on the interest of his lecturing fund. Here is his report: 'During the year I have lectured one hundred and twenty-one times, as follows: Five lectures in Washington for $50, $10 each; thirty-seven in New York, $121, about $5.50 each; thirty-five in Vermont, $78, about $2 each, twenty four in New Jersey, $91, about $4 each; thirteen in Pennsylvania, $52, $4 each; four in Deleware, $20, $5 each; and three in Connecticut, $13, about $4.50 each; total, $425, or less than $3.50 each. It has cost a good share of this to pay my travelling and other expenses. . . . . My income tax never troubles me, and probably none of our speakers are much more troubled on that score than myself."

Comment on this statement is unnecessary, save to express a hope that the following piece of statistical information will prove of a more acceptable character.

At a convention held at Baltimore by the Catholics of the United States, some of their most prominent dignitaries stated, upon "accurate and reliable bases of information," that the believers in Spiritualism on the American Continent had reached the almost incredible number of *eleven millions, or one-third of the population of the United States!*

If such are the beginnings of this giant movement, where, what, and when will be the end? If the pious pulpit and sanguine press, who are perpetually reporting the death and burial of Spiritualism, cannot answer us, perhaps the Harvard professors, followers of Brewster and Faraday, or the fine gentlemen of the "Dundreary" class, who represent such a large proportion of the fashionable brains of England, can supply us with the information.

CHAPTER XXVII.

SPIRITUALISM IN PENNSYLVANIA.

"The mightiest souls of all time hover o'er us,
Who labored like gods amongst men and are gone;
Like great bursts of sun on the dark way before us,
They're with us, still with us; our battles fight on."
GERALD MASSEY.

SPIRITUALISM IN PHILADELPHIA—DR. H. T. CHILD'S REPORT—FLOATING IN THE AIR AT A PUBLIC MEETING—MR. M. B. DYOTT AND THE CHILDREN'S LYCEUM—SPIRITUALISTS' FUNERALS—SPIRITUALISM IN CORRY, TITUSVILLE AND MEADVILLE—MCFADDEN, THE HEALING MEDIUM—DR. JOHN NEWCOMER—NORRISTOWN—PENTECOSTAL SCENES IN ROULETTE—BALTIMORE AND WASHINGTON—MRS. DANSKIN'S CIRCLES.

WE must now present a brief sketch of the rise and progress of Spiritualism in Philadelphia; and though our space will only admit of a slight glance at its external movement, we shall be able to offer a faithful picture of its origin and present status, by referring to a compendius notice which appeared in the columns of the *Religio-Philosophical Journal* of 1866, drawn up by a gentleman equally celebrated as a noble spiritualist, aud as one of the most talented and inspired writers of spiritualistic literature, namely, Dr. H. T. Child, of Philadelphia. The report in question is as follows:

"A BRIEF HISTORY OF MODERN SPIRITUALISM IN PHILADELPHIA.

"The undersigned were appointed by the 'First Society of Spiritualists,' in Philadelphia, to prepare a history of modern Spiritualism in this city: Henry T. Child, M. D.; Isaac Rhen, Peter Osborn, Dr. J. L. Pierce, and George D. Henck. The following report was read on Sunday, September 3, 1866, by the chairman, and directed to be published in the *Banner of Light*, and *Religio-Philosophical Journal.*

"'There is probably no better illustration of one of the prominent teachings of modern Spiritualism than that which is given in the history of the movement in different localities. And yet, we believe it is well to record its history while it is fresh in our memories. . . . . . . In our times, the free thought of the age, born of our noble institutions, was lifting mankind into higher conditions, when Andrew Jackson Davis gave to the world his 'Nature's Divine Revelations,' a volume which, though it contains much that is speculative and uncertain in our present state of unfoldment, was evidently the most suggestive work, not only of its inspired and faithful author, but of the age itself.

"'We believe that but few of us have realized the value of this book, marking as it did an era in human history, and especially in the history of our cause in this city. Soon after its appearance, the Psychological Society of this city, most of whose members have since been identified with our cause, believed it to be right to bring this book prominently before the public, while at the same time they desired to study it critically; hence they rented a hall on Fourth street, known as Keim's Hall, and during the winter and spring of 1848 and 1849, three evenings in the week were devoted to reading this book. The plan adopted — which we think might be pursued with profit with other profound works — was to read one hour and devote the remainder of the evening to criticisms by the audience of the portions read. These meetings were eagerly attended, and we have no doubt were productive of much good. The spirit of inquiry which had been awakened was spreading with rapidity; a new era was dawning; one which had been predicted by Mr. Davis in the book above alluded to, in which intelligent communications were brought to this world from the dwellers of the inner life.

"'The manifestations at Hydesville, New York, known as the Rochester knockings, which had commenced in 1848, although not new, were connected with the most important event of the century, namely, the discovery of an intelligence behind these, which not only attempted to explain their cause, but gave evidence of the identity of individual spirits who had passed from this sphere. On the 9th of October, 1850, the first circle was formed in this city, and for four months numerous meetings were held, without eliciting a single response.

"'On the evening of February 10, 1851, the sounds were heard, and the manifestations which have since become so common over the entire civilized world, were introduced.

"'About the 15th of February, 1851, the writer,* who, as a physician, was attending Mary Ann Wiggins, a young lady, who was a very sensitive clairvoyant and magnetic subject, was informed that for some time past the family had heard the sounds around her bed. On this day, he was told that a brother in spirit-life had promised the medium that he would rap. Having waited for some time in vain, he was about to leave the room when three loud raps were heard upon the wall, at some distance from the bed of the patient. In a few days, these manifestations occurred readily and many persons were enabled to witness them.

"'The circle above alluded to, and others which were subsequently formed, met during the summer of 1851 and the following winter. There were also some lectures given before the Psychological Society at Keim's Hall. In the April of 1862, some of the friends met, and in accordance with the directions given by the spirits at one of the circles, the 'Harmonial Benevolent Society' was formed. The society held meetings every week, and on the 5th of May, 1852, appointed a committee, consisting of one member from each of six different circles, to draft a plan of organization. On the 2d of June, the committee reported a short constitution, which was adopted, and twenty members joined the society, the object of which was of a benevolent character, and for the holding of spiritual meetings. Lectures were delivered by the members, and communications received of the circles were occasionally read. On the 9th of June, 1852, the committee decided to rent Franklin Hall, Sixth street, for lectures on Sundays, for six months, from the first of July.

* Dr. H. T. Child.

During this time conferences were held, and at almost every meeting new members were added. . . . . . .

"'At a meeting held on the 6th of March, 1853, it was moved that the board be instructed to procure Concert Hall for Sunday meetings for six months, if practicable. . . . . The arrangements were subsequently made for one year, and an agreement entered into to pay one thousand dollars for the year; but when the friends assembled on the Sunday morning, they found it closed against them. Preferring to yield peaceably rather than maintain their rights by a legal controversy, they concluded to return to Franklin Hall. . . . . . .

"'On the 23d of September, 1854, Aaron Comfort reported a proposition to hire Sansom Street Hall at a rent of five hundred dollars a year; and in September, 1855, the rent of Sansom Street Hall — which was occupied by the association for regular Sunday meetings — was reduced to four hundred dollars per annum.

"'Numerous changes occurred in the committee by death, removal, or resignation, and new members were added. The board continued to arrange for lectures, conferences, etc., depending upon subscriptions, and a fee of five cents at the door, until the 2d of August, 1864, when a report was made by them to a new organization, offering to disband the association, if they would assume the engagements, accept the debt, take the hall, etc.; which being acceded to, the board adjourned *sine die*. Before noticing the action of 'the new organization, namely, the 'First Spiritualist Association,' which succeeded the board that for nine years arranged and carried out, very successfully, courses of lectures in Sansom Street Hall, it may be interesting to record the names of the various lecturers who occupied their rostrum. They were, Dr. Hallock, L. Judd Pardee, Dr. Robert Hare, Rev. T. L. Harris, Judge Edmonds, Rufus Elmer, J. H. Toohey, Charles Partridge, Rev. S. B. Britain, Joel Tiffany, Rev. Adin Ballou, Rev. R. P. Ambler, Mr. G. Stewart, A. J. Davis, Emerson Bennett, Mary F. Davis, Miss Emma Jay, Dr. J. B. Dodds, Professor Mapes, Miss Sprague, Rev. William Fishbough, T. F. Coles, William D. Wharton, Miss Beebe, Dr. T. Orton, Isaac Rhen, Mr. Huntley, Mrs. Tuttle, S. J. Finney, W. S. Courtney, Peter Osborn, A. B. Whiting, Mrs. Emma Hardinge, Mrs. E. J. French, Mrs. Henderson, Mrs. Hyzer, Mrs. Hatch, R. P. Wilson, Dr. J. L. Pierce, Rev. John Pierpont, Thomas Gales Forster, Mrs. M. S. Townsend, Miss Lizzie Doten, Dr. H. T. Child.

Besides the lectures, conferences were held during the summer months, in which various subjects were discussed, from time to time, by members of the society and others. Of the value of the lectures, embracing, as they have, a vast range of thought, often clothed in the most eloquent and impressive language, we need say nothing; the continued and increasing interest in the meetings is evidence that they have been appreciated; and those who have attended them regularly have noticed that each year we have many new faces in our audiences; so that while only hundreds can attend our meetings, thousands have received some portions of the truth sown by the various laborers. . . . . . .

"'The history of Spiritualism in this city will not be completed without a reference to other meetings. We have alluded to the six circles, of which the first society was formed. Many others, both public and private, have existed since. Of the latter, we may not speak, except to say that their influence has been eminently calculated to benefit those who are seeking for a knowledge of the relations which subsist between the spirit-world and our own. The public circles, by furnishing tests and other means of developing media, have been very useful; several of these have been continued and well attended for years.

"'We shall conclude this brief sketch by a reference to the present organization, under whose auspices the meetings are held, entitled 'The First Association of Spiritualists.' This society was formed by the adoption of a constitution on the 24th of July, 1864. It numbers several hundered members and contributors. Its officers are: Dr. J. L. Pierce, President; M. B. Dyott and Louis Belrose, Vice-Presidents; James Trueman, Secretary; Henry T. Child, M. D., Treasurer; and the following Board of Directors: Mrs. M. B. Dyott, Isaac Rhen, Mrs. Belrose, Mrs. M. A. Stretch, Mr. and Mrs. Ballenger, Mr. and Mrs. Shumway, Mrs. A. B. Wilson, Mrs. H. C. Chase.

"'One of the first acts of this association was to abandon the fee of five cents at the door and depend upon voluntary subscriptions and donations to meet the expenses of the lectures. . . . . . .

"'Having received notice that Sansom Street Hall was to be used for other purposes, the committee were obliged to seek another place of meeting. After considerable inquiry, we have concluded to rent Washington Hall for the present; though we are fully aware it will not accommodate all who wish to attend the lectures this winter; yet it was the most desirable hall that could be obtained. We hope that the historian of next year will be be able to record the fact that the Spiritualists of Philadelphia, who now number several thousands, will possess a hall of their own capable of accommodating all who may desire to hear their lectures.

"'Among the most practical features of the spiritual movement, the children's progressive lyceum must rank foremost.* The success of these institutions in our city has been highly gratifying to all the friends of human progress who have witnessed these operations. The lyceum number one, under the conductorship of Mr. M. B. Dyott, with an able corps of leaders, and nearly two hundred children in the groups, has a reputation second to none in our country: it will be continued in this hall, and we hope with increasing success.

"'Another institution which owes its origin and success to our philosophy is the 'Penetralium,' a society which was organized in October, 1864, for the purpose of extending the investigation of scientific subjects into the realm of the spiritual.

This society has held regular weekly meetings. The plan pursued is to have a short lecture, and then allow ten minutes to each speaker to present their views upon the subject under consideration. Of the utility of such a course there can be no doubt, and the success thus far has been very apparent. The audiences have been large and the range of subjects quite extensive. Amongst the lectures arranged for the coming winter are: one by Dr. Pancoast, on the 'structure, development, and functions of the nervous system;' one by Isaac Rhen, 'on the forces of nature,' to be illustrated by extensive experiments; and one by Dr. Child, 'on life—its origin and objects.'

"'A prominent feature of the spiritual movement, which we must briefly notice, is the admission of woman to an equal position on the rostrum and in the executive with man; an experiment which is no longer doubtful. Some of our best lecturers are to be found amongst those whom the Apostle Paul denied the right to speak in church, and whom the church has almost universally excluded.

"'In thus tracing the history of about eighteen years of our cause, one prominent fact is apparent: whereas, at the beginning of that period there were no Spiritualists, liberal and progressive minds were still looking and praying for the coming of a new era, to-day hundreds of thousands, it is said millions, are enrolled under our banner and within the ranks of Spiritualism. To say we believe such are happier and better for this knowledge is but to express the almost universal feeling of this very large class, who, having been introduced into a practical knowledge of the near relation and communion between the two worlds, the physical and the spiritual, feel that they have been blessed indeed, and that life has become a more important reality by a knowledge of its intimate connection with the life hereafter, which is still more real.'"

Let it not be supposed that this sketch—which we have necessarily abridged from the original in some statistical details—comprehends all of the history of Spiritualism in Philadelphia, or indeed any other portion of it than the mere external features of its progress.

The movement in that city has been pre-eminently distinguished for its stability, utility, and influence. All the best spirit mediums and speakers in America have visited Philadelphia, and ever found in the houses of its warm-hearted citizens, the most hospitable, generous and practically Christian treatment.

To go to Philadelphia to give lectures or manifestations of spirit power,

* A full account of the rise and progress of the admirable movement known as the Children's Progressive Lyceum will be given in our second volume.

required *a priori*, in the mediums, a good capital of spiritualistic endowments. Nothing less would be, or ever has been, tolerated amongst this refined and educated community; but once satisfied of the value and genuine character of the phenomena displayed, no people have extended to the unresting feet of the wanderer, a nobler or more refreshing welcome, nor has any community done more to sustain the hands of the laborers, whether in mortal or spirit life, than the faithful Philadelphians.

Our limits have compelled us to omit many of the lecturers' names who have graced the Philadelphia rostrum since the formation of the last society on record, but we should fail to do justice to the genius of the movement, did we pass over that of one of the most constant and highly appreciated of the speakers who have occupied the desk of late years, namely, Mrs. Augusta Currier. This lady, without possessing any of the natural or acquired advantages that arise from wealth and educational preparation, may be regarded as one of those phenomenal children of the spiritual movement, who form in themselves a complete evidence of supra-mundane power and guidance. Youth, a pleasing external appearance, and naturally graceful bearing, were the little lady's only claims to public attention; yet, springing from a position of humble respectability only, she made her way through all the various stages of strong physical test mediumship, clairvoyance, and other remarkable spiritual gifts, until, without human aid, instruction or patronage, she gravitated to her legitimate place, as one of the most brilliant, eloquent, and attractive speakers of the day. Those who prepared her for, and placed her in this exalted position, where wholly unseen in this world, unknown to men, and in fact not "of the earth, earthy;" yet the most profound logicians, renowned scientists, and accomplished orators, have paled before this once-obscure young woman, and looked with marvel and fruitless curiosity for the source of her unearthly power. Never have the promises of the prophets and apostles been more wonderfully fulfilled than in this gifted medium, who has truly testified, that "the weak things of earth should confound the wise," and "the ignorance of the foolish put to shame the understanding of the prudent."

As Mrs. Currier's various gifts have been gradually unfolded, her experience has proved a remarkable exception to the general rule, that "one endowment supersedes another;" her "gift of tongues" has been superadded to that of her physical mediumship, but the latter has not failed in consequence, and it has been one of the attendant charms of her eloquent addresses, that the mystic raps sound through them, in frequent and emphatic chorus to her sentences. As a more extended notice of this interesting medium will be found hereafter in our book of biographical sketches, we need only further add that her frequent ministrations on the Philadelphia rostrum have been as acceptable as beneficial to the cause in that city.

Another of the fair missionaries who helped to dispense the bread of spiritual life, though unnamed in the preceding quotations, was Miss Mattie C. Beckwith, a highly-esteemed favorite of the refined Philadelphians; also, Mrs. Middlebrook, late Mrs. Henderson, of whose noble services in the cause of Spiritualism we shall hereafter make further mention.

As the original favorites of the rostrum were gradually removed, by calls to the higher life or changes in their own earthly arrangements, the promise of old, that "the very stones would cry out" in testimony for the truth, seemed to be realized, for fresh inspirations continued to pour from the mouths of "babes and sucklings" or animate the most unlooked-for instruments to arise and dispense the bread of life to hungering souls.

Philadelphia has herself been rich in internal missionary labor. Besides that giant of the movement, Dr. Robert Hare, Dr. H. T. Child, Mr. Iasac Rhen, Mr. M. B. Dyott, Dr. Pancoast, and several other gentlemen of learning and intellectual endowments, have filled the spiritual rostrum with quite as much acceptance as the lecturers from abroad. Thus, the movement has never slumbered in that city, or lacked the oil by which the lamps of immortality could be kept brightly burning. In no part of the States has the celebrated movement entitled the "Children's Progressive Lyceum" taken so deep a hold on the people, or performed so great a missionary work, as in Philadelphia. Without desiring to appear partial in selecting individuals for notice, where all have labored so long and faithfully, it is but justice to own that this pre-eminence is due to the indefatigable labors of Mr. and Mrs. M. B. Dyott, whose lives for several years past seem to have been mainly devoted, with a self-sacrifice, disinterestedness, and endurance, beyond all worldly praise or appreciation, to the success of this deeply, important undertaking. When it is remembered that in these "lyceums" are laid the very corner-stone, and foundations upon which the faith of future generations is to be built; that in their early training, and habitudes of spiritual thought, is to be found the corrective for the bigotry, superstition, and ignorance of the past, and the bitter persecutions through which the present generation have had to struggle,—the vast and momentous influence of this movement may be prophetically felt, and something of the stupendous debt which posterity will owe to its founder, A. J. Davis, and such workers as Mr. and Mrs. Dyott, be conceived of. Amidst much of worldly ingratitude, misconception, and ancient bigotry, lingering even amidst the spiritual ranks, it is gratifying to be able to record, that the lucid intellects of the young generation, springing up around us, brightened into quick perception by the day-beams of Spiritualism, have in part realized the value of these unselfish labors: witness a handsome service of plate, which quite recently was presented, in the form of a genuine surprise party, to Mr. and Mrs. Dyott, by the grateful teachers and members of the Philadelphia Progressive Lyceum.

Highly interesting features of the movement, connecting the "Progressive Lyceum" with the most sacred interests of Spiritualism, have been the interments — funerals we cannot call them — which have consigned the mortal remains of those broken caskets, from which the bright spirits have escaped, to the dust from which they were temporarily gathered up, as moulds for the formation of immortal blossoms. At these ceremonies, all the sweetest, holiest, and withal the most consolatory exercises of the Progressive Lyceums have been introduced; groups of fair young children, whose blossoming beauty was in itself a prophecy of life immortal; processions of mature people, chiefly arrayed in, or adorned with pure white and floral emblems, typical of the love and truth, life, light, and beauty of the spirit country, into which the freed soul had been born,—all these spoke not of gloom, sorrow, or impenetrable mystery; no more of death, bereavement, and agonizing grief, made hideous by the awful panoply of external signs, but of deep sympathy with the bright, holy, and happy change, by which some beloved one had been made glorified, and which consigned the worn-out garments of mortality back to its kindred earth.

No over-strained or unnatural tokens of rejoicing have been manifested at these "spiritual birthdays." The decorum of the processions, the solemn order of the ceremonial, the pathetic, yet elevating songs and recitations, of the children, the highly exalted tone in which the orators pronounced the valedictory to the departing soul, all displayed the tenderest sympathy for the great heart-wrench involved in such a change, and a glorious assurance of continued life and a bright progressive future for the enfranchised soul.

Besides many mediums of the highest intellectual character, Philadelphia has been visited by all the best travelling physical mediums, some of whom have been occasional residents there. Amongst these was the celebrated Henry Gordon, of whom Dr. Hallock related, at the New York Conference, the following striking evidence of phenomenal power, exhibited during one of his (the Doctor's) Sunday discourses in that city:

"Dr. Hallock stated that on the previous Sunday afternoon, at the commencement of a lecture he was delivering before the Spiritualists of Philadelphia, there was a great deal of spirit manifestation in the form of rappings, etc., which attracted much notice, and created such a disturbance in the minds of the audience, that at one time he was a little annoyed lest due attention should not be paid to what he was saying, and his effort would be lost if that state of things continued. But he soon forgot his concern, and went on with his remarks, and succeeded in entirely fastening the attention of the congregation upon the subject he was presenting; and while, as he believed, every eye and all thoughts were directed towards him, Mr. Henry Gordon the well-known physical medium, who then sat at some distance from, but in front of him, in the perfectly well-lighted room, rose in the air without any human aid, till the speaker beheld him floating so high that his feet just grazed the top of the seat, above which he hung in the air, where he swayed about from side to side and turned partly around. By this time the attention of the entire congregation was rivetted on him, when he sank to the ground. The manifestation was imperfect on the part of the power that lifted him up, because it was afterwards declared by the spirits that they intended to have carried him over the heads of the entire congregation, and landed him on the rostrum, had the conditions permitted, but it seemed that the intense astonishment and agitation of the audience had broken the conditions of passivity necessary for the fulfilment of their design, and so he sank suddenly to the ground. Still there remained the phenomenon of his having been lifted up and suspended in the air without mortal aid, in fact, in a manner which no mortal could have achieved. . . . . . . The effect of this marvellous operation of spirits in a crowded assembly and the full light of day, instead of attracting the attention of the audience from the address, intensified it to the utmost degree. 'I think I may say,' added Dr. Hallock, 'that I never was in an assembly where so much serene joy and spiritual exaltation was manifested. Each one felt that it was good to be there. I cannot describe that Pentecostal scene in words."

Our limits compel us here to close our notice of Spiritualism in Philadelphia. We need scarcely say, the half has not been told; neither do these brief sketches define the extent of the movement throughout the vast area of the State of Pennsylvania, where numbers of places we cannot pause to notice cherish the faith with strong and zealous affection. In Corry, a small but flourishing town in the oil regions, spiritual meetings are regularly held each Sabbath. Some very excellent mediums are to be found there, and an abundance of phenomena is exhibited.

Titusville, a neighboring town, is also a stronghold of the belief. A curious evidence of healing power was exhibited in this place, and one which served greatly to popularize the cause of Spiritualism. The wife of Mr. B., a gentleman of large means and influence, residing in Titusville, had become, through a painful complication of internal ailments, a confirmed invalid; in fact, though quite a young woman, Mrs. B. had been confined to her bed for a period of over three years. Enduring the most intense suffering, and her case baffling all the skill of such medical aid as that wild district could supply, the unhappy lady cherished but one wish in her forlorn and hopeless condition, and that was, that death would speedily terminate her mournful existence, and relieve her friends and family from what she could not but feel was a heavy burden upon them. Her tender and devoted companion, having become interested in Spiritualism, joyfully hailed the approach of all who professed that faith, in the hope that some amongst them, spiritually guided, might bring relief to his long-suffering partner, but months, and at length years, glided by without any realization of their vain hopes, which finally gave way to resignation on the part of the husband, and despair on that of the wife. One day a singular couple of itinerants, husband and wife, presented themselves at the residence of Mr. B., claiming, rather than requesting, hospitality, on the ground that the male traveller was a healing medium, and had been sent there by the spirits "to effect some great cure."

The man, whose name was "McFadden," did not seem even to know the sex or quality of the patient he was to operate upon, yet he insisted that he had "a work to do there," and as his mild and gentle wife seconded his affirmation, Mr. B., though without any very strong prepossession in their favor, consented to receive them for a while into his house. For the best interests of truth, it is well that the whole circumstances of this strange case should be fully understood.

McFadden was represented to the author, not only by the parties most nearly concerned in this narrative, namely, Mr. and Mrs. B. themselves, but also by others well acquainted with him, as a man of repulsive manners and appearance, and one, moreover, so addicted to the use of profane language that he seemed scarcely able to speak without expressions painful to the sensitive ear to listen to. His wife was mild, unassuming, and benevolent, and except for her association with her strange companion, would, doubtless, have proved a welcome visitor anywhere. When first introduced to the bedside of Mrs. B., a highly refined and sensitive person, the medium was literally thrown back from her couch, as if with an electric shock, by the force of repulsion which the lady at once conceived for the strange operator. His wife, who stood by at the time, besought Mrs. B. to make an effort to overcome this intense disgust, frequently declaring that "they had been sent to cure her and must do their work, although her repulsive feeling would for a time inevitably hinder them." In vain the lady strove to accept of this kindly assurance, and conquer her aversion to the rude operator. No sooner would he approach her than he fell back with the same singular magnetic force as before; and the two poles of a battery, scientifically arranged to exhibit the nature of repulsion, could not have operated with more marvellous power than the patient and her would-be healer. And still he persisted in his attempt, swearing, even with oaths, that he must and would effect a cure; that for such a purpose he had been sent, and without its accomplishment he might not depart on his way.

On a certain occasion, after a long and hitherto ineffectual trial, the rough doctor, aided by his gentle companion, succeeded in producing, by distant manipulations over the couch of Mrs. B., the the charmed magnetic sleep. Awaking from this delightful somnolence, refreshed and invigorated, Mrs. B. remarked that she had not been so free from pain for three years, and that at length she was convinced the true physician to her malady had arrived. From this time the spell was broken. The intense magnetic repulsion being overcome, kindlier and more receptive influences supervened. The strange healer performed his work with grateful appreciation on the part of the lady, and rugged determination on his own, and within six weeks the bed-ridden invalid was once more in the midst of her family, performing, in perfect health and renewed strength, her household duties, with as much ease and capacity as if they had never been interrupted by her long and perilous years of suffering. Her cure was effected solely by the laying on of those hands from which a few weeks before she had shrunk with such loathing, but which she now humbly and gratefully acknowledged had come to her freighted with the inestimable boon of life and health. Mr. and Mrs. B. related this circumstance at a Pentecostal gathering, which had assembled to meet the author when lecturing for a few days at Corry, *en route* for the far West. The snow was two foot deep on the ground and still falling fast. The roads were almost impassable, yet the once bedridden lady had travelled in that inclement season above fifty miles to attend the author's lectures, and bear her grateful testimony to the beneficent character of Spiritualism and its missionaries.

The conversation had turned on the prevalence of "spiritual mountebanks" and itinerant vagabonds, who, scouring the country in every direction, used the talismanic word "Spiritualism" as their *open sesame* to the hospitalities of the credulous. It was these remarks that called forth the history above detailed, which, being related by Mr. and Mrs. B. with tears of deep emotion, and verified by several of their acquaintances present, who were personally cognizant of the facts, was summed up by the husband in the assurance that though he believed there were many impostors ranging the country and attempting to deceive people out of a maintenance by false professions, yet for the sake of the one divinely guided missionary who had brought in his hand the life of his best beloved, *all* had since been welcome who had crossed their threshold in the sacred name of "the spirits." "I can never again close those doors against the wanderer," he added, "which have been opened to 'entertain an angel unawares.'"

In Meadville, Pennsylvaina, a numerous body of Spiritualists may be found, who, although laboring under many disabilities peculiar to the advent of a new and unpopular movement, have struggled on bravely, and given a tone to the belief of these wild and remote districts where the name of Spiritualism is no longer regarded as a bugbear, but rather as a warranty for strange and beneficent powers, whose possession invests their owner with gifts which are deemed worthy of investigation and respect.

In Meadville resides Dr. John Newcomer, a gentleman who unites in his own person the many gifts of inventor, mechanic, herbalist, doctor, healing medium, lecturer writer, astronomer, designer of certain remarkably ingenious astronomical instruments, and originator of a most singular prophetic scheme of the earth's destiny. Besides these varied accomplishments, Dr. John Newcomer plays on two or three musical instruments, one of which, of a lute fashion, originated in his own fertile genius and mechanical skill. In an office open for the sale of various healing compounds, all originated by himself, the visitor would find it difficult to think of any articles of domestic use, herbs, minerals, drugs or machines, even models of the earth, orreries and musical instruments, which are not to be here found, on "improved principles;" in fact this wonderful sanctum is the *omnium gatherum* of a very comprehensive mind, which represents itself and the universe in equally microcosmic characters. As Dr. Newcomer is a very uncompromising Spiritualist, the other world and its interests come in for an equal share of illustrative talent, the full scope of which appears in a hall which Dr. Newcomer has fitted up, and hires at his own expense, for the purpose of devoting freely to the service of Spiritualism.

This building will accommodate about two hundred persons; is neatly furnished with a small platform and seats, whilst the walls are adorned with a large collection of oil-paintings executed by the versatile proprietor of the hall, highly colored and elaborately finished. They form, altogether, a serial and pictorial commentary on the biblical account of creation, together with the artist's own views of the hereafter, as derived from the popular teachings of

Spiritualism. Although Dr. Newcomer's pictures and the opinions they illustrate, like every other production of his remarkable genius, are strictly original, and form no direct affinity with any other person's acts or works or words, that the most cosmopolitan visitor could ever have encountered, the theological views they suggest cannot fail to remind the beholder more immediately of Tom Paine, Volney, and the English Robert Taylor, than of the Patriarch Abraham and the Apostle Paul; nevertheless, these and other "sacred" personages are freely represented on Dr. Newcomer's glowing canvas; but as they generally figure in the same scene where certain Divine personages are represented as pronging souls out of heaven with celestial thunderbolts, whilst other diabolical personages stir them up in burning broth with brimstone pitchforks, and the "everlasting Yankee" is introduced with the hook and line of combined benevolence and ingenuity, fishing them up and restoring them to earth, it may be supposed that these biblical illustrations are not designed on the most approved theological pattern. They are very numerous, however, and highly suggestive.

The ludicious and the horrible are represented in terribly faithful proximity; and a more graphic commentary on the heavens, hells, saints, sinners, angels, and demons, brimstone and blue fire, in which ancient orthodoxy delighted to revel, from the gloomy Calvin to the stern Emmons, and which modern orthodoxy has not altogether quenched in the tides of modern progress, has never surely found a more fearless or imaginative illustrator than this same singular Pennsylvania artist. It need scarcely be hinted that Dr. John Newcomer is not popular with the church-going community of his district, and as his very direct and peculiar methods of propagating his opinions have obtained for him a wide-spread notoriety and most obnoxious reputation, they have served to isolate him even from many worldly persons who sympathize in part, though not entirely with his extreme views.

In the author's visit to Meadville for the purpose of delivering two lectures in that collegiate town, she realized most painfully the lines of demarcation which strongly marked idiosyncracies draw between their professors and mankind in general. The progressive spirit which already animated at least one half of the young students and professors of a fine Unitarian college at Meadville, induced their attendance at the lectures, and manifested itself in a noble complimentary testimonial which a few high-minded and talented young men presented to her in grateful acknowledgment of her definition of "the beautiful faith and philosophy of Spiritualism;" and yet these brave and aspiring young spirits were driven off with repelling force from the strange old philosopher, who could have suggested, aye, and taught them so much that their eager souls were hungering for, had not himself and his methods of presenting the truth been so eminently distasteful to their sense of propriety and refinement. Dr. John Newcomer was also an excellent healing medium. His strong hands, freighted with health, and his kind heart would gladly have spread abroad this blessing to all around him. The indescribably odd old man might be seen any day with basket on arm, gathering up medicinal herbs and plants of healing virtue, which would have been cheerfully drawn forth from the shelves of his wonderful little museum for the free use of the afflicted, were there not a ban on the place, and a breath of evil signing the dark stairway which led to it, with an invisible yet potent circle, into which it was deemed ill for the foot of good repute to enter.

Strange isolation of a kind heart, ready hand, and highly endowed brain! Strange and cross-grained woof of human destiny which has converted an instrument of blessing into a tool of offence! Dr. John Newcomer and the world, require the bright transfiguration of the land of light, truth, and charity, to understand, mutually forgive, and mutually appreciate each other.

Our limits will only permit us to notice two more points of interest in Pennsylvania, although the whole State abounds with such, in the history of Spiritualism; the first of these is Morristown, near Philadelphia, less remarkable however, for its little faithful band of Spiritualists than as having been the residence of one of the most talented advocates of the cause, Miss Belle Bush, the charming poetess and writer, whose gems of thought have contributed so largely to the reputation of spiritual literature. The second and last noteworthy point which we can notice in this noble State, is Brookfield, famous as the scene of a great spiritual outporing, which occurred quite early in the modern movement under the following circumstances.

Amongst the Methodists, Shakers, and other fervid sects of religionists, marked and preternatural tokens of a spiritual afflatus had been frequent ever since the famous revival which preceded the Rochester knockings by some ten years. Certain sections of country, called "the burnt districts" from having been swept by the action of the Pentecostal fires, still preserved the evidences of the mighty visitation in the strange and apparently fanatical associations which sprang up amongst them. Spiritual philosophers attributed many of the eccentricities both of the revival and spiritual movements to the effect of magnetism, stimulated into violent and irresistible action by the contagion of the times. Unphilosophical religionists called them the work of the "Holy Ghost" or the "Evil One," according as their sectarian prejudices inclined. The following narrative, reprinted in part from the *Spiritual Telegraph*, is a well-anthenticated account of one of these singular revival fevers, the details of which seem to be so closely allied to Spiritualism, that it claims its legitimate place in our notice of that movement in Pennsylvania. Mr. Partridge, in his editorial account of what follows, states that the Rev. John Crapsey was a minister of the high ecclesiatical school at Brookfield, Tioga County, Pennsylvania, and that, at a meeting which he was holding in Roulette, Potter County, Pennsylvania, just as he was quoting the words of Jesus on the cross, "*Eli, Eli, lama Sabachthani.*"

"A mighty invisible power seemed suddenly to possess him, and a luminous appearance scintillated upon and around his hand, shining with brilliant effulgence in the eyes of all beholders. 'Under an impulse which I could not resist, I sprang,' says Mr. Crapsey, 'from the desk out upon the middle of the floor into the midst of the congregation; great signs and wonders then ensued and were witnessed by all.

"'Fire, and pillars of smoke and luminous light rose up bodily in our midst; men, women, and even stammering children were seized, speaking with new tongues, and uttering prophecies. Prayers and exhortations were poured forth in abundance, and many of the congregation broke out into the most marvellous and heavenly singing.'"

But the demonstrations of this Pentecostal hour did not terminate with the close of that meeting. They came together again and again, meeting sometimes each day and occasionally in the night, when similar manifestations accompanied their gatherings, and continued up to the date of the *Telegraph's* report, about June, 1855. Mr. Crapsey goes on to say that at times, certain of the persons affected, who were chiefly young people from ten to thirty years of age, would come to him, and enact in pantomime a spiritual or prophetic drama, showing that he would be subject to much persecution. Sometimes also the house where they were assembled would shake, and "even rock about as if in a gale of wind, although the air without was as still as death." They usually held their meetings in a building, the lower portion of which was used as a school, and the shaking of the house became so violent that the teachers were compelled to dismiss the scholars, as "they could not write and feared to remain upon the premises."

After this excitement had continued until the whole neighborhood became stirred by it, a public meeting was held in the place, and a committee appointed to wait on Mr. Crapsey and request him to quit the neighborhood. This he refused to do, when the prophetic warnings of the spiritual drama were realized by Mr. Crapsey's arrest on a false charge of his having assaulted some members of his congregation. A trial ensued, but as nothing reprehensible could be proved against the minister, and not a witness could be found who did not take part with him in this strange excitement, he was ultimately discharged; but as the disturbances continued with greater force than ever, a fresh committee waited on him, with the offer of a sum of money, conditional upon his instant departure, an offer which he promptly and indignantly rejected. Finding their efforts to drive him out or quench the obnoxious manifestations in vain, Mr. Crapsey's opponents now began to resort to open violence and a continued series of persecutions. Himself and his congregation were denied entrance to any building in the neighborhood, and when they sought shelter in woods, groves, or forests, they were set upon, the woods fired, and themselves stormed and hooted at.

And yet it often happened that the bands of disturbers who set upon these gatherings were so struck with the flashing of the preternatural lights, the rocking of the trees, trembling earth, and the pathetic appeals of the entranced speakers, that their acts of violence were changed into tones of prayer, and they joined the revivalists in their celebrations, leaping, singing, shuddering, and praying, under the same inevitable afflatus as themselves.

Mr. Pendleton, a gentleman who was at that time a resident of Brookfield, and an eye witness and participator in their Pentecostal meetings, affirmed that himself and many others saw angelic beings moving about in their midst, and that often "the spirits of dead persons" were seen and described with such accuracy that their friends and relations could not doubt but that "truly their loved and lost ones were arisen from the grave, and come back in life amongst them." The phenomena of mediumship which would account for the preternatural lights and movements around them, no less than the open vision which recognized the forms of the beloved departed, had not yet become sufficiently well known and understood in those remote sections of country to resolve themselves into a part of an orderly and universal movement, hence for a long time their manifestation, as above narrated, was regarded as a special Pentecostal outpouring, which predicated the speedy approach of the long expected "millennium."

As the report of kindred phenomena, occurring in other parts of the State, reached the "possessed district," its preternatural characteristics disappeared, the excitement subsided, and the orderly development of medium powers in and amongst Mr. Crapsey's congregation changed the fever into the normal and healthy tone of Spiritualism.

Our space will not allow us to pause longer on the progress of the spiritual movement in Pennsylvania, or to notice, except *en passant*, its many remarkable developments in Washington and Baltimore. Frequent allusions to the extraordinary mediumistic gifts displayed in both cities will be found scattered through these pages, and a brief notice of the highly-gifted Laurie family in Washington, and Colonel Danskin and his amiable lady in Baltimore, will be given in our biographical sketches.

For the present we can only pause to remark that amongst the many excellent mediums in Baltimore, the most distinguished for her professional services was a Mrs. Morrel, a superior rapping, writing, physical, and test medium. Amongst other singular phases of intercourse between the two worlds, a very striking one was exhibited in Baltimore also, through the mediumship of Mrs. Danskin, a lady moving in the first circles of the city, but who, in her fidelity to the cause of Spiritualism, nobly ignored the scoffs and sneers of her associates, and devoted her remarkable powers as a trance medium to the service of those who could not be satisfied to investigate through a professional source. Besides gifts of clairvoyance, psychometry, and healing, Mrs. Danskin was peculiarly distinguished as a medium through whom "dark" or "undeveloped" spirits could return and manifest to earth the deplorable shipwrecks which crime and ignorance had made of their souls. The interviews with these suffering, earth-bound beings were often thrilling and full of warning and instruction.

These circles, as well as others of a similar kind held in various parts of the country, made a profound impression on the community, and induced many persons, from motives of curiosity no less than interest, to inquire more closely into the relations sustained between the inhabitants of earth, and the dwellers of the spirit country. The vague notions so loosely inculcated by theology on the conditions of compensation and retribution in the hereafter, were entirely put to flight by the revelations of these circles. The idea that earthly criminals could continue such as spirits, and receive the same benefit from human counsel as they could have done had they remained in the form, was a doctrine so entirely subversive of all preconceived opinions on such subjects, that their promulgation was met with the most profound scepticism, and sometimes even by indignant denial. It was only, then, by the persistent efforts of such respected missionaries as Mrs. Danskin, and other ladies who held circles for the progression of "undeveloped spirits," that this singular phase of the communion between the two worlds began to be understood, and the possibility that we are "all ministering spirits," slowly to dawn upon the minds of earth's inhabitants, not as a mere biblical phrase, but as a solemn and divine mission which we should endeavor to put into practical reality for the benefit no less of spirits in the form than for the sake of those whom the disabilities of false systems have sent from earth still in conditions of ignorance and crime.

As this portion of the spiritual philosophy must be reserved for a more full and special notice, we shall now pass on to consider, in detail, the Spiritualism of those vast sections of country so graphically entitled "the mighty West."